THE EMIL AND KATHLEEN SICK LECTURE-BOOK SERIES IN WESTERN HISTORY AND BIOGRAPHY

Under the provisions of a Fund established by the children of Mr. and Mrs. Emil Sick, whose deep interest in the history and culture of the American West was inspired by their own experience in the region, distinguished scholars are brought to the University of Washington to deliver public lectures based on original research in the fields of Western history and biography. The terms of the gift also provide for the publication by the University of Washington Press of the books resulting from the research upon which the lectures are based. This is the sixteenth book in the series. A complete listing of the books in the series appears at the end of this book.

SHADOW

Andrew H. Fisher

CENTER FOR THE STUDY OF THE PACIFIC NORTHWEST *IN ASSOCIATION*

TRIBE

THE MAKING OF COLUMBIA RIVER INDIAN IDENTITY

WITH UNIVERSITY OF WASHINGTON PRESS ■ SEATTLE AND LONDON

© 2010 by University of Washington Press
Printed in the United States of America
Designed by Pamela Canell
15 14 13 12 11 10   5 4 3 2 1

University of Washington Press
PO Box 50096, Seattle, WA 98145, USA
www.washington.edu/uwpress

Center for the Study of the Pacific
Northwest, PO Box 353587,
Seattle, WA 98195, USA

Library of Congress Cataloging-in-Publication Data
Fisher, Andrew H.
Shadow tribe : the making of Columbia River Indian identity /
Andrew H. Fisher. — 1st ed.
p. cm. — (The Emil and Kathleen Sick lecture-book series
in western history and biography)
Includes bibliographical references and index.
ISBN 978-0-295-99020-0 (pbk. : alk. paper)
1. Indians of North America—Columbia River Valley—History.
2. Indians of North America—Columbia River Valley—Ethnic identity.
3. Indians of North America—Columbia River Valley—Government relations.
4. Tribal government—Columbia River Valley.
5. Columbia River Valley—Ethnic relations. I. Title. II. Series.
E78.C64F57 2010   323.11970797—dc22   2010002144

CONTENTS

PREFACE AND ACKNOWLEDGMENTS

Three Native American men pose with backs to the camera, their bodies wrapped in Pendleton blankets and their faces hidden or shadowed by the broad-brimmed "reservation hats" popular among western Indians at the turn of the twentieth century. A pair of safety bikes leans together in the foreground, dating the scene sometime in the early 1900s. The photographer's intention in juxtaposing Indians and bicycles is unclear, though similar images from that time suggest an attempt to evoke the idea of progress overtaking primitivism. The Columbia River and the forested hills of the Columbia Gorge stretch out in front of the scene, yet unmarked by the highways, bridges, and dams that would further displace the area's Native residents. The men are watching the activity at the ferry landing in Hood River, Oregon, more than a hundred miles from the nearest Indian reservation. They are part of everyday life in the community, but the photograph sets them apart as idle observers. It also renders them anonymous. Contemporary viewers would have seen them only as types, as symbols of a fading frontier and a vanishing race. Their identities remain shadowy, and that ambiguity captures the subject of this book.

Shadow Tribe grew out of conversations with Native people—initially uncomfortable conversations in which my flawed assumptions about them became apparent. One of the earliest occurred following the publication of my first article, which related the history of an agreement between Indians I had identified as Yakamas and representatives of the U.S. Forest Service regarding access to huckleberry fields within the Gifford Pinchot National Forest. Átway Frederick Ike, Sr., the head of the Rock Creek Longhouse and a member of the Yakama Tribal Council, invited me to the annual huckleberry feast at the Cold Springs campground. To my surprise, he also asked me to speak to the group assembled beneath a makeshift arbor of wooden beams and plastic tarps. After stumbling through a brief speech, I was approached by a woman who told me bluntly: "We don't like people making assumptions about us. We're not Yakama Indians." Her declaration puzzled me because Ike and many others in the crowd lived on the Yakama reservation and even worked for the tribe. I put on the face of the discerning scholar, though, venturing my best guess about her possible affiliation within the "confederated tribes and bands" of the Yakama Nation: "Are you Klickitat?" "No," she replied, "we're Columbia River Indians." I nodded vaguely, unsure of what to say. I had never heard of any such people, as Columbia River Indians are neither a federally recognized tribe nor an aboriginal group noted in the ethnographic literature. It took a few more awkward conversations for me to realize that the tribal framework I had used in my early research did not fully capture the lived experiences and identities of the people about whom I wrote. Born of curiosity and the desire to correct past mistakes, this book traces the development of Columbia River Indian identity and explains its significance within the broader context of Native American history.

I am indebted to Átway Frederick Ike for starting me down this path, and I regret that he did not live to see the project to completion. Many other Native people have offered invaluable advice and information along the way, especially Vivian Adams, George Aguilar, Sr., Yvonne Colfax, Carol Craig, Roberta Conner, Ed Edmo, Johnny Jackson, Lewis Malatare, Anita Nez, Louie Pitt, Ron Pond, Marilyn Skahan-Malatare, Wilbur Slockish, Jr., Wilson Wewa, Deborah Winnier, and Galen Yallup. Although I am still very much an outsider looking in, I deeply appreciate their interest, feedback, and guidance over the past ten years.

Much of the archival research for this project was financed by a Castles Fellowship from the Center for Columbia River History, a Graduate Research Support Grant from Arizona State University, and a Phillips Fund Grant for Native American Research from the American Philosophical Society. Friendly and knowledgeable archivists at federal, state, and university repositories ensured that my time and money were well spent. First and foremost, Joyce Justice of the National Archives branch in Seattle paid me the great kindness of not retiring before I could take advantage of her vast expertise. When she did finally step down, John Ferrell, Susan Karren, and Patty McNamee did an excellent job of filling her shoes. Additional thanks go to the many helpful staff members I encountered at the High Desert Museum, the National Archives in Washington, DC, the Northwest Museum of Arts and Culture, the Oregon Historical Society, the Oregon State Archives, the Portland Library, the Washington State Archives, the Washington State Historical Society, the Yakima Valley Regional Library, and the special collections departments of the University of Idaho, the University of Oregon, the University of Washington, and Washington State University. I also owe a huge debt of gratitude to Forest Service archaeologists Cheryl Mack and Rick McClure, Carol Craig of the Yakama Nation, and Keith Hatch from the Portland Area Office of the Bureau of Indian Affairs for sharing their personal files with me.

From the start, this project and my academic career have benefited from the gentle direction, inexhaustible patience, and unflagging confidence of my graduate advisor, Peter Iverson. I could not have asked for a better mentor. Great thanks go as well to the other members of my dissertation committee—Margaret Connell Szasz, Robert Trennert, and Philip VanderMeer—and to the many friends and colleagues who have helped shape the manuscript. Four anonymous peer reviewers provided important feedback and saved me from some embarrassing errors, as did Tom Hampson (ONABEN) and attorneys Gary Berne and Peter Parnickis, who not only read but lived through the events in chapter 7. Katrine Barber and David Rich Lewis read individual chapters, and David kindly published a version of chapter 3 in the Winter 2001 issue of the *Western Historical Quarterly*. Robert Boyd, Alexandra (Sasha) Harmon, and Bruce Rigsby graciously plowed through the entire manuscript at the dissertation stage. Their comments and suggestions, along with their own scholarship, pushed me to think about the topic in new ways and contributed to a number of important insights. Bruce Rigsby deserves special thanks for introducing me to Deward Walker, another influential commentator, and for providing Sahaptin transliterations of numerous personal and place names in the text. I am further indebted to Sasha and my editor, Marianne Keddington-Lang, for allowing me to publish portions of chapter 6 in *The Power of Promises: Rethinking Indian Treaties in the Pacific Northwest* (University of Washington Press, 2008) and in the Summer 2004 issue of the *Oregon Historical Quarterly*. Marianne deserves credit for shepherding my manuscript through the long acquisitions process, but I must also thank Julidta Tarver for expressing early interest in the project and offering me an advance contract when I was still a lowly graduate student.

Speaking of which, my graduate school cohorts at Arizona State University must be acknowledged as well for challenging me intellectually while also helping me to see the lighter side of academic life (including the light at the end of the tunnel). Special thanks go to Jaime Aguila, Steve Amerman, Elizabeth Carney, Myla Vicente Carpio, Wendel Cox, Wade Davies, Brian Frehner, Leah Glaser, John Heaton, Andrew Honker, Elizabeth James, Tracy Leavelle, Doug Seefeldt, Jeff Shepherd, Adam Sowards, and Tara Wood. Remarkably, we all got jobs, but it's too bad we only get to see each other once or twice a year at most. The History

Department and my colleagues at the College of William and Mary were kind enough to take me in and offer helpful feedback through several brown-bag lectures.

Last but not least are the members of my family. My father and mother taught me the importance of good writing and caring about the world, my sister blazed the trail through graduate school, and my brother urged me on with the appropriate mixture of concern and wisecracking. I cannot thank them and my in-laws enough for their love and support. By far the biggest debt is owed to my wife, Lisa, who shouldered much of the load on this long road and made the whole trip worthwhile. It is to her and our daughter, Lindsay, that I dedicate this book.

ANDREW H. FISHER
Williamsburg, Virginia

SHADOW TRIBE

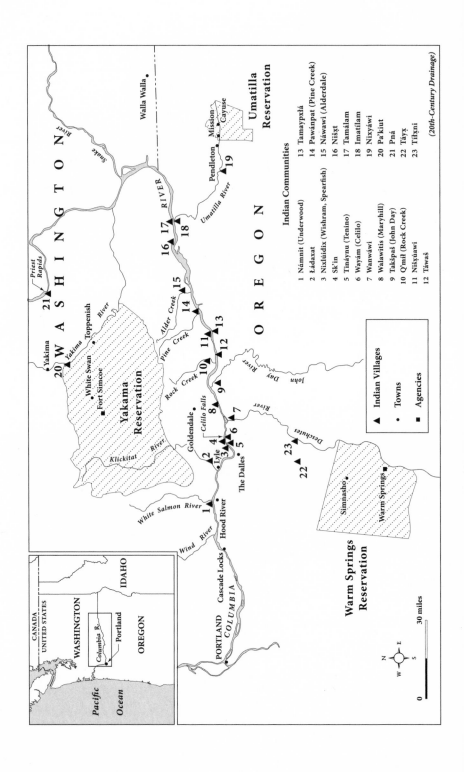

Indian Communities

1 Námnit (Underwood)
2 Łádaxat
3 Nixłúidix (Wishram, Spearfish)
4 Sk'in
5 Tináynu (Tenino)
6 Wayám (Celilo)
7 Wanwáwi
8 Walawítis (Maryhill)
9 Takápaš (John Day)
10 Q'míł (Rock Creek)
11 Nix*ú*awi
12 Táwaš
13 Tamaypxłá
14 Pawánpat (Pine Creek)
15 Náwawi (Alderdale)
16 Niš*x*t
17 Tamálam
18 Imatílam
19 Nixyáwi
20 Pa'kiut
21 Pná
22 Táy*x*
23 Tíł*x*ni

Indian Villages ▲

Towns •

Agencies ■

(20th-Century Drainage)

0   30 miles

INTRODUCTION

I n the summer of 1985, a group calling itself the Chiefs and Council of the Columbia River Indians filed a motion to appear as *amicus curiae* (friend of the court) in a legal dispute between the Bureau of Indian Affairs and several Native American families living in the Columbia Gorge. The BIA had recently ordered their eviction from three tribal fishing sites that the Army Corps of Engineers had built to replace

---

Facing page: Mid-Columbia Indian Reservations and Selected Off-Reservation Communities, 1850s–1880s (20th-century drainage). This map is not comprehensive but shows major Indian villages mentioned in the text. Adapted from maps appearing in *The Handbook of North American Indians*, vol. 12, pp. 362–63, 379, 396.

locations flooded by Bonneville Dam. Bureau attorneys insisted that the sites belonged to the federal government and had never been intended for permanent occupation. The residents fought back, arguing that their treaties and their traditional way of life gave them the right to stay. "We are not going to abandon what is ours from the beginning," declared Johnny Jackson, a member of the Chiefs and Council of the Columbia River Indians. "Our forefathers used this area and lived and fished here, it was passed down from generation to generation, and we are a part of that land and river." The families had hoped to receive support from the governments of the confederated tribes of the Warm Springs, Umatilla, and Yakama reservations. In this case, though, the tribal councils sided with the BIA and urged the residents to leave. The Chiefs and Council of the Columbia River Indians saw no choice but to intervene. "Although this governing body is not 'officially' recognized by the U.S. government," explained attorney Gary Berne, "it is recognized by the appellants as a tribe in which they hold citizenship. This governing body has had, and continues to have, a strong voice in the affairs of its people along the Columbia River. [They] contend that this voice should be heard in support of its people and their rights to live and fish in their ancestral ways."[1]

The motion for *amicus* participation annoyed the BIA. While agency attorneys were willing to allow the council's intervention, Regional Solicitor Vernon Peterson pointedly noted that most of the Indians involved were members of the Yakama Nation and therefore ineligible for enrollment in another tribe. "Surely," he chided, "these appellants do not intend their membership in the group known as 'Chiefs and Council of the Columbia River Indians' to be regarded as equivalent to tribal membership in the Yakima Indian Nation, so as to jeopardize their enrollment in that recognized tribe." As far as Peterson was concerned, the Columbia River Indians did not exist. "In consequence," he concluded, "whatever status the group may have as a private organization or association of individuals, it is not appropriate to characterize it as a tribe with protected treaty rights or with sovereign authority over its membership." The matter seemed quite simple from a legal standpoint, and Peterson ignored the deeper questions raised by the council's request. If these people were not a tribe, then what were they? Why did they wish to speak with their own voice? How had they come to see themselves as distinct from the tribes to which they nominally belonged? What did it mean to be a Columbia River Indian?[2]

Answering these questions requires us to turn from law to history. Neither a cohesive aboriginal group nor a federally recognized tribe, Columbia River Indians are the product of social and political processes triggered by Euro-American colonization.[3] Between the imposition of the reservation system in the mid-1850s and the destruction of Celilo Falls in 1957, off-reservation River People developed a strong sense of difference from the recognized tribes to which federal policies had assigned them. Initially, the label "Columbia River Indian" designated nothing more than a scattered assortment of "renegades" living between the Cascade Rapids and Priest Rapids.[4] They came from many different villages and continued to identify with those settlements long after the treaties had established new residences and new roles for them to occupy. Over time, the shared experience of being off the reservation and at odds with the recognized tribes pushed these persistent river communities into a loose confederation called the Columbia River Tribe or the Mid-Columbia River Tribe. Environmental changes and political pressures eroded their autonomy in the second half of the twentieth century, yet the River People continued to honor a common heritage of ancestral connection to the Columbia, resistance to the reservation system, devotion to cultural traditions, and detachment from the institutions of federal control and tribal governance. At times, their independent and uncompromising attitude has challenged the sovereignty of the recognized tribes, earning Columbia River Indians a reputation as radicals and troublemakers. But many have also become active members and even leaders of the treaty tribes, adding legal and political strands to the intricate web of kinship that binds them to the reservations. "Family ties remain primary," notes Plateau ethnographer Eugene Hunn, "and the tribes are like very large families, not always happy with one another, but still family."[5]

■ ■ ■

It is tempting to describe Columbia River Indians as merely a faction within the recognized tribes because they are so intertwined with the people of the reservations and they do not readily fit into any other category that scholars generally accept. Academics yearn to categorize and classify, even when they criticize colonial powers for placing indigenous people in boxes of alien design. Especially in the social sciences, there is a latent expectation that groups and histories will conform to established models and theories of ethnogenesis. Anthropologists might call the Columbia River Indians a "hybridized group coalition," which Patricia C. Albers places at the middle of a "merger continuum" between "polyethnic alliance formations" and "emergent ethnic communities." In a hybridized group coalition, she writes,

> intermarriage and coresidency become so pervasive that local settlements with dual ethnic origins begin to constitute a sociopolitical body whose interests and actions stand apart from those of either parent bloc. In the process, they take on hybrid ethnic identities as well. At this point, ethnogenesis is not yet completed because the hybrid populations still retain some sort of umbilical connection (i.e., in language preference, economic dependency) to either or both parental blocs.[6]

This model appears to suit Columbia River Indians at particular points in their history, yet it is still too neat and clean for a group whose boundaries are nebulous and whose members come from dozens of distinct communities. It seems best, then, to describe them with a metaphor rather than to force them into an academic mold.

Columbia River Indians constitute a shadow tribe, part of and yet separate from the tribal bodies whose fortunes they share. Cast by the imperfect light of federal policy and dimly perceived by the colonial gaze, their shadowy presence has followed the treaty tribes down the difficult historical path marked out by the dominant society. Much of the time, River People have moved in harmony with the recognized tribes, their shadow seeming to fade altogether as their interests align with those of the reservations. But then a threatening change of direction throws their shadow into stark relief as it tugs against the course set by the treaty tribes or drags them along behind. Although unable to break free entirely, Columbia River Indians have even formed a shadow government that spars with tribal councils and non-Indian powerbrokers.

The shadow tribe's inability to achieve an enduring, substantive form has led outsiders to deny that it is there at all. This sense of invisibility lies at the heart of the history of Columbia River Indians. They are not a tribe, many have said, but a political faction or interest group within the "real" tribes acknowledged by the federal government. It is true that the River People have often behaved as a faction, particularly after their enrollment in the reservation tribes foreclosed the possibility of formal recognition. Nevertheless, no bureaucratic category or academic model adequately explains why they have periodically insisted on being called a tribe when everyone else claims they are not.

Because of their unofficial status, the Columbia River Indians have largely escaped scholarly notice. With a few exceptions, most notably the work of Eugene Hunn and Roberta Ulrich, the bulk of the anthropological and historical literature about the Columbia Plateau subsumes the River People under the tribal headings established by the federal government. This study strives to restore their visibility by charting the historical development of their identity and explaining its significance within the broader context of Native American history. The story of Columbia River Indians is interesting and important in its own right, and it also encourages a fuller, more complex understanding of modern Indian history and identity.[7]

■ ■ ■

Despite increasing scholarly attention to modern Native American history, the popular narrative still ends with the confinement of tribes to reservations during the late nineteenth century. As the story goes, Indians valiantly but vainly resisted American expansion in a dramatic series of "Indian Wars," typically exemplified by the Battle of the Little Big Horn and the flight of Chief Joseph's Nez Perce toward Canada. With the tragic massacre of Lakota Ghost Dancers at Wounded Knee in 1890, the military contest ended, and Native peoples were forced, in the words of one account, "behind the curtain of oblivion on the reservation."[8] Even in current U.S. history textbooks, there are few references to Indians or Indian issues beyond that point. Although it is true that many Native Americans ended up on reservations, the emphasis on exclusion serves to remove them from the master narrative of U.S. history.[9] With Indians out of the way, it seems, the "real" story of Euro-American progress can proceed. The narrative of dispossession also overstates the extent of state power and ignores the persistence of Native people in off-reservation settings, where they continued to interact with both reservation Indians and non-Indians in complex ways. The point here is not to diminish the significance of reservations, which have become cherished tribal homelands, but rather to stress that Indian history exists beyond their boundaries and that reservations are not required for either the preservation or creation of Indian identities.

One of the major ironies of Native American history arises from the reservation system's tendency to foster new Indian identities at the very time the federal government hoped to erase "Indianness" altogether. Forced into drastically reduced territories, diverse aboriginal groups mingled and merged to form new social and political entities. Until recently, however, processes of identity formation and nation-building among Native Americans received little attention because of a general tendency to portray Indian identity as timeless and unchanging. The term "tribe" has a primordial feel to it, suggesting a tightly bounded group of people sharing a clearly marked territory and a fixed body of ancient traditions. This view is essentially ahistorical, yet historians have helped perpetuate the dangerous assumption that change destroys Indian identity. Fortunately, more and more scholars challenge outmoded notions of indigenous "authenticity" and produce increasingly sophisticated analyses of the emergence of modern Indian nations. I seek to advance that trend by developing two significant but slighted themes in Native American history.[10]

8

First, the River People's story confirms the incomplete nature of Indian removal and the continuing presence of Indians beyond the reservation. Although several scholars have examined the experiences of urban Indians, who now comprise over half the Native American population in the United States, off-reservation communities remain neglected and poorly understood.[11] Most recent books about tribal identity and nation-building focus on particular reservations and recognized tribes.[12] Indians who stray beyond reservation boundaries tend to fade from view. They are also generally seen as exceptions, yet in many areas off-reservation Indians comprise a substantial minority or even the majority. In the 1870s, roughly a third of the people assigned to the four southern Plateau reservations (Warm Springs, Yakama, Umatilla, Nez Perce) had either refused to settle there or stayed only part of the year. A century later, some 2,800 of the 7,300 Indians enrolled in those tribes lived off-reservation. Similar patterns prevailed throughout the Pacific Northwest, as Native Americans frequently defied both geographic confinement and tribal classification. Reservation boundaries remained porous, and Indian enclaves survived amid the burgeoning non-Indian population, effectively blurring the racial and tribal lines the government sought to inscribe. The history of Columbia River Indians helps explain this larger pattern while also illustrating the particular ways in which one group coped with radical changes, challenged federal authority, and altered the outcomes of national policy.[13]

Second, the River People's history adds to the growing body of literature on the construction of ethnic and racial categories in the United States. Like scholars in other fields, Indian historians have begun to describe identity as a dynamic process rather than a primordial essence. State power still shapes the discussion, but scholars now acknowledge that Native Americans have frequently contested the dominant society's racial and tribal designations. "Within the framework of laws and federal policies," notes historian Alexandra Harmon, "various descendants of aboriginal people have taken the initiative to define themselves, trying to fashion identities that make sense to them." These identities, like all human identities, have multiple layers or positions that shift depending on the situation. Individuals create and continually rearrange their own hierarchy of identities, but ethnic affiliations necessarily develop in a group context and exist in relation to other groups. "Columbia River Indian" originated as an administrative category for the ethnically diverse peoples who refused to leave their ancestral homelands and adopt the roles prescribed in their treaties. Over time, through a process of negotiation with other Indians and non-Indians, this label gradually evolved into a distinct tribal consciousness that sometimes complements but often conflicts with recognized tribal identities.[14]

Interactions within and among Native communities have been central to the formation of Columbia River Indian identity. Although federal policy and law have limited their options, Native Americans have vigorously debated questions of group membership and self-definition among themselves. They have played an active role in defining who they are and have not simply defined themselves in opposition to Euro-Americans. Ethnographers such as Morris Foster and Loretta Fowler have urged scholars to pay closer attention to Indian-Indian interactions, but historians have been slow to move beyond the dualistic perspective of Indian-white relations, in part because of the limitations imposed by documentary sources. When they have done so, scholars have generally focused on the growth of pan-Indian identities in boarding schools and urban communities. By examining intra-tribal divisions as well as external pressures, I aim to highlight the creative but often contentious efforts of colonized peoples to gain control over their history and identity.[15]

Because of the colonial context in which Indian history is produced, any discussion of tribal identity must begin with the acknowledgment that divisions and disagreements among Native Americans do not necessarily make their identities less real or worthy of recognition. All ethnic and national identities are socially constructed, and most have been contested by insiders as well as outsiders. To borrow an example from theorist Edwin Wilmsen, "There are no 'ethnic' Italians in Italy—when Italy was created, Italians had to be created to people it . . . and they were created from the heterogeneous polities that then speckled the Boot of Europe." The same holds true for countless other nationalities, including Americans; indeed, the debate over who and what is "American" remains a pervasive theme in U.S. cultural and political discourse.[16] The principal difference with modern tribal identities is the history of colonialism that forced American Indians to grapple with powerful legal fictions imposed by outsiders. Anthropologist Jonathan Hill explains,

> As independent states expanded across the Americas in the nineteenth century, the European concept of nation-state informed state policies toward indigenous peoples at local and regional levels, resulting in a cultural landscape of relatively fixed ethnic, or tribal, groups. . . . What was left out of that picture was the tremendous fluidity and sheer magnitude of interethnic relations among culturally and linguistically differentiated indigenous peoples.[17]

In other words, the U.S. government did not give Native Americans their identities any more than it gave them land or sovereignty. Rather, in the process of seizing Indian land and abridging tribal sovereignty, the United States attempted to simplify and standardize indigenous forms of social and political organization to suit its own purposes. In doing so, federal policy and law triggered the formation of new tribes. Although Columbia River Indians have never received formal recognition as a tribe, they have continued to think of themselves as a distinct community. Their story deserves to be told.

Of course, there are limits to what a historian can learn about the Native American past. Although I have conducted or read more than a dozen interviews with Indian people, I do not presume to understand fully what it means to *live* the history and identity about which I write. With time and patience, however, a scholar can interpret what indigenous people have said in the course of their own discussions of identity. "Ethnicity has a strategic function that fosters public dialogues," writes Alexandra Harmon. "Distinctions between Indians and non-Indians or between different kinds of Indians have been integral to some people's strategies for survival, economic gain, or self-respect; and groups do not formulate strategy without debate." By searching archives and oral histories for representations of group consciousness, I have aimed to reveal the primary markers of Columbia River Indian identity as they have developed over time. Because it is in part an identity of opposition, forged in conflict with recognized tribes, I have often been compelled to write about events and issues that remain controversial among Indian people today. My purpose in recounting this history is not to inflame old wounds, but rather to show how those wounds were inflicted and how Native people have tried to cope with them. I sincerely hope that, in doing so, this book will prove useful both to scholars and the Indian communities concerned.[18]

The people and communities that are represented by the
Mid-Columbia River Council are the children of the ancestors
who were created in these lands, along side the rivers and creeks,
and in harmony with all other life in this part of the world.
Our existence represents an uninterrupted history that dates
back to the time of our creation within these lands.

—MID-COLUMBIA RIVER COUNCIL,
STATEMENT OF UNIFICATION, 1990

1 ▪ ▪ ▪

PEOPLE OF THE RIVER

On the morning of April 18, 1806, William Clark woke from a fitful sleep in the village of Nixlúidix (Wishram), on the banks of the Columbia River. The co-captain of the homeward bound Corps of Discovery had arrived there two days earlier, seeking horses to ease the expedition's upriver portage around the treacherous Long Narrows. Although the local "Skillutes" had furnished few pack animals, they had welcomed him and asked him to spend the night. "Great numbers of Indians from defferent [*sic*] directions" passed through the Kiksht-speaking community during his brief stay. "Among other Nations who visit this place for the purpose of trade is the *Skad-datt's*," he wrote, noting the arrival of a group that "bantered the Skillutes to play at a Singular kind of game . . . Composed of 9 men on a Side."

They Set down opposit to each other at the distance of about 10 feet. In front of each party a long pole was placed on which they Struck with a Small Stick to the time of their Songs. After the bets were made up which was nearly half an hour after they Set down, two round bones was producd about the Size of a mans little finger or Something Smaller and 2¼ inches in length, which they held in their hand Changeing it from one hand to the other with great dexterity. 2 men on [each] the Same Side performed this part, and when they had the bone in the hand they wished, they looked at their advosarys Swinging arms around their Sholders for their advosary Guess which they pirformed by the motion the hand either to the right or left.

Clark watched them gamble for hours, impressed by their sleight of hand and the volume of goods exchanged, but the rules of one contest ultimately baffled him. "This is a very intricate game," he confessed in his journal entry for the day, "and I cannot Sufficiently understand to discribe [*sic*] it."[1]

More than the nuances of the stick game eluded Clark that day. Despite their keen powers of observation, he and his companions never grasped the full complexity of aboriginal society along the Columbia River. They certainly recognized that the area between The Cascades and Celilo Falls served as a "great mart" for the indigenous peoples of the region. The desire to deal had brought the Corps of Discovery to Nixlúidix ("coming-together place") just as it had drawn representatives of the diverse "Tribes" and "Nations" Clark encountered during his stay. The "Skadatts," however, came from Łádaxat, a nearby Klickitat village with a mixed population of Sahaptin and Kiksht speakers. The visiting Indians probably had relatives among the "Skillutes," and personal ties clouded the tribal labels applied by the American explorers. The boundaries separating Native communities along the Columbia River were rarely as clear-cut as the parallel lines of the stick game would suggest. Largely hidden from view, like the bones passed among the Indian gamblers, an intricate kinship network stretched across the Mid-Columbia region and beyond. Lewis and Clark caught glimpses of this network during their sojourn, but they never understood it well enough to describe it.[2]

The co-captains and their government failed to understand because they tried to fit Native communities into a simplistic model of social and political organization. As the first whites to cross the Columbia Plateau, Lewis and Clark began the process of dividing its indigenous population into discrete "tribes" and "bands" with which the United States government could deal efficiently. Before contact with Europeans, however, Indian relations along the Columbia River flowed through channels quite different from those the newcomers constructed. The names listed in Lewis and Clark's journals did not represent distinct "tribes" in the modern sense of the word, but instead denoted autonomous winter villages. These self-governing communities typically formed the largest political units in a regional social network bound together by shared territory, cultural affinity, economic exchange, and extensive intermarriage. Family ties crisscrossed the Columbia Basin, bridging both geographic barriers and linguistic boundaries, and individuals moved in and out of different social groupings during the year. In this world of interconnected communities, Indians had multiple affiliations and multifaceted identities that would complicate future attempts to place them in singular tribal categories.[3]

■ ■ ■

The roots of Columbia River Indian identity tap the river itself. Called Nch'í Wána in Sahaptin and Wi'mahl in Upper Chinookan (Kiksht), "the Big River" has sustained life and shaped culture in the rain shadow of the Cascade Mountains for at least ten thousand years. The Indians of the dry plateau country relied on the river for much of their water and food. Mutual dependence forged a common human bond to the Columbia that belied its later use as a boundary between tribes, territories, and states. While modern history has invested this line with power and meaning, the separation of peoples and polities in aboriginal times was neither so neat nor natural as maps suggest. In fact, the waters of the Columbia River typically united rather than divided human populations. At The Dalles, the region's largest fishery and main commercial center, Indians from across the Plateau gathered to trade for salmon and other valued commodities. Salmon tied people to each other and linked them all to the river. As one elder explained in 1915, the Columbia formed "a table for [Indians on] both sides of the river. It laid right in between them, and they came and ate and were gone." Those who lived on its banks became known in the Sahaptin language as Wanałáma or Wánapam, "people of the river," a name that connotes a spiritual connection as well as a spatial relationship. In the words of Johnny Jackson, a current leader of the River People, "All our traditional values are along the Columbia River."[4]

Mid-Columbia Indians expressed their ties to the river through shared oral traditions that stretch back over centuries and across different groups. Several stories describe an epic battle between two sets of brothers representing the cold east winds and the warm west winds that blow alternately through the Columbia Gorge. In one version of the story, the trickster Coyote intervened and established a balance between the warring sides. In another, the victorious west winds dictated terms to their vanquished winter rivals:

From now on you will no longer be a person and go around freezing people. You can blow once in awhile, then I will come and overpower you. Rain will be your enemy too. You will blow and freeze everything, but then he and I will come; we will thaw out the ground, warm everything up, and make the earth green and beautiful again.

Significantly, some of the groups occupying the gorge had known its prevailing air currents for so many centuries that their dialects lacked words for "north wind" and "south wind."[5]

Geological events made a similar impression on indigenous cultural memories. Around eight hundred years ago, a huge chunk of Table Mountain slid into the Columbia River, temporarily damming it and blocking the salmon runs. The people living upstream felt the impact deeply. Generations later their descendants still related stories about the time Coyote freed the salmon from a pair of sisters who had imprisoned them behind a dam. To punish the women for their selfishness, the trickster transformed them into swallows, whose return each spring heralds the arrival of the first salmon runs. Linguists traditionally assigned different versions of this tradition to particular tribes, but Native groups swapped stories as frequently as they traded goods. Mid-Columbia Indians told similar tales because they had shared the same places, the same experiences, and the same traditions for such a long time.[6]

Archaeological evidence confirms the ancient presence of Native Americans along the Columbia River. The ancestors of the people who met Lewis and Clark etched petroglyphs such as Tsagiglalal, "She Who Watches," into the basalt cliffs overlooking the Long Narrows. They buried their dead in the talus slopes beneath or on islands in the river. Their garbage accumulated in huge middens such as Wakemap Mound, near the village where Clark witnessed the stick game. In the 1950s, just before The Dalles Dam flooded one of the oldest living communities in the world, scientists dug through thirty feet of camp refuse at a site across the river. The upper layers contained modern trade goods, similar to those Lewis and Clark carried, while the lowest levels held material dating back more than ten thousand years. The precise extent and timing of cultural change in the intervening period remains a subject of debate among archaeologists, who often differ with the Indians themselves. Still, most scholars agree that the defining characteristics of the contact-era Plateau culture had developed at least two thousand years before the Corps of Discovery first described it.[7]

The peoples of the Columbia Plateau shared a way of life based on the seasonal harvesting of fish, game, and wild plant foods. Naturally, the details of the annual subsistence cycle varied across the region, with some groups relying more than others on particular resources. Those living closest to the great fisheries of the Columbia River depended most heavily on salmon and often traded their surplus catch for other foodstuffs, whereas their interior neighbors placed slightly greater emphasis on hunting and gathering. In most years, the seasonal round also afforded room for individual choice. One family might remain in the Cascade Mountains until October, hunting and harvesting berries, while another hastened back to the Columbia River to meet the fall salmon runs. Those too old or too sick to travel typically remained on the river year-round, perhaps shifting between a winter village and temporary summer fishing camps. Generally speaking, though, Plateau Indians traced familiar patterns on the landscape and through time as they followed the familiar rhythm of the seasons.[8]

During the dreary winter months, when overcast skies blanketed much of the region, families congregated in village sites along major rivers and tributary streams. Subsisting primarily on dried food stores, they used this time for storytelling, spiritual renewal, and the maintenance or manufacture of tools. Families often traveled to neighboring villages to participate in a regional complex of ceremonial dances and shamanic performances. By the early 1800s, some groups from eastern Oregon spent the entire winter at The Dalles, where they traded and worshiped with the local population. Besides breaking the monotony of cold-weather confinement, visiting had a vital economic function, as people met to plan their foraging activities and redistribute local food surpluses through feasting. As much as the Indians enjoyed these festivities, they welcomed the arrival of the warm Chinook winds in early March. Rising temperatures and melting snow signaled the start of a new seasonal round, when families left their winter lodges to begin a period of increased mobility and social activity.[9]

Mid-Columbia Indians harvested subsistence resources as they became available. Drawing on an encyclopedic knowledge of local ecology, they adapted the size and distribution of task groups to best exploit seasonal variations in the abundance of traditional foods. Wilbur Slockish, Jr., has described the land as a vast grocery store, with different places representing separate aisles stocked with particular goods. The patterns of aboriginal "shopping" reflected Plateau gender roles. Depending on their specific location within the region, women fulfilled between 50 and 70 percent of a village's dietary needs through the gathering of wild plant foods. They also preserved and prepared most of the game and fish that men procured. Euro-American observers perceived such work as evidence of "squaw drudgery," but economic parity gave Mid-Columbia women greater status and influence than that of their contemporary American counterparts. Although few women became village chiefs, they often led task groups and ceremonial gathering expeditions.

Women knew the locations and uses of important plant resources, and they knew precisely when to harvest them.[10]

Plateau women broke the long winter fast with the first fresh foods of the season. In early spring they gathered bitterroot and lomatiums (Indian celeries) in the hills near their villages, while men caught spawning suckers in the rivers and streams. This fare whetted appetites for the runs of spring chinook, which generally arrived in late April and continued through May. Lewis and Clark witnessed the start of the season and marveled at the amount of fish the Indians landed. Each village between The Dalles and Celilo utilized a cluster of traditional fishing stations, typically composed of rocks, islands, and cliffs adjoining the falls and rapids in the river. At such points, where the current forced the fish into eddies and narrow channels, Indian men gaffed, speared, seined, or dip-netted salmon, depending on the site and the stream conditions. Women cleaned and dried the fish on racks, then packed them into bundles or pounded them into "salmon flour." Walking among the towering stacks of dried salmon at Wishram, Lewis and Clark estimated that the villagers had processed some ten thousand pounds of fish.[11]

The local Indians earmarked much of this salmon for trade. Long before the Corps of Discovery passed through the region, The Dalles had developed into one of the greatest commercial centers in North America. Every year during the salmon runs, the area's permanent population swelled by several thousand people. Indians traveled to the fisheries from across the Plateau and beyond to swap goods, ideas, and genes with the local residents. In exchange for dried salmon, Indians from the Lower Columbia River traded eulachon (candlefish), cured shellfish, and wapato. Interior Plateau peoples contributed venison, roots, and berries from their own territory as well as buffalo meat from the Great Plains. These food items mingled with a wide array of other commodities, including dentalia shells, obsidian, canoes, baskets, mats, furs, hides, and horses. Some people also purchased captives taken from enemies to the south, who were generally traded as slaves to downstream neighbors and visitors from the Northwest Coast.[12] During the late eighteenth century, blankets, glass beads, metal tools, guns, and other Euro-American manufactured goods became a regular part of the bargaining process. More than just a prime fishery, The Dalles served as the focal point of a vast economic and social network. It was, in the words of one American writer, "the Billingsgate of Oregon," a reference to the London market famous for its foul-mouthed fishwives.[13]

The first trading season ended in late May or early June, when spring runoff rendered the rivers too high and muddy for fishing. At that time, many families stored their catch and moved on to root-digging grounds in the Cascade foothills or the Blue Mountains. Following the receding snow and the ripening of plants at higher elevations, women gathered roots and berries, while men hunted deer, elk, and other game. Families progressed from camp to camp until they reached their traditional camas meadows and enjoyed another opportunity for large social gatherings. Kittitas, Fox Valley, and Camas Prairie hosted hundreds or even thousands of Indians each year. "The gathering was for the purpose of digging these roots," recalled Chief William Yallup of Rock Creek. "[The Indians] killed game and they fished and had a big time." "A big time" included gambling, trading, socializing, and (after about 1730) horse racing. Some families also arranged the marriages that tied Plateau communities together and underpinned friendly relations.[14]

This pattern of economic and social exchange among village groups continued throughout the seasonal round. In late June and early July, falling stream levels and returning salmon brought many people back to the river for another round of fishing and trading. Heavy runs of chinook, sockeye, and steelhead generally kept them there for several weeks, though some women left to harvest chokecherries and other berries during the slack periods. In mid-August, many families moved off into the huckleberry meadows along the crest of the Cascade Mountains. At places such as Indian Heaven, near Mount Adams, various groups congregated to gather their favorite fruit, hunt deer and elk, and participate in more social activity. Some families stayed in the mountains until the first snowfall; others returned to the rivers in September to fish the fall chinook runs and prepare their village sites. The fall fishery witnessed the peak trading period, and many people took the opportunity to supplement their winter stores. By November, when the cold east winds began to whistle through the Columbia Gorge, the Indians had completed their seasonal migrations and settled in for the long months ahead.[15]

In most years, the systematic harvesting of diverse subsistence resources produced enough food to last through the winter. Plateau Indians did not take abundance for granted, however, and the peoples of the Mid-Columbia River prefaced each stage of the seasonal round with familial or communal rituals intended to guarantee future security. "At the beginning of each season," explained Vivian M. Adams of the Yakama Nation in the early 1990s, "a special group of people was selected for the first gathering of that season's offerings." Chosen for their skills and intimate knowledge of particular resources, these ceremonial leaders fasted and prayed to ensure their people's success in the coming harvest.[16] Although the antiquity of specific rites is uncertain, the first non-Indians to visit the Mid-Columbia noted the ceremonial practices that surrounded salmon in the early nineteenth century. Heading back upriver in April 1806, members of the Lewis and Clark expedition observed a "first-salmon feast" in the village of Wishram:

> There was great joy with the natives last night in consequence of the arrival of the Salmon; one of those fish was caught; this was the harbinger of good news to them. They informed us that these fish would arrive in great quantities in the course of about 5 days. This fish was dressed and being divided into small pieces was given to each child in the village. This custom is founded in superstitious opinion that it will hasten the arrival of the salmon.[17]

Traditionally, no one could catch or consume any of their own fish until this ceremony had been performed. As the Methodist missionary Henry Perkins further explained in the early 1840s,

> The tu-a-ti-ma [twáti-ma, "Indian doctors"]—or medicine men—as they are sometimes called by the white—practice a sort of invocatory ceremony on the first arrival of the salmon in the spring. Before any of the common people are permitted to boil, or even to cut the flesh of the salmon trans-

versely for any purpose, the tu-a-ti [twáti] . . . assembles the people, & after invoking the "Tah" [taax] or the particular spirit which presides over the salmon, & who they suppose can make it a prosperous year or otherwise, takes a fish just caught, & wrings off its head. The blood, which flows from the fish, he catches in a basin, or small dish, & sets it aside. He then cuts the salmon transversely into small pieces, & boils. The way is thus opened for any one else to do the same. Joy & rejoicing circulate through the village, & the people now boil & eat to their heart's content.[18]

After five days—a ritually proscribed number—the blood of the first fish was "carried out, waved in the direction in which they wish the fish to run, & then carefully poured into the water." Then the general fishing season could begin.[19]

Scholars have since recognized that the practices these explorers and missionaries derided as "superstition" in fact served an important ecological purpose. By delaying the start of the regular harvest for several days, religious ritual allowed the upriver escapement of salmon that might otherwise fall prey to Native nets. Anthropologists still debate whether this form of resource conservation was an intentional or incidental result of Plateau first-food feasts. The matter cannot be settled with the available sources, but there is little doubt that the ceremony's core message of respect for the gifts of the Creator served to discourage waste. "Myths, ceremonies, and taboos restrained individual and social consumption," argues environmental historian Joseph Taylor, "while settlement patterns and usufruct rights restricted access to salmon." Thus, despite highly efficient fishing techniques and historically large catches, "Indian culture and economy produced a sustainable tension between society and nature."[20]

At Celilo Falls, an important fishery adjoining the villages of Sk'in (Skin) and Wayám (Wayam/Celilo), the enforcement of traditional rules ultimately became the responsibility of a special salmon chief. The antiquity of this title, like the age of particular rituals, is a subject of some disagreement. Anthropologists generally consider it a modern creation, called into being by declining salmon populations and increasing competition in the late nineteenth century, whereas most Mid-Columbia Indians insist on earlier origins. Howard Jim, the late chief of Celilo Village, informed Congress that the position had existed "from the time beginning, no one knows how long ago it was, but as long as it has been in existence the fishing was always regulated by the chief." Evidence from elsewhere on the Plateau suggests that it was an aboriginal title whose importance became magnified as changing circumstances raised the stakes. By the time Tommy Thompson assumed the role in the early 1900s, it had evidently become a hereditary position with well-defined rights and responsibilities. As he explained in the early 1940s, the salmon chief set the fishing seasons and enforced prohibitions against fishing at night, on Sundays, and after drowning deaths (a fairly regular occurrence in the turbulent rapids of The Dalles–Celilo reach). In addition, said Thompson, the salmon chief "was the one who would say who should use a place when there was no one in the family to whom it had belonged capable of making use of it and that the decision of the Chief was final and respected by all the other Indians."[21]

■ ■ ■

As Lewis and Clark noted in their journals, the dramatic falls at Celilo marked the upper end of a cultural and linguistic transition zone between Sahaptin-speaking and Kiksht-speaking Indians. Within the Plateau culture area, linguists have identified four major languages and at least sixteen distinct dialects that existed at the time of European contact. Although some peoples had lived there longer than others, the diversity of dialects and the depth of environmental vocabulary suggest many centuries of continuous occupation by the present groups. The majority of Mid-Columbia Indians spoke the Sahaptin language, which includes three dialect clusters with fourteen known variants. Some 8,400 Northwest Sahaptins (Kittitas, Yakama, Klickitat, and Taitnapam) inhabited the interior valleys to the north and west of the Columbia River. Between them and the linguistically distinct Nez Perces and Cayuses lived approximately 7,500 Northeast Sahaptins (Walla Walla, Lower

Snake, Palouse, Wánapam). Another 7,000 Columbia River Sahaptins (Tenino, Tygh, Wayám, Rock Creek, John Day, and Umatilla) occupied villages along the mainstem Columbia and the lower reaches of its tributaries from the Umatilla River to The Dalles. Those communities comprised the heart of the Wanałáma, the "people of the river" whose descendants came to identify as Columbia River Indians, but many also traced their ancestry to Wánapam, Walla Walla, Klickitat, and Upper Chinookan villages. Upper Chinookan (Kiksht) is part of a different language group that stretched up the Columbia as far as The Dalles, where Sahaptin-speakers mingled with roughly 10,000 Wascos, Wishrams, and Cascades. Multilingualism was common, and language differences did not create impermeable social barriers. While linguistic groups create a convenient framework for classification, they fail to convey the fluid nature of aboriginal ethnic distinctions then and now.[22]

Plateau Indians lived in a world of independent but interconnected villages, not cohesive linguistic tribes. Each language or dialect encompassed a number of semi-permanent winter settlements and associated seasonal camps, which became the "tribes" and "bands" of Euro-American usage through a process of creative misunderstanding. As anthropologist Verne F. Ray noted in 1939, "Early settlers, traders, missionaries, and government officials carried with them from the east the notion that all Indian groups were of necessity organized along tribal lines. Upon learning a village name from a native the whites immediately and indiscriminately applied it to all Indians of the vicinity." Some labels represented self-designations, such as Wayám and Tináynu (Tenino), but others derived from neighbors with different languages or dialects. The Kiksht-speaking Wishrams, for example, acquired the name for their principal village from the Sahaptin word Wišxam. Few indigenous names survived transliteration without some degree of corruption and variation. The Wascos alone had nineteen synonyms for their name in early Euro-American writings. Using such labels therefore requires the caveat that they are historical creations with changing forms and ambiguous definitions.[23]

The confusion surrounding tribal names compounded Euro-American misperceptions of Plateau political organization. Villages, not broader linguistic or ethnic categories, constituted the largest political units with any significant structure. Although several neighboring settlements might unite under a particularly charismatic leader to form a loose confederacy, larger alliances rarely occurred except in times of war. Even then, individuals and families retained considerable autonomy. A strong class system, reflecting Northwest Coast influences, allowed Upper Chinookan headmen and their families to control the lives and labor of slaves. Most Sahaptins did not practice slavery, however, and their chiefs (*miyúux*) had little power to command others. Both societies premised leadership on proven ability. The title of chief could be inherited, but only men who displayed the requisite chiefly qualities of eloquence, generosity, self-discipline, and wisdom could expect to assume the position. Leading by example and exhortation, headmen exercised authority through spokesmen and sometimes made decisions in concert with informal councils of respected elders, both male and female. The presence of sub-chiefs and specialized task leaders, including shamans and war chiefs, further diffused power within Plateau communities. People who disagreed with their headmen were free to leave and live with relatives in another village.[24]

Multiple bonds of blood and marriage superseded loyalty to a particular village or ethnic group. Mid-Columbia Indians traditionally counted more than forty kinds of relatives, whereas most Euro-Americans recognize about thirty. Consequently, each person had a large number of kin designated as aunts, uncles, and siblings, all of whom deserved special consideration in social and economic matters. This broad network of mutual obligation encompassed one's in-laws, and marriage provided the primary means of linking different villages and "tribal" groups. Although most Plateau weddings joined communities sharing contiguous territory, kinship ties bridged geographical and political boundaries. The residents of Sk'ín and Wayám "considered themselves one big family," in the words of Chief Yallup, despite occupying opposite banks of the Columbia River and acknowledging separate headmen. Close relationships with distant groups developed less frequently, but wealthy families endeavored to arrange such unions whenever possible. A prominent chief might have several wives from different communities. As a result of these marriage practices, individuals could visit freely with relatives across the Plateau. Indians often lived in several villages during their lifetimes, and many settlements had ethnically and linguistically diverse populations. This constant shuttling of people between communities wove a thick social blanket that insulated families against adversity and directed their movement across the landscape.[25]

Kinship ties structured access to resources, especially at the prime fisheries of the Columbia River. While the residents of particular villages tended to utilize the same fishing grounds, specific sites belonged to individuals and families. The rights to a particular cliff, rock, island, or scaffold descended through inheritance, and the owners had to grant permission for others to use it. Fishing rights thus created a major incentive to marry outside one's village, enabling a person to acquire rights to several sites across a wide area. Relatives took priority over strangers at the fisheries, but few visitors went away empty-handed. "If the visiting Indians did not have anything to trade for fish," explained Celilo chief Tommy Thompson in the 1940s, "the local people would either give them some of their own supply or else they would lend them the necessary equipment and permit them to catch all the fish they needed from one of the established fishing stations belonging to the local people." This system of generalized reciprocity provided security for all while preserving local prerogatives. As Thompson witnessed during his long lifetime, though, the pressures produced by American colonization would strain traditional arrangements to the breaking point.[26]

■ ■ ■

Significant changes had already swept the Plateau by the time Lewis and Clark arrived in Wishram seeking horses. Those animals, acquired from the Shoshones and Flatheads to the east, appeared in the region around 1730 and quickly became integral to Native culture. By the mid-nineteenth century, the prophet Smohalla would insist that Indians had always possessed horses. Though less important to River People, who tended to remain more sedentary than their interior neighbors, the *kúsi* (literally, "dog") became a standard of wealth and greatly expanded the range of the seasonal round. Families could now travel farther, move faster, and carry heavier loads. Horses also introduced new items into the regional diet and culture. Nez Perces and Cayuses—accomplished horse breeders in their own right—occasionally joined Yakamas, Walla Wallas, and Umatillas in buffalo-hunting expeditions on the northern Great Plains. Other Columbia River Sahaptins may have participated in these forays, but the usual abundance of salmon made such trips unnecessary. As William Clark witnessed during his visit to Wishram, river residents could usually trade for bison skins and the Plains-style regalia that Plateau people increasingly favored as clothing and adornment.[27]

The same horses that transported hunters east of the Rockies carried Plateau raiders deep into enemy territory. Mounted parties of Klickitats, Columbia River Sahaptins, and Upper Chinookans captured or purchased slaves from groups in southern Oregon and California to exchange at The Dalles. Taking advantage of horses and guns, as well as the terrible impact of disease on western Indians, Klickitat groups also expanded their range into the Willamette Valley during the 1830s and 1840s. In turn, Plateau communities suffered escalating attacks from mounted Shoshones in the Great Basin. By 1805, fear of "Snake" raids had caused some Sahaptin villages to relocate from the south bank of the Columbia River to new sites on midstream islands or the north shore. Even enemies occasionally came to trade, however, and periodic hostilities did not overturn the norm of peaceful relations among Plateau villages.[28]

The diseases that ravaged Indian communities during the period of Euro-American contact proved far deadlier than warfare. Although scholars disagree on the timing and origins of these imported epidemics, most believe that the first known epidemic of smallpox, spread from Northwest Coast or Plains sources, hit the Plateau between 1775 and 1782. Another wave of smallpox swept down the Columbia in 1801, carrying off a fresh generation of victims and reducing the aboriginal population to perhaps half its pre-contact level. During the 1820s, a Wasco prophet reportedly foresaw a day when many Indians would "lay dead like drift-wood along the shores of the [Big River]." The depleted numbers recorded by Lewis and Clark fell even further in subsequent decades, as fur traders and colonists introduced influenza, malaria, whooping cough, and other diseases to which indigenous peoples had no immunity. Some Cayuses retaliated in 1847, killing the missionaries Marcus and Narcissa Whitman in the wake of a measles epidemic. Still, Plateau Indian populations continued to decline throughout the nineteenth century.[29]

The social and cultural impacts of earlier epidemics remain difficult to determine. Clearly, the deaths of so many people in such a short time traumatized families and disrupted kin networks along the Columbia River. When disease killed relatives and in-laws, many people lost their links to other communities. Elders died in droves, depleting the rich stores of knowledge and memory that supported social identities and cultural traditions. More immediately, some groups probably lost the ability to remain independent. As residents succumbed to illness or sought refuge with relatives living elsewhere, many nuclear families and winter lodges broke apart. Consequently, some villages may have collapsed or combined with neighboring settlements, reprising a story that had played out across the continent since the earliest days of European colonization. At the western end of the Columbia Gorge, the Middle and Lower Cascades people formed a single village following the malaria and influenza epidemics that decimated their ranks in the early 1830s. Similar migrations and mergers likely occurred above The Dalles. In 1854, following another outbreak of smallpox, American observers found the Yakima River "lined with the vestiges of former villages, now vacant," though these may have been confused with seasonal camps. Still, most Plateau communities weathered the invasion of foreign microbes better than their coastal neighbors did. Damaged but not destroyed, the web of kinship stretching between villages continued to order social relations along the Columbia River.[30]

Hard on the heels of pestilence followed a growing procession of non-Indian newcomers eager to claim the country Lewis and Clark had placed on the map. Within a decade of their visit, Plateau Indians met

the first of many British and American fur traders, missionaries, emigrants, soldiers, and bureaucrats. Each group had its own agenda, but
all shared the desire to control or change Indian behavior in some way.
They also shared a set of ideas about Indians—often erroneous and mis-
leading—developed through centuries of interaction with Native peoples
across North America. While aware of differences among Indian groups,
Euro-Americans generally assumed that existing knowledge and experience could effectively guide their dealings with any and all Indians they
encountered. In particular, the newcomers believed that Indians every-
where had a similar form of social and political organization based on
"tribes" and "chiefs." Where such entities did not exist or did not function
in the desired fashion, Euro-Americans endeavored to change the current forms or create entirely new ones. Mid-Columbia Indians responded
to these efforts in a variety of ways, but rarely with the expected results.[31]

British fur traders, the first non-Indians to arrive in significant numbers, attempted fairly minor modifications to the Plateau social system.
Their light touch came not from any special respect for indigenous cultures, but from the limited nature of British interests in the region. The
basalt canyons and sagebrush deserts of the Mid-Columbia produced
few furs for the booming European and Asian markets of the nineteenth
century. The traders' main concern was the river itself, which provided a
vital link in their expansive commercial chains. In 1818, the North West
Company (NWC) established Fort Nez Percés at the mouth of the Walla
Walla River to support its lucrative operations in present-day British
Columbia and the Upper Snake River country. Six years later, following
its merger with the NWC, the Hudson's Bay Company (HBC) founded
Fort Vancouver near the western end of the Columbia Gorge. The stretch
of river between these posts served as the primary shipping route for the
combined fur production of the interior Northwest. Accordingly, company employees had to maintain friendly relations with Native people.[32]

Mid-Columbia Indians tolerated the "King George men," as they
called the British, but most had no interest in trapping furs for trade.
River dwellers generally treated hunting as a supplemental activity and
kept animal skins for their own use. Even Indians who relied more on

hunting, such as the Nez Perces and Palouses, deemed trapping beneath their dignity. Still, some people sought closer relationships with the strangers and found new opportunities at the forts. Klickitats worked the company farm at Fort Vancouver, while Walla Wallas performed various chores at Fort Nez Percés. Cayuses and Nez Perces looked down on "fort Indians" but supplied horses and venison to the company in return for guns, ammunition, and other valued items. Farther down the Columbia River, Wascos and Wishrams preserved their traditional role as middlemen by assisting HBC parties with their portages around the rapids of The Cascades and The Dalles. The failure of early Astorian and Nor'Wester parties to respect Indian control of the river had caused friction and even armed conflict. By the 1820s, however, a fragile "middle ground" had developed that usually enabled Natives and newcomers to conduct business on predictable, mutually acceptable terms.[33]

Even so, the British believed that the Indians could use improvement, and HBC officers tried to change the indigenous institutions they found unpleasant or inconvenient. After the Crown's abolition of slavery in 1833, the company worked to end the practice among the Upper Chinookan population near The Dalles. Pierre Pambrun, the chief trader at Fort Nez Percés, introduced Indians to Christian concepts that later became part of the Washani, or Dreamer, faith. The company also moved to strengthen the authority of its client chiefs in order to simplify diplomacy and assert more control over Indian behavior. At Fort Nez Percés, the traders staged an annual "clothing of the chiefs" ceremony to encourage Native leaders and their people to trap beaver. Only a few Cayuses agreed to that request, yet the ritual of recognition increased British influence with some groups. HBC officials further enhanced the power of particular leaders by expanding their traditional role as mediators in village disputes. Unhappy with the perceived "lawlessness" of Indian society, the company aimed to create formal tribal courts in which chiefs judged offenses and "floggers" administered punishment for lesser crimes. The result, HBC officers assumed, would be the swifter and surer enforcement of company rules.[34]

30   These early attempts at guided culture change made little headway

among Plateau peoples, who accepted, adapted, or rejected British rules as they saw fit. Speeches condemning slavery and plural marriage generally fell on deaf ears, and the Indians openly opposed the imposition of flogging by tribal courts. Although Plateau villages traditionally employed a "whip man" to discipline wayward children with a willow switch, adults considered flogging shameful and beyond the bounds of chiefly authority. Tawatoy, the "paramount chief" of the Cayuses, vigorously enforced the practice only to see his following disintegrate. When the Walla Walla headman Pyópyo Maqsmáqs (Piupiumaksmaks) whipped his people, they recalled their recent religious instruction and declared that God would punish him. Mid-Columbia Indians respected those who held the esteem of powerful outsiders, but they did not discard their own standards of leadership. The "head chiefs" identified by the British still had to earn the allegiance of their own people, and they still had clear limits to their authority. Consensus and individual choice, not coercion and chiefly rule, remained the governing principles of Plateau politics.[35]

The most significant cultural changes of the fur trade era occurred informally, through the daily interaction of Natives and newcomers along the river. In addition to obtaining trade goods and contracting foreign diseases, some Mid-Columbia Indians acquired cattle and started their own herds. Others began raising barley, corn, melons, potatoes, and squash in irrigated gardens. The exchange of animals, plants, commodities, and labor encouraged the development of intimate social ties. Both the British and the Indians understood that marriage cemented friendly relations and provided access to valuable resources. Consequently, with HBC permission many Native women wedded British, French Canadian, Iroquois, or Métis employees. The children of such unions, as well as those of more illicit encounters, often assumed the role of cultural liaisons in adulthood. Moreover, they began the process of racial mixing that would further blur the boundaries of tribal and Indian identity.[36]

The missionaries who followed the fur traders into the region lived in close proximity to the Indians but avoided intermarriage with them. Besides holding strong racial views, many Protestant missionaries came as married couples. In 1836, Henry and Eliza Hart Spalding established a

Presbyterian mission at Lapwai, in Nez Perce country. Their friends, the Whitmans, settled among the Walla Wallas and Cayuses at Waiilatpu. In 1838 Methodist minister Henry Perkins joined Daniel Lee in founding Wascopam Mission near The Dalles. The Catholic Jesuits answered with their own missions on the Mid-Columbia, and the race for Indian souls began. Each denomination scored initial successes that fueled high expectations. During the winter revival of 1839–40, for instance, the Methodists claimed to have converted a thousand people. Their influence soon waned, however, and the first phase of missionary activity had a relatively superficial impact on Plateau Indian culture.[37]

The short lifespan and limited reach of the early missions resulted from a variety of factors. Some Indians had hoped to acquire spiritual power from the outsiders; instead, they received sermons against gambling, polygamy, and other "heathen" practices. Protestant missionaries, convinced that Christianity and American "civilization" must advance together, paired religious instruction with agricultural training. They found some converts willing to follow both the plow and the Lord, but most Plateau people remained loyal to the seasonal round. Sectarian squabbling over whose Lord they should follow further undermined the Indians' faith in the missionary message. As Chief Joseph of the Nez Perces later explained, it seemed that churches would only teach them "to quarrel about God, as the Protestants and Catholics do. . . . We do not want to learn that." The most damning indictment against the missions arose from their growing association with the spread of white settlements and white diseases. Watching their own people sicken and die while the Whitmans greeted wagon trains, many Indians concluded that the preachers had more power to harm than to help. By 1847, when the so-called Whitman Massacre forced the temporary abandonment of most stations, Christian missionaries had influenced Plateau patterns of work and worship but had barely touched the underlying social structure.[38]

Greater changes were already in the making. From 1839 onward, a growing contingent of American emigrants embarked for the Oregon Country, challenging both the British claim to the region and the rights of its Native inhabitants. Although most of the "Bostons" settled in the verdant Willamette Valley, the Oregon Trail passed through the southern Plateau and exposed Mid-Columbia Indians to new challenges and opportunities. Some Cayuses, Walla Wallas, and Umatillas served as guides or traded their garden produce to hungry travelers in exchange for clothing and other commodities. Štáqułay (Stocketly), a Wayám headman, did a brisk business ferrying emigrants across the Deschutes River. To most Indians, however, transient whites represented unwelcome and ungrateful intruders. Despite their relative wealth in livestock and other goods, they burned firewood, consumed forage, and hunted game on Native lands without permission or compensation. Consequently, some Indians sought to enforce reciprocity and extract payment through the pilfering of small items and the theft of stock. Between the Umatilla River and The Dalles, overland parties lost numerous animals to Sahaptin and "Snake" raiders. Distressed emigrants joined the beleaguered Protestant missionaries in calling for the extension of U.S. jurisdiction over the Oregon Country. In 1842, the federal government took a step in that direction by appointing an agent named Elijah White to regulate relations with the Indian groups west of the Rockies.[39]

Although he lacked both administrative support and military backing, White hurriedly launched the first American attempt to reorder Mid-Columbia Indian society along tribal lines. In late 1842, he visited the missions at Lapwai, Waiilatpu, and Wascopam to announce the imposition of a new legal and political order intended to curb Indian "lawlessness" and increase tribal accountability. His ambitious plan involved the appointment of a single head chief and several subordinate chiefs and constables to govern each tribe. Together, these men would enforce "all of [the head chief's] lawful requirements, which they were at once to have in writing, in their own language, to regulate their intercourse with whites, and in most cases with themselves." The eleven proposed laws listed several crimes, ranging from murder and arson to theft and property damage, along with their equivalent penalties. Depending on the offense, the designated chiefs would have the authority to fine, imprison, flog, or hang the guilty party. Like the Hudson's Bay Company before him, White believed that centralizing judicial authority would simplify and systematize relations with Native peoples. Some Nez Perces, Cayuses, Walla Wallas, and Upper Chinookans accepted his "civil compact," in part because it resembled familiar fur trade practices, but they struggled to reconcile it with their own institutions. Most groups ignored the code entirely, and it never attained the region-wide application White had envisioned.[40]

The "Nez Perce laws," as he labeled them, clashed with indigenous practices of political power and dispute resolution. In Plateau legal tradition, the relatives of the injured party investigated an offense and imposed the appropriate sanctions against the perpetrator or a relative. By vesting judicial authority in a set of supreme leaders, White's law code shifted social control from kin groups to political figures with unprecedented powers. Although White allowed the Indians to select their own chiefs and sub-chiefs, the prerogatives he purported to give them threatened Plateau norms of individual and village autonomy. Traditionally, headmen could not speak for or give orders to members of other villages. Some of the leaders chosen to fill the new roles welcomed the opportunity because it enhanced their status and authority. Others found it embarrassing and routinely protested that they could not represent all of their people. Many of their peers and followers expressed similar misgivings. Among the Wascos, affluent men who deemed themselves social equals of the head chief refused to accept flogging without compensation. The law code thus created or aggravated personal divisions within the groups that adopted it, while failing to produce a radical transformation of Native social and political practices.[41]

If White's reforms fell short of the mark, they nonetheless indicated the nature of things to come. The practice of naming principal chiefs, already a trademark of European-Indian diplomacy, would continue under U.S. jurisdiction. In 1846 President James Polk negotiated a complete British withdrawal from the new Oregon Territory, officially opening the road for American colonization and subjecting the Native population to policies framed in Washington, DC. To regulate Native relations in the region, the Office of Indian Affairs installed a bureaucratic hierarchy of territorial superintendencies, regional districts, and local agencies. A new era was dawning. At the end of the 1840s, however, the American nation-state and its citizens had little power to remake the indigenous peoples of the Columbia Plateau. Despite the dramatic changes of the previous century, Mid-Columbia Indians continued to live in a world attuned to the seasons and structured according to their own social categories. The "intricate game" that William Clark had dimly perceived in 1805 still followed Native rules.

Several times we sat with the new people and tried to put together
agreements that would accommodate the needs of both of our peoples.
Each time it was we who gave privileges to the new people. We gave
them the privilege of a place to live, we gave them the privilege to
fish and hunt, we were open to sharing the gifts of the Creator.
But the new people were not of the same mind.

——MID-COLUMBIA RIVER COUNCIL,
STATEMENT OF UNIFICATION, 1990

2 ▪ ▪ ▪

MAKING TREATIES, MAKING TRIBES

William Chinook worried about the future of his people. From his farm near The Dalles, where an American military post and settlement had recently sprouted among the rocks, the Wasco headman watched apprehensively as an endless column of emigrants rolled off the Oregon Trail. His own travels in the East, accompanying the explorer John C. Frémont, had revealed the size and strength of the United States. Billy Chinook knew that armed resistance offered little hope, and he tried to live as the whites instructed. Raised near Wascopam Mission, he had adopted the Methodist faith and acquired a reputation as a "progressive" Indian. He had built a house, planted a garden, purchased a herd of cattle, and learned to read and write the English language. Yet the newcomers seemed no less determined to displace him and his fellow Indians from their homes along the Columbia River. In 1853, his concerns drove him to demand an explanation from the Oregon superintendent of Indian affairs: "Now we wish to know whether this is the land of the white man or of the Indian. . . . If it is our land the whites must not trouble us. If it is the land of the white man, when did he buy it?" The emigrants behaved as if they already owned the territory, and Chinook feared they would "take possession of the very spots we occupy." "Where will we go," he wondered, "where will we make our homes? If we lose our country what shall we do?"[1]

There is no record of an official reply to his questions, but the government gave its answer soon enough. In July 1855, Chinook and twelve other Native leaders signed a treaty ceding ten million acres to the United States and creating a reservation for the Warm Springs and Wasco "tribes." Similar treaties, concluded two weeks earlier in the Walla Walla Valley, established new homelands for groups that ultimately became the Yakama Nation, the Confederated Tribes of the Umatilla Indian Reservation, and the Nez Perce Tribe. Reservations emerged during the 1840s and 1850s as the government's solution to its perceived "Indian problem." By extinguishing aboriginal title to the land and removing Indians from the path of white colonization, federal officials hoped to prevent unregulated contact between the races until Native peoples could take their place in American society. Reservations would supposedly serve as "nurseries of civilization," where Indians could learn to till the soil and embrace the values of Euro-American culture without interference from unscrupulous whites. Even friendly progressives such as Billy Chinook would have to leave their ancestral homes. All Indians, regardless of their individual desires and dispositions, belonged on reservations because of their presumed inferiority and inability to coexist with American emigrants.[2]

Even as it placed Native Americans in a single racial category, the reservation policy drew lines that divided the aboriginal landscape and fragmented Indian communities. In order to make treaties, the Office of Indian Affairs (Indian Office) had to identify the signatory tribes, demarcate their various territories, and select the proper "head chiefs" with whom to negotiate. This process, driven by political expediency rather than the reality of Indian life, entailed a radical reordering of indigenous institutions. On paper, the treaty commissioners purported to divide kinship networks, reassign political loyalties, and restructure group rights. Acting with little knowledge of Plateau social organization and less regard for Indian interests, they partitioned the region into ceded areas and assigned each tribe to a particular agency. In this way, the government attempted to create a system it could comprehend and control. Native people understood the treaties quite differently, however, and they did not instantly behave as unified groups. Even during the war that followed the treaty councils, individual Indians made their own decisions about whether and with whom to fight. The treaties gave birth to modern Native American nations, but tribal confederations did not immediately replace earlier forms of social and political organization. At the end of the 1850s, Mid-Columbia Indians still had many different ways to identify themselves and many different responses to federal policy.

■ ■ ■

The implementation of the reservation system started with the construction of a suitable tribal taxonomy. Between 1846 and 1855, federal officials revised and refined the ethnic classifications developed during the previous forty years. Using pieces of the aboriginal pattern, now tattered by disease, they patched together a plain tribal quilt to replace the intricate social blanket shared by the Native peoples of the region. Indian Office maps and reports turned villages into bands and grouped bands into tribes, which usually took their names from a specific aboriginal community. Wasco (or Wascopam), for example, emerged as an umbrella term for the various Upper Chinookan peoples living south of the Columbia River. Their Sahaptin neighbors from The Dalles to the Palouse country became known collectively as Walla Wallas, even though they spoke several different dialects and never applied such a broad label to themselves. Some tribal designations eventually acquired significance for the people they supposedly described, just as "German" or "Italian" came to have meaning for the diverse immigrants from those countries. During the mid-nineteenth century, however, the tribes and bands of the Middle Columbia existed primarily for the diplomatic and administrative convenience of the U.S. government.[3]

The practice of classifying Indians involved more than simply naming the tribes and marking their territories. Federal officials also made judgments about the character of each group and its prospects for "civilization." Some observers, such as Agent Robert Newell, considered river residents "quite poor and full of conceit." Compared to the Nez Perces and Cayuses in particular, Columbia River Sahaptins and Upper Chinookans owned few horses and therefore lacked the principal source of wealth that whites recognized among Indians. Instead of hunting buffalo, they stayed near their fishing stations and subsisted mainly on salmon, which most Americans still regarded as a food of last resort. River dwellers seemed less colorful, less like the resplendent Plains warriors that the public would grow to admire. They also seemed less honorable than the equestrian peoples of the eastern Plateau. Echoing the opinions of Lewis and Clark, who had wrangled with the shrewd Native traders at The Dalles, Indian agent and amateur ethnographer George Gibbs deemed the Yakamas and Klickitats "much superior to river Indians [in regard to moral character] . . . they are more strict in respect to their women, particularly the married ones, and they are far less thievish." Such ethnocentric generalizations ignored the cultural context for Native actions and overlooked the intimate ties between "horse Indians" and "fish Indians." In particular, the people Gibbs identified as Klickitats had a foot in each camp, with some ranging far and wide on horseback while others stayed close to their ancestral villages and fisheries. Regardless, American officials often presumed that each tribe had certain innate qualities—an essential nature—that determined its place in an imagined racial hierarchy.[4]

During the 1840s, as traffic increased along the Oregon Trail, the River Indians' reputation grew worse among whites and the demands for their removal grew louder. In 1849, Agent Newell stated, "All those Indians from The Cascades to near Walla-Walla have annoyed the Emigrants much and no doubt have been disturbed occasionally in return. I have all confidence that if a proper strict and kind system was adopted with these bands, it would be beneficial to them as also to the whites." The following year, Congress passed two pieces of legislation that promised to benefit whites far more than it did Indians. Under the Oregon Donation Land Act of 1850, every adult male citizen could claim 320 acres from the public domain; married couples could claim 640 acres. The Indian Treaty Act, also passed in 1850, belatedly prepared the way for this land grab by authorizing commissions to liquidate aboriginal title and relocate Indians on reservations. By 1853, when Washington became a separate territory, only a few tribes west of the Cascade Mountains had surrendered their lands. Isaac I. Stevens, the territory's first governor and superintendent of Indian affairs, moved to complete the process as quickly and cheaply as possible. Together with General Joel Palmer, the Oregon superintendent, he would draw the lines that dramatically changed the contours of Native life along the Columbia River.[5]

Stevens did not let the details of Indian social and political organization hinder his treaty preparations. On the contrary, he freely engaged in social engineering for the sake of bureaucratic efficiency. The boundary between Oregon and Washington presented an obvious dilemma. East of Wallula Gap, the line left the Columbia River and ran along the 46th parallel, cutting directly through the territories of several indigenous groups. Stevens blithely suggested rearranging Indian allegiances to avoid jurisdictional conflicts: "Could not those of the Walla Wallas living north of the Columbia be placed under control of the Yakama chiefs, the Cayuses removed entirely into Oregon and the Nez Perces divided into two bands, one under the direction of each [agent] and separated say by the Snake and Kooskoskie [Clearwater] rivers?" Palmer discouraged such action prior to the signing of treaties, but he had no qualms about using the Columbia River to divide the Indians dwelling downstream. Wascos and Wayáms would go to a reservation south of the river while their Wishram and Skin relatives removed to the north. The Columbia formed a natural tribal boundary in the eyes of the commissioners, and they treated it so despite evidence that Native social networks spanned the stream.[6]

Where nature had not seen fit to demarcate coherent tribes, Stevens readily assumed the role of creator. In his instructions to Andrew J. Bolon, the agent in charge of the Central District, the governor explicitly outlined the procedure for appointing Native spokesmen:

> You will assemble the chiefs, and as many of the men as possible, and if sufficient organization does not already exist in the tribe, endeavor to establish it. Where it is practicable you will bring about the selection of one great head chief for each tribe (conferring on him as extensive powers as the rest will submit to) and also of such number of lesser tyees [headmen] as in your opinion may be expedient, having reference to the size of the tribe and the number of different villages or grounds occupied by them. . . . *In any case however you will throw the weight of your influence in the scale of those chiefs who are best affected toward the American government & people.*

Henceforth, the United States would hold these men responsible not only for the conduct of their own people, but also for that of any other group the government assigned to them. "Wherever you find small detached bands with no head or union among themselves," Stevens continued, "you will endeavor to unite them under a principal chief, taking care to bring together such as are naturally alike. You will recognize no one who has merely a remnant of a tribe under his authority. In the case of a single detached party, you will try to make them coalesce with some larger neighbor." The Indian Office wanted to deal with a small number of compliant tribes, not an unpredictable mass of independent communities. Stevens would make sure that it did so.[7]

Even as Agent Bolon labored to reconstruct Plateau society along imagined tribal lines, the Indians contemplated political changes of their own. During the early 1850s, several Yakama headmen attempted to join their independent villages in a loose alliance that could better resist Šuyápu encroachment.[8] To the north of Wenas Creek, in central Washington, Tyáyaš (Teias) and Áwx̣ay (Owhi) led the Upper Yakama confederation. To the south, their nephews Kʼamáyaqan (Kamiakin), Šklúum (Skloom), and Šáwaway (Showaway) presided over the Lower Yakamas. Kamiakin, a headman of mixed Palouse and Yakama heritage, became particularly influential on the eve of treaty negotiations. He closely monitored events west of the Cascade Mountains—where Governor Stevens hastily concluded several treaties in 1854—and he sent emissaries throughout the Plateau to encourage opposition to land cessions. Kamiakin also staged a large intertribal council in the Grande Ronde Valley of eastern Oregon, where leaders from numerous Native groups met to consider unified and possibly armed resistance to American expansion. Historians disagree over the timing and outcome of this council. Andrew Splawn, Kamiakin's biographer, claimed that it took place before the treaty councils and that the Indians agreed to unite under major leaders who would speak for all concerned. More recent studies by Alvin Josephy and Theodore Stern suggest that the meeting occurred after the treaty councils and that the tribal delegates adjourned without resolution.[9] Whatever the result, Native responses to the treaties revealed that Mid-Columbia Indians found it difficult to behave in the manner Stevens expected. Their traditions of autonomy and self-sufficiency would not easily give way to collective action.

In any event, Stevens and Palmer did not allow much time for the Indians to learn new modes of thought. During the spring of 1855, the commissioners sent two delegations to arrange for treaty councils with the interior tribes. Stevens's secretary, James Doty, covered the territory north of the Columbia River, while agent Robert Thompson traversed the Oregon side. Indian mobility greatly complicated their mission. When they reached the country above The Dalles, they discovered that most winter villages had already dispersed for the seasonal round. Doty missed a significant portion of the Klickitats because they had gone west of the Cascade Mountains to hunt, trade, and visit. Some had even settled there during the 1830s and intended to stay. Palmer ordered those found in the Willamette and Umpqua valleys to return to their designated territory and participate in the councils, but many refused or escaped notice. Thompson failed to contact the so-called John Days (Takšpášłáma), a Columbia River Sahaptin group, because they had temporarily moved to the north shore and out of his jurisdiction. Although messengers located some people at their root-digging grounds, only a fraction of the affected Indians heard firsthand of the government's plan to purchase their lands and place them on reservations. The majority received notice through their social networks, and a significant minority did not learn of the treaties until the ink had dried. Ultimately, their absence made little difference to the treaty commissioners, who required merely the appearance of full representation to accomplish their goal.[10]

Stevens and Palmer came to the council grounds determined to secure the largest possible amount of land through the smallest possible number of treaties. To meet this paradoxical objective, they compressed the Plateau's diverse indigenous population into a handful of confederated tribes. Officially convened on May 29, 1855, the Walla Walla council attracted some five thousand Indians from the southern Plateau. Two weeks of tense negotiations produced three treaties embracing eighteen officially recognized tribes and bands. Of those, fourteen were joined to form a single body known as the Yakama Nation.[11] Stevens had planned to attach the Walla Wallas, Umatillas, and Cayuses to either the Yakama or the Nez Perce agency, but strong Indian opposition compelled him to create a separate treaty and reservation for those tribes. The largest group in attendance, the Nez Perces, signed the last of the Walla Walla treaties on June 11.[12] Two weeks later, on his return trip through The Dalles, Palmer concluded a fourth agreement with roughly nine hundred Indians representing seven confederated bands of Wascos and so-called Walla Wallas (Warm Springs).[13] It had taken the commissioners less than a month to acquire over thirty million acres of land in three future states. In doing so, they had laid the legal foundations of new political entities and added a fresh layer to the shifting sands of Indian identity along the Columbia River.[14]

The crowds at the council grounds bore only a vague resemblance to the tribal confederations that developed over the next century. Although the treaties furnished the founding documents of modern Native American nations, Stevens and Palmer did not negotiate with the complete, coherent tribes they had sketched on paper. On the contrary, as historian Alexandra Harmon observed in her analysis of the councils on Puget Sound, "subdivisions of the populations encompassed by the treaties were far more numerous and ambiguous than the Americans wanted to admit."[15] At Walla Walla, the mass of humanity surrounding the U.S. delegation mingled Indians from dozens of autonomous villages, including several groups not directly involved in the negotiations. Even at the smaller Wasco council, Palmer had trouble determining tribal numbers. "The accurate enumeration of the Indians is very difficult," he conceded, "as an entire tribe can seldom be collected at one point." Some Indians confused the issue by attending both meetings, while others stayed away entirely. By one estimate, more than eight hundred Indians failed to appear for the council at The Dalles. Some may have gone to Walla Walla and not returned in time, but upwards of two thousand people missed that meeting as well.[16] Whether defiant or indifferent, unaware or preoccupied, many of these people lacked direct representation in the proceedings. Consequently, some Mid-Columbia Indians later insisted that they had never sold their lands and that the treaties held no power over them.

The Yakama treaty offers a case in point. At first glance, the document has a deceptive symmetry, with fourteen signers for the fourteen tribes and bands of the nation. Upon closer inspection, this tidy arrangement dissolves into a much hazier set of relationships. Kamiakin received the arbitrary label of head chief, even though he personally identified with only the Yakamas and Palouses. Another Palouse headman, Kla'túš (Kahlotus), came to the council to announce that his people would not participate; Stevens roped him into co-signing for the entire Palouse tribe.[17] Laxúmt (Lahoom) served the same purpose for the Salish-speaking Wenatchis, while Owhi and Skloom represented the Upper and Lower Yakamas, respectively. The remaining signatory chiefs hailed from villages along the Columbia River. Q'álwaš (Colwash), Schanooa (Skannowa), and Šláq'iš (Slockish) made their marks on behalf of the people designated as Wishrams and Klickitats in the treaty. Wiyašknípic (Wishochkmpits) lived at Wishram but came from the village of Rock Creek (Qmíł), also the home of Šiyakát (Sheeahcotte), who in turn had ties to the people of Maryhill (Wálawitis). Both of these headmen also counted relatives from Sk'in, which produced the signers Maná·ynak (Meninock) and Takí·l (Tuckquille/Tahkeal). Ilaytp'á·ma (Elit Palmer) has been variously identified with the villages of Náwawi (Alderdale),

44

Sk'in, Maryhill, and Wayám—the last of which would place him on the "wrong" side of the river in relation to the Yakama treaty.[18] No one expressly represented several unnamed Columbia River Sahaptin communities. The Wánapams did not appear in the treaty either, although it enfolded much of their territory. Nevertheless, Stevens confidently reported that "the concurrence of the several tribes in establishing the [Yakama] nation is universal."[19]

The other treaties followed a slightly different pattern but still excluded a significant portion of the Indian population. In each case, the number of signers greatly exceeded the number of tribes and bands listed in the document. Twenty-eight men besides the principal chiefs marked the agreement with the Cayuses, Umatillas, and Walla Wallas. Fifty-eight Native names appear on the Nez Perce treaty and 151 on the Wasco treaty. The reason for this surplus of signatures remains a matter of speculation. Among the status-conscious Upper Chinookans, some heads of household probably expected the Americans to request their permission and thereby recognize their standing in Native society. The evidence suggests that Palmer did so to protect the government against charges that it had cheated the Indians. As he told the parties to the Umatilla treaty, he desired not only the names of the chiefs and headmen, but "also the name of every man on the paper that the President may see every man's name and know that they have given their consent."[20]

Obviously, he could not collect every man's name if some of them skipped the councils. For additional insurance, he inserted a provision in the Umatilla and Middle Oregon agreements stating that the Indians who signed would receive compensation on behalf of those who failed to accept or abide by the treaty terms. Palmer never explained this confusing clause to tribal representatives, however, and he pointedly ignored the one outright refusal he heard at the councils. Wallachin, a Cascades headman, declined to sign the Middle Oregon treaty, "alleging as a reason that his people could not subsist away from the Columbia River, and declaring, 'I have said that I would not sell my country and I have but one talk.'" Unable to find a more compliant leader to replace him, Palmer listed his name anyway, giving the assurance "that he and his people will

45

ultimately desire to be embraced in this treaty." The government had made an offer the Indians could not refuse.[21]

The treaty commissioners' inflexible demands placed the signatory chiefs in an unprecedented and uncomfortable position. As a representative of a centralized nation-state, Stevens had no desire to parley with every "petty tyee" on the Plateau. He would talk "with chiefs only," meaning the select group of headmen approved or appointed by the commissioners themselves. These leaders were not mere puppets of the federal government; the Indians generally understood the commissioners' expectations and chose representatives of genuine prominence in Native society. Many chiefs probably found this recognition flattering, since it confirmed and enhanced their status as men of prestige, but it also conferred upon them powers none had contemplated before. Although most of the signatory headmen had links to multiple communities, few exercised or even asserted authority beyond their own villages. As Meninock's son and successor said of Kamiakin sixty years later, "He was not over our people on the Columbia River. He was only over part of the Yakimas the other way, but not down to the Columbia River . . . he was not a head [man] over them." The British and the Americans had named principal chiefs in the past, but those men had not been asked to surrender huge tracts of territory. Such a radical proposition required Indian leaders to think and act in ways entirely alien to them.[22]

Several chiefs balked at this burden of responsibility. They knew that many of their people had not attended the treaty councils, and they anticipated the criticism that would surely follow if they ceded lands without popular consent. "My people are far away," protested Owhi. "They do not know your words. This is the reason I cannot give you an answer now." Pressed to speak on behalf of the entire Yakama Nation, Kamiakin also pleaded for more time: "The place that I am from there are but few Indians. All have gone to the Calapooya country [Willamette Valley]. Some are at Nisqually and some at Taih [Tygh]. That is the reason why I have deferred speaking till I see my Indians." The prospect of selling land demanded thorough discussion because it cut against the grain of indigenous culture. Although each village occupied and utilized an extensive territory, usually in concert with other communities, Plateau people did not view land as a commodity that could be bought and sold. The idea that the government could purchase the earth they lived on confused and alarmed many Indians. The worldly Wasco headman Billy Chinook, now reconciled to the loss of his country, urged Palmer not to rush them: "How could we say yes when there is only two of us that agree. [If] I had said yes, it would be like leaving my people. . . . I know that you buy the land from us, but my people do not think so, they think you are taking it away from us. It is true that we are long talking about it but by talking slowly, we will all understand it." Though licensed by federal officials to wield arbitrary authority, the signatory chiefs struggled to reconcile their actions with Native political norms.[23]

The government's proposal also clashed with Indian religious beliefs. Some of the more acculturated headmen, such as Billy Chinook, accepted the notion that land could be purchased. During the 1850s, however, most Native leaders shared the spiritual concerns voiced by Owhi:

> God named this land to us, that is the reason I am afraid to say anything about this land. I am afraid of the laws of the Almighty, this is the reason I am afraid to speak of the land. . . . Shall I steal this land and sell it? Or what shall I do? This is the reason that my heart is sad.
>
> My friends, God made our bodies from the earth as if they were different from the whites. What shall I do? Shall I give the lands that are a part of my body and leave myself poor and destitute? Shall I say I will give you my lands? I cannot say. I am afraid of the Almighty.[24]

Mid-Columbia Indian religion, though increasingly influenced by Christian ideas and imagery, tied people to the earth on which they lived. The Creator had given them land (*tiičám*) to supply their sacred foods and shelter the graves of their ancestors. To trade away this gift, the chiefs feared, invited divine punishment as well as political turmoil and economic hardship.[25]

Columbia River Sahaptin and Upper Chinookan villages had the most to lose from signing the treaties. The government wanted them off the Oregon Trail and away from the railroad route Stevens had surveyed in 1854.

Accordingly, the treaty commissioners selected reservations distant from the Columbia River. Some of the Yakamas, Cayuses, and Nez Perces would not have to relocate because their winter villages stood within reservation boundaries. The prime fisheries lay in ceded territory, however, and all the river communities faced removal to relatively unfamiliar and inhospitable locations. Indian leaders responded by arguing for reserves that encompassed their ancestral homes. "I think the land where my forefathers are buried should be mine," contended Young Chief of the Cayuses. "That is the place that I am speaking for. . . . That is what I love, the place where we get our roots to live upon. The salmon comes up the stream." At the Wasco council, Štáqulay (Stocketly) stubbornly insisted on retaining territory near his home village of Wayám : "My heart is to have that country that I spoke of, from [Deschutes] to John Days River, from the Columbia River to the Blue Mountains." Other chiefs made similar requests, but Palmer refused to modify his plans, claiming that the president had directed him "not to make a reservation, here, there and all over." His predecessor, Anson Dart, had tried that approach in the Willamette Valley only to see Congress reject the treaties. Palmer would not make the same mistake. "We propose to do you good," he assured the Indians. "But if you live scattered all over the country, we cannot do you any good."[26]

The treaty commissioners weakened Native resistance to removal with a steady barrage of promises and threats. Invoking the spirit of Manifest Destiny, Palmer portrayed American settlement as an elemental and inexorable force bearing down on the Indians:

Can you stop the waters of the Columbia River from flowing on its course? Can you prevent the wind from blowing? Can you prevent the rain from falling? Can you prevent the whites from coming? You are answered no! Like the grass hoppers on the plains, some years there will be more than others. You cannot stop them, our chief cannot stop them, we cannot stop them.[27]

If they made treaties now, he warned, the commissioners could at least prevent whites from overrunning the reservations and leaving the Indians homeless; otherwise, they would be swept away by the tides of progress. Trying to sweeten this bitter pill, the government pledged to provide schools, sawmills, blacksmith shops, farm implements, and other accoutrements of Euro-American culture. Still, many Indians remained skeptical. Pyópyo Maqsmáqs (Piupiumaksmaks), the head chief of the Walla Wallas, observed, "Goods and the earth are not equal; goods are for using on the earth. I do not know where they have given land for goods." Tohsimph, a Cascades headman, wondered how his people would use the sawmill on the proposed Warm Springs reservation: "There is no wood there, what shall we saw?" Regardless of their future value to reservation residents, such things seemed a poor trade for the land that had nurtured indigenous people for thousands of years.[28]

To most Indians, the only promise that mattered was the one ensuring continued access to off-reservation subsistence resources. Although Stevens and Palmer regarded the treaties as tools of assimilation, they recognized that the tribes would require time to adjust to an agricultural lifestyle. Allowing people to fish, gather, and hunt at their traditional sites would ostensibly soften the shock of land cessions and save the government money during this cultural transition. Moreover, the commissioners knew that tribal leaders would not sign a treaty that failed to guarantee their rights to salmon and other staples. In 1854, Agent George Gibbs had advised against confining the Plateau peoples on reservations because they required "the liberty of motion for the purpose of seeking, in their proper season, roots, berries, and fish, where those articles can be found, and of grazing their horses and cattle at large. . . . In like manner, the use of their customary fisheries, and free pasturage for their stock on unenclosed lands, should be secured." Stevens ignored Gibbs's advice concerning reservations but judiciously incorporated his other suggestions into the treaty provisions.[29]

During the councils, many Native representatives specified the resource sites they wished to retain for their people. William Yallup, a descendant of the treaty signer Wiyašknípic, recalled hearing that each of the river chiefs at Walla Walla gave "a description of what they had reserved in the way of food." Their statements went unrecorded but likely echoed those made at the Wasco council, where several headmen expressed special concern for their food sources. "Our fishing place on the Columbia we wish to keep," declared the Tenino chief Alexis. "The country you have shown us we are glad to live on it. That is all I have to say. I only came to talk of the fishing ground." Simtáštaš (Simtustus), a Tayxłáma (Tygh) spokesman, went into greater detail:

> The [Deschutes] have sustained us in fish. The Falls where we catch the fish, we would like to reserve it. You have seen our country where we get our roots, this is the country I spoke about. I wish to keep the country beyond the Tygh about the Mutton Mountain and between the Mutton & Jefferson Mountains, where we gather our berries.[30]

The Indians had no intention of surrendering their means of survival, and the commissioners agreed to provide the necessary protection.

The provisions that secured Indian subsistence rights also sowed the seeds of future controversy. The treaties did not *give* the tribes any special privileges, as critics later claimed, but the language of the treaty documents subtly restructured aboriginal rights in significant ways. Like the treaties on Puget Sound, which Stevens used as a model, all of the Plateau agreements contained a virtually identical version of this article:

> The exclusive right of taking fish in all the streams, where running through or bordering said reservation, is further *secured to said confederated tribes and bands of Indians*, as also the right of taking fish at all usual and accustomed places, *in common with the citizens of the Territory*, and of erecting temporary buildings for curing them; together with the *privileges* of hunting, gathering roots and berries, and pasturing their horses and cattle upon open and unclaimed land.[31]

By vesting subsistence rights in the confederated tribes and bands, this clause implicitly transformed individual and familial entitlements into tribal ones, leading to future disagreements among Indians about who could fish where. At the same time, it raised the prospect of competition from American citizens through the phrase "in common" and introduced a false distinction between "rights" and "privileges." The treaty commissioners anticipated the continuance of fishing but presumed that the Indians would abandon other off-reservation activities as cultural assimilation proceeded and whites filled the surrounding country. The Indians had far different expectations, and they left the councils with a vastly different understanding of their treaties.[32]

As members of an oral culture, tribal leaders absorbed the verbal explanations of the treaty terms rather than the words written in the official documents. They did not recognize the legalistic difference between rights and privileges, and the commissioners made no such distinction in their descriptions of the "fishing clause." Using a chain of mixed-blood interpreters and Indian criers, Stevens informed the assembly at Walla Walla:

> You will be allowed to pasture your animals on land not claimed or occupied by settlers, white men. You will be allowed to go on the roads to take your things to market, your horses and cattle. You will be allowed to go to the usual fishing places and fish in common with the whites, and to get roots and berries and to kill game on land not occupied by the whites. All that outside the reservation.

At the Wasco council, Palmer likewise assured the Indians that they "would always have the privilege to hunt, gather roots and berries, and fish."[33] These promises placed all subsistence activities on equal footing and set no explicit limits on the purpose, time, or method of harvesting resources. Insofar as the Indians understood the phrase "in common with the whites," they probably expected to exercise control over American citizens at the fisheries. They certainly never anticipated the usurpation of their traditional sites or the imposition of federal, state, and tribal laws on a system regulated by custom and kinship. John Skannowa, a nephew of the Wasco signatory Koshkeelah, recalled, "The way we understood, the white man wouldn't have any use for salmon, the berries and the roots; the white man wouldn't eat that and didn't know what that food was . . . Joel Palmer indicated that there would be no interference with the Indians' fishing rights at all; that the white men just weren't interested in fishing."[34]

The right to obtain food at usual and accustomed places, without interference from non-Indians, implied the freedom to stay off the reservation for extended periods of time. Even after the advent of agriculture, most Plateau families spent six to eight months of the year engaged in the seasonal round. The treaties ensured their ability to pursue this lifestyle, and the Indians saw no conflict between ceding pieces of their territory while continuing to use them. Therefore, they perceived reservation boundaries as permanent but porous, denying entry to unwelcome outsiders while permitting residents to pass through on legitimate business. As John Skannowa explained, his people believed that the treaties safeguarded "the right to secure hunting grounds, berries and roots and fishing along the Columbia River, which should remain all the time after that. Indians who were removed to reservations would be allowed to come back to the Columbia River during [salmon] runs and would have all the River secured to them." State and federal officials later challenged this construction of the agreements, but it survived in Native oral traditions and inspired resistance to the reservation policy.[35]

Some Indians evidently believed that the treaty terms gave them license to avoid the reservation entirely. Noting the difficulty of accurate translation at the councils, ethnographer Eugene Hunn has argued that "the treaties were not understood as prohibiting continued residence at or adjacent to [the] Columbia River fisheries." The fishing clause allowed Indians to erect "temporary buildings" or "suitable houses" for curing salmon. In Hunn's opinion, these words probably translated into the Sahaptin language as "house" (*niit*) or "winter village, settlement" (*nišáykt*) rather than as "fish drying shed" (*tyáwtaaš*).[36] Since families often hung fish to dry in their homes, the distinction between the two structures seems blurry indeed. Johnny Jackson, a current member of the Mid-Columbia River Council, has never doubted what his ancestors told him: "We never moved because when the treaties were signed by chief Slockish at Walla Walla we reserved the right to live at our usual and accustomed sites along the river. These sites were reserved because they hold all of our religious sacred sites, cemeteries, gathering sites, fishing sites and where we have always maintained our livelihood." When Slockish and his fellow river chiefs accepted the treaties, they likely did so on terms quite different from those the government proposed.[37]

■ ■ ■

The initially tenuous nature of the agreements became clear in the months following the councils. Many Indians reacted to news of the treaties with anger and disbelief. Upon arrival in their home villages, Palmer reported, the Yakama headmen "were beset by their people and denounced as traitors to their tribe. Two of the chiefs, Owhi and Skloom, evidently signed the treaty with great reluctance, and after returning home and meeting with their friends, were easily induced to join in opposition to adhering to its provisions." Kamiakin, who claimed to have "touched the pen" merely as a gesture of peace and friendship, quickly renounced the title of head chief and revived talk of war against the whites. Of the various tribes assigned to him, the Klickitats in particular "were much enraged at the sale of their country without their knowledge or consent, and declared they would not abide by an agreement in which they had no voice." Far from ensuring harmonious relations between Indians and whites, the treaties had heated the situation to the point of explosion.[38]

Stevens and Palmer promptly lit the fuse. During the councils, they had assured tribal leaders that the treaties would not take effect for two to three years, pending Congressional ratification and completion of the promised improvements. In the meantime, the Indians still owned the land and did not have to move onto reservations. Within a month of the Walla Walla meeting, however, Stevens ran advertisements in three territorial newspapers declaring the ceded areas open for settlement. Palmer had helped draft the notice the day after the council, apparently forgetting his earlier warning "that the settlement of the country, prior to the extinguishing of the Native title to the soil, is in most cases, attended with serious difficulties and embarrassments to the Government, with annoyances and danger to the settlers, and proves fatal to the best interests—the improvement and civilization of the natives." News of the "highly advantageous" treaties competed for attention with stories announcing the discovery of gold in the Colville district of northeastern Washington Territory. By mid-summer, an invading army of settlers and prospectors had marched over the mountains or streamed up the Columbia River—straight into the territory of the smoldering interior tribes.[39]

This sudden influx of intruders, before the Indians had seen any material benefit from the treaties, made war virtually inevitable. Although the commissioners expected the tribes "to allow white people to come and settle in the country anywhere outside the reservations," many Indians assumed that the government had broken its word. Open hostilities flared after Yakama warriors killed several miners for stealing horses and assaulting Indian women. When Agent Bolon went to investigate, a party of Yakamas murdered him as well. Major Granville O. Haller led a punitive expedition from Fort Dalles, only to be routed by a force of seven hundred Indians under Kamiakin. Nearly simultaneous outbursts of violence in the Rogue River and Puget Sound regions convinced many citizens of a "savage" conspiracy to drive them from the Northwest. "*War!*" screamed the *Oregonian* in the wake of Haller's humiliation. "Aye, a WAR of *extermination*, has been declared by the combined tribes against the whites on the Pacific slope."[40]

The general uprising described in the newspapers never actually materialized. In reality, the so-called Yakima and Coeur d'Alene wars of 1855 to 1858 unfolded as a sporadic series of skirmishes involving only a portion of the Plateau's indigenous population. Apart from an Indian attack on The Cascades in 1856, the main battles occurred in the Yakima Valley and the eastern reaches of Washington Territory. By 1857, when General John E. Wool temporarily closed the interior to settlement, the majority of Mid-Columbia Indians had already made peace. Native attempts to expand the conflict brought limited returns. In the early stages of the war, Kamiakin and his allies sent messengers to all the surrounding groups to enlist support for a united campaign against the Americans. If anyone refused, Joel Palmer reported, the "hostiles" vowed to treat them as enemies and enslave their children. Palouse chiefs tried a different approach after fighting resumed in 1858, giving horses to the leading men of the Klickitats "to make their hearts good towards the hostile Indians and bad towards the whites." Neither the carrot nor the stick garnered many recruits, Palmer noted, "but individual members of the several bands have joined them." With few exceptions, the decision to fight remained a personal one, not a matter of tribal policy. Hostile headmen coaxed and threatened but could not force others into battle, although some evidently detained people suspected of aiding the whites. Press reports to the contrary, Mid-Columbia Indians failed to make common cause on either tribal or racial grounds.[41]

The divisions within Native communities became readily apparent to federal officials. Shortly before the opening battle, a Wasco chief informed Joel Palmer that the Klickitats had split over the question of war, with "the greater portion of those recently returned from the Umpqua and Willamette valley having joined the Yakimas, whilst a majority of those heretofore residing in the country have declined to do so." Similar rifts opened among the Columbia River Sahaptins. Repudiating the authority of their signatory chiefs, some Tyghs and Wayáms headed north of the Columbia to join with Skin warriors loyal to Elit Palmer. Meanwhile, Meninock rebuffed the numerous emissaries sent to break the neutrality of the remaining Skins. Angered by his stubbornness, belligerent Indians stole horses and destroyed property, as well as "continuously threatening to attack and burn their villages and take them prisoner if they did not forsake the whites and join them in hostilities."[42]

Native people had diverse reasons for staying out of the fray. Many shared Billy Chinook's opinion that they could never defeat the Americans. To drive that point across in council, the well-traveled Wasco reputedly "took up his hands full of sand and said: 'I saw this many white people, and more. The Indians are no more than ten against all these people I saw, the white man. Let the Yakimas fight, but we will not fight.'"[43] Other Indians, especially Upper Chinookans, feared jeopardizing the treaties and their beneficial relations with white neighbors. The absence of former employers and trading partners placed some families in dire straits, and they struggled to repair the cultural bridges damaged during the war. In 1856, for example, a Wasco delegation approached Agent R. R. Thompson to request the return of a certain Mr. Jenkins, who had fled the region following the outbreak of hostilities. Thompson stated:

> They have promised me that if he will return that they will keep guard as they have done on former occasions, give him all the information they can gather, deliver to him all their guns, destroy the old canoes and take the others to his house, and if at any time he should consider it expedient for his or their safety to leave, they will cheerfully come with him to the Dalles.[44]

More than a dozen Indians, including some Klickitats and Columbia River Sahaptins, went further and volunteered to scout for the U.S. Army. By doing so, they demonstrated that the racial and tribal lines marked in the treaties were easily crossed even in times of war.[45]

Many Americans, ignoring such evidence of amity and neutrality among the Indians, made no distinction between "friendlies" and "hostiles." Consider the sentiments expressed by the editor of the *Oregonian*:

> There are NONE who are friendly. FEAR is the only principle which controls their action—cupidity and cruelty their natural instincts—war, rapine and blood their favorite vocation. Then why cry, "Lo! The poor Indian!" Why have sympathy for a race who are strangers to justice, deaf to the cry of anguish, and blind to the principles of integrity. The only way now is, a war of extermination against all who have not placed themselves under the protection of the whites.[46]

Taking this advice to heart, nervous homesteaders and trigger-happy volunteers preferred to shoot first and ask no questions whatsoever. Indians tending their herds or traveling to the fisheries reported being fired upon without provocation or warning. Spencer, a Klickitat scout and future head chief of the Yakama Nation, lost his father as well as his wife and six children at the hands of vengeful whites. Similar reprisals took place following the skirmish at The Cascades, a critical point for the movement of troops and supplies upriver. Outraged by the surprise attack on their settlement, local residents killed one Indian for each of the twelve white casualties. The Oregon Volunteers summarily tried and executed nine more, including the friendly headman Chenoweth, who had tried in vain to warn his neighbors of the impending danger.[47]

Military officers condemned such behavior but found it easier to restrict the peaceful Indians than to reign in overzealous volunteer units. To protect the neutrals from both hostile influences and vigilante action, the government concentrated them in makeshift internment camps near the Columbia. In the fall of 1855, Palmer designated three sites for the Middle Oregon tribes and the friendly groups from north of the river. Other Indians remained under guard at Fort Vancouver and The Cascades until the summer of 1856, when Stevens moved them to a temporary reservation between the White Salmon and Klickitat rivers. The neutrals generally accepted confinement despite the considerable hardships it imposed. Forced to answer daily roll calls and forbidden to leave without passes, they became virtual prisoners of war. Fear of attack discouraged some people from leaving to gather food, particularly after the military disarmed them and destroyed the property they had left behind. Meanwhile, their livestock fell prey to rustlers or wasted away on the limited pasture within the reserves. The Indian Office distributed rations and farming supplies to those in need, but tight-fisted superiors continually ordered agents to cut expenditures. Asked to justify his inflated costs during the winter of 1856, White Salmon agent Alfred Townshend explained that many of his charges "were almost wholly destitute, and entirely dependent on the Indian [Department] for the assistance which had been promised them." In 1858, some neutrals grew so frustrated with camp conditions that they contemplated joining the hostiles rather than submitting to further privations and restrictions.[48]

In spite of widespread discontent, it seems that at least one of these temporary reservations raised Indian hopes of remaining on the Columbia River. The White Salmon agency lay within the traditional territory of several Klickitat villages, and some people wished to stay there when the war ended. In 1856, a spokesman named Yocatowit told Governor Stevens, "I want to go into the country between the White Salmon, Klickitat, and Yakama rivers. There is plenty of fish, roots, berries, game and everything we want. It is also our own country—the Klickitats' country, and here we wish to go and live." The following year, his people declared that they would not willingly remove to the proposed Yakama agency at Fort Simcoe. Although Stevens repeatedly stressed the provisional nature of the White Salmon reserve, which he had chosen largely for logistical reasons, his subordinates may have inadvertently fostered a sense of permanence by encouraging the Indians to plant crops and build fences. When American citizens began staking claims to land inside reservation boundaries, the residents immediately complained to their agent, who turned away the prospective homesteaders for the time being. The Indian Office refused to allow a permanent reserve adjoining the Columbia River, however, and the White Salmon agency closed in 1859. By that time, many Indians had already relocated to the Warm Springs and Yakama reservations.[49]

The Americans who watched them leave haughtily assumed that the war had settled matters once and for all. They construed the Native withdrawal from armed conflict as a confirmation of their racial dominance and national destiny. Henceforth, the Indians had to obey the will of the United States. They must go to the reservations and begin their transformation into ordinary Americans, proclaimed Agent Robert H. Lansdale, "or disperse before the superior race as the mist disperses before the rising sun. . . . History plainly teaches this lesson; I need but refer to it to secure the assent of all." Most indigenous people would have begged to differ. They did not interpret the hostiles' military defeat as a sign of collective racial disgrace or complete political subjugation. Nor did they universally accept the treaties that had sparked the war in the first place. In fact, a month after the war ended, Lansdale reported that roughly two thousand Yakamas, Klickitats, and "Columbia River Indians" still resented the loss of the territory "ceded without their consent in 1855." Though no admirer of Indians, even he recognized the "injustice and impolicy of seizing upon the lands of several tribes because their leading men falsely signed a treaty ceding lands that did not belong to them." To correct the situation, he recommended discarding the original Yakama treaty and negotiating a new one "with all the tribes and people interested." The Indian Office ignored his suggestion, and in 1859 the Senate finally ratified the treaties made four years earlier.[50]

■ ■ ■

Today, those treaties stand as vital symbols of tribal sovereignty and nationalism, akin to the Constitution that upholds them as "the supreme law of the land." They forged binding legal links between the federal government and the tribes, links that few modern Indians wish to see broken. At the end of the 1850s, however, the meaning of these documents seemed less clear to the indigenous peoples of the Plateau. Through the treaties, the United States had secured title to vast tracts of land and established new homelands for a specified number of tribes. Yet many people challenged the legitimacy of the agreements and questioned the authority of the political units they had created. Mid-Columbia Indians accepted or rejected the treaties on their own terms, and they continued to think of themselves as members of extended families and autonomous villages rather than as constituents of confederated tribes. New points of reference and identity had emerged but had yet to command loyalty from the people they supposedly described. Far from simplifying Indian society, the treaties had merely paved the way for complex and unexpected developments in the decades to come.

Among those who would come to identify as Columbia River Indians, the collective memory of the treaties and the war is a tale of innocence, betrayal, and defiance. "While we agreed to treaties that protected our rights and lands," insisted the members of the Mid-Columbia River Council (MCRC) in 1990, "they [the whites] wrote treaties that say we gave, or 'ceded' our lands and rights away. Soon they were telling us that we had to move off the river, that we had to abandon our way of Life." During the fighting that followed,

They came amongst our people and murdered elders, men, women, and children. They attempted to herd us like cattle. But there were many who refused to abandon the gifts of the Creator and their ancestors who had gone on ahead who are buried along the river.

In spite of these injustices, the River People "did not wage war against the white settlers and U.S. army during the Yakima wars because our ancestors were very religious people. They practiced their religion to the fullest. We believe that taking another human's life is the greatest sin in the world." Significantly, though all three of the chiefs who signed this statement were enrolled in the Yakama Nation, they shared the view that the "Yakima wars" had been essentially a Yakama affair from start to finish.[51]

For future generations of Columbia River Indians, the historical contrast between Yakama belligerence and their own pacifism became a useful way of distancing themselves from the largest and most powerful of the recognized tribes. Their ancestors had neither started the war nor fought in it, but they had suffered nonetheless. American troops had attacked innocent people, placed them in concentration camps, and destroyed their property under the mistaken assumption that it belonged to the hostile Yakamas. This would not be the last time, as contemporary River People see it, that Yakama actions caused them undeserved grief at the hands of white society. Still, their ancestors had stayed true to their principles and kept the peace even in the face of grave injuries and threats. Moreover, by refusing to join the Yakamas in battle, they had asserted their autonomy within the tribal system just established under the treaties. As the MCRC declared in 1990, "Our ancestors' hands were clean, they did not spill blood of the settlers or the U.S. Army. Therefore, we are not Yakima, Warm Springs, or Umatilla Indians. We do not and will not accept the Yakima or any other tribe as having authority or jurisdiction to speak for us."[52]

Although this interpretation glosses over many complexities and delivers a clear political message—as nationalistic narratives usually do—it does reflect certain historical realities that inform the River People's sense of themselves. The war had begun after a series of extreme provocations, when outraged Yakama warriors killed white miners and ambushed Agent Bolon near Satus Pass. Many different Indians had then joined Kamiakin's alliance, including individuals from Sk'in, Wayám, and other river villages. The war had divided their communities, but even Army and Indian Office reports conceded that most people along the Columbia chose neutrality. If government officials took this as a sign of compliance with American plans, they soon learned that many river Indians had no intention of being penned up on reservations and placed under the jurisdiction of alien "head chiefs." On the contrary, their descendants would turn defiance of federal power and distrust of tribal authority into hallmarks of Columbia River Indian identity.

We are the people who have inherited the sacred words and songs
that were given to our ancestors so that we may celebrate our life
within this place. We have never abandoned or relinquished
these lands or the rights given to us by the Creator.

—MID-COLUMBIA RIVER COUNCIL,
STATEMENT OF UNIFICATION, 1990

3 ▪ ▪ ▪

THEY MEAN TO BE INDIAN ALWAYS

n November 1878, as the Bannock War raged in eastern Oregon and
Idaho, a company of U.S. soldiers escorted a small, bedraggled band
of Takšpašláma (John Day Indians) onto the Warm Springs reservation. These so-called renegades had taken no part in the hostilities;
in fact, they had reportedly fled the Umatilla reservation to escape the
bloodshed there and had tried to warn white settlers of the danger. Nevertheless, Agent John Smith considered them unwelcome troublemakers. Except for a handful, he protested, "These Indians do not belong to
this reservation, having never been compelled to move onto it until this
time. They are said to be very destitute, and it is evident some provision
must be made for them." Smith would let them stay if they agreed to
start farms and conform to agency rules, but he had no faith in their

leader, X̣áyx̣ni Hehaney (or Hackney), an inveterate "vagabond" whom the army had temporarily imprisoned at Vancouver Barracks. "I put him in irons four different times," Smith complained, "and he always made fair promises when he was set free. . . . I am almost in hopes he will be sent to the Indian Territory. If sent here he must obey or be sent off."[1]

He did not obey. In the spring Smith reported that Hehaney had left without permission, taking many people with him and crossing the Columbia River ostensibly to make a home on the Yakama reservation. He did not stay there either, and the agent at Fort Simcoe later identified him among a group of off-reservation Indians who declined to provide any information for the tribal census. Hehaney's band had pulled the same stunt at the Umatilla agency, claiming "to belong [to] no reserve, that nobody has any control over them and their association with reservation Indians has the effect of creating a dislike on the part of the latter to reservations, Agents and the government." Hehaney was a bad apple, an incorrigible and ungrateful spoiler of the government's well-laid plans to uplift his race. "He means to be an Indian always," huffed Smith, "in the fullest sense of the character attached to that name."[2]

Hehaney and his followers represented a larger class of Mid-Columbia Indians who refused to accept that the treaties bound them to any single reservation or recognized tribe. Between 1860 and 1885, federal officials complained that many of the people assigned to the Umatilla, Warm Springs, and Yakama agencies remained at large on the public domain. Despite petitions from white citizens and threats of forced removal, these "renegades" never abandoned their ancestral village sites, cemeteries, and fishing stations along the Columbia River. Reservation residents often mingled with them and shared the same practical concerns, cultural commitments, and spiritual beliefs that kept them from settling down in the tribal homelands. Yet, as the years dragged on, the Office of Indian Affairs increasingly viewed off-reservation Indians as a coherent group bent on undermining federal authority and corrupting their reservation kin. By the 1870s, the government had labeled them "Columbia River Indians," a term describing both an official category for off-reservation bands and a potential tribal identity. Although ties of kinship and exchange continued to bind reservation and off-reservation communities, many of their members began to develop a sense of difference from the other. Seeing themselves as more authentically Indian than reservation residents, River People purposefully stayed outside the lines that demarcated tribal territory and defined tribal identity under the emerging colonial order.

■ ■ ■

In 1859, following the end of the Plateau Indian wars and the ratification of the Mid-Columbia treaties, the United States expected all Plateau Indians to move to their respective agencies. Many complied within the one-year deadline, but many others stayed away or routinely crossed reservation boundaries for decades to come. In 1870 Lieutenant W. H. Boyle noted that only 837 of the 1,622 Indians in his charge had relocated to the Umatilla reservation. When he visited the groups scattered along the Columbia River to demand their removal, they denied belonging to his agency by treaty and refused to recognize his authority. In 1881, by the government's own count, roughly a third of the 3,400 Indians assigned to the Yakama agency still lived off the reservation entirely or resided there only in winter. Another third had permanent homes on the reservation but left each year during the fishing season. Their continuous movement and mingling made clear that federal policy had failed to erect impermeable racial barriers or freeze the fluid identities of Mid-Columbia Indians.[3]

Native mobility and autonomy frustrated efforts to restrict each tribe to its proper reservation. While the treaties produced new places of residence and new political affiliations, existing social ties remained intact as Indians moved freely between communities where they had kin. The Indian Office struggled to conduct tribal censuses and to determine which people belonged where, because reservation populations fluctuated dramatically from season to season and year to year. In 1873, Umatilla agent Narcisse A. Cornoyer stated that "a portion of the Indians belonging to these tribes still remain on the Columbia River, and some of these occasionally come on the reservation and profess to have come to remain; they will stay a short time and then leave again for the Columbia." Seven years later, Indian Inspector William Pollock declared that only four of the fourteen tribes named in the Yakama treaty had any members on that reservation. Agent James Wilbur no longer enumerated the individual groups, which he said had become hopelessly mixed by intermarriage, yet Pollock thought it entirely possible to do so. By his estimate, exactly 501 legitimate agency Indians mingled with some 300 to 850 others "near and remotely related to, and affiliating with, but not clearly traceable to any particular tribe." He further predicted that the current census would "show more than can properly be called Reservation Indians" after the "wandering vagrant Columbia River Indians are, by the rigors of winter, driven to the Reservation to subsist upon their more provident relatives."[4]

Agents did not necessarily wish to claim these people—particularly if they appeared likely to cause problems or sap limited reservation resources—but officials had trouble distinguishing between residents and "renegades." Reservation Indians could switch roles in a matter of days. As Wilbur's successor, Robert H. Milroy, noted with obvious distaste, "Nearly all [renegades] have relatives living here. When one of my Indians desires to free himself from the restraints of wholesome discipline, all he has to do is go to the Columbia River, join the Non Reservation Indians, and the agent's authority over him ceases, and he can gamble and get drunk as he likes."[5]

While correctly noting the ease of the transformation, Milroy's description distorted the reasons for interaction between these groups. Mid-Columbia Indians had always shared resources with kin, and they continued to do so despite efforts to discourage their "usual habit of roaming & visiting neighboring tribes." In the spring and summer, many reservation residents traveled to traditional fishing and gathering sites, where they mingled with "renegades" and often acquired that label. During the winter, off-reservation Indians joined in ceremonial dances and feasts at the agencies. On such occasions, reservation residents could redistribute some of the government rations, agricultural produce, and livestock that confirmed their status as wealthy people. Thus, when Agent Wilbur allocated treaty annuities in 1872, "runners were sent out in all directions and a grand rally made to gather in as many Indians as possible." It was hard to tell whether all the people who showed up actually belonged to that agency or whether they subsequently shared their supplies with visiting relatives. The government became, in effect, a sponsor of traditional Plateau "giveaways."[6]

Not even the lure of federal largesse could convince diehard "renegades" to affiliate with a specific agency. Though some wintered on the reservations or sought refuge there in times of danger, they avoided claiming tribal membership for fear of jeopardizing their freedom. Hehaney and his people spent most of 1878 on the Umatilla reserve but kept their names from the agent to prevent being reported as permanent residents. Other "renegades" insisted that they had never set foot inside reservation lines or accepted any treaty benefits "for the reason that they believe by so doing they would admit the principle of having sold their right to occupy land." If they belonged to a particular agency, the Indian Office could demand their removal or compel their children to attend school. Distance and detachment partially relieved the pressures of forced assimilation, and some reservation residents used their off-reservation relations to foil federal policy. In 1884, for instance, Agent Milroy staged a roundup of pupils for the reservation boarding school only to discover that "all the school children of the Cotiahan [Kútayax̣an, Kotiakan] band have been run off among the wild Indians along the Columbia River, some 90 miles distant, to pass out of the reach of my police."[7]

Native people knew enough about the federal bureaucracy—including its limitations and internal divisions—to play different agencies and departments against each other. The rivalry between the Office of Indian Affairs and the Department of War furnished particularly fertile ground in which to sow discord.[8] When Agent Milroy sent his Indian police in pursuit of the "renegades" and their children, they immediately appealed to the Military Department of the Columbia. At a council with Captain F. K. Upham, who merely intended to explain the procedure for taking off-reservation homesteads, several headmen "continued to insist upon a complaint against the reservation, with a request that the [department commander] might be informed. . . ." According to Upham:

> Buscappa [Pášxapa, Pascappa], cheif [sic] of a small band living near Alder Creek, and Ko-tai-a-kon [Kotiakan] were particularly anxious that their grievances should be known; which were in effect, that while they, as a matter of principle, would not go to the reservation, and had never received any benefits or annuities therefrom, the agent at the Yakima reservation continued to send the Indian police after them, and particularly their children, insisting that they should be taught at the reservation schools, and [learn] the religion of the agency, and that their hair should be cut.[9]

Milroy grudgingly complied with orders to confine his police to the reservation. His tirades against military interference irritated the army, however, and local officers responded sympathetically to further complaints about his draconian policies. Fearing an outbreak if Milroy remained in charge, Major General John Pope recommended his immediate suspension. In 1885, the secretary of the interior requested Milroy's resignation, and the Indian Office forbade the use of agency police beyond reservation boundaries. The "renegades" and their reservation kin had won a small but significant victory over the agency that nominally controlled them.[10]

Agents tried with little success to regulate off-reservation travel through a system of official passes. Like devious students, Indians found various ways to slip off without permission. In 1870, for example, a Tygh headman named Kʷíyapama (Queahpahmah) reportedly "dreamed that he was to leave Warm Springs" and demanded a pass, citing as reasons both his vision and the lack of good land on the reservation. When the agent refused, Queahpahmah "boldly announced to the Indians—though not to the Agent—that he was going and 'never would come back again.'" He returned in 1878, evidently of his own accord, to assume a position of leadership among the Warm Springs Indians. In the interim, however, he evaded capture and continued his "vagabond mode of life." Indians who did receive passes often took similar liberties, staying away for longer than allowed or failing to appear at the promised destination. In 1879, the same year that Hehaney absconded from Warm Springs, Pascappa and another "renegade" chief known as Stock asked to move their people from the Umatilla reservation to Fort Simcoe. Agent Narcisse Cornoyer issued the requisite passes, along with instructions to proceed straight to the agency, but they ignored his directions and stayed on the Columbia River.[11]

Fugitives from the reservations blended smoothly into the permanent "renegade" population. The Indian Office did not systematically enumerate off-reservation Indians until the mid-twentieth century, but during the 1870s most estimates pegged their number between 1,800 and 2,000 people. Large villages persisted at Wishram, Celilo, Sk'in, Rock Creek, and other aboriginal sites upstream, while smaller settlements dotted tributaries from The Cascades to the Umatilla River. Movement among these far-flung communities created new social networks embracing a wide range of indigenous ethnicities and tribal affiliations. The Indian Office recognized the disparate origins of the off-reservation population but increasingly grouped them together under the shorthand label "Columbia River Indians." By the early 1870s, this broad geographic category had become standard in government correspondence and census reports, where it often appeared next to tribal designations such as Umatilla, Wasco, and Yakama. By 1890, "Columbia River Indians" also appeared in the U.S. decennial census, identified as "a number of Indians who have never been on any reservation. They live in huts along the river and subsist almost wholly on salmon. As a rule they are dirty and lazy." Such negative characterizations show that "Columbia River Indian" had become virtually synonymous with the term "renegade" in the official lexicon. Not every off-reservation individual was a Columbia River Indian, of course, but all Columbia River Indians were renegades in the eyes of federal agents.[12]

Irate whites generally associated "wild Indians" with the nearest agency and complained accordingly. While squatters and stockmen violated reservation boundaries throughout the late nineteenth century, the refusal of Indians to stay inside the lines infuriated their American neighbors.

They vented their anger in letters, petitions, and editorials detailing the alleged abuses of the "renegades" and demanding immediate action from federal authorities. In 1874, forty settlers in Wasco County, Oregon, sent a letter to the Warm Springs agent stating that "a large number of Indians belonging to his reservation" had hunted illegally, stolen livestock, destroyed range land, and frightened local families. If the agent could not control them, the writer warned, "we will be compelled to hunt for relief in some other quarter."[13] One of the most impassioned pleas came from E. S. Penham, a former Wasco County judge, who in 1878 called attention to the Columbia River Indians living near The Dalles:

> Since you have declined to remove them they are worse than ever, and the result is they have burnt up my neighbor's grain stack, tools, etc. A poor man, illy able to sustain the loss. Beside are driving his wife, a sickly nervous woman, to the grave or insanity by her constant fears. In fact none of us in our neighborhood feel very safe. Our farms are in their line of travel from Dalles to Celilo and the fisheries, and they pass from town all times night and day in troops, and most of the time *crazy drunk* hollering and yelling as only drunken Indians can. . . . I hope you will look into the matter at an early day, as we would like to realize [for] once the fact that we are not toiling for vagabond Indians."[14]

Penham and his fellow "pioneers" played the role of injured innocents with great conviction, but their letters tell only a fraction of the story. From the perspective of off-reservation Indians—especially those who considered themselves party to no treaty—the newcomers were the real renegades. Besides taking game without permission, some citizens rustled Indian stock or filed homestead claims on Native-occupied land. Meanwhile, American-owned horses, cattle, and sheep trampled root-digging grounds and consumed pasture that Columbia River Indians still regarded as rightfully theirs. Even those who accepted the treaties possessed the right to pasture their stock on "open and unclaimed lands," which included most of the public domain. When Indians drank, it had much to do with the ready availability of alcohol from local saloons and peddlers operating in defiance of federal trade and intercourse laws. After investigating a complaint against some Natives living near The Cascades, Agent Wilbur determined that "the men who had signed the petition for the immediate removal of the Indians (a part of them) had been giving them whiskey, running horses, gambling and using their women. The whites have been the cause of all their trouble. The things stated in the petition in regard to the Indians having designs of hostility are in my judgment without foundation." The people crying "wolf," it appeared, could often be wolves in sheep's clothing.[15]

Some citizens intentionally exaggerated the threat of Indian outbreaks to encourage removal and advance their own claims to Native lands. During the Modoc War (1869–1873), in which some Columbia River Indians served as army scouts, rumors surfaced that two thousand renegades had gathered at White Bluffs in preparation for an attack on American settlements. By spreading such stories, Agent Wilbur suspected, "a club of inhospitable whites" in eastern Washington Territory planned to provoke a war that would lead to the dissolution of the reservation. If nothing else, ranchers hoped that a little Indian scare might frighten off pesky sodbusters.[16] In 1883, two farmers in Klickitat County told Agent Milroy that local whites had fled their homes in fear of an uprising by four hundred armed renegades. The Columbia River Indians in the area denied the allegations, declaring that "they never had a thought of going to war, that they are not fools and do not want to see their families scattered and themselves hanged." But Milroy had little interest in their version of events. "Whether these complaints are true or not," he informed the local military commander, "my duty to these Indians requires me to use all efforts to remove them from these constantly recurring disputes and troubles with white settlers." When Captain Thomas McGregor went to investigate, he concluded that the two white men had started the rumor in a bid to seize the Indians' land. Far from supporting the scheme, McGregor reported, "it is the wish of all the rest of the whites living in the vicinity of the Columbia River Indians that they be *let alone*."[17]

Fear and hostility were but two features of a more complicated and conflicted relationship between Natives and newcomers. While some

Americans anxiously avoided or greedily exploited their indigenous neighbors, others coexisted peacefully and even productively with local Indians. Both sides had strong economic incentives for cooperation. Unable to recruit adequate help from the small non-Native population, whites employed Indians as pack handlers, farm laborers, ranch hands, and domestic servants. By the mid-1880s, some Columbia River Indians had likewise hired emigrants to tend their crops and cattle. One government observer called these Native entrepreneurs "remarkable for their prompt cash payments for such labor." Other Indians shunned agriculture and wage work but readily traded horses or peddled fish, venison, and berries in American settlements. Whites often perceived these activities as a sign of Native dependency, but the existence of both a market and a marketable surplus suggests quite the opposite. Less self-reliant than they liked to believe, Americans confronted Indians who remained more self-sufficient and more hospitable to strangers than contemporary racial stereotypes allowed.[18]

Many of the newcomers further confounded racist assumptions by consorting with Native women. Faced with a shortage of potential spouses and sexual partners, European and American men had looked to local Indian communities for female companionship since the days of the fur trade. The resulting relationships ran the gamut from prostitution to marriage, which occurred routinely despite state and territorial statutes prohibiting interracial unions. Through cohabitation or marriage "in the Indian custom," settlers gained entrance to Native social networks and access to Native resources. In turn, the relatives of Indian brides obtained valuable sources of information and assistance in their dealings with the government and the wider American society. Some unions quickly cracked under the strain of differing cultural expectations, but even those often produced an enduring legacy in the form of mixed-heritage children. Today, familiar surnames such as McKay, Olney, Van Pelt, and Switzler testify to the presence of white fathers in many nineteenth-century Plateau families. Their offspring and the adult children of earlier unions shared an ambiguous position in the racially stratified society of the United States. As "half-breeds" or "mixed-bloods" in contemporary parlance, they straddled the cultural and legal divides that separated Indians from mainstream American society. Nevertheless, their growing numbers illustrated a simple fact: for better or worse, Natives and newcomers had become deeply intertwined.[19]

Economic cooperation and personal contact with Indian neighbors gradually softened the racial attitudes of some whites. Lingering ambivalence easily flared into antagonism, especially during the various Indian wars of the 1870s, yet many newcomers tolerated or even defended the presence of Indians. Some clearly did so out of self-interest. Farmers and ranchers worried that overzealous agents would deprive them of the Native labor that sustained their operations. In frontier towns such as Pendleton, Oregon, merchants eager for Indian commerce argued that off-reservation transactions fell outside of federal trade and intercourse laws. Not all Americans had such mercenary motives, however, and a few went so far as to side with Indians against other whites. In 1884, when an aggressive homesteader chased the family of an Indian called "Salmon Man" off their land along the Columbia River, a group of non-Indian neighbors testified that the Indians "were known to be honest, industrious and self-supporting, and that they had always occupied the site taken from them." The year before, as rumors of an imminent outbreak raced around Klickitat County, more level-headed whites had requested that Agent Milroy call off his police and leave the local Natives alone. Though hardly starry-eyed idealists, these individuals set aside abstract notions of racial solidarity and tried to coexist with Columbia River Indians.[20]

The Indian Office, rather than applauding such behavior, actively discouraged racial fraternization. According to J. W. Perit Huntington, the Oregon superintendent of Indian affairs during the mid-1860s, unregulated contact made Native Americans "an intolerable nuisance to the whites, and the effect upon themselves is most pernicious."

They are always drunken and debauched, their women become prostitute, and all soon become infected with loathsome diseases. There are found in every community a few [white] persons vile enough to associate with them and desire their presence. These persons naturally acquire the good will of the Indians and have much influence over them. By enticing them to leave the reservation, notifying them of the approach of the agent, and assisting them to conceal themselves from him, they often defeat the object of the government of keeping the white and red races apart. Another class of citizens, who are respectable, and do not furnish them whiskey or debauch their women, thoughtlessly encourage their presence to secure their services upon their farms or at other labor. But once away from the reservation, and beyond the control of the agent, they unavoidably come in contact with immoral influences, and the effect is the same as if the motive was bad.[21]

To prevent these unwholesome effects, Huntington recommended punishing both the Indians who left the reservation without consent and the whites who abetted them. E. S. Penham, the former Wasco County judge, would have gladly enforced such sanctions against his fellow citizens. The majority of the white population wanted the Indians removed, he insisted, "and they should not be permitted to roam at large . . . even if a few interested parties desire them to remain." But roam they did. Two decades after Huntington's dire warning, the Warm Springs agent still fretted about an annual rendezvous at the Cross Hollows stage station, where people from his agency and the Umatilla reservation met with "renegades" and white cowboys to race horses, gamble, drink whiskey, and engage in other "immoral practices." Year after year, the spectacle of Indians working and playing with their non-Indian neighbors belied the basic premises of the reservation policy.[22]

In 1865 Superintendent Huntington had tried to plug the legal loopholes in the system with a fraudulent treaty foisted on the confederated tribes of Warm Springs. Taking aim at the off-reservation rights reserved in the 1855 Treaty of Middle Oregon, he tricked tribal leaders into signing a supplemental agreement intended to prevent reservation residents from leaving home to harvest traditional foods. Although he did so with Indian Office approval, his methods raised serious questions about the legality of the final document. During the talks, he never mentioned giving up the subsistence rights guaranteed under Article 1 of the 1855 treaty.

Instead, he told the Indians that the new agreement simply required them to obtain passes before traveling off the reservation. It sounded reasonable enough to the handful of headmen at the council, who remembered his verbal description of the agreement, but the version Huntington sent to Washington contained an additional clause stating that the tribes had relinquished their off-reservation hunting, fishing, and gathering rights for the paltry price of $3,500. Congress ratified the altered document in 1867, giving it the stamp of legitimacy, and Huntington promptly ordered Agent Smith to "collect in all the straggling Indians" he could find. When tribal leaders later discovered the scam, they objected bitterly to "the great wrong and swindle that was inflicted upon them and endorsed by the Government in the supplemental treaty." Subsequent agents never enforced its terms and often advocated its repeal, yet the legal implications of Huntington's handiwork would haunt the confederated tribes of Warm Springs through the twentieth century.[23]

Agents on other reservations generally shared Huntington's frustration with the treaties, if not his lack of scruples. Robert Milroy, eager to absolve himself of blame for the existence of "renegade" Yakamas, pointed to the off-reservation fishing clause as the source of his apparent impotence. As much as he would like to arrest them, he told one group of petitioners, "the Agent is unable to *compel* these Indians to come to the Reservation without a violation of the plain provisions of a treaty—a responsibility that of course no Government officer would dare to take." Milroy chafed under these restrictions, which he deemed unnecessary since the "open and unclaimed lands" specified in Article 3 had supposedly "ceased to exist." To make matters worse, he suspected that "some lawyers and other whites" had planted the idea that the fishing clause "gave the Indians the right to remain off the reservation as they pleased." Hehaney and the Walla Walla chief Xúmlay (Homli), among others, reportedly sought legal advice from local attorneys. By indicting the counselor instead of the client, however, Milroy ignored Native initiative and dismissed the possibility that Indians already had working knowledge of their treaty rights. Like military officers who arrogantly poked their noses where they did not belong, lawyers and other meddlesome civilians constituted a "pernicious" external influence on Indians and Indian affairs. Blaming them made it easier for agents to overlook their own shortcomings and those of the reservation system itself.[24]

■ ■ ■

Critics of Indian "roaming" tended to ignore the many practical reasons Native people had for doing so. For one thing, they had to eat. Most showed little interest in farming, which conflicted with their traditional lifestyle, and early agricultural ventures often failed due to Native inexperience, inadequate equipment, and poor growing conditions. Since the government could not feed them adequately, even staunch "progressives" had no choice but to harvest wild foods. In 1869, for example, both the Warm Springs and Umatilla agents permitted Indians to leave the reservations because their crops had withered and they lacked sufficient rations.[25] Two years later, the Wasco chief Pianoose expressed frustration with the resulting contradiction:

> The Government has tried to do something for us, but the ground will not raise anything. So we must go outside and hunt deer on which to live. Then the news goes to the President that the Indians are wandering off their reservation troubling everybody. If we would live we must go outside, for the land is poor and will not raise anything.[26]

Agents faced an equally impossible situation. Caught between hungry Indians, angry citizens, and impatient but parsimonious superiors, agency officials struggled to reconcile national policy with the terms of the treaties and the demands of humanity. In 1878, when the Indian Office forbade Indians to leave their reservations without approval from Washington, DC, Agent Smith respectfully disobeyed on the grounds that his charges "still need to go after their annual supplies of soft and dried salmon [and], in fact, by treaty stipulation they are entitled to permits to do so."[27]

The threat of enemy depredations gave Mid-Columbia Indians another reason for avoiding the reservations well into the 1870s. The struggling farmers on the Oregon reservations made easy and attractive targets for Snake raiders. Consequently, even when residents managed to raise a good crop or amass a decent herd of cattle, they risked losing the fruits of their labor to Shoshone, Bannock, and Northern Paiute attacks. In 1859, the Warm Springs agent reported that many of his charges had deserted the reservation due to repeated assaults. Striking the isolated outpost with little fear of reprisal, Snake raiders had kidnapped women and children, stolen livestock, trampled crops, and burned houses and barns. Three years later, the local Indians were still "unwilling to remain on the reservation except in the immediate vicinity of the agency building, where they can be protected." Similar problems plagued the Umatilla agency, especially during the Bannock War of 1878. Fearing violence from avenging whites as well as from Snake war parties, Indians fled to the reservation only to discover that its lines could not shield them. In fact, the agent reported, "Some of the most industrious and worthy Indians on the reservation have been reduced from comfortable circumstances to poverty by their losses." Many people, including Hehaney and his band, preferred to take their chances on the public domain. Unfortunately for them, a handful of Columbia River Indians joined the hostiles, thereby feeding fears of a massive uprising and inviting retaliation against peaceful families.[28]

For reservation residents, feelings of insecurity also developed from the uncertain status of their new homes. Responding to pressure from American farmers and ranchers, who coveted Yakama and Umatilla lands in particular, Congress and the Indian Office considered several proposals to abolish one or more of the Plateau reservations. As early as 1859, Agent Andrew Cain recommended eliminating the Umatilla reservation and dispersing its residents to other agencies. His proposal went nowhere, yet Indian Inspector Felix Brunot again raised the subject at an 1871 meeting. When tribal leaders unanimously rejected the idea, Brunot instead suggested eliminating the Warm Springs reservation. At an 1876 council there, all but one of the Indians present expressed strong opposition. Still, the government would not relent, and in 1885 Congress forced the allotment and sale of Umatilla lands over tribal objections. Fearing a similar fate, Yakama leaders voiced "a strong desire that those living off the reservation be returned" to boost the tribal population. Agent Milroy dispatched emissaries and advocated the use of military force to compel removal, but few off-reservation families had heeded the call by the time he resigned in 1885.[29]

To many Indians, it probably seemed foolish to start a new life on a reservation that might soon disappear. White people obviously could not make up their minds about where Indians belonged. Some citizens demanded their swift removal from the public domain; others clamored for the immediate dissolution of the reservation system. Meanwhile, ranchers and homesteaders ignored reservation lines that remained largely unsurveyed and unmarked for decades after the treaties. All of the Mid-Columbia reservations had disputed boundaries, which collectively cast a cloud over tribal title to hundreds of thousands of acres. The tardy resolution of these disputes discouraged some Indians from settling in the tribal homelands, or at least gave them an excuse for not doing so. Investigating the status of the so-called McQuinn Strip, Indian Office Inspector T. D. Marcum reported:

> There are about 100 Warm Springs Indians who now reside off the reserve along the Columbia River, who want to locate on that part of the reservation now in controversy, but will not go upon the land until the north boundary line is definitely established, and will not do so if this land is cut off of the reserve.[30]

The government seemed more concerned with keeping Indians on the reservation than with keeping whites off, and it had done little to make the reserves into hospitable homes. "I gave up [my lands] and moved and came here on this reservation," grumbled Cayuse headman Howlish-wampo in 1871. "I have been here 11 years and all that [Governor Stevens] promised I have not seen. I think it must be lost." Given the circumstances, many Indians had little faith in the "Great Father" and little incentive to make the reservation a permanent residence.[31]

Even so, some "renegades" did express willingness to settle down if they could receive reservations adjoining the Columbia River. During an 1873 council with Inspector E. C. Kemble, the Walla Walla chief Homli suggested relocating his followers from the Umatilla reservation to a narrow tract of territory between Wallula and Priest Rapids. Luls, a Umatilla headman also in attendance, explained that he would remain along the "Big Water running" because the Creator had made it for his people and it listened to their prayers. Still, Kemble looked askance at the proposed reservation, calling it land in which "the horned frog could scarcely subsist" and noting that the Northern Pacific Railroad had already withdrawn most of it from the public domain. In his report to the Indian Office, he recommended merely allowing the Indians continued access to their fisheries as a means of gradually reconciling them to reservation life. Homli and Tygh headman Queahpahmah ultimately accepted it, giving some credence to Kemble's prediction that time and pressure would grind away the remaining "renegades." "They are certainly not increasing in strength," he wrote, "and there is pretty good reason to believe that a work of disintegration has begun among them which is diminishing their numbers every month." He misjudged the holdouts, however, just as the Indian Office underestimated the resolve of tribal leaders to keep their reservations.[32]

The passion with which seemingly compliant chiefs defended their reservations demonstrated that some Indians had already come to value them as homelands. "Since we have been brought here we have become attached to this land as though tied by a rope, and this is first and last our home to stay in," explained Takolus, a Sahaptin resident of Warm Springs, during the council with Inspector Brunot. "If we are outside to run around and shift for ourselves there may be trouble and bloodshed and that would be wrong." John Mission, a Wasco, could not understand why the government sought to relocate them a second time: "When we first made a treaty we did not want to go so far away from our homes. We asked for some land between here and The Dalles, but the Commissioner said ['No'].... Now I don't want to remove again and go to Simcoe. ... I do not crave any other country or speculate on the desirability of other places; this is my country." Instead of abandoning Warm Springs, the Indians suggested, the government should fulfill its promise to help them. "We do not want to hear anything more about leaving," insisted a Wasco called Tadshaw. "We only want our mill and other things fixed up so that they will be more serviceable to us here."[33]

The Indians on the Umatilla and Yakama reservations expressed similar sentiments during their meetings with Inspector Brunot. Aeneas, an influential Yakama headman, put it quite bluntly: "The treaty assigned us this land, and we will remain on it." The Umatilla tribes, facing a more immediate threat, responded with equally firm words. "I do not wish to sell any land or throw it away, as long as I live I will not sell it," declared Pierre, a Umatilla treaty signer favored by the government. "My heart will always be the same. That is all I want written. I am Indian." Howlish-wampo confirmed this sense of attachment to a clearly bounded Indian space: "I am holding on to my land that I am living on. The country that is marked out for us we see with our hearts and with our eyes. . . . The land that we have here we hold with our bodies and our souls." Reservation Indians had planted crops and built homes. They had shed blood defending those homes against the Snakes. They had buried their dead in reservation ground. Boundaries now mattered to these people, even if they frequently crossed them for economic and social reasons. They did not want the lines erased.[34]

Differing attitudes toward the reservation gradually created divisions between residents and Columbia River Indians. Fearful of losing their homes, some agency Indians criticized their kin for refusing to settle down on the lands set aside for them. Their presence on the public domain riled up the Americans, making it harder to defend the reservations against claims that Indians had broken the treaties or kept too much land for themselves. To make matters worse, reservation residents often shouldered the blame and suffered the consequences for problems caused by Columbia River Indians. "If the people were all good, white men would not trouble us," lamented White Swan (Joe Stwire), the head chief of the Yakama Nation. "Some of my people are wild and get into trouble with the whites. I am ashamed of them, because they are my people." A "renegade" named Frank, evidently feeling ashamed of himself, confessed his sinful ways to Inspector Brunot:

> I lived long ago at [Fort] Simcoe. My heart was, as it were, asleep. I used to hear good talk while I lived here. I was like a good man. Mr. Wilbur gave me good advice and I took it. Now it is like as if I had thrown away good things. I went away; I went away among those who did all that was wrong. My heart was sick. . . . When I see the white men, they are my friends. I don't steal white men's cattle. I don't want to steal; I want to do well, to farm; but I am away by myself among bad people.

Brunot obligingly pointed the way to salvation. To keep the reservations, he warned, "you must tell the absent [people] what is good, and get them to do what the President wants all to do. . . . You can make it sure that you will always live here by cultivating the land and getting others of your tribes to do so."[35]

Tribal leaders tried to fulfill this mandate. Through formal requests and personal appeals, the headmen and residents of Warm Springs repeatedly urged the people at Celilo "to come upon this reservation, take up land and make homes," but to no avail. After settling down himself, the former "renegade" Queahpahmah intervened to secure Hehaney's release from jail. Expressing regret at having "worked against the good" in the past, the Tygh chief assured Agent Smith that Hehaney "will be a good man after he sees all the Indians are gathered up, for he will have no place to go, except here. If he comes back, we agree to see that he carries out his promises." Hehaney saw things differently and soon embarrassed his former friend by bolting from the reservation. In 1883 he and five other Columbia River Indian headmen received a visit from Stick Joe, a Klickitat emissary sent to encourage their removal to Fort Simcoe. Acting on the orders of Agent Milroy, "Joe suggested to them that it would be much better for them all to come to the Reservation, and locate themselves there." They preferred to remain on the river, near the fisheries and the graves of their ancestors, and Milroy's antics merely hardened their resolve. In 1885, during a showdown with his Indian police, the off-reservation chiefs vowed that they would never willingly leave the river. To do so, they believed, would compromise their culture and identity.[36]

Columbia River Indians equated the reservations with assimilation and "whiteness" because many agency residents favored acculturation and celebrated the progress they had made since signing the treaties. "We were Indians then, not men as we are now," stated Thomas Pearn, a Klickitat preacher at Fort Simcoe. "We know the President assigned us this country. We did as the agent said, and we received an education. I am a man. I have a new heart. The old heart we received from our fathers has passed away." "I believe we are prospering and advancing," agreed Billy Chinook, who had once wondered what would become of his people if they lost their land. "I would not for anything go back to what we were." In the same breath, however, he reiterated his tribe's commitment to retaining the reservation: "This is our home and it is as dear to us as anyone's home can be to them." The strength of this commitment confounded the Indian Office, which regarded the reserves as temporary nurseries of civilization. As soon as Native people outgrew their "Indian" traits and adopted those of the whites, the nurseries would be closed. Most reservation residents saw a future of continued separation. As Wenapsnoot (Winanpšnút), a Umatilla treaty signer, put it to Brunot, "I think now that we will raise our children together, we on the reservation and you outside."[37]

Agency Indians tied the survival of their communities to the preservation of a land base. Even when they spoke approvingly of becoming like the whites, they did not necessarily intend to remove all the barriers separating them from American society. They wished to "improve" themselves, to achieve equality with the whites, but they wished to do so in their own place. Pianoose, head chief of the Wascos, articulated this position in an appeal to President Ulysses S. Grant:

With your help a great work can be done here. My desire is to bring my people up. We are poor creatures trampled under foot by the whites and I cry to you for help for my people. . . . We are not going to abandon this reservation. It is first and last our home. We want farming utensils and we want schools and also a man to teach us in spiritual things. Then we want a good saw mill and cattle and sheep that we may manufacture to supply some of our necessities. I want you to be a safe shelter for my people on which they can rely for assistance. If you will give my people these things I will see that they improve them and we will be ready to listen to your instructions.

By following instructions and proving their good faith, reservation residents hoped to retain a small sliver of Native space. They wanted to stay inside the lines, separate from American citizens, because they still considered themselves Indians.[38]

Columbia River Indians wanted to stay outside the lines for the same reason. As centers of federal power and control, reservations embodied the assault on indigenous culture and identity. Indian police and jails, Christian missionaries and churches, teachers and schools, agricultural instructors and farms—all of these things placed reservation life in opposition to traditional "Indianness" as then defined on the Columbia River. Consequently, despite continuing interaction and intermarriage, many off-reservation people began to see themselves as more authentically Indian than agency residents. "[Their leaders] profess to look with contempt on the reservation Indians, calling them whites and half-breeds," observed Agent Cornoyer. "By thus appealing to the passions and pride of the Indians, they hold a control, not only on those living on the Columbia River, but on large numbers who reside upon the several reservations." Hehaney, in a bid to draw people away from Warm Springs, ridiculed his former ally Queahpahmah "for having given up his plurality of wives and Smohalla religion, telling him he might as well give up his food." Real Indians, he implied, subsisted on fish and the natural products of the earth; only white men lived by cultivation of the soil. Such criticism shows that Indians and agents alike made inflexible distinctions between "progressives" and "traditionals," between "civilized" reservation residents and "wild" renegades. While each group assigned different values to those labels, both used them to define themselves and shape their relations with the federal government.[39]

The sharp contrasts made between reservation and off-reservation Indians concealed significant diversity within each group. Among reservation residents in particular, varying degrees of acculturation generated friction along ethnic and religious lines. At Warm Springs, the Wascos generally lived nearest the agency and expressed the greatest interest in learning white ways. Many became devout Christians and looked down on the "heathen" Sahaptins, who kept to the northern portion of the reserve and showed little inclination to farm or build homes. The Wascos opposed Hehaney's return in 1879, while the so-called Warm Springs welcomed him with open arms. Neither group cared much for the Northern Paiutes the government placed on their land later that year. Meanwhile, on the Yakama reservation, Methodists and Catholics clashed with one another and with the traditionalist Dreamers. "This does not give us good hearts," explained George Paul, a Klickitat member of the Methodist congregation. "We do not all agree, and come to get good advice. . . . We would like the others to be separated from us, and those that are left would be as one." Similar conflicts occurred on the Umatilla reserve, where Agent Cornoyer supported Catholic Indians against those who had either joined Protestant churches or remained faithful to indigenous spirituality. Thanks to the early missionaries and the Peace Policy of the 1870s, which assigned each agency to a different denomination, Native Americans had indeed learned to fight about God. Although their agents often described them as a single group, reservation residents rarely displayed as much harmony or homogeneity in their behavior.[40]

Among "renegades," religion provided a unifying force and the underpinning for an incipient Columbia River Indian identity. Whereas many reservation residents had converted to Christianity, most off-reservation Indians followed the nativistic teachings of Smohalla (Šmúxala) and his disciples. Born about 1815 in a Wánapam village on the Columbia River, Smohalla rose to prominence during the 1850s as the head of a powerful religious revitalization movement. Already deemed a potent *iyánča* ("one who trains or disciplines") by his own people, he attracted numerous followers from across the Plateau by promising them deliverance from the American onslaught. His creed, called Wá·šani (Washani, meaning "dancers" or "worship"), mingled indigenous beliefs with Christian concepts but explicitly renounced white culture. Known for the power of his visions—obtained during deep, death-like trances in which he professed to visit the afterworld and receive instructions from the Creator—Smohalla declared that Indians must stop tilling the soil or face divine retribution. When an army officer attempted to convince him otherwise, he retorted:

> It is a bad word that comes from Washington; it is not a good law that would take my people away from me.
>
> You ask me to plow the ground! Shall I take a knife and tear my mother's bosom? Then when I die she will not take me to her bosom to rest.
>
> You ask me to dig for stone! Shall I dig under her skin for her bones? Then when I die I can not enter her body to be born again.
>
> You ask me to cut grass and make hay and sell it, and be rich like the white men, but how dare I cut off my mother's hair?[41]

The Creator would reward obedience to this creed with world renewal. If Indians faithfully performed the *wá·šat* ("dance"), the whites would die off or disappear, deceased relatives would return to life, and the land would revert to its pristine state. In the meantime, Smohalla declared, Indians must cast off white ways, reject the reservation system, and seek wisdom in dreams. Although he also preached nonviolence, his religion gave spiritual sanction to the defiance of federal authority.[42]

To the government's dismay, the revitalized Washani faith (Wá·šat; also called the Dreamer or Seven Drums religion) spread far beyond Smohalla's winter village at Priest Rapids. His vision appealed to Indian communities reeling from the impact of Euro-American colonization, and a host of disciples carried his creed up and down the Columbia River. Although some modified Washani symbols and ceremonies, all retained the basic belief that Indians must remain free of white influences and return to traditional ways. "Their model of a man is an Indian"; cursed one exasperated official; "they aspire to be Indian and nothing else." Accordingly, many Dreamers stayed off the reservations, beyond the reach of agents and their Indian police. Lishwailait and Ashnithlai preached among the "renegade" Klickitats along the White Salmon and Klickitat rivers. Waltsac, a Umatilla čá·ča·ni (holy man, prophet), traveled with around a hundred followers between the John Day River and Priest Rapids. Skamia (Sx̱imáya), a resident of Sk'in, held ceremonies there and reputedly foretold the construction of the dam that would drown the fisheries and villages along The Dalles–Celilo reach. With an estimated 250 followers in 1873, he ranked as one of Smohalla's greatest contemporaries and one of the Indian Office's biggest headaches. Thumbing their noses at the promise of "civilization," Dreamers challenged the reservation system and reaffirmed the Indian identity of their followers.[43]

Agents and missionaries, acting in concert with sympathetic Christian Indians, responded with a crusade to crush Washani. According to stories told on the Warm Springs reservation, Presbyterian Wascos ordered Queahpahmah to stop performing the Washat ceremony. When he refused, soldiers allegedly tossed his drum into the fire, then dragged him behind a horse and threw him into the agency jail at Warm Springs. He continued to sing, even after they cut off one of his braids. In 1878, Homli complained that Agent Cornoyer and the Roman Catholics at Umatilla persecuted his followers, "which makes their hearts sore, and [they] cannot stay on the reservation if they are not left alone, and allowed to worship God in their own way." Seven years later, numerous Yakama families abandoned their reservation farms after Agent Milroy clapped Kotiakan in irons and imprisoned him at hard labor for six weeks. "Runners have been going throughout the outlying country, and the Indians [are] generally very much excited," cautioned Captain James MacMurray. "Many advocate armed resistance and attack on the Klickitats who live near the Agency and constitute the Indian police force." Far from silencing the Seven Drums, coercion merely drove its followers underground or off the reservation, while also driving wedges between Columbia River Indians and their Christian kin.[44]

The exodus of Dreamers to off-reservation sanctuaries confirmed official suspicions that Smohalla and his disciples were actively luring Indians away from the agencies. The threat clearly existed, although the government tended to exaggerate the Wánapam prophet's personal control over his followers. According to Agent Cornoyer, Smohalla had "emissaries constantly visiting the different reservations, corrupting the minds of the well-behaved and peaceable Indians and endeavoring to induce them to leave and go with him." Other Dreamer prophets followed his lead and aggressively proselytized their reservation relatives. In doing so, they became another pernicious outside influence, an external scapegoat that beleaguered agents could blame for their troubles. "Until these Indians are placed under proper control," Cornoyer declared, "there will be no material improvement among the several reservations in Eastern Oregon and Washington." Agent Smith concurred: "There should be something done to rid the community of this nuisance and the agents of the annoyance of having such a class [of Indians] in so close proximity to his own people, for the influences that come from there are all bad."[45]

Frustrated with the limited reach of their authority, agents continually urged the mobilization of military power to push "renegades" inside the lines. "It is useless to persuade this class of Indians to remove to reservations," complained Cornoyer. "It has been tried again and again to no avail. The only way in my estimation to deal with them is to remove the principal medicine-men from their midst and compel the others to go on reservations and keep them there by force, if necessary, until they learn obedience." Inspector William Vandever, a former soldier himself, recommended giving Columbia River Indians a choice between exile on the Colville reservation or banishment to the Indian Territory. But the Military Department of the Columbia rarely countenanced such drastic action except in times of war. Off-reservation Indians remained peaceful enough, and their lands undesirable enough, that the army saw little reason to incur the trouble and expense of rounding them up. As Colonel Charles Grover, the commanding officer at Fort Walla Walla, explained in 1885:

> They are not *in fact* Reservation Indians, and never have been. They are a quiet peaceable people and have as good a natural right to their own homes as anybody else, and if they are unceremoniously expelled from them, it will probably result in an unnecessary and costly Indian War.

Even if the army managed to remove them without provoking armed resistance, the Indians would not stay put unless constantly policed. Reservation boundaries remained too porous and other priorities too pressing. Consequently, by the early 1880s, military officers had become leading advocates of allowing off-reservation Indians to select homesteads on the public domain.[46]

■ ■ ■

Without firing a shot, Hehaney and his fellow Columbia River Indians had escaped the fate of more famous "renegades" such as Chief Joseph, Crazy Horse, and Geronimo. They had also earned the lasting enmity of the Indian Office. No longer a neutral geographic designation, the term "Columbia River Indian" now connoted a negative attitude toward federal policy and American society. Agents stopped short of calling them a tribe but described them as "a class, who were at heart hostile—refusing to live on the Reservation or to recognize the authority of the Agent, and rejecting all efforts to conciliate them." Cornoyer fumed: "All the small bands of Columbia River Indians are worthless vagabonds, roaming from place to place, drinking, gambling, stealing horses, etc." Never one to mince words, Agent Milroy branded them "wild animals that go wherever they can obtain a subsistence with the least exertion and most securely. They are lazy and indolent, [having] retained all the vices of their savage ancestors and absorbed largely the grosser vices of the whites." His counterpart at Warm Springs could only add, "They are nearly all a worthless, ignorant, and superstitious lot of people; as much so as they possibly can be." Grounded in the ethnocentric assumptions of the colonizers, this poor reputation persisted for decades among federal officials and tribal authorities alike. Yet many Columbia River Indians took pride in their defiance, and many eventually adopted the government's label as an alternative tribal identity.[47]

This new identity emerged slowly and incompletely between 1860 and 1885. Aboriginal affiliations persisted, and most off-reservation Indians still associated with one or more of the confederated tribes and integrated the reservations into their seasonal movements. Native identities remained complex and multifaceted. The federal government had merely added a new dimension with the creation of a separate category for Columbia River Indians. Eager to distinguish them from "good" reservation residents, agents gave off-reservation "renegades" a collective name that underscored both their opposition to the federal policy and their attachment to a particular place. The term Columbia River Indian implied a level of unity and organization that did not yet exist among the widely scattered communities on the public domain. For those who already considered themselves "people of the river," however, the label proved a natural fit. In time, many off-reservation Indians would become aware of the name and apply it to themselves. A shadow tribe had emerged, faintly visible as a presence standing in opposition to the Indian Office and, occasionally, the reservation tribes. This sense of difference rested on a common heritage of resistance, which later generations proudly invoked in defense of their rights. As Yakama tribal member Mike George declared in 1993, "I prefer to call myself a Columbia River Indian. There were Indians that never wanted to go on the reservation, and we're some of them."[48]

It has been the long standing goal of the people to achieve some

form of recognition for our community needs from the three tribes

to which our people belong. The three tribes use our head count to

obtain federal funds, but provide very limited services to our people.

—MID-COLUMBIA RIVER COUNCIL, APPLICATION
FOR FEDERAL ASSISTANCE TO THE ADMINI-
STRATION FOR NATIVE AMERICANS, 1993

4 ▪ ▪ ▪

PLACES OF PERSISTENCE

Agent Robert Milroy's mood matched the black ink from his pen as he wrote the Fort Simcoe agency's first monthly report of 1885. The previous summer, that "military fool," Captain James W. MacMurray, had conferred with a band of "renegades" without Milroy's knowledge or consent. Thanks to this "clandestine council," some of *his* Indians had pulled their children out of school and left the Yakama reservation in anticipation of taking homesteads on the public domain. He could not pursue them because the Office of Indian Affairs forbade the dispatch of agency police beyond reservation boundaries. Rather than force their removal, the army filled their heads with nonsense about filing claims on what Milroy considered to be "refuse and worthless lands." An erstwhile advocate of Indian homesteading, Milroy soured

89

on the idea when it involved Columbia River Indians and their reservation allies. "As a general rule," he charged, "they are among the most ignorant, superstitious, and vicious among all those that belong to this agency." Reading back over the sentence, he took a moment to insert the word "lazy" above the line and then continued his diatribe. These people had no intention of improving their property or themselves. They sought homesteads, he insisted, "not for the sake of the *lands* but for the *papers*, which *free* them forever from the jurisdiction of the U.S. Agent, and leave them and their children, while any of them survive, to vegitate [*sic*] amid vice, ignorance, and squalor."[1]

Milroy's tirade was among the last gasps of bureaucratic resistance to Indian homesteading. By 1885, most policy makers and reformers had grown disillusioned with the reservation system. Despite the concerted efforts of agents, missionaries, teachers, and boss farmers, the balance of the nation's Native American population still shunned the light of "civilization." Reservations, the ultimate symbol of racial separation, appeared to be hindering rather than helping the process of assimilation. Most tribes held their homelands in common, and reformers increasingly placed this practice at the root of the persistent "Indian problem." In 1886, Commissioner of Indian Affairs John D. C. Atkins proclaimed: "[The Indian] must be imbued with the exalting egotism of American civilization so that he will say 'I' instead of 'We,' and 'This is mine' instead of 'This is ours.'" The Indian Homestead Acts of 1875 and 1884 encouraged Native people to sever their tribal relations and take up their own land away from the reservations. The General Allotment Act, passed in 1887 with support from self-styled humanitarians and land speculators alike, targeted the reservations themselves. Better known as the Dawes Act, the law mandated the division of tribal holdings into individual parcels and the sale of "surplus" lands to white role models. In theory, allotment in severalty would teach Indians the value of private property and transform them into productive American citizens. In practice, the policy caused severe economic disruption, cultural distress, and the loss of some ninety million acres from the tribal land base. Congress finally abandoned allotment in 1934, but many reservations still bear the scars of this misguided experiment in social engineering.[2]

Historians have roundly and justly criticized allotment for its harmful impact on Native Americans.[3] Ironically, though, the Dawes Act and the Indian homestead laws that preceded it also gave "renegades" the chance to legitimize their presence off the reservation. By taking advantage of this legislation, Columbia River Indians largely relieved the pressure for their removal and secured a measure of freedom from government interference.[4] Many families never built homes or started farms on their property, and some ultimately lost it. Even so, public domain allotments and homesteads served an important purpose. In the shadows that stretched between the reservations, Columbia River Indian identity gained strength and developed new layers. Isolation fostered a sense of independence and self-sufficiency, yet government neglect also accentuated feelings of resentment toward the Office of Indian Affairs and reservation residents. These conflicting sentiments added to the confusion created by shifting administrative jurisdictions and crisscrossing ties to the reservation tribes. Passed from agency to agency and often treated as outsiders, Columbia River Indians began to feel that neither the federal government nor the tribal councils adequately represented their interests. They retained both personal and political ties to the reservations, however, and Columbia River Indian remained one among many identities available to the indigenous peoples of the region.

■ ■ ■

Policy makers considered Indian identity of any kind to be incompatible with full membership in American society, and they wrote this assumption into public land laws. The Homestead Act of 1862 permitted only citizens and those who had registered for citizenship to claim quarter sections (160 acres) of the public domain. This limitation virtually excluded Native Americans until 1870, when Secretary of the Interior Jacob Cox ruled that the Fourteenth Amendment gave "civilized" Indians equal rights under the law. By severing tribal ties and foreswearing all treaty benefits, they could achieve "civilized" status and make homestead entries just like American citizens. Few Indians managed to file the necessary papers before Cox's successor temporarily slammed shut the window of opportunity. In 1874, Secretary Columbus Delano decreed that only an explicit act of Congress could grant Indians access to the land laws, as legislators had not intended the Fourteenth Amendment to confer such benefits. Congress obliged with the Indian Homestead Act of 1875, which confirmed legitimate entries under the existing laws and extended homestead privileges to any Indian "born in the United States, who is the head of a family, or who has arrived at the age of twenty-one years, and who has abandoned, or may hereafter abandon, his tribal relations." The act allowed applicants to receive shares of tribal money and property, but in time they would ostensibly forswear all claims to Indian identity and merge into American society.[5]

Supporters hoped that the Indian Homestead Act would induce Native Americans to leave the reservations and pursue the Jeffersonian dream of a small family farm. Urging local agents to hasten the process, one Northwest newspaper editor predicted that the law would "free us forever from the confusion and expense of the Indian question, by leaving him to work out his destiny alongside of other men." Congress did not specify the procedure for granting homesteads to Indians, however, and nearly two years passed before the Interior Department developed regulations. To enter land under the act, applicants had to file an affidavit with the proper district land office swearing that they had abandoned tribal relations and adopted "the habits and pursuits of civilized life." A second affidavit offered corroborative testimony from two "disinterested witnesses," and a third vouched that the Indian had actually improved the claim. After the applicant made final proof, the government would hold the homestead in trust for five years to protect against rapid sale or seizure. At the end of that period, the owner would receive a fee patent and "step into the open door of citizenship." "He can do it as well as the freedman," proclaimed the *Oregonian*. "No one can do it for him. If he has not seen or does not see it—which is probable—let his friends in every place tell him of it; explain the facts; help him up out of his darkness."[6]

The War Department, seeking an alternative to the costly conflicts of recent years, led the charge to locate off-reservation Indians on homesteads. In 1878, fresh from his pursuit of Chief Joseph's non-treaty Nez Perce, General Oliver O. Howard distributed instructions from the General Land Office to military commanders in the Department of the Columbia. The Bannock War created more pressing priorities, however, and most Plateau Indians remained unaware of the act at the end of the decade. The real impetus for action came when American emigrants began claiming lands occupied and cultivated by Columbia River Indians. In 1884, for example, Salmon Man complained that a white intruder had seized his family's property near Umatilla, "driving the Indians off and threatening them with the law if they trespassed on his 'homestead.'" Blind Jim, the local headman, demanded that the army "explain to them whether the settlers who are coming in fast have any right to crowd them off the Government Land. They want to live where they always have and not be disturbed by any one." Agent Milroy cited these events as cause to remove the Indians, but the War Department chose to protect them. The previous year, in response to similar problems in Arizona Territory, the Interior secretary had directed the General Land Office to refuse all entries filed on lands "in the possession of Indians who have made improvements of any value whatever thereon." After investigating the trouble on the Columbia, General Nelson A. Miles applied successfully to extend this order to his department.[7]

Deflecting the threat of preemption proved easier than placing Native families on homesteads. In March 1884, as the War Department worked to block white claim jumpers, Captain F. K. Upham met with a group of off-reservation Indians and informed them that "occupying surveyed government land, or even improving it, was not sufficient and did not give them a title to it, no matter how long it had been occupied by them, and that no Indian could expect to be protected in such a claim or title." In other words, they must either take homesteads or move onto the reservations. Three months later, Captain J. W. MacMurray left Fort Vancouver in a wagon loaded with plat maps and survey equipment. Accompanied by a driver, interpreter, and engineer, he visited Indian communities along the Columbia River and further explained the provisions of the law. Many of the people he encountered already possessed houses, gardens, and corrals. Some assumed that these things ensured their rights to their property and were disappointed to learn otherwise. The concept of land ownership still puzzled them, and the procedural details of the law only increased their confusion. "[The Indian] thinks the survey and plat are ample security," noted MacMurray, "and [he] is lost in the maze of other things he has to do to make his title as good as a white man's."[8]

Some Columbia River Indians objected to the very idea of homesteading. As followers of the Washani faith, they believed that people could occupy and use land but should never buy and sell it. When Captain Upham said they must file claims or lose their homes, the Indians replied "that they would not do so for the reason that it was one of the principal tenets of their religion that there was no such thing as property in land. . . . This principle they said they could not violate, whatever the consequences might be." Dreamers especially disliked paying entry fees and commissions, which smacked of buying land and imposed a financial burden on many applicants. Instead of taking homesteads, they wanted the government to affirm their rights to their traditional territory along the Columbia River. Captain MacMurray's interpreter, a non-Indian "squaw man" named Chapman, evidently led some people to believe the military would grant their wish. According to Cyrus Beede, the Indian Office agent sent to assist Indian homesteaders, the prophet Skamia insisted that Chapman had "told us to remain as we were, our lands would be given back to us; our understanding is that we were to have all the lands on both sides of the Columbia." This interpretation may have resulted from garbled translation, deliberate misrepresentation, or wishful thinking. Beede, in the best tradition of jealous bureaucrats, took it as a sign that the War Department had again interfered with Indian Office business.[9]

Some agents opposed Indian homesteading no matter which office planted the survey stakes. Shortly before retiring from his post at Fort Simcoe, James Wilbur condemned the policy because it removed Indians from official supervision and exposed them to "designing white men." His successor, Agent Milroy, spent the last three years of his career cursing the Indian Homestead Act and the army. An enthusiastic supporter of homesteading during his tenure as Washington superintendent of Indian affairs, he turned against it after Congress changed the rules and Columbia River Indians challenged his authority. On July 4, 1884, legislators had passed a second Indian Homestead Act that waived all entry fees and extended the trust period to twenty-five years. Enacted in the midst of Milroy's bout with the renegades, the new law made it easier for applicants to acquire and retain homesteads without making significant improvements. He contended that the "vicious, anti-civilization" Indians would file under false pretenses, thereby depriving American citizens of lands the government had purchased for their benefit. Meanwhile, vastly superior acreage on the reservation would go to waste and "renegades" would continue to annoy white settlers, who would in turn pester the agent with complaints. Now a firm believer in the need for continued racial separation, Milroy advocated reversing the "mistaken and pernicious policy" of Indian homesteading. "Civilization is a plant of very slow growth," he preached, "especially during the struggling period while starting from barbarism." In his opinion, most Indians still needed their reservation greenhouses.[10]

Milroy's arguments resonated with many of his colleagues and fellow citizens, but the pendulum of federal policy had already swung too far. In September 1884, the Interior Department ordered agents not to interfere with Indians seeking homesteads on the public domain. A similar directive to General Land Office employees stated that "every facility practicable should be afforded the Indians to enter and settle upon homesteads." Native interest grew as news of the revised law spread along the Columbia River. Although the strictest Dreamers still shunned private ownership, the promise of secure title and relief from coercive agents helped some Indians overcome their ambivalence. Supportive non-Indian kinsmen and neighbors offered additional encouragement and assistance. Beyond explaining the procedures and signing the required affidavits, a few even defended Native homesteaders against white legal challenges and claim jumpers. During the troubles with Agent Milroy, for example, an American settler named Jade Switzler wrote letters on behalf of the headman Blind Jim and served as an interpreter at meetings with local Columbia River Indians. The Indian Office still received petitions from disgruntled whites demanding removal, but their protests failed to stop the policy shift. By the time Milroy stepped down in 1885, homesteading had become a legitimate way for Native Americans to remain off the reservation.[11]

Congress opened a second avenue of opportunity with the General Allotment Act of 1887. Praised by Theodore Roosevelt as "a mighty pulverizing engine for breaking up the tribal mass," the Dawes Act provided for the division of reservations into individual parcels, or allotments, to be distributed among tribal members. Each head of family could claim 160 acres, and single persons over the age of eighteen and orphans under eighteen could receive eighty acres apiece. Their allotments would be protected from alienation during a twenty-five-year trust period, but any remaining reservation land could be sold to non-Indian applicants. Thus surrounded by white exemplars and given the dual blessings of private property and American citizenship, tribes would supposedly dissolve and Indians would cease to exist as a distinct race. Section 4 of the Dawes Act extended these presumed benefits to non-reservation Natives by allowing them to select allotments on the public domain. Reservation residents could also opt for land away from the reservation, as policymakers assumed that would be all the better to speed their assimilation into American society. Ultimately, through Section 4 and the existing homestead laws, more than 650 individuals and families filed applications with government land offices in Vancouver, Walla Walla, and The Dalles.[12]

The distribution of off-reservation homesteads and allotments proceeded fitfully from the mid-1880s to the early 1920s. The Indian Office preferred that applicants take "fourth section" allotments because they required less documentation than homestead entries and could not be contested by white claimants. Indians filing homestead entries had to complete several affidavits and "prove up" their claims before the General

Land Office would issue a trust patent, whereas Indian allottees obtained a trust patent immediately after the Indian Office submitted the necessary paperwork. The distinction between these forms of property eluded many Indians, however, and local land offices continued to issue homesteads into the early twentieth century. Ironically, this dual system allowed people to obtain homesteads by forswearing their tribal relations while at the same time taking allotments as tribal members. Mid-Columbia Indians ultimately filed about 120 homestead claims in The Dalles and Vancouver land districts, with allotment becoming the norm in the 1890s.[13] After a few false starts, special allotting agents visited the area periodically over the next three decades. The majority of Columbia River Indians received their trust patents between 1893 and 1909, with the largest concentration issued from 1900 to 1905. Then, rising concerns about fraudulent applications began to slow the process. In 1906, the General Land Office investigated fifty-five public domain allotments to determine whether white men had acquired them illegally through their Indian wives and mixed-heritage children. Although the inquiry found no evidence of fraud in those cases, the Indian Office suspended allotment from 1913 to 1917 pending the approval of stricter regulations. Under the new rules, which required stronger proof of tribal identity, the last sixteen Columbia River applicants obtained trust patents in 1920 and 1921.[14]

The story of these final allotments reveals the familiar blend of sympathy and self-interest that led some whites to assist their Native neighbors. In 1889, Oregon rancher W. G. Flett notified the Indian Office that a small group of Columbia River Indians in his vicinity wished to secure allotments on the public domain. Flett had lived in Gilliam County for nearly three decades and had married a mixed-blood woman, which probably helped him gain the confidence of the local indigenous population. His wife may have asked him to take up the cause of landless Columbia River Indians, but Flett also had his own fortunes in mind. In 1901, a decade after Congress lifted restrictions on the leasing of allotments, he offered his services as an interpreter and surveyor to an Indian Office allotting crew working upriver from Celilo Falls. "I am 48 years among these Indians," he later boasted, "and my activity has resulted in 300 alottments [*sic*] being made to the tribe and [I] am very anxious to settle those who are homeless." By 1914, he seemed especially keen to settle a small group of "homeless" Natives along the nearby John Day River. Frustrated by the moratorium on fourth-section allotments between 1913 and 1917, Flett wrote letter after letter warning the Indian Office that aggressive sheepmen would run the Indians off and ruin their land unless the government acted promptly.[15]

When the Indian Office finally dispatched an agent to the area, he began to suspect the mixed motives behind Flett's ardent advocacy of public domain allotments. Nearing eighty years of age in 1919, the veteran stockman had nominally retired from the ranching business. His two sons stayed in the saddle, however, and they owned large spreads adjoining Hay Creek Canyon, where the General Land Office had set aside acreage for Indian entries. "In an effort to acquire a monopoly of the range," charged Special Agent Charles E. Roblin, "the Flett family has endeavored to get the Indians of the Columbia River district interested in this land and to claim it for allotment. As an inducement toward this end they have been paying a small 'rental' to such Indians as would come in and claim lands in the canyons." Once allotted, the owners could make formal leasing arrangements with the Fletts to effectively exclude other stockmen from previously open range. "The Indians have made no use of the lands themselves, and not one has made any bona fide attempt to make *any* settlement on the lands selected," complained Roblin, a firm believer in the benefits of allotment. He could hardly blame them, for the country in question was an "inconceivably rough" expanse of rocky plateaus and deep gorges, but Congress had intended the Dawes Act to promote permanent use and occupation of allotted lands. Accordingly, the Indian Office regarded Flett's scheme as flagrant abuse of the law and the Indians alike.[16]

Local sheep ranchers also resented his ploy and tried to block the allotments. Accustomed to wintering their flocks in the reserved district, they accused the Fletts of angling "to get control of that land for personal gain only." "They are anxious to get rid of everyone else in that vicinity," insisted a representative of the rival Barker estate, "and have even gone so far with the Indians as to advise them to say that they did not want any sheep on the lands." The Indian Office had stumbled into the middle of a classic Western range war. Seizing upon the government's mistaken identification of the applicants as members of the Klickitat tribe, the local Grange issued a resolution opposing allotment on the grounds that "the said Klickitat Indians are in the State of Washington, and the State of Washington has plenty of public lands to supply her own Indians." In fact, most of the candidates considered themselves Takšpašłáma (John Day Indians), and the Indian Office wisely ignored this attempt to turn its own faulty assumptions against them. It did not ignore that many of them had already received allotments on one of the reservations or elsewhere on the public domain. Where Flett perceived some two hundred homeless Indians in need of land, Special Agent Roblin found a mere twenty eligible to apply. "The fact that I denied the requests of some of the Indians offended them all," he noted, "and at first those who were entitled to allotments refused to take them." In the end, only fifteen secured land, leading an embittered Flett to conclude: "When this government will act in Colusion [sic] with renegade Sheep Men to defeat efforts of a lot of half starved Indians, it is time for Cattle men to get out."[17]

■ ■ ■

Flett's description of the Indians as hapless victims of bureaucratic corruption ignores the intelligent role they played in the selection of homesteads and allotments. Far from being mere pawns in a stockman's game, Columbia River Indians had their own ideas about where to acquire land and why. The fifteen John Days allotted in 1920 knew full well that their plots in Hay Creek Canyon would never support agriculture. They wanted the lands to raise cash—a scarce commodity in their communities—and Flett had agreed to pay in advance. When Roblin informed them that they must have Indian Office approval, the Indians "stated that if they could not lease [the land] it would do them no good." A reasoned estimate of economic worth also inspired Chief Tommy Thompson's unsuccessful request for an allotment on the wheat-growing benches above Celilo Falls, which he insisted the whites had stolen from his people. By fair means and foul, Euro-Americans had appropriated the lion's share of the arable land on the dry Columbia Plateau. Tommy Thompson's son, Henry, concluded that his parcel near Rock Creek was not "fit for anything. I guess that is why the Government gave me that land for an allotment." A few Indian homesteaders managed to secure good agricultural acreage along the Klickitat and White Salmon rivers, but most Columbia River Indians received allotments designated as grazing land. Although inadequate for commercial ranching operations, a 160-acre parcel might furnish enough pasture, garden space, and rental income to make it worthwhile.[18]

For many River People, time-honored subsistence patterns and cultural practices took precedence over the economic potential of an allotment or homestead. Accordingly, they sought to acquire land in places of traditional significance, regardless of the agricultural prospects there. Assigned to the Columbia River district in 1902, Special Agent George A. Keepers encountered numerous people "averse to removing any distance from their old locations for the purpose of securing allotments, hence it is difficult to secure desirable lands for them, especially as the country is being very rapidly settled up by whites." A decade earlier, during a visit to The Dalles, Special Agent George P. Litchfield had met several Indians "whose Fathers were buried here, and they want to be buried here also." They initially expressed little interest in allotment but later reconsidered and asked for land adjoining the Tumwater fishery, where white homestead claims had seriously reduced river access. To their dismay, Litchfield found nothing suitable along the rocky shoreline. After consulting with Joe, the local headman, he agreed to leave any vacant tracts open for tribal camping and grazing during the salmon season. While these Indians could do without allotments, if necessary, they would not surrender the ancient fisheries and cemeteries of their people.[19]

Ultimately, hundreds of Columbia River Indians went without allotments or homesteads of their own. True to the original tenets of the Washani religion, many Dreamers steadfastly refused to acquire property in land. They held the division of the earth to be a sin, and they repeatedly rebuffed the government officials sent to convince them otherwise. Meanwhile, an unknown number of people missed the opportunity to secure land because they happened to be away when allotting agents passed through their territory. The semi-nomadic lifestyle of Columbia River Indians made them difficult to track down, especially during the spring and summer months, and the Indian Office passed over many people entitled to fourth-section allotments. According to W. G. Flett, who accompanied the Keepers crew in 1901, the family of George Selam received no land at that time because they were off in the mountains. They got a second chance in 1919, but Selam's parents had neither an allotment nor any apparent desire to obtain one. Unlike reservation residents, who frequently had selections made for them, Columbia River Indians remained free to decide whether they would participate in the government's latest scheme to improve their lives.[20]

Some of those who failed to secure land on the public domain accepted allotments on the reservations instead. For various reasons, and with varying degrees of enthusiasm, individual Indians drifted in to submit applications throughout the 1890s and early 1900s. Agency officials assumed that these prodigal sons and daughters had seen the error of their ways and had come back to stay. In 1893, for example, Umatilla agent George W. Harper smugly reported the presence of sixty "Indian tramps or renegades, who wandered off years ago . . . [but] now see the benefits arising from holding land in their own name and are anxious for the privilege of getting in, even in the garret, as the ground [floor] is all taken." Certainly, some Columbia River Indians chose this course after hearing promises of better land and ample assistance to be had on the reservations. In many cases, however, they were not drawn to the agencies so much as driven from their preferred places of residence. Recalling the decision to leave his ancestral home, Frank Seelatsee said, "I am of the Wish-hom tribe, raised on the Columbia River. White people crowded in, and I changed my mind and came to the Yakima Reservation." Ki-li-ish (James Takawpyciks) sought an allotment at Umatilla for the same reason. At the venerable age of eighty, he could no longer provide for himself in the traditional way because "white men [had] taken up lands outside the diminished reserve over which he was wont to hunt and fish and dig roots, and he [had] no abiding place." Such examples testify more to the increasingly difficult conditions faced by off-reservation Indians than to the inherent appeal of allotment.[21]

Reservation allotments provided security against the loss of property on the public domain, where Natives and newcomers alike often struggled to meet the requirements of the public land laws. Either from lack of interest or ability, dozens of Native homesteaders had their entries canceled by the General Land Office after failing to make final proof on their claims. The Indian Office also retired some fourth section allotments when agents belatedly discovered that the lands "were practically abandoned and the improvements allowed to fall into decay." In most cases, however, the Indian Office preferred to track down heirs and renew trust patents repeatedly rather than strip people of their property and lease income. The exposure of double allotments invariably produced demands to surrender one or the other, which added to the reluctance of many heirs to testify in probate proceedings. Other Indians voluntarily relinquished their public domain lands in exchange for superior reservation parcels, lost their property to tax foreclosure, or sold it to non-Indians. The generally poor quality of fourth section allotments and the increasingly complicated inheritance situation tended to discourage buyers, but white homesteaders and railroad corporations periodically challenged Indian entries on the public domain. Several families lost all or part of their land as a result. Still, during the 1930s, at least 296 Indian allotments and homesteads remained in The Dalles and Vancouver districts.[22]

Even Indians who chose land on the reservations did not necessarily settle down there. Many had no real interest in agriculture and left almost immediately; others abandoned the experiment after months or years of frustration. Historian Barbara Leibhardt has noted that on the semiarid Plateau, "Successful farming depended upon far more than an individual's ability and inclination to take up Euro-American practices. Land quality, access to water, cash for tools, seeds, and water charges (if the land was within a reclamation project) all affected the productivity of a particular allotment." Indians with low-quality land and little capital often wandered away to seek their fortunes elsewhere.[23] In 1902 Yakama superintendent Jay Lynch reported,

> Many of the allottees here were and are scattered over the State. Many came here for allotments, expecting the Government would build them irrigation canals, houses, etc., which was not done, and they could not make a living upon the land allotted to them without water to irrigate, and they have been compelled to go where they could live. The most of them went along the Columbia River, where they could fish for their own subsistence and for the markets, and it is impossible to obtain an accurate census of these.[24]

Forced to hazard a guess, Lynch estimated that roughly 1,300 of the 1,600 Indians on the reservation actually lived there all the time. Phantom residents haunted the other agencies as well. In 1906, for example, the Warm Springs agent counted eighty-three permanently absent allottees. More than a few Indians knew they had land somewhere but could not identify it or even remember the correct agency.[25] The Dawes Act clearly had not rooted these people in the soil. By taking allotments on a reservation, however, they had participated in an important defining ritual for the recognized tribes.

■ ■ ■

The process of allotting tribal members marked a significant but ambiguous moment in the emergence of modern Native American nations. Besides threatening tribal homelands and plunging many groups into economic dependency, the Dawes Act introduced the concept of blood quantum and effectively codified the assumption that an Indian could belong to only one tribe. To ensure the orderly distribution of allotments, the Indian Office conducted reservation censuses and compiled official tribal rolls, which became the baseline for determining future tribal membership.[26] Only enrolled members could obtain allotments, and nobody could receive more than one allotment either on or off the reservation (except through inheritance). This rule, though clear enough on paper, conflicted with the realities of Indian life on the Columbia Plateau. Many people had family members on several reservations, including agencies outside the region, as well as connections to various off-reservation enclaves. Frequent travel and intermarriage among these communities could make pinpointing tribal membership a dicey proposition. Some Indians appeared on two or more tribal rolls, often under different names, and others appeared on none at all. Corresponding errors in the assignment of allotments caused a great deal of confusion in the decades to come.

Native naming practices and kinship ties greatly complicated efforts to confine each person to one tribe and one allotment. Many people had both English names and Indian names, which could change over the course of a lifetime, and an individual might be known by different titles in different communities. Pressed for time and generally unfamiliar with the populations they served, allotting agents struggled to spell indigenous words and assign tribal affiliations with consistency.[27] A single passage from Indian Office correspondence suggests how muddled matters could become:

> Inspector Lonergan reports that Slutu-us, Warm Springs allottee No. 69 is also Mart Meninick, Yakima No. 1263; Lizzie Slutu-us, Warm Springs allottee No. 70 is also Leescresh Meninick, Yakima No. 1264; Hokh-hote, Warm Springs allottee No. 716 is also Low-push, Yakima No. 847; Tulalakas Wesley, The Dalles No. 13 is also Tulagus, Vancouver No. 158; Charlie Pistolhat, Warm Springs No. 980 is also Suplowis, The Dalles No. 55; and that Andy Spencer, Warm Springs No. 971 is also The Dalles No. 32.[28]

Not everyone benefited from cases of mistaken identity; in 1940, for example, the Indian Office revoked the trust patent of Jim Charley (Sanout Charley) and evicted his family because he had allegedly received another allotment under the name Snawat—who turned out to be an entirely different person. This comedy of errors led one off-reservation leader to remark that "all 'you white people' do is to get the Indians' names mixed up," but some of the confusion likely resulted from Indian manipulation of the system. Raised in a world of frequent movement, where kinship granted access to distant resources, many Mid-Columbia Indians saw nothing wrong with acquiring land wherever they had relatives. By employing different names and exploiting family connections, dozens of individuals circumvented Indian Office restrictions and secured multiple allotments on different reservations or the public domain.[29]

To guard against such abuses, the Indian Office enlisted tribal leaders to help screen out ineligible applicants. If a person's name did not appear on the base roll, he or she had to request enrollment in a recognized tribe or band before receiving an allotment. The details of this procedure changed over time and varied between agencies, but all of the southern Plateau reservations submitted enrollment applications to tribal councils or committees composed of prominent individuals from the community. Federal officials could not determine on their own which candidates had legitimate claims to tribal property, so they relied on the judgment of local chiefs and headmen. In doing so, historian Alexandra Harmon has found, the government initiated an unprecedented cross-cultural dialogue concerning Indian identity. In effect, reservation leaders had to decide what made someone a member of a particular tribe. Did affiliation depend primarily on the possession of "Indian blood" or on the maintenance of "tribal relations"? How much blood? What kind of relations? To answer these difficult questions, Harmon writes, "The Indians had to consider both their own conceptions of tribal ties and the government definition. Additionally, they had to consider conditions that had unraveled some people's community and family ties." The conclusions they reached had far-reaching consequences for both the people welcomed into the reservation community and those left outside.[30]

Contemporary notions of race figured prominently in enrollment decisions. In spite of allotment, which the tribes had fruitlessly opposed, many reservation leaders hoped to preserve their lands as distinctly Indian spaces. To that end, they encouraged "full-bloods" to return home, claim their shares of tribal property, and thereby reduce the amount of "surplus" acreage available to whites. In 1893, the year after allotment began on the Yakama reservation, the tribal council issued an invitation through the agent, stating,

> Sir: We . . . the head men of Yakima Reservation, agree that our own full-blood Indians will come into this reservation and take land, all different tribes. We will let our own Indian friends come in, too. This reservation we open for our red friends.[31]

Federal officials later discovered that the councilmen had construed "red friends" to include people from other reservations. Ignoring the government's narrow definition of tribal relations, they sent delegations to agencies west of the Cascade Mountains to invite friends and relatives to take land on the Yakama reservation. Approximately ten percent of Yakama allottees hailed from remote origins, but tribal leaders did not recruit members indiscriminately. The emphasis on "full-blood Indians" and "Indian friends" admitted persons of obvious Native ancestry while implicitly excluding mixed-bloods. Although numerous people of Indian-white parentage successfully applied for tribal membership, general distrust of "half-breeds" became a common theme in councils regarding allotment and enrollment.[32]

Tribal leaders worried that unscrupulous strangers would use dubious Indian heritage and superior knowledge of the system to acquire reservation lands. These concerns had merit, and they grew in response to a steady stream of mixed-blood claimants, some of whom were reputed to be "tough characters . . . [already] driven from other reservations" in the region.[33] A Cayuse spokesman called Captain Shumpkin voiced a common fear in 1905, when he spoke against opening the Umatilla agency's unallotted acreage to new applicants:

> When the half-breeds were allotted there was many of them unknown to these Indians on the Reservation, and that is still going on—they are not known by any of these Indians here. . . . If the half-breeds will be unknown by the Indians here, and then they will go out and get a lawyer and try the best they can to get an allotment here on the reservation.[34]

Twelve years later, when the matter came up again, Albert Minthorn charged, "These white people, so called mixed bloods, are not claiming the Indian blood, but are claiming the tribal land. In the case land should be given to the children [of allottees], these very people mentioned will be the very first people to select the very best land there is left on the tribal land." Umapine, a Umatilla chief, did not want mixed-bloods even in the room during the discussion. Like the reservation boundary, around which these men hoped to build a fence, racial lines had come to matter.[35]

But race was rarely the sole consideration. To many Indians, blood quantum mattered less than bonds of culture, kinship, and community.[36] Although some full-bloods remained suspicious of any and all "breeds," mixed-bloods with clear connections to the reservation or its residents could achieve a measure of acceptance and earn the right to participate in tribal affairs. At the same council where Umapine tried to exclude "breeds," the Walla Walla headman No Shirt made a crucial distinction between known and unknown persons. Addressing the mixed-bloods in attendance, he declared, "I know you people are entitled to this tribal land as much as the full blood Indians. You belong to the reservation and have rights on the reservation. . . . Let's all get together and hold this land as it is." Sabina Morton, a mixed-blood enrolled by the previous generation of tribal leaders, promptly reiterated the importance of group solidarity and kinship ties:

> There must be no unfriendliness among the full bloods and the half breeds, or mixed bloods. The full bloods are here because of their blood. In our Council when Homily, Peopeomoxmox and Kash Kash accepted us all, we were of their family, [and] that cannot be changed now.[37]

Applicants like Morton stood a good chance of gaining tribal membership regardless of their racial background. By contrast, those who applied late or lacked strong community ties frequently shared the fate of Margaret Jetté, a mixed-blood whom Umatilla leaders rejected in 1909. Despite the presence of nine half-siblings, who had received allotments in 1892, the tribal council considered her a stranger. "None of them knew the woman," reported the agency superintendent, "and they strongly opposed that she should be enrolled upon the ground that she does not live here, and is not known."[38]

The desire to protect the remaining tribal domain from unknown "outsiders" prevented some Columbia River Indians from obtaining land on the Umatilla reservation. In 1905, thirteen years after the agency closed its original base roll, Umapine and No Shirt traveled to Washington, DC, to request allotments for some thirty-five families that had previously lived near the mouth of the Umatilla River. At a meeting with the commissioner of Indian affairs, Umapine presented a letter explaining their plight and "told him I had pity on the outside Indians because they had no place to stay." The Umatillas and Walla Wallas largely supported this attempt to settle their fellow river Indians on the reservation, as did their agent, but Cayuse leaders opposed the plan and accused Umapine of going behind their backs. Although most of the applicants were full-bloods with family ties to the reservation, many councilmen had doubts about permitting former "renegades" to carve allotments from the dwindling tribal estate, which had once been Cayuse territory. The ensuing debate exposed significant divisions within the reservation community concerning the character and status of Columbia River Indians.[39]

The arguments for and against the allotment of "outside Indians" reflected the competing ethnic allegiances, cultural positions, and economic priorities of tribal leaders. Even though they had shared the same land for fifty years, reservation residents had different ideas about who belonged on it and how it should be used. Most council members agreed that mixed-bloods had no business there, and Cayuse opposition rested partially on the premise that opportunistic "half-breeds" would snatch up the land if the tribes opened it for anyone. Umapine and his supporters countered by noting that only affiliated full-bloods would receive consideration. Such people had rights at Umatilla, insisted Amos Pond, "and purposely for them we all held the reservation." Poker Jim added, "The Indians that want to have their allotments here, they are known by these Indians here, and the Government knows them too." But the Cayuses refused to relinquish an acre for the sake of those they considered strangers. Their headmen had weaker connections to the river and stronger ties to Christianity, which may have colored their opposition to an influx of "heathen" fish Indians. Moreover, many Cayuses owned large herds of livestock that depended on the tribal range, and they did not want to lose any of it. "The pasture lands and the unallotted lands here are very small," explained Pete Calitan. "This is the reason why we don't want to open allotments. We love it, and we can't open it for allotment." Ultimately, the council voted twenty-one to fifteen against admitting Columbia River Indians. To some residents, they had become outsiders beyond the pale of tribal responsibility.[40]

Even on the much larger Yakama reservation, where full-bloods usually received a warm welcome, late-coming Columbia River Indians stirred mixed emotions. At an 1897 council to discuss the sale of so-called surplus lands, the aging head chief White Swan clung to the hope that "renegades" would return to claim allotments. "I don't care how few was to come in," he told the impatient federal negotiators, "we want them to come in and get their land on this reservation. . . . We will go out to the Wenatchee [River] and go out to the Columbia and see the Indians and if they say they don't want to come into the reservation, then we won't ask you for any more time."[41] At the same meeting, however, Klickitat preacher Thomas Pearn lashed out at the spokesman for off-reservation Wishrams after he proposed selling the unallotted acreage:

> You see that man (Captain Simpson), he has got to have half a dozen interpreters for people to understand him. . . . That Indian man he belongs to the Columbia river. He is a citizen. He had a homestead at Goldendale. This treaty on this reservation won't allow that man to get up and talk on this reservation. That man from the outside come into this reservation and lives 2 or 3 years and he wants to be head of all this tribe that belongs to this reservation.[42]

Thomas Simpson had actually been on the reservation for a decade, serving as the chief of Indian police, but the Wishrams had chosen him to represent their interests before the tribal council. Pearn considered him an outsider who belonged on the river, not the reservation. Simpson had not lived there long enough nor learned enough of white ways to warrant a voice in tribal affairs. Paradoxically, he seemed too Indian and not Indian enough at the same time. Certainly, his willingness to surrender tribal lands did little to enhance his popularity, but other Columbia River Indians would confront similar prejudices well into the twentieth century.[43]

Off-reservation homesteaders and allottees had similarly ambivalent relations with their non-Indian neighbors. Although calls for Indian removal died down in the 1890s, cultural differences and economic competition continued to generate friction. Along the river, white land claims crowded out Native occupants and impeded access to traditional fishing sites. In the mountains, sheepmen invaded Indian huckleberry fields and tried to exclude Indian livestock from public lands, and traditional root-digging grounds succumbed to the plow or the trampling hooves of Euro-American cattle.[44] Problems with livestock also emerged on off-reservation allotments. Some white lessees failed to pay rent or ran more animals on the land than their contacts allowed; others simply let their cattle and sheep roam across unfenced Indian properties. In turn, Indian horses and root-digging parties trespassed on Euro-American homesteads.[45] The resulting clashes reinforced familiar racial stereotypes on both sides. Whites complained about the "shabby" appearance of Native settlements and characterized Indian men as habitual drunkards. Natives indiscriminately branded whites as liars and thieves with little regard for treaty rights. As one Indian wryly told Yakima agent Thomas Priestley in 1886, "He was getting to be the same as a white man and would soon be just like one; that he had 'learned to steal a little and lie a good deal.'"[46] If racial confrontation no longer produced rumors of violent uprisings, it still hindered the development of mutual trust and respect.

Even so, by the early 1900s most Euro-Americans had come to accept the presence of Indians off the reservation. They often interacted with one another on a daily basis, and individual relationships could grow quite cordial over time. A. A. Ames, whose family farm embraced the village of Walawatis (Maryhill), recalled in 1913 that his parents "imployed [sic] the Indians a great deal in gathering and caring for our crops, and working with them as I did I learned their own language so well as the choonuck language [Chinook jargon] that I could carry on a good conversation with them." He spoke fondly of having "many dear friends among them" who even invited him to attend their dances, funerals, and religious meetings. In 1918, Warm Springs superintendent Omar L. Babcock was likewise "pleased to report that the Indians at Hood River are spoken of very highly by the people with whom they come in contact. They are industrious and moral, and law-abiding citizens and have a distinct place in the community."[47]

Skookum Wallahee, an Indian homesteader in the Klickitat Valley, became a neighborhood celebrity of sorts. He rented pasture to white families on equitable terms, and they opened their farms to his people during the annual huckleberry pilgrimage.[48] He reputedly loved a free lunch, yet he peddled surplus berries, salmon, and orchard produce in local towns. During these visits, a white neighbor recalled, Wallahee enjoyed stopping by the one-room schoolhouse to scare the pupils:

> He would creep up to the windows, rise up, make awful faces, and give out an awful yell. He got a thrill out of seeing the children rush up to the teacher, who was usually not much older than they, and try to hide behind her. He would finally go inside, smiling and friendly, but the children did not quite trust him. Older folks who grew up in those times tell how the mothers used Skookum as a threat when the children disobeyed.[49]

Such tales challenge the old model of constant racial conflict, yet they also suggest the danger of romanticizing Indian-white relations in this period. To the average Euro-American, Indians such as Wallahee remained the exotic other, friendly and familiar yet still strange and vaguely frightening. For every story about the mischievous Klickitat "chief" who swapped apples for apple pies, local whites told another of Indians begging, drinking, or otherwise violating Euro-American notions of propriety. Native people could become true friends, but they more often became objects of contempt, ridicule, and pity.

■ ■ ■

Pity moved some Euro-Americans to question why the government did not do more for Columbia River Indians. Troubled by real or imagined signs of poverty and exploitation, conscientious whites periodically pressed the Indian Office to help their Native neighbors. During the winter of 1925, W. T. Jordan asked the Yakama agency to remove four Indians from the home of Sallie Moses, who lived on his land near Maryhill. Her guests belonged on the Warm Springs reservation, he insisted, and they should "not be allowed to settle down here on Sallie and Teeminway [her daughter] and expect to be fed as they have the past winter." Jordan clearly had good intentions. Moses's visitors may have been her relatives, however, and Jordan may have failed to recognize that obligations to kin crossed tribal boundaries. A more astute observer, linguist Melville Jacobs, also acted out of sympathy when he contacted the Yakama agency in 1928 on behalf of Native contacts. While conducting fieldwork in the area of Husum, Washington, he had become "exceedingly distressed" at the condition of the aged Hunt family. "At times, before some kind neighbor chances along," he wrote, "these old Indian people frequently come close to starvation." He suggested that the agency provide emergency funds for their relief. Superintendent Evan W. Estep refused, claiming they were "really not Yakima Indians and do not appear on our tribal rolls at all. . . . These people have always looked after themselves. We simply look out for their lands." Such excuses did not impress Indian Office Inspector P. T. Lonergan. "I do not know a solution of the difficulty for these poor Indians," he chided after a visit to the region, "but I know they need better supervision."[50]

Criticism of this kind irritated superintendents because they lacked the resources to provide more oversight. Most of the public domain allotments and homesteads in The Dalles and Vancouver districts lay upward of ninety miles from the agencies, across rugged terrain and primitive roads. Visits to these far-flung settlements strained the budgets and taxed the patience of overworked officials. By late 1918, Superintendent Babcock had exhausted his annual travel expenses for The Dalles district, which stretched nearly

200 miles from Hood River to the Burns Paiute colony in eastern Oregon. He thought it unfair to use reservation funds "for the purpose of visiting outlying bands of Indians that have been added to this jurisdiction but who have no share in the benefits." Two years later, his travel account still contained only 200 dollars for the entire district. Time was an even scarcer commodity. Agency personnel had enough trouble managing reservation business, yet their superiors frequently denied requests for additional staff or special agents to handle off-reservation matters. Then, Indian inspectors and other "uninformed" white people had the audacity to pass judgment on the performance of agency employees. By the 1930s, the administrative headache had grown so severe that local superintendents began advocating the creation of a sub-agency on the Columbia River.[51]

In the meantime, frequent jurisdictional changes further complicated efforts to look after Columbia River Indians. Originally, the three Mid-Columbia reservations shared responsibility for The Dalles and Vancouver allotments. In 1909, the Indian Office transferred The Dalles district to the Roseburg agency, located some two hundred miles from the river on the other side of the Cascade Mountains. When that office closed in 1918, control reverted to the Warm Springs Agency, but the Vancouver district remained under Yakama jurisdiction. Responsibility rested there until 1936, when the Indian Office passed both The Dalles and Vancouver allotments to the Umatilla agency. This game of administrative hot potato confused and frustrated its participants. At times, even agency superintendents seemed unsure of their bureaucratic boundaries. In a 1913 letter to the Roseburg office, Warm Springs agent Gilbert L. Hall offered to take care of various problems at Celilo, including a property dispute between Annie Wesley and an alleged white squatter. Hall did not know if the village fell within Warm Springs jurisdiction, however, and he had no desire to "butt in" on his colleague's territory. The Roseburg superintendent reminded him of the 1909 switch and promised to send a clerk to the agency within thirty days. Until then, Annie Wesley and the other issues at Celilo would have to wait.[52]

Besides delaying the federal response to off-reservation issues, the shuffling of papers and people among agencies seriously compromised the property interests of Columbia River Indians. Six months after taking control of The Dalles district in 1918, Superintendent Babcock had received neither maps nor plat books for the allotments under his authority. Without them, he could not locate disputed tracts, much less settle their boundaries. In 1936, after moving to the Umatilla agency, Babcock found himself in the same situation when The Dalles and Vancouver allotments suddenly dropped into his lap. To make matters worse, his single lease clerk lacked the records necessary to process rental agreements and probate Indian estates. By 1936, most of the original allottees and many of their primary heirs had passed away, usually without leaving wills. Because the records of the Vancouver district stayed at the Yakama agency, Babcock had to request typewritten copies in order to determine ownership and inheritance. "The Yakima office needs the records for their own use," he griped, "and since the same records are needed for administration of the Vancouver allotments, we are seriously handicapped." By their own admission, agents rarely knew the individuals involved or even the precise number of allotments and homesteads in their jurisdiction. As a result, rents often went unpaid or ended up in the wrong accounts, and many estates remained unsettled for years or even decades after the deaths of their owners.[53]

The disbursement of rental income became a particular annoyance to allottees and administrators alike. Since most Columbia River Indians remained nominal wards of the federal government, with their lands held in trust, the Indian Office generally managed their lease agreements and deposited their rent payments in Individual Indian Money accounts. To obtain a check, public domain allottees had to contact the responsible agency and wait for the lease clerk to process the request. If the Indian in question could not read or write, he or she had to ask someone to draft a letter or else visit the agency in person. Some made the trip only to find that the office had no funds to their credit or would not release them due to questions of ownership. Others could not remember which agency kept the account and wasted precious time corresponding with various officials. The tendency of Indians to move frequently created further difficulties. Anniapum (Jennie George), a John Day allottee, received no rent checks for two years because the Indian Office did not have her current address. While agency employees blamed these problems on Native habits, Indians resented having to bank with their local Indian Office branch. For people with limited cash incomes, even small delays could cause significant hardship. In a 1913 letter, Skookum Wallahee spoke for many off-reservation families when he demanded: "Why not [let] Indians their [sic] have lease money now; old man and woman [they're] just waiting for money but agent he would not let have their money. He helding in his office for over month. I don't like that myself."[54]

Some Columbia River Indians disliked the system enough to begin leasing their lands directly to non-Indians. Although fee-patented homesteaders and "competent" allottees had the right to make such arrangements, agency officials often discouraged the practice because it further confused their records and invited mutual exploitation. Whites negotiated unfair deals or defaulted on their payments. Indians rented the same allotment to two or three different stockmen each year. In addition, reported Superintendent Babcock, "There had been a considerable amount of land leased by people who were not the owners, nor even participants in the ownership. It is needless to say that the funds received by the Indians who leased land in this way were never distributed to the rightful owners." Nevertheless, many public domain allottees preferred direct leasing because it enabled them to receive more money faster, without having to bother with meddling bureaucrats. When the Indian Office attempted to intervene in these arrangements, Indian owners complained of government interference and asked to be left alone. By 1927, at least one reservation superintendent agreed that "it would be better for the person desiring to use the land to make his deals direct with the Indians."[55]

The preference for direct leasing reflected a widespread sense of autonomy and self-sufficiency among Columbia River Indians. They rarely saw agency officials off the reservations, and that generally suited them just fine. "For the most part," noted Yakama superintendent Don M. Carr in 1921, "they are independent and rather resent supervision at all. The crowd at Celilo and Fallbridge [Sk'in] particularly so." He had also visited the communities at Sundale and Rock Creek to offer clothes and supplies from the agency, "but they simply would not have anything to do with anything which was in the nature of a gratuity." William Yallup, the headman at Rock Creek, objected to Indian Office probate proceedings because they interfered with his traditional practice of collecting and distributing the rental income of deceased allottees along the Columbia River. In 1922, upon hearing a rumor that county assessors planned to levy taxes on the John Day allotments, Yallup and thirteen men calling themselves the Columbia Tribal Council requested copies of the pertinent trust patents. They gave no reason in their letter, signaling their intention to handle the problem on their own, but the Indian Office promptly intervened. However much the river communities might wish to govern their own destiny, government paternalism remained a fact of life.[56]

Chief Yallup's efforts to look after his people's interests demonstrated his continuing importance as the recognized leader (*wiyántcha*) and spokeperson (*sanwi-ła*) for several off-reservation communities on the north side of the Columbia River. By the mid-1920s, he appeared regularly in government correspondence as the voice of the closely related villages of Rock Creek, Sk'in, and Wapáykt. Many of his duties escaped the notice of Indian Office employees. As traditional chiefs had done for generations, Yallup presided over community events such as funerals, weddings, and first-food feasts. He also worked to settle disputes within and between villages without triggering outside intervention. As treaty rights became a source of friction, however, Yallup was often called upon to explain and defend Columbia River Indian positions in dealings with tribal, state, and federal officials. A descendant of Wiyašknípic, the Rock Creek headman who signed the Yakama treaty, Yallup had been versed in the Native interpretation of the promises it contained. He spent the last thirty years of his life fighting to have them upheld. James Selam, a former resident of Sk'in, recalled that "whenever any problems came to our village, he [Yallup] stood up to them and told them. He pointed his finger and told [them]: this is ours. Don't bring any problem to us." During the 1920s, Frank Slockish and Tommy Thompson filled the same role for the off-reservation Klickitats and Wayáms, respectively. Their names did not yet appear on the list of Columbia Tribal Council members, but the time was coming when the scattered off-reservation communities along the river would band together for mutual protection.[57]

■ ■ ■

Caught between freedom and dependence, Columbia River Indians developed a conflicted relationship with the agencies that administered their lands. While some chafed at Indian Office restrictions and intrusions, others felt ignored and unprotected. Agency officials bossed them around, yet off-reservation families could not seem to get help when they needed it. "I will let you know about our Superintendent from Yakima," grumbled Skookum Wallahee in a 1913 letter to the commissioner of Indian affairs. "He has made lots times promis [sic] that he would take [a] look all over on Indians homestead but he never com [sic] out here . . . that makes me feel bad that is not right." Superintendent Carr insisted that he endeavored to care for his off-reservation charges "in the best possible way," but criticism continued to roll in from the river. In 1915, another Klickitat named Caples Dave scolded Carr for failing to help him gain clear title to a disputed allotment: "You told us you would help us to get that land and we tell you alright you can help us to get that land back. Then you don't do that. What is that money you take in Fort Simcoe for?" Such complaints may have had some effect, for in 1916 Carr inquired about the possibility of using agency funds to assist elderly, indigent Indians in the Vancouver district. Another twenty-three years passed before the Indian Office finally established a sub-agency at The Dalles. By that time, a sense of alienation and neglect had already become part of Columbia River Indian identity. As the Celilo headman Tommy Thompson saw things near the end of his life, "We never did have any Indian service for assistance, no time anywheres."[58]

The Indian Office's habit of punting public domain Indians from agency to agency did little to erase this feeling. No one consulted off-reservation communities or even notified them in advance of the changes, and the resulting confusion intensified their frustration with reservation authorities. The agencies claimed them for certain purposes but not for others, and reservation leaders seemed interested in them only if it served tribal purposes. In 1936, when the Indian Office placed Celilo Village under Umatilla jurisdiction, the residents of Warm Springs lodged a complaint with their superintendent. They believed that Celilo naturally belonged to them "inasmuch as many Warm Springs Indians traditionally occupy that village during the fishing season, and those who remain at Celilo permanently, are Warm Springs and not Umatilla Indians. Apparently, the transfer was made without the knowledge of the Indians, and under the circumstances, the action was very disappointing to them." Celilo Village had become a "political football," in the words of one former resident, alternately crushed in the scrum of competing tribes or tossed away and ignored. Residents of other off-reservation communities began to feel the same way. Even as the Indian Reorganization Act of 1934 (IRA) revitalized tribal governments with the promise of self-determination, the River People's shadow continued to lengthen and gain definition. The informal Columbia Tribal Council never had the opportunity to organize under the IRA, but its existence as early as 1922 suggests that River Indians had begun to organize politically.[59]

Allotment had done little to fix their identity in reservation cement. Certainly, in the decades since the Dawes Act first encouraged them to enroll in specific tribes, Columbia River Indians had learned to appreciate the power and importance of tribal distinctions. Federal bureaucrats expected them to deal with their assigned agencies, and reservation allotments gave them a tangible stake in tribal affairs. Among those still living on the river, however, a separate identity competed with the official categories created by treaty and confirmed by allotment. In 1942, eight years after Congress ended Senator Dawes's disastrous policy, Rock Creek resident Willie John Culpus could still declare that "he [did] not consider himself a true Yakima Indian even though his father and mother took allotments for themselves and himself on the Yakima Reservation . . . he follows the customs of the Columbia River Indian people."

Agent Milroy must have spun in his grave to hear such words spoken more than fifty years after he blasted the "mistaken and pernicious policy" of Indian homesteading. In some ways, his dire prediction of 1885 had come true. Although they lived between the reservations, surrounded by whites, Columbia River Indians had not shed their Native identities. On the contrary, their sense of racial and tribal distinctiveness had grown stronger and developed new layers. Columbia River Indians continued to interact with reservation residents on a regular basis, but decades of distance and detachment from the agencies deepened the divisions evident in the 1880s. Much had changed since the days when Agent Milroy sent his police charging off at the first sign of trouble. Indeed, by the 1940s, communities once hounded by reservation authorities had difficulty getting any sort of attention from the Indian Office. This lack of supervision bred frustration and resentment but also encouraged independence and self-reliance. More importantly, it enabled Columbia River Indians to escape the most coercive aspects of the government's "Americanization" program. Although still subject to federal paternalism, the Native places scattered between the reservations often served as cultural bastions that resisted assimilation, maintained a degree of economic independence, and sheltered a new tribal identity.

We are a traditional people, and we live under the traditional laws

and the ways of the river life. . . . We live off the land. We live by our

unwritten laws. And today those unwritten laws are being ignored.

—JOHNNY JACKSON, KLICKITAT SUB-CHIEF, 1988

5 ■ ■ ■

SPACES OF RESISTANCE

The phrase "come hell or high water" may have occurred to Wasco County truant officer T. J. Smith as he gazed across Three Mile Rapids in November 1922. Swelled by fall rains, the rising Columbia River had foiled his latest attempt to catch several Indian children from the small community on Williams Island, a narrow sliver of rock just upstream from the city of The Dalles. Nine months earlier, Smith had hesitated to act while school officials and federal administrators debated the question of jurisdiction. Omar Babcock, the Warm Springs agent, wanted the children in class but could not force them to go because they lived off the reservation. The Oregon superintendent of public instruction assumed that his officers had no power to compel the attendance of Indian wards.

Frustrated with the apparent impasse, Babcock fretted that the state's position "left a wide open door whereby the Indians living off the reservation might evade sending their children to school." A gust of bureaucratic wind quickly slammed the door and empowered local authorities to pursue the truants, but the river offered them sanctuary. At low water, Smith could have walked to Williams Island across a dry side channel. Now, until he found a boat, the children could continue to dodge the education that Babcock deemed essential for "development of the [Indian] race."[1]

Williams Island constituted one of many off-reservation refuges where Columbia River Indians weathered the storm of Americanization. From the 1880s through the 1920s, the U.S. government subjected Native Americans to an intense program of religious instruction, educational training, and land reform designed to destroy their cultures and absorb them into the dominant society. The time had come to "make the Indian at home in America," one reformer declared with no sense of irony, and few indigenous communities would survive the onslaught unscathed. With the blessing and assistance of federal officials, Christian missionaries continued their long crusade to crush indigenous spirituality.[2] Meanwhile, a national network of church and government schools worked to stamp out Native languages and lifeways before they took root in younger generations.[3] Although religious persecution and compulsory education had deep and often damaging effects on tribal cultures and identities, the government never fully achieved its goals. Indian resistance and adaptation ensured that policies meant to speed assimilation instead produced unforeseen and even contrary results.

The off-reservation allotments and homesteads of the Columbia Plateau offer a prime example of Native resilience in the face of federal pressure. As Agent Robert Milroy and other critics had feared, Columbia River Indians showed little inclination to improve their lands on the public domain. Many allotments sat empty and unused, while those with permanent residents often hosted activities banned or discouraged by the Indian Office. Contrary to conventional wisdom, off-reservation people were not necessarily more acculturated or more "progressive" than reservation residents.[4]

In fact, Columbia River Indians typically maintained strong ties to their aboriginal culture even as they adjusted to changing economic and environmental conditions. Largely free of agency supervision and missionary meddling, they continued to follow a modified seasonal round and to practice indigenous forms of medicine, marriage, and religious worship. Although these customs also survived on the reservations with greater difficulty, many off-reservation communities became centers of resistance to Americanization. By the 1940s, when the Indian New Deal had created a climate of relative tolerance and self-determination, traditionalism had become a primary marker of Columbia River Indian identity.

Recently, the concept of "traditionalism" has fallen on hard times among scholars. When applied to Native American cultures in particular, the word implies an ancient, static, and essential collection of aboriginal traits. It allows little room for change and fails to acknowledge the hybrid nature of many "indigenous" practices. If a group's defining customs and characteristics are lost or altered, it is assumed, then the people who once possessed them cease to be authentic Indians. The term "traditional" becomes even more problematic when paired with its opposite, "progressive," which implies the desire to assimilate and the abandonment of Indian identity. Scholars now recognize that such polarized models of acculturation tend to obscure understanding of cultural change and identity.[5] Even so, the words retain some descriptive power, particularly as they relate to processes of self-identification. Myra Sohappy certainly knew what she meant when she said in 1984, "I live like an Indian and I will stay an Indian. I am proud of my heritage." Her son, David, credited her for raising him "to be a traditional Indian and eating the salmon, roots, berries, water." Native people rarely bracket the words "Indian" and "tradition" like scholars do. In this chapter, therefore, the scare quotes are dropped and traditionalism is used in the sense given by Plateau ethnographer Helen Schuster, who defines it as "a pattern of cultural beliefs, values, customs, and activities that are perceived as indigenous and 'Indian' by both conservative and acculturated members [of an Indian community]." The issue here is not whether a particular way of life is unquestionably "traditional," but whether the people who follow it accept that label.[6]

The traditionalism of Columbia River Indians owes much to their historical detachment from the reservations, which bore the brunt of the assault on Plateau culture. Although many reservation residents fought assimilation with equal determination, their proximity to the agencies placed greater constraints on their behavior. They lived under the watchful eyes of government personnel and within the reach of Indian police, who periodically hauled "agitators and violators" before special courts of Indian offenses. Starting in 1883, the Indian Office established reservation tribunals to maintain order and prosecute crimes that hindered Americanization. Although misdemeanors such as theft and intoxication filled the typical docket, the courts also enforced rules against "heathenish dances," indigenous marriage practices, and Indian doctoring. Native judges chosen by the agent could impose fines or jail time on those convicted of perpetuating "savage and barbarous practices." The courts did not always render the desired verdict, nor did Indian police always obey orders, but they effectively projected Indian Office authority into Native American communities. However incomplete and contested, federal power regularly intruded on the lives of reservation residents. Columbia River Indians, by comparison, had considerable latitude to follow old customs or adopt new ones as they saw fit.[7]

The contrast between conditions on and off the reservation became particularly evident in the realm of religion. In a time of rapid and unsettling change, many Mid-Columbia Indians took comfort in syncretic spiritual movements that raised the hackles of missionaries and government officials. The Dreamer Religion, the oldest and most traditional of these movements, survived despite federal persecution and the dawning realization that Smohalla's prophecies would not come to pass. As its nativistic message faded, the Dreamer faith evolved into the modern Washat religion, which remained a powerful source of hope and a primary symbol of Indian identity. By the early 1900s, however, two new sects had begun to compete for the hearts and minds of Plateau people. Like the Dreamer Religion, the Indian Shaker Church and the Feather Religion originated amid the suffering and turmoil of the reservation period. Yet, also like Smohalla's creed, they developed in off-reservation settings and then spread to surrounding agencies. All three faiths had aboriginal elements and overlapping membership, but they were not strictly or equally indigenous in form and content. Indian Shakers espoused an indigenous form of Christianity and criticized Washat for its devotion to traditional customs, even as they identified their own faith as an Indian religion. While federal officials recognized such differences, they attempted to suppress aspects of Shakerism as well. Unless reservation residents belonged to a mainstream Christian church, they had no guarantees of religious freedom even after becoming U.S. citizens in 1924.[8]

Agents and missionaries leaned most heavily on Washat, which they blamed for obstructing federal policy and Native progress. Since the 1860s, the Indian Office had tried to stifle the "Smohalla religion" by disrupting Longhouse meetings and arresting ceremonial leaders. Neither those tactics nor Smohalla's death in 1895 destroyed Washat, but the government and its allies kept trying for another thirty years. In 1901 and again in 1921, the Indian Office reiterated its opposition to Indian dances and feasts that perpetuated "heathen" customs and distracted people from the business of "civilization." Although the bans proved unpopular and difficult to enforce, they gave agents license to curtail Indian social and religious activities. Washat ceremonies presented an obvious target because they revolved around dancing and feasting. They also provided regular opportunities for people to mingle with friends and relatives from off reservation. Agents particularly disliked the large summer celebrations, which lasted for weeks and featured Washat ceremonies as well as social dances. While trying to downplay their religious content, Yakama superintendent Even Estep described them as "a place where [the Indians] can come together in a crowd, camp, gamble, drink some, and engage in other objectionable practices and make the boys and girls who have attended school over into pagans." Native dancing and "paganism" seemed to go hand in hand. Therefore, even as the crusading zeal of individual agents waxed and waned, the Mid-Columbia reservations witnessed recurrent efforts to regulate the behavior of "dance Indians."[9]

The government's campaign against Washat and its associated customs played out as a seesaw battle with no clear victor. Using a combination of punishment and persuasion, the Indian Office achieved some success in convincing tribal leaders to limit the number and duration of traditional gatherings. By the early 1900s, reservation Indians reportedly held only two dances a year—one during the first week of July and the other in late December—with an additional root feast in the spring. The timing of the dances corresponded with Independence Day and Christmas, as Mid-Columbia Indians attempted to evade Indian Office regulations by wrapping traditional celebrations in the trappings of American patriotism and Christianity. Many agents saw through this disguise but consoled themselves and their superiors with the assurance that younger, mixed-blood, and "progressive" Indians no longer accorded the ceremonies any spiritual significance. Some officials confidently predicted that tribal dances would die out with the older generations. "If we can hold this down for another year or two," wrote Superintendent Estep in 1927, "it is likely there will be no more 'celebrations' in midsummer." Decades of harassment by church and state took their toll on Washat, which only recently returned to the Umatilla reservation after decades of absence, but rumors of the religion's demise were greatly exaggerated.[10]

On the Warm Springs and Yakama reservations, where Washat followers comprised sizable minorities, the faithful pushed back against the limits imposed on them. In 1917, for example, a group of Longhouse members from Warm Springs sent a petition to the commissioner of Indian affairs requesting the freedom to practice their traditional religion. They had attended the Presbyterian church at Simnasho, on the northern portion of the reservation, but they found the services lacking. Now, they asked, "We want our way to pray to God and sing a song for we do not understand the white-men's songs. Therefore, we pray to you that we may have rights to serve God in our way." The commissioner turned a deaf ear. "I should not want to see you leave a church that was being conducted for your welfare," he said, "and return to old customs that are not in keeping with the advancement which you have made." Ten years later, Yakama leaders reacted angrily when their agent refused to allow two weeks for their annual July celebration. During a tense, two-hour council, they pressed Superintendent Estep for at least a ten-day event, "and when they failed to gain their end they advised that there would be no celebration at all as they were going to the other reservations where the Indians were celebrating. . . . A good many of them left that day for other points." Estep took their departure as a sign of their defeat, but it would be more accurately interpreted as an act of defiance. Rather than accept additional constraints, they packed up and went elsewhere, taking advantage of the kinship connections that still linked Indian communities on the Columbia Plateau.[11]

Evidence from the Warm Springs reservation suggests that Estep merely succeeded in passing the buck to his counterpart there. Stung by criticism from an irate Presbyterian missionary, Superintendent F. E. Perkins asked the local boss farmer to gather information about the 1930 Fourth of July gathering at Simnasho. The hapless fellow later reported that Indians had started arriving on July 2 but did not actually begin celebrating for another four days:

> On July 6 they held what they called a religious service in the Long House. It consisted of beating the Tom Tom, singing and some Pagan ceremonies. This service was all in the Indian language. On Monday, July 7, they began their real celebration and continued all that week, until July 12.

In addition to holding large feasts, parades, and horse races, the Indians played stick game, which the superintendent's not-so-secretive spy rightly suspected to be a form of gambling. Every time the Indians saw him coming, "they would scatter, and when I asked them what they were doing, their answer would be, 'nothing.'" Fed up with these shenanigans, the farmer tried to convince an agency policeman and the local headmen to break up the party on July 8, "but they stated that they had invited their friends from other Reservations and they would have to entertain their friends during that week." Following another religious ceremony on July 13, the Indians finally began to disperse, taking most of the next two days to break down their camps. Their officially sanctioned three-day celebration had lasted nearly two weeks.[12]

This polite but open display of defiance says two important things about the social and religious constraints faced by reservation Indians. On the one hand, it shows that they could bend and break the government's rules, too; there was no neat cultural divide separating compliant reservation residents from their disobedient, off-reservation relatives. In fact, as Superintendent Perkins recognized, among the people gambling and performing "pagan ceremonies" on the reservation were "many of the Columbia River Indians who reside in and around Celilo Falls."[13] The local leaders who refused to send their friends away—John Powyowit, Isaac McKinley, and Frank Queahpama, Sr.—ranked among the most "progressive" in the Simnasho district. On the other hand, their confrontation with the farmer showed that reservation residents found it difficult to escape federal surveillance, even on a holiday dedicated to American freedom. As late as 1930, when many policymakers and bureaucrats had already lost their passion for forced assimilation, the people of Warm Springs still had to put up with constant supervision and frequent interference. They had to be deceitful just to celebrate their "independence" in their own way, and then they had to tolerate the snooping and scolding of white men whose very correspondence testifies to the intrusiveness of federal power. Ironically, when the visiting River People crossed the reservation boundary on their way home, they entered a world where it was often easier to be an Indian.

Followers of the Washat religion had long known that Indian Office authority diminished beyond reservation boundaries. After escaping from jail in 1885, the dreamer-prophet Kotiakan had moved his longhouse just over the reservation line to avoid further conflict with the Yakama agency. Some of his people accepted reservation allotments after his death in the early 1890s, but most remained in the vicinity of Pa'kiut Village or joined the remnants of Smohalla's band near Priest Rapids. Farther downstream, Washat services continued without interruption at Wallula, Rock Creek, Celilo, Wishram, and Husum. Although at least three of these longhouses stood on Indian allotments or homesteads, the Indian Office could do little to prevent people from gathering there. Agency employees had neither the time nor the money for regular visits to off-reservation communities. When officials did travel to river settlements and fishing camps, they worried more about the problems of drinking, gambling, and truancy than they did about stopping Washat ceremonies. Indian police had limited power to act off the reservations, and breaking up Longhouse meetings was hardly a priority for local law enforcement. Columbia River Indians thus evaded restrictions on Washat worship and other indigenous forms of dancing. Scant references to off-reservation religious activity in federal records is itself evidence that, insofar as federal policies succeeded in silencing the Seven Drums, they succeeded only within reservation lines.[14]

■ ■ ■

Similar patterns prevailed in the case of the Indian Shaker Church, which spread to the Columbia Plateau from the shores of Puget Sound. In 1882, a middle-aged Sahewamish man named John Slocum (Squ-sacht-un) fell ill and appeared to die after years of hard drinking. During his funeral, he suddenly sat up and declared that he had traveled to paradise, only to be turned away because of his wicked behavior. Angels then gave him the choice of either going to Hell or returning to Earth to preach among his people. Slocum wisely chose the second option and directed his family to build a church, where he exhorted followers to worship Jesus Christ and forswear the evils of alcohol, gambling, profanity, and shamanism. He soon fell back into his old vices, however, and within a year he again lay on the verge of death. While praying for his deliverance, his wife, Mary, began to shake uncontrollably, an episode she attributed to divine possession. She then went to her husband's bed and shook over his body while others held candles and rang bells. He revived, and as news of his recovery spread, Indians began flocking to the Slocum home. There, assisted by Louis Yowaluch (Mud Bay Louis), they held services featuring bells, candles, crucifixes, and other Christian symbols, as well as chants, dances, and songs reminiscent of aboriginal spirit ceremonies. In 1892 this blend of Catholic, Presbyterian, and indigenous influences became legally organized as the Indian Shaker Church.[15]

Shaker worship came to the Plateau through Native kinship networks. In 1891, John Slocum, Mud Bay Louis, and three converts visited the town of White Swan, on the Yakama reservation, to cure the sister-in-law of church elder Alex Teio. From there, the faith traveled east to Teio's home in Toppenish and south to the Columbia River. By 1900, Shaker congregations had formed in Hood River, White Salmon, and The Dalles, where a group of Wasco converts built a church at Lone Pine. Their minister was Sam Williams, a man of Cowlitz-Yakama heritage who had learned the faith from his uncle, Mud Bay Louis. Born near present-day Longview, on the Lower Columbia, Williams migrated to Hood River in the early 1890s and married a Wasco woman. In 1896, they moved to The Dalles and assumed leadership of the church, which later relocated to their homestead on Williams Island. Although enrolled and allotted on the Yakama reservation, Williams had closer ties to the residents of Warm Springs, and it may have been members of his church who carried Shakerism to that reservation. The Wascos seemed more receptive to the new religion than did Warm Springs people, but Williams opened his doors to all. On any given Sunday, especially during the fishing season, his congregation might include Indians from across the Northwest.[16]

Except for an occasional white observer, Williams's parishioners appear to have worshipped with few intrusions from the dominant society. This situation owed something to the church's remote location, but it also reflected a measure of tolerance among local non-Indians. While they generally scoffed at Shaker curing practices, many whites appreciated the church's emphasis on sober and upright living. "Wherever Shakerism has gone," testified missionary Sarah Ober, "drunkenness, gambling and other kindred vices disappeared and their places are taken by Christian virtues and better citizenship."[17] Williams, himself a former drinker, tried to calm the boisterous atmosphere of the fisheries. At the entrance to his church, he posted a sign reading:

INDIAN SHAKER CHURCH
You are welcome, Please be orderly
NO ROWDYISM ALLOWED

Inside, he conducted quiet, dignified services that included Catholic chants played on a phonograph.[18] His neighbors had little cause to complain, and the local paper even praised Shaker missionaries for "teaching Christianity, morality, civilization and temperance" to the residents of nearby reservations.[19] The Indian Office viewed Shakerism with greater ambivalence, yet there is no evidence of federal interference with Williams's church. As a citizen living on private land outside reservation boundaries, he enjoyed virtual immunity from Indian Office persecution.

By contrast, Shakers living within reservation boundaries practiced their faith at the whim of bureaucrats and established Christian churches. Even after its formal incorporation, the Indian Shaker Church faced an uphill struggle for recognition. Some agents tolerated the new religion because of its Christian foundations and commitment to temperance, but many attacked it as a thinly veiled form of Indian doctoring, which the government had banned in the 1870s. Traditionally, Plateau people hired shamans to cure illnesses resulting from evil sorcery or the desertion of one's guardian spirits. Indian doctors healed by using their more potent spirit powers to restore the lost guardians or drive out the destructive forces afflicting the patient. Although practices varied, the curing ceremony often involved multiple participants who sang, chanted, and drummed while the shaman uttered incantations, shook rattles, and "pulled out" the sickness. To an uncritical observer, Shaker rites appeared virtually indistinguishable from the old ways. The close resemblance probably made Shakerism more attractive to Native people, yet Slocum and his followers rejected Indian doctoring as "superstition" and denied that they had merely dressed it in Christian vestments. "We have been falsely reported," protested Harry Miller of Warm Springs in 1920. "Indian medicine man and Shakers are two different things." Regardless, the Indian Office prosecuted numerous church members in the courts of Indian offenses.[20]

The reaction to Shaker activities varied among the three Mid-Columbia agencies. On the Yakama reservation, where it first appeared, the religion had gained some acceptance and security by the early twentieth century. In 1908, an ISC delegation led by Thomas Simpson and Alex Teio appealed to Superintendent Jay Lynch for a parcel of land on which to erect a permanent church. He gave them seventy-nine acres near White Swan, affording the Yakama congregation a property right, yet some of his successors still eyed the Shakers with skepticism. "The Shakers may be classified as Christians," sniffed S. A. M. Young in 1911, "though much superstition and irrelevant matter is connected with their worship." Meanwhile, Shakerism struggled to achieve even a toehold on the Umatilla reservation in the face of concerted opposition from its Christian congregations. In 1912, Shaker minister Enoch Abraham accepted an invitation to visit Pendleton, presumably to explain the faith and advise potential converts. He believed that the Shakers could "carry our religion same as whites because we have white's education in us," but the tribal welcoming committee disagreed. Instead of asking Abraham to preach, a panel of Presbyterian Indians subjected him to an inquisition before sending him back to the Yakama reservation empty-handed. Although a few Umatilla tribal members traveled there to attend services at White Swan, the Umatilla agency never had to deal with an independent church.[21]

At Warm Springs, the Indian Office and the Shakers clashed sporadically for nearly two decades. First brought to the reservation by Wascos from the Columbia River, Shakerism attracted few followers until 1904, when Alex Teio converted about fifteen individuals during a series of revival meetings. By 1912, the congregation had grown sufficiently to alarm the reservation's Presbyterian minister, who helped some of his converts draft a petition denouncing the "Shaker superstition" and calling its adherents "the lowest among Indians here." Remarkably, the Indian Office inspector sent to investigate the matter sided with the Shakers and issued a call for religious toleration. Trouble erupted again in 1918, however, when Superintendent A. M. Reynolds issued a memorandum prohibiting Shakers from gathering in the homes of sick people. Although claiming to have no objection to their faith per se, he interpreted "religion" in the narrowest possible terms: "By the term Religious worship, I mean a religion founded on the Holy Bible and not of man's origin. There can not be a religion or religious organization without using the Bible as a rule and guide to Faith and Practice." When the Shakers ignored his order, he had minister Warren McCorkle arrested and tried in the tribal court, where "he posed as a Christian martyr [and] said he would go to jail but would not give up his religious practices." To Reynolds's dismay, the judges dismissed the case. Fearing that this example would encourage further defiance, he requested authority to imprison the Shakers anyway. Failing that, he suggested, the Indian Office might consider taking their allotments out of trust and "letting them shift for themselves," for the threat of losing their lands to taxation "would do more to keep them in subjection than anything else."[22]

Acting Commissioner E. B. Merritt rejected such extortionate tactics, but he gave McCorkle a stern warning and refused to permit any curing ceremonies. The ban weighed heavily on the Shaker community. Writing to a friend on the Klamath reservation, Harry Miller lamented, "I suppose you know by now that here at Warm Springs we can't shake anymore. . . . On our Superintendent's account we have been neglecting our church." In the midst of its struggle with the Indian Office, the Warm Springs congregation had allowed its corporate status to lapse. Omar Babcock, the new superintendent, threatened to shut down the church entirely unless they renewed its charter. Bishop Garfield Jack, the head of the Indian Shaker Church of Oregon, promptly sent a letter to Babcock asking him to respect the Indians' constitutional right to freedom of conscience. Babcock brushed off the appeal, but the Shakers had another card to play. Unable to sway the Indian Office on their own, they enlisted the support of James Wickersham, the judge who had helped the church gain legal status in 1892. Now a territorial representative for Alaska, Wickersham intervened on the Shakers' behalf and convinced the Indian Office to call off the "officious agents and employees" who had "misunderstood these people." Still, another decade would pass before the church received lasting guarantees of religious toleration.[23]

Sam Williams did not stand aloof from this fight. The treatment of his co-religionists troubled him enough that he attended a special ISC convention at White Swan in 1918. After listening to Klamath and Warm Springs delegates express their desire for liberation from agency supervision, he told the assembly: "Now [in] Hood River the light of Shaker religion is nearly out. Here of late the laws of our country is chasing us like a

Fort Walla Walla, 1853. This outpost of the Hudson's Bay Company heralded the transformation of Native life along the Columbia River. Sketch by John Mix Stanley, Washington State Historical Society, 2005.0.21.37.

Walla Walla treaty council, 1855. Federal commissioners at the council began the process of dividing Mid-Columbia Indians into discrete "tribes" and "bands" for the purposes of diplomacy and administration. Governor Isaac Stevens and General Joel Palmer are visible under the arbor in the center. Sketch by Gustav Sohon, Washington State Historical Society, 1918.114.9.39.

Štáqułay (Stocketly), the headman at Wayám. Stocketly ran a ferry across the Deschutes River for American emigrants, but he opposed relocating his people to a reservation. Sketch by Gustav Sohon, Washington State Historical Society, 1918.114.9.50.

Columbia River Indian dwellings in about 1900. Despite white complaints and official pressure, many Indians refused to abandon their ancestral villages and camping sites along the Columbia River. This picture suggests why the U.S. Army saw little reason to force them off land deemed unfit for American settlement. Photograph by Lee Moorhouse, University of Oregon Special Collections, PH 036-5276rb.

Yakama police and agency employees in 1880. Tribal police helped enforce Indian Office proscriptions against indigenous religious ceremonies, healing practices, and marriage customs. After 1885, however, they could not leave the reservation to interfere with off-reservation communities. Photograph by C. Haines, Northwest Museum of Arts and Culture, L93-75.66.

Skookum Wallahee on his homestead in the Klickitat Valley, 1911. One of the few Native homesteaders to receive decent agricultural land, Wallahee enjoyed cordial relations with his non-Indian neighbors. Oregon Historical Society, OrHi 37602.

Facing page, top: Smohalla (Šmúxala), the Wánapam prophet of the Dreamer Religion, with a group of disciples in 1884. Smohalla's creed encouraged Columbia River Indian resistance to the reservation system and federal assimilation policies. National Anthropological Archives, Smithsonian Institution, 02903A.

Facing page, bottom: Unidentified Native women in Hood River, Oregon. Some local whites saw off-reservation Indians as a valuable source of business and labor, while others condemned "renegades" as a nuisance and threat to Euro-American settlement. Oregon Historical Society, OrHi 52501.

Chief William Yallup, his wife (not identified), and their son Thomas attending the National Indian Congress in Spokane, Washington, 1925. As the descendant of a treaty signer and the recognized leader of several off-reservation communities in Washington, Chief Yallup regularly defended Columbia River Indian interests in dealings with tribal, state, and federal officials. Photograph by Frank W. Guilbert, Northwest Museum of Arts and Culture, L97-2.3.

A group of Indian Shakers near The Dalles, Oregon. The man second from left may be Sam Williams, the minister of the Shaker church at The Dalles until the early 1920s. Unlike their co-religionists on the reservations, Indian Shakers along the Columbia River experienced little interference with their sect's healing ceremonies, which government officials deemed a form of "Indian doctoring." Photograph by Lee Moorhouse, University of Oregon Special Collections, PH036-4567

Native leaders, including Chief William Yallup (second row, center), meet
with Forest Service officials concerning access to traditional huckleberry fields
in the Columbia National Forest, August 1935. The determination of Columbia River Indians to continue their seasonal subsistence activities on public
lands brought them into conflict with non-Indian priorities and made them
into champions of tribal treaty rights. Significantly, though Native women
were primarily responsible for the berry harvest and directly interested in the
negotiations, they are not represented in the photograph. Photograph by Ray
Filloon, U.S. Forest Service. Courtesy of Cheryl Mack and Rick McClure, Gifford Pinchot National Forest.

Yakama hop pickers in 1893. Many Mid-Columbia Indians enjoyed picking hops because it mimicked traditional gathering activities and provided cash for goods and services they could not get through the seasonal round. Photograph by Kelly Photo, Northwest Museum of Arts and Culture, L94-27.26.

Cableways at Celilo Falls, 1956. Starting in the 1930s, cannery owners and Indian fishers began installing cableways to access the islands at Celilo Falls. Disputes occasionally erupted when individuals or companies tried to restrict the use of their cables. Photograph by Clarence Colby, Northwest Museum of Arts and Culture, L95-66.1.

Linda George, Flora Thompson, and Chief Tommy Thompson pose overlooking Celilo Falls in 1956. For more than thirty years, Thompson had tried to protect the familial rights of resident fishers against a rising tide of reservation "comers" and non-treaty Indians. He also opposed the dam that flooded Celilo in 1957. Northwest Museum of Arts and Culture, L97-5.26.

The Celilo Fish Committee, 1940. The Fish Committee tried to regulate the fishery at Celilo Falls and reconcile the competing interests of its many users. Andrew Barnhart and Henry Thompson are standing second and third from the left. Photograph by H. U. Sanders, National Archives and Records Administration-Seattle.

Willie John Culpus, Henry Thompson, Tommy Thompson, and John Whiz meeting in Condon, Oregon, 1948. According to the local newspaper, the men had convened to announce Columbia River Indian opposition to outside interference at Celilo Falls. Oregon Historical Society, CN 015009.

Indian being cited for illegal fall fishing, 1978. Despite recent court victories favoring treaty rights, the states cracked down heavily on "renegade" tribal fishers as salmon runs neared their lowest levels on record. Photograph from *Oregon Journal*, Oregon Historical Society, OrHi 93190.

David Sohappy, Sr., during his trial by the Yakama Nation in 1987. Although the tribal court acquitted him and the other defendants, the spectacle of avowed traditionalists being prosecuted by their own government outraged many Columbia River Indians. Photograph by Max Gutierrez, Oregon Historical Society, CN 020037.

Cascades chief Johnny Jackson and Klickitat chief Wilbur Slockish, Jr., at
Lyle Point in 2009. Acting in concert with the local Indian community and
non-Indian activists, Jackson and Slockish helped stop the construction of a
33-home subdivision on the Point, which contains a former village site, graves,
and tribal fishing scaffolds. In 2007, the Trust for Public Lands transferred the
property to the Yakama Nation. Photograph by Nancy Kittle, Trust for Public
Lands

Children eagerly await Satuyah Slickpoo's signal to grab their gifts during the giveaway portion of the 2007 memorial for the flooding of Celilo Falls. As the traditional "whip man," Slickpoo was responsible for overseeing their behavior during the ceremony in the Celilo Village longhouse, which the Army Corps of Engineers recently rebuilt as part of a belated redevelopment project. Photograph by Carol Craig, Trust for Public Lands band of dogs." Williams feared the loss of his ministerial license, which depended on state recognition of the church, but Shakers continued to worship at The Dalles until he moved to Hood River in the early 1920s. Although the reasons for his departure remain obscure, there is nothing to suggest that it resulted from a direct confrontation with state or federal authorities. In fact, during this period, the Indian Office became his ally in a dispute over property and fishing rights at The Dalles. The personal setbacks he suffered in this contest likely had more to do with his return to Hood River. Not content to let his religion's light fade from the river, Williams became a bishop in the Oregon corporation of Bible-reading Shakers and stayed active in the ministry until his death in 1933. Only a year before, his old congregation at The Dalles had asked for and received Yakama agency assistance in building a new church.[24]

■ ■ ■

The mingling of Shaker, Washat, and shamanic healing traditions produced a third spiritual movement known in Sahaptin as Wasklíki ("spin") or Wáptaši (Waptashi, "having a feather, feathered"). Its prophet, Jake Hunt, was born around 1870 in a Klickitat village near Husum, Washington, on the White Salmon River. Although raised in the Dreamer faith, Hunt drifted from its teachings as a young man and began cutting his hair short and wearing Euro-American clothes. He learned of Shakerism around 1904, when his son became deathly ill and the healer Wasco Jim visited the village to attempt a cure. Wasco Jim failed to save the boy's life or to convert the distraught father, yet he still influenced Hunt profoundly. In a vision, Wasco Jim said, he had learned that all religious ceremonies should employ feathers and be conducted in buckskin clothing. Neither of these elements played any role in the Indian Shaker Church, which eschewed such traditional symbols, but they became an integral part of the curing cult that Hunt created following the death of his second wife, Minnie Coon, only a month after their son's passing.[25]

Known colloquially as the Feather Religion, Waptashi emerged in opposition to the Shakers yet borrowed liberally from them while remaining closely associated with Washat. Hunt briefly converted to Shakerism in hopes of saving Minnie's life. In his grief, however, he withdrew from the church and even threatened to kill Wasco Jim. As he mourned over his wife's grave, Hunt experienced a pair of powerful visions that laid the foundation for an alternative faith. In the first vision, Hunt beheld the deceased Klickitat prophet Lishwailait standing on a disc of light that symbolized the earth (*tiičám*) sacred to Washat believers.[26] Lishwailait wore buckskin clothing, along with two eagle feathers in his hair, and he carried a hand drum like those used in Longhouse ceremonies. In the second vision, Hunt's departed loved ones told him to stop griev-ing and go on with his life. They were followed by his ancestors, who instructed him to worship with a rawhide drum and to convert people in seven lands. Hunt then awoke and, dressed in buckskin, entered a home where the Shakers had gathered for a meal. After reputedly overturning their table with a wave of his hand, he banished them from the village with the order "Never perform this work here again." Like the Shakers, though, Hunt stressed the prohibition of alcohol and the practice of cur-ing. He also retained the songs and first-food feasts central to Washat while expanding the traditional use of eagle feathers, which he said had the power to cleanse souls. With the addition of a dramatic initiation cer-emony—featuring rapid spinning and ritualized vomiting to purge one's sins—Waptashi became truly distinct from its predecessors.[27]

The Hunt family's homestead near Husum served as the spiritual center of the new religion. Now calling himself Ti·čámnašat (Tiicham Nashat, "Earth Thunderer"), Hunt erected a longhouse to host Washat ceremonies. Aided by his four sisters, who reportedly played key roles in developing the faith, he began performing successful cures and win-ning converts among his fellow villagers. Word of these exploits brought a demand for his services and a stream of potential initiates from nearby communities. In turn, Tiicham Nashat began carrying his cult to "seven lands," as his ancestors had instructed in the vision. In 1904 he journeyed to Spearfish (Wishram) and healed a young girl, prompting the conver-sion of most residents and the construction of a new longhouse. Tii-

cham Nashat married a local woman and lived there periodically for the remainder of his life, but his spiritual calling kept him on the move. Several months after his initial trip to Spearfish, he traveled to the community of Rock Creek, where he picked up additional followers and tallied the third of seven "nations." Then, having built a strong base among the Columbia River Indians, he turned to the surrounding reservations.[28]

As Tiicham Nashat ventured into areas under Indian Office control, his movement encountered resistance from Indian agents, established Christian churches, and the fledgling Shakers. These forces may account for his relatively disappointing returns on the Yakama reservation, where he managed to convert only fourteen households over the course of three visits. Although the Methodists and the Shakers shared his commitment to temperance, they did not necessarily agree with Tiicham Nashat's view that Feather worshippers and Christians "should all work together and not meddle with the belief of others."[29] His trip to Warm Springs around 1905 produced better results. While attending the annual Fourth of July celebration at Simnasho, he received an invitation to address a Washat meeting. His speech so impressed the group's leader, the former renegade Queahpahmah, that he allowed Hunt to stay for the full two weeks of services. As one Native witness recalled:

> The old chief got interested and let him talk. [Hunt] said openly he was not compelling people to join but they should come of their own accord. Some people tried to tempt him with drink, but he refused. Some laughed at him, but quite a few believed. He got about five members at that first meeting.[30]

Tiicham Nashat never went to Warm Springs again, yet the seeds he had planted bore fruit. His followers there stayed in contact through visits to the Columbia River, and the Feather Religion thrived in the Sahaptin community around Simnasho. It also made headway in the small Paiute colony of Seekseequa, in the southern portion of the reservation, where two earlier converts had settled. Among the Wascos and Teninos nearest the agency, however, Waptashi never seriously challenged the Presbyterians and the Shakers. According to Wilson Wewa, a current reservation resident, both groups reported Feather healers and Indian doctors to the agency authorities, forcing them to be secretive about their meetings.[31]

The Christian Indians of the Umatilla agency presented an even greater barrier. In January 1906, the Walla Walla chief No Shirt called on Tiicham Nashat to cure his ailing wife. Accompanied by ten disciples, including his Wishram wife and his sister Waiet, Tiicham Nashat initially received a warm welcome. On the day of his arrival, said one observer, "Twenty-eight or thirty rigs went out to meet him and many people went on foot. Everyone was excited. They brought their sick to him and followed him wherever he went." His reception soured when tribal judge and devout Presbyterian Jim Kash Kash reported Tiicham Nashat's activities to Superintendent O. C. Edwards. At the insistence of the leading "progressive" Indians, Edwards had Tiicham Nashat brought to the agency for interrogation. He seemed harmless enough, so the superintendent released him—only to have the tribal court order his removal from the reservation. When Edwards carried out the judges' wishes, a group of "dance Indians" led by No Shirt and Umapine voiced their determination that Tiicham Nashat would return to "practice his healing art." Edwards conceded that he might do so if he stayed near the agency, where the superintendent could keep an eye on him, but the chiefs argued that Tiicham Nashat could not work effectively under such scrutiny. With neither side willing to give ground, Edwards instructed his Indian police to arrest the "medicine man" if he set foot on the reservation again.[32]

On the surface, the fracas over Tiicham Nashat's presence seemed like a simple dispute over religion. At a deeper level, however, it showcased competing conceptions of Indian identity in the early twentieth century. Just a month before Tiicham Nashat's arrival, tribal leaders had split over the question of whether Columbia River Indians should receive allotments on tribal land. Many of the so-called progressives had fought to maintain the reservation as Native space by denying property to mixed-bloods and other "outsiders." Now they called for the expulsion of a "medicine man" they deemed too traditional, too Indian, for their Indian community. They accused Tiicham Nashat of "turning the children from the schools and away from progressive ways" and of "teaching a new dance which teaches the Indians to follow the old

Indian ways." Although much of Waptashi was actually quite innovative, detractors and supporters both identified it as a traditional religion. To those who defended Tiicham Nashat and favored allotting former "renegades," being Indian meant following the "old Indian ways" embodied in Washat and Waptashi. The intra-tribal debate sparked by the prophet's appearance merely intensified an ongoing controversy over whose vision of Indianness would govern the Umatilla reservation.[33]

Ultimately, the agency superintendent and his tribal allies prevented Tiicham Nashat from fulfilling his spiritual quest. When he returned to Umatilla in the spring of 1906, the police accosted him and took him to the agency. There are differing accounts of what happened next. According to Superintendent Edwards, Tiicham Nashat had sent a letter following his first ejection, in which he claimed "I have cured George Marshall of drinking, you can watch him and if he drinks, you can do what you please with me." Edwards saved both the letter and a bottle of whiskey later taken from Marshall by police in the border town of Pendleton. Clearly savoring his triumph, Edwards wrote:

I confronted Ne Shut with this evidence of his failure and told him that upon his own written proposition I wished to cut his hair; that if he was a man of his word, he would follow me over to the boys' building where I was going to cut the hair of two school boys (aged 14 and 16) whom he had with him and whom I was placing in school. He followed me and I 'removed his ornate locks' without any opposition or protest on his part. I laughingly told him that the large ear-rings which he had in his ears would look just as well in his nose. Upon which he removed them from his ears and retained them.

After humiliating Tiicham Nashat in this way, Edwards offered him the choice of either leaving the reservation or going to jail. Tiicham Nashat departed voluntarily but later "attempted to secure the services of several attorneys at Pendleton to have his imaginary wrongs redressed."[34] Ethnographer Cora DuBois recorded a slightly different version of events during the 1930s. According to her informants, the reservation authorities had proposed a test of Tiicham Nashat's healing power to prove that he was a charlatan. If he could cure a young Nez Perce man in the terminal stages of consumption, they said, he could continue to practice among them. If he failed, he would accept punishment at the hands of the tribal court. Jim Kash Kash, the chief judge, reported that both the agency physician and a doctor from Pendleton had given the patient only a day to live. After singing and dancing over the man, Tiicham Nashat predicted that he would last at least forty-eight hours. Around noon the following day, as hundreds of Indians anxiously awaited the outcome, the patient died. The agency police seized Tiicham Nashat, cut his long hair, and destroyed his ceremonial regalia. Given a choice between imprisonment and banishment, he and his followers left the reservation and returned to Husum in disgrace.[35]

   Whichever version is closer to the truth, the story ends with Tiicham Nashat shorn of his hair and his reputation by the sharp edge of colonial power. "No one believed in him after that," said DuBois's tribal contacts, and Waptashi never achieved a wide following on the Umatilla reservation. Some residents even claimed that Tiicham Nashat's humiliation precipitated his untimely death. Although he made two more trips to the Yakama reservation, a debilitating infection forced him to abandon plans to visit the Nez Perce tribe, the seventh nation to which he would have proselytized. He spent his final years at Spearfish and passed away in about 1914. By 1940, no Feather worshippers remained in the village, but the prophet's religion did not die with him. About a dozen families kept the faith on the Yakama reservation, and it blossomed at Warm Springs despite the antagonism of agents and missionaries. In 1918, Superintendent Babcock added a ban on Feather worship to the existing prohibition of Shaker curing rites, but Native appeals to the Indian Office eventually overturned his orders. Meanwhile, people from Husum and Rock Creek conducted Waptashi rituals and Washat ceremonies without federal interference. The remaining members of the Hunt family hosted religious meetings into the 1920s, and their homestead retains spiritual significance to Feather worshippers today. During the 1990s, Johnny Jackson of the Mid-Columbia River Council described it as a sacred site and expressed the desire to rebuild the longhouse that once stood there. Revered as the birthplace and base of a Native spiritual movement, the Hunt homestead has become a historical symbol of Columbia River Indian traditionalism.[36]

▓ ▓ ▓

The reluctance of Mid-Columbia Indians to abandon their own religions and healing methods was matched by their allegiance to traditional marriage practices. Although polygamy had virtually disappeared by the end of the nineteenth century, many Native people wed, divorced, and remarried without obtaining the licenses or filing the papers required under state laws. Instead, they followed the aboriginal custom of the "wedding trade," whereby the families of the bride and groom exchanged gifts to formalize the union. An anonymous Yakama woman recalled that she and her husband got a license only after his uncle, a justice of the peace, "forced the old people to have us legally married first. My mother and father didn't want it. They said, 'We're Indian. We want Indian marriage.'" Indian divorces also circumvented the bureaucratic "white tape" of the dominant society. When one partner (or both) decided to end the marital relationship, husband and wife simply returned to their respective families or took new spouses. The Indian Office and the courts vacillated on the legitimacy of "Indian custom marriages and divorces," particularly when it came to settling Native estates, but most agents considered them a grave legal and moral problem. By criminalizing indigenous cultural norms, they hoped to simplify questions of inheritance and "civilize" the Indians at the same time.[37]

Agency officials pressed charges of bigamy and illegal cohabitation both on and off the reservations, but with differing degrees of success. The majority of cases passed through the courts of Indian offenses, which handed out fines and jail terms of sixty days or more. If the offending parties lived off the reservation, agents enlisted the help of the local authorities and county courts. In 1919, for example, a Warm Springs tribal member named George Smith received a six-month sentence for bigamy from a Wasco County judge. "We want to make an example of Smith," Superintendent Babcock told *The Dalles Chronicle*. "Many of the Indians have been led to believe that they are not amenable to the white man's law and there has been too much laxity in the enforcement of the laws governing the marriage relations." The following year, he reported that the Indians of his reservation now obeyed the rules, whereas "in the Burns and The Dalles bands they do not do so, if convenient to do otherwise. Their nomadic habits make it easy for them to avoid trouble for disregarding the State laws in this matter." Although Babcock probably exaggerated the extent of compliance at Warm Springs, his statement suggests that agents perceived significant differences in the behavior of off-reservation Indians. Of all the groups under his jurisdiction, he claimed, "The more immorality exists among those of the Columbia River." The Indian Office simply could not control people living so far from the agencies. In Babcock's opinion, law and order would be established among Columbia River Indians "only by having some employee in immediate supervision of them and their activities." Almost twenty years passed before the Indian Office finally followed through on his suggestion.[38]

In the meantime, agents expressed similar concerns about cracks in their education program, which many bureaucrats and policy makers viewed as the cornerstone of Americanization. In the late 1870s, the federal government and the churches began expanding the boarding school system. By 1900, the Indian Office boasted twenty-five industrial schools off reservation and eighty-one schools on reservation with a nationwide enrollment of over 17,000 students. An additional 9,000 pupils attended the growing number of reservation day schools, mission schools, and contract public schools. Some Mid-Columbia Indians went to flagship institutions, such as Carlisle in Pennsylvania and Chemawa in western Oregon, but the majority passed through reservation boarding schools. Yakama children generally attended the one at Fort Simcoe, which operated from 1861 to 1922, and Umatilla students chose between the Catholic mission school and the agency boarding school. On the Warm Springs reservation, the Indian Office ran two boarding schools until 1895, when the Simnasho building burned down and the government consolidated educational facilities at the agency. Although small and ill-equipped in comparison to the major industrial schools, all of these institutions shared basic methods and objectives. Using a mixture of military discipline, vocational training, and academic instruction, they worked to "kill the Indian and save the man" within their students.[39]

The first step lay in recruiting and retaining enough pupils to fill the classrooms. Agents, who usually held the title of school superintendent after 1903, employed a variety of carrot-and-stick techniques to encourage regular attendance. They began by advising Indian parents "to avail themselves of the great opportunities now offered to them by the Government of securing for their children, without expense to themselves, the inestimable boon of an English education, including board, clothing, and care while sick." If parents did not respond to friendly persuasion, agency superintendents tried withholding travel passes, lease payments, and employment opportunities. When all else failed, the Indian Office granted superintendents full authority to compel attendance. By the early 1900s, however, agents rarely resorted to the strong-arm tactics of the nineteenth century. Superintendent J. E. Kirk considered using force in 1901, when a group of Warm Springs Indians swore they would fight rather than put their children in school, but the captain of police refused to participate and resigned his post. Five years later, the Umatilla superintendent avowed, "I have not used any force in the matter of placing the children in school nor do I believe that sheer force should be used to accomplish this end." He might have added that it had become far less necessary to do so. Although some reservation residents continued to resist the government's educational advances, they generally accepted schooling more readily than did their off-reservation relatives.[40]

The attendance gap between these groups widened as the century progressed. By the early 1920s, superintendents generally reported that all the eligible children of the reservation had enrolled in school, although many started late because their families spent the fall away from home. This habit irritated agency officials, yet they typically had no trouble meeting school quotas. In fact, they occasionally turned students away for lack of space. Some pupils came from off-reservation communities, but Columbia River Indians easily evaded school if they chose not to go. The Indian Office did not begin systematically tracking attendance at public schools until the 1910s, and even then agents could not accurately monitor the enrollment of off-reservation children. In 1925 Superintendent Estep admitted that, thanks to absentee families, there was "a goodly number of children of school age on our rolls that we know but little of, so far as school attendance is concerned." At Warm Springs, annual school census reports from The Dalles District noted: "These people are nomadic in habit and it is impossible to keep track of them." Even if agents knew where the Indians were, they could do little to prevent truancy. Superintendent Babcock managed to secure the enrollment of some children from Rock Creek by freezing trust accounts until their parents produced evidence of school attendance. In the long term, though, he despaired of much improvement unless the Indian Office assigned a permanent employee to the Columbia River or the agency received better cooperation from local authorities.[41]

Legally, local school districts had the authority and the responsibility to compel the attendance of Indians residing off reservation. As Superintendent Babcock informed one county administrator, "We have little, or no, chance to force them to place their children in school but they are directly amenable to the laws of the state in which they live regarding the education of their children." Starting in 1891, the Department of the Interior paid tuition for Indian students in public schools because, as federal wards, their parents contributed no property taxes to support education. The original contract system proved unnecessarily cumbersome, however, and some school officials seemed unaware that they could receive payments or require the attendance of Indian children. As late as the 1930s, agency superintendents had to walk district administrators through the process of applying for tuition and remind them of their jurisdiction over Indian truants. Instead of appreciation, agents received complaints from parents and school boards accusing Indians of hitching a free ride on the backs of taxpayers. Even on the Yakama reservation, where public schools depended on Indian tuition, the idea that Indian students got something for nothing proved impossible to dispel. More than mere ignorance kept it alive. For those who wished to promote a de facto form of school segregation, the tax issue furnished a useful propaganda tool.[42]

Racial prejudice partially explains both the hesitance of school administrators to pursue Indian truants and the reluctance of Indian parents to enroll their children. Although the districts gladly accepted tuition payments, many white parents and teachers had no desire to see Native American pupils in the classroom. In 1922, the storekeeper at Celilo informed the Warm Springs agency that a local man "would not send [his] little girl to school on account of the Indian children going. He has been to the school board, the [county superintendent], and even took it up with the [state superintendent] to have them put out." Twelve years later, the school board in The Dalles still opposed the attendance of Indian children from Celilo, although board members insisted they did so only because the terrible sanitary conditions in the village made it "a hotbed of epidemics." White residents of the Goodnoe Hills district made no such excuses in 1940, when some "stated that they were going to attempt to frighten the Indians from attending the school by telling them that they would be required to vote and thus lose all their rights as Indians." Teachers and administrators often joined the chorus calling for the exclusion of Indians from public schools. Due to their spotty attendance, wrote the Arlington district superintendent, "They are very backward in their work and are a decided burden on the class. . . . I wish to ask very frankly if we must keep these children in school here or whether they should attend some Indian school." Such feelings were not lost on Native parents. As Frank Seelatsee said to Superintendent Estep in 1930, "The white people do not want my children in school. He just wants the money you pay."[43]

Given the strength of anti-Indian sentiment in local white communities, parents had good cause to doubt the quality of their children's education. With the exception of the Celilo school and some reservation districts, Indian students formed a minority at public institutions. None employed Native American teachers—unlike many boarding schools—and multicultural education had yet to be invented. The standard history textbook in Oregon primary schools from the 1920s through the 1950s described Indians as "true savages." Although acknowledging some tribal distinctions, the authors declared "it cannot be said that any of them possessed more than the rude beginnings of civilization. . . . They were always poor, always hungry and miserable."[44] Fortunately, Indian students read, their Hobbesian ancestors had gradually disappeared:

> The red man once lived undisturbed in Oregon; his villages once filled every valley. Now, however, his thousands of warriors and hunters, his dark-eyed maidens and careless children are no more. . . . Today only a remnant remains. They are wards of the Nation, carefully watched over, their wants provided for. Those of the new generation, born on the reservations, have become reconciled to the new plan of life. If they can do what their ancestors could not achieve, they may survive. For, after all is said, the Indian vanished because he could not learn the ways of the white man. He could not survive in competition with the dominant race.[45]

Even after the Indian New Deal introduced a measure of cultural pluralism to federal policy, public school children continued to read about helpless Indian wards confined to reservations and coddled by a benevolent government. As Johnny Jackson recalled of his schooling during the late 1930s and 1940s, "American history was all about George Washington, Abraham Lincoln, and Thomas Edison, and all those. . . . There was none about no natives." Jackson also remembered frequent fights with white boys who insulted Indian children. He eventually learned to box, but that could not protect him from the physical and psychic blows landed by his teachers.[46]

The treatment of Indian students in public schools reflected their marginal status within Euro-American society. Although some instructors probably tried their best to reach Native children, others treated them with contempt and hostility, even to the point of physical abuse. In 1931, Bessie Quiemps of Underwood, Washington, wrote the Yakama agency "to report the trouble of my little Boy in school. The teacher beat him on the head and face in a fit of temper." Johnny Jackson's teacher "used to hit us on the hand with a ruler if she caught us talking to each other in our own language." Meanwhile, a nine-year-old Indian student in nearby

Maryhill got in trouble for not talking at all. Clarence G. Davis, the Indian Office field agent sent to determine whether the boy was "demented," found instead "that he plays normally at home, talking and shouting like any other children, but that at school he 'seeks shelter within his shell not unlike a turtle.'" Whereas his aunt explained this behavior as shyness, a white neighbor deemed the student "just dumb like lots of Indians," and the teacher dismissed him as "a terrible draw-back to her school." In such an inhospitable environment, it hardly seems surprising that Native children frequently failed to thrive or even stay in the classroom.[47]

For many Columbia River Indians, simply getting to and from class each day proved difficult. Scattered along the river and in remote side canyons, their homes often stood a considerable distance from the nearest public school. The temporary closure of the Wahkiacus, Washington, school in 1928 gave the Indian students there no choice but to walk four miles, "up hill and a steep hill at that," to a school on the bench above the Klickitat River. Passing up the opportunity to regale their future children with stories of the hike, they opted to play hooky instead. During the same period, pupils from Rock Creek had to walk six miles down a narrow, winding road to attend class in Goodnoe Hills. The district had provided a small bus by the late 1930s, but it could not accommodate all the students, and the Indian driver had a drinking problem that threatened their safety. One afternoon, rather than wake him from a drunken slumber and risk another wild ride, they opted to go home on foot. Led by William Yallup, the headman at Rock Creek, a group of concerned parents demanded that the district hire a new driver and even proposed their own replacement. Inexplicably, the school board dragged its heels for more than two years, possibly in hopes that the Indians would give up and stay home. Frustrated by this irresponsible behavior, Chief Yallup asked the Indian Office to build a day school at a convenient point within the Rock Creek Valley. Although his people had never moved to the Yakama reservation, he considered Indian education to be "peculiarly the function of the Indian Service and not of the States and says that he never 'put my mark on any paper that said the Indian children should go to State school.'"[48]

Yallup's request offers two valuable insights into the River People's complex and evolving attitude toward Euro-American education. First, it illustrates the feelings of mistrust and neglect held by many off-reservation Indians, who judged public schooling to be both inadequate and a breach of the federal government's trust responsibility. Second, his statement shows that Columbia River Indians did not categorically oppose sending their children to "the school of the white man." In 1939, Yallup declared himself "very much in favor of them attending such schools, being taught to think well and secure the benefits of a rudimentary education such as reading, writing and being able to handle figures. And he believes that he has the backing of all Indians in this district in this [regard]." Understandably, they did object to the practice of treating sick children at boarding schools, without parental consent, "and then notifying the Indian parents that their child is dead and asking such parent to come and get their dead child." Besides leaving families "deeply shocked and wounded," such callous conduct robbed their people of potential leaders. Yallup, like many Native Americans, believed that education should serve Indian interests first and foremost. As Field Agent Davis reported:

> He is very much opposed to [the] trend to fill the mind of the child so full of impractical teachings that the child cannot do any good either for himself or his people when he returns, and that the trend is to wean him away from the idea of using his newly acquired knowledge for the benefit of the Indian people—to help protect the rights of the Indian.

This commonsense approach to education also informed the advice of Ella Jim's grandmother, a contemporary resident of Rock Creek. She had not attended school herself but urged Jim to go with the warning, "White society will never be happy until you're walking down the road a hobo with no more country." If used wisely, formal schooling could give River People the tools necessary to fight their colonizers and secure their future in a changing world.[49]

The desire to obtain education without compromising their own identity presented Columbia River Indians with a difficult dilemma, especially with regard to language instruction. Public school teachers, like their counterparts in the boarding schools, expected students to speak English only—even if the teacher in question did not. Ella Jim remembered with bitter irony the German American woman at the Goodnoe Hills schoolhouse, who spoke her native language fluently while forbidding Indian children to speak theirs. Parents and grandparents often tried to counteract such pressure, with mixed results. Mavis Kindness, a childhood resident of Rock Creek, had hoped to attend the Chemawa boarding school; her mother withheld permission for fear that she would forsake their ancestral tongue. Kindness kept it and now teaches in the Yakama Nation's language preservation program, but other children were not so lucky. Johnny Jackson started school speaking only Sahaptin but left knowing very little. Although he could still understand his parents and his grandmother, who refused to converse with him in English, he soon began to use the new language exclusively. "We never tried to talk our own language or anything in school anymore," he noted in a 1999 interview. "But later on, after we start forgetting a lot of things we were supposed to know, well it kind of bothered us." In trying to reclaim Sahaptin and other traditional knowledge as an adult, he generally turns to elders from the off-reservation community around Rock Creek whenever he "gets stuck with something."[50]

For Jackson's family and others, the proper balance between the "old ways" and the new became a subject of debate among adults and a source of confusion for children. Walter Speedis, who grew up at Rock Creek, went to school because his mother wanted him "to know what white man's feelings is . . . she was talking about ulterior motives." When he spoke English to his elders, however, they whipped him and scolded: "Don't talk English to me, I'm not a white man!" Other adults simply pretended not to hear children unless they "talked Indian." Speedis's neighbor, Elsie Gibson, willingly sent her boys off to class only because she "wanted them to learn [to] read and write and [interpret for] me." Highly practical in their approach to education, many River People subordinated the pursuit of "white" knowledge to the obligations of family and the preservation of culture. By the 1940s, they had accepted formal schooling insofar as it enhanced their ability to meet threats and deal with outsiders. They rejected education to the degree it promoted assimilation and endangered their conception of traditional Indianness. Some also remained skeptical of its potential to ensure fair and honest dealings from white society. "Yeah, I know how to read and write," said Ella Jim's cousin, "but those words on the treaty they never live up to and probably never will."[51]

■ ■ ■

Whether or not they supported public schooling, most off-reservation households curtailed their children's attendance as a matter of economic necessity. Limited cash incomes and continued loyalty to the seasonal round dictated a migratory lifestyle, with families moving regularly among customary resource sites and to wage labor opportunities. Children generally left school in March or April and returned in late September or October. In the interim, they worked alongside their parents, contributing to the family economy and acquiring the skills necessary to support themselves as adults. When agency officials complained about truancy, Columbia River Indians made their priorities clear. In 1941, Clarence Davis wrote,

> The attitude seems to be reflected in a statement made to me by Willie John [Culpus], who said that he knew what was best for the children; that he would teach them how to hunt and fish like their forefathers did, and when such seasons were finished he would take them back to school, the latter part of October. He said it was more important for them to learn to hunt and fish than to learn what the whites teach them.[52]

Vera Jean Jackson put it even more bluntly, telling Davis "that she would get her children in school when she was good and ready and what was [he] going to do about it." William Yallup softened this challenge with the observation that "many of the Indian people out there who have children [in school] are physically unable to harvest the root crop without the aid of their children. . . . The Chief does not wish to offend the School Authorities but can see no other way than to allow the children to remain away from school in order to help keep the family alive by assisting in the root harvest." No sudden converts to white education, Columbia River Indians continued to weigh its costs and benefits against their own economic and cultural prerogatives.[53]

The majority of off-reservation families followed the same basic subsistence cycle from the 1880s to the 1940s. Even after they had taken homesteads and allotments, agency officials reported that it remained "the exception rather than the rule in [the] case of the public domain Indians for them to be specially interested in agricultural pursuits." Instead, wrote the Yakama superintendent in 1917,

> They rent their surplus allotments for grazing purposes at an average rental of 10¢ per acre per year. Some raise a few ponies. They go in very much for fishing from early spring until early fall. During this period some of them can be found at any time along the Columbia River at their usual fishing places.[54]

River People also continued to dig roots, pick berries, and hunt game in traditional locations. At the same time, however, they modified aboriginal subsistence patterns to accommodate seasonal wage work and summer entertainment venues such as fairs, rodeos, and powwows. The advent of affordable cars, like the earlier appearance of horses, made even poor families highly mobile. "With such transportation at their command," noted one agent, "it is relatively easy for them to travel from fishing place to fishing place, and from one orchard to another, to the hop fields, potato country, etc. Thus our Indians are doing the thing that they like best. . . . not necessarily the things that would be for their best interests." The automobile became a primary symbol of modernity in the early twentieth century, yet it could also be made to serve traditional ends.[55]

Mid-Columbia Indians preferred communal work such as digging potatoes or picking apples, cherries, and hops because it resembled traditional gathering activities. At harvest time, the expansive fields and orchards of the Columbia Basin hosted lively intertribal gatherings such as those held in the camas meadows and berry patches. Arriving by car and by train, on horseback and on foot, Indians came from as far away as Canada and Oklahoma to mingle with "fruit tramps" from the local reservations and the public domain. Growers left the camps largely unsupervised, and pickers filled their off hours with dancing, drinking, gambling, horse racing, and gossiping. Some also sold traditional handicrafts to white onlookers or charged fees to have their photographs taken. As historian Paige Raibmon has said of similar gatherings in western Washington, "Indian watchers saw a romantic spectacle when they looked at Indian hop pickers, but spectacle encompassed only a fraction of these workers' lives. Migration to hop fields was part of a larger indigenous network of economy, politics, and society that ensured Aboriginal survival." A strategic concession to the modern market, harvesting crops helped make ends meet—if just—for people without ready access to cash or credit. Together with lease payments and the sale of salmon, income from agricultural labor and curio sales gave many families the only hard currency they had to purchase clothing, groceries, medicine, and other goods not afforded by the seasonal round.[56]

Columbia River Indians shared this transient way of life with a large number of reservation residents. Although some agency families dutifully farmed their allotments or raised livestock for market, others adopted the same economic strategy as their off-reservation relations. In 1928, Superintendent Estep observed that "even the old, helpless Indians would rather go to the berry fields than stay at home on three full meals a day. It is not poverty that causes them to make these trips . . . but they go just the same, hundreds of them each year." On the Yakama and Umatilla reservations in particular, the Dawes Act had done little except channel arable land and irrigation water into non-Indian hands.[57] Estep's 1929 report on allotment lamented:

As a general rule our Indians are not farmers and spend much of their good weather time away from the reservation; down on the Columbia River during the salmon run where they sell some fish for money and dry and smoke their winter supply; they go to the mountains for roots and berries and some remain for the deer hunting season, while others come down and go to the hop picking and potato harvesting. The most of them prefer this kind of life to farming. Even the good, steady fellows who do like to farm "go to the mountains" for a short time. "Going some place" is the occupation of 90% of our lessors.[58]

In terms of subsistence, as in other areas of Native culture, reservation boundaries never inscribed a clear line between "progressives" and "traditionalists." Reservation residents and river Indians remained highly diverse, flexible, and interconnected. Neither group could lay exclusive claim to a single standard of authentic "Indianness." At the end of the Americanization era, however, Columbia River Indians largely continued to live as they believed traditional people should. "That's what identifies us," insisted Elsie David, a member of the Rock Creek longhouse, during a recent oral interview. "I don't think I would know a great deal of my culture if I just lived on cow and non-traditional food. My grandma used to say, 'You're not going to know anything about our people if you don't eat our food.' If you're going to eat cows, you're going to be dumb like a cow."[59]

David's reference to her grandmother suggests that the continuation of a modified seasonal round helped perpetuate traditional Plateau gender roles. In the harvest camps, work followed the customary division of labor, with women and children doing the bulk of the picking while men relaxed, hunted, and prepared for the next salmon run. Women also continued to process the fish and game procured by their husbands, in addition to cooking meals, tending livestock, growing gardens, and canning produce for winter storage. "The women were real strong in them days," observed Flora Thompson, Chief Tommy Thompson's second wife, with obvious pride. Agency officials, echoing the words of early traders and missionaries, complained of male loafing and female drudgery. They hoped that allotments and boarding schools would produce simple nuclear families headed by solid patriarchs. Throughout the Americanization era, however, Mid-Columbia Indians stubbornly preserved what Plateau ethnographer Lillian Ackerman has called "a necessary balance." Even in more sedentary farm families, she notes, "Women maintained their traditional role of owning and managing all foods and their distribution within and outside of the family and keeping surpluses for trading purposes." Women also owned their personal property and often took responsibility for the family's cash flow, including major purchases. Political affairs remained largely a male domain, thanks in part to the expectations of white power brokers, but women's economic clout gave them a high degree of autonomy within the family.[60]

Columbia River Indian women also continued to play an important role as culture bearers. Long after alternative technologies appeared, they made tule mats for lodges and twined cedar-root baskets, which could be used for plant gathering or sold to white collectors. Such skills were not confined to off-reservation families, but women from river communities were especially well regarded for their basketry. Women likewise preserved and passed down the ecological knowledge that underpinned traditional handicrafts as well as the harvesting and processing of traditional foods. Young children learned by hearing, watching, and helping their mothers and female relatives at work. When kids left home to attend school, many did so with "Indian roots and Indian food for their lunch," as Elsie Gibson boasted of her boys during the 1930s. Reservation families still ate large quantities of wild food, too, but many had more varied diets because they owned farms and ranches. Wilbur Slockish, who spent his early years on a family allotment in the Klickitat Valley, recalled that his meals "depended on where I was at. When I was over on the Columbia, it was the traditional food supply. And when I was over on the reservation, it was a mixed diet. My grandmother on the reservation . . . she had both sides, pork chops, chicken and steaks, beef, like that."[61] As providers and teachers, women helped sustain the "old ways" that defined Indian identity for River People. David Sohappy, Jr., probably spoke for many when he thanked his mother for bringing him up "to be a traditional Indian and eating the salmon, roots, berries, water."[62]

Columbia River Indian claims to a more authentically indigenous identity rested on a set of contrasts between their lifestyle and their perception of reservation conditions. The presence of Indian farmers and ranchers, like the existence of churches and schools, made reservations seem more "progressive" to agents and Indians alike. However few in number, the "steady fellows" who made a living from agriculture or ranching exemplified the changes wrought by federal policy. As such, they provided a convenient foil for Columbia River Indians, who compared their own idealized image of Indianness to the acculturated appearance of reservation folk. Chief Thompson expressed this sense of difference in 1941: "Me, I am poor and do not have any home on a Reservation and no allotment, and I have to live from fish I catch at Celilo." "We ain't no rich people," agreed his ally, Chief Yallup, "and whatever we fish we live on that, and it is not very much—just enough to get by. And the Indians that live on the reservations have lot of income from their land and we are not that way." The reality was more complex. Even the most affluent reservation residents looked rather poor by Euro-American standards, and many Columbia River Indians had land on the reservations or the public domain that furnished rental income. On the plane of perception, however, real and imagined differences in cultural orientation and economic status helped shape the contours of Columbia River Indian identity.[63]

Despite decades of assimilation policy, the people claiming this identity in the 1940s possessed the markers of traditional Indianness as then defined on the Columbia Plateau. Primarily "full-bloods" with strong ties to river communities, they continued to hold the federal government and the dominant society at arm's length. Most remained faithful to Washat, which became known colloquially as the "traditional" or "Indian" religion. Many also still believed in the guardian spirit complex that informed Indian doctoring and the derivative Feather Religion. Though initially hostile to Washat and Waptashi, the Indian Shaker Church ultimately came to coexist with those forms of worship and healing. Similar patterns prevailed in the spheres of marriage and education, where off-reservation Indians obeyed the dominant society's laws selectively or not at all. Although not necessarily opposed to practical schooling, they placed greater emphasis on the retention of language and the transmission of knowledge and skills central to the seasonal round. In the shadowy spaces between the reservations, where the searchlight of federal scrutiny passed infrequently, Columbia River Indians found ways to accommodate modernity without surrendering their core values and customs.

For this reason, modern tribal leaders often seek out River People for advice regarding indigenous beliefs and practices. Tribal language programs are full of people from river communities, and river longhouses are widely regarded as the most traditional. Their members happily embrace this distinction and do not hesitate to correct reservation people whom they deem less knowledgeable about Native history and culture. "It isn't 'was.' It still is today," snapped Ella Jim when the college-educated director of a tribal culture center stated that Indian communities had been pushed off the river. "I can talk because I've seen all the longhouses on the river. . . . They're still there yet." Proud and prickly in defense of the old ways, Columbia River Indians are renowned as traditionalists because of their off-reservation upbringing—not in spite of it—and this reputation has become a pillar of their identity. Testifying before Congress in 1988, Klickitat sub-chief Johnny Jackson declared: "We are a traditional people, and we live under the traditional laws and the ways of the river life. . . . We live by our unwritten laws. And today those unwritten laws are being ignored. But we will not forget it."[64]

The Mid-Columbia River Council has been the governing authority
for the river and its people. The chief, sub-chief, and councillors
were responsible for coordinating the activities of the people,
resolving disputes, and providing for the unity of the bands,
tribes and nations along the river. Their authority was recognized
as the political/spiritual jurisdiction over affairs on the river.

—MID-COLUMBIA RIVER COUNCIL,
STATEMENT OF UNIFICATION, 1990

6 ■ ■ ■

HOME FOLK

On a hot July day in 1941, Yakama tribal members Henry Charley and Pete Soctillo opened a soda pop stand on Chief Island,
one of the prime fishing areas at Celilo Falls. No one could
fault their business instincts. Fishermen grew thirsty on the shadeless
rocks and scaffolds, despite the spray from the thundering Columbia
River, and many would gladly pay for a cold soft drink. The budding
entrepreneurs committed a cultural faux pas, however, by failing to ask
permission of Tommy Kuni Thompson, the local headman and salmon
chief responsible for regulating the fishery. Thompson immediately complained to the Yakama agency: "I don't want these Yakima people to put
out such stands on Chief's Island without notifying me. I'm living there
at Celilo—just barely getting along, and short of money sometimes—

because too many people come there to fish." If anyone was to run a franchise on his island, it should be a local Indian rather than a "comer." Then, at least, the River People might use the proceeds to fund trips to Portland and Salem, Oregon, where they had pressing business with the federal and state governments.[1]

Speaking in support of his cousin and fellow river chief, William Yallup of Rock Creek voiced concerns that went far beyond the concessions stand:

> Whatever Indians come around here from different reservations, these Indians just call us down. Whatever we tell them they won't listen. . . . Our two sons live right there and it seems to me they ought to have more to say than any one else, and whatever we say about fishing rights it is all for their own good. I don't like to have anybody come from some other place and talk against them—I don't like to hear that. . . . We never entered reservations— just stayed on the river where we have our fishing rights. We are going to hold that place as long as we live. We [are] staying right there until we pass away.[2]

Soda pop seems an unlikely trigger for such an eloquent fountain of words, but the offending stand was only the latest in a long series of provocations. By the 1940s, decades of mounting conflict and frustration had pushed the pressure at Celilo to the point that even a slight disturbance could uncork a stream of recrimination rivaling the roar of the falls.

The primary source of this turbulence was the Euro-American colonization and commercialization of the fisheries during the second half of the nineteenth century. Between 1887 and 1939, the federal government filed four lawsuits defending the off-reservation fishing rights of Mid-Columbia treaty tribes against white encroachment and state interference. The Indians prevailed each time, yet the controversy only grew as the salmon runs dwindled. Among Native people, the struggle underscored the importance of tribal membership. Although river residents often led the fight, litigation made it clear that the government construed off-reservation fishing as a tribal right belonging to the reservation-based confederations named in the treaties.[3] Federal officials preferred to deal with tribal leaders and treated fishing sites as tribal property, practices that clashed with indigenous traditions of village autonomy and family ownership. Thus, even as the courts upheld treaty rights and encouraged tribal unity, they also set up conflicts between the recognized tribes and the off-reservation communities near the fisheries. At Celilo Falls, the tension between river-dwelling "home folk" and reservation "comers" accelerated the development of a distinct Columbia River Indian identity. Overwhelmed by an army of outsiders, river residents increasingly defined themselves in opposition to the reservations and attempted to mobilize as an independent political body. By the mid-1940s, they had banded together to articulate and advance their separate interests as the confederated Columbia River Tribe.

■ ■ ■

The non-Indian assault on treaty fishing rights resulted from the introduction of salmon to the capitalist marketplace. Starting in the mid-1860s, the application of industrial processing and canning techniques transformed the legendary runs of the Columbia River into a lucrative commodity. Initially, the remote location and swift currents of the middle river shielded local Indians from direct competition with white commercial interests, which focused their activities in the estuary. In 1879, however, the introduction of the fishwheel made it possible to catch salmon in the upstream rapids where traps, seines, and gillnets generally could not function. Wheels, either fixed to the bank or attached to scows, scooped fish from the river with shocking efficiency. When the Northern Pacific Railroad reached The Dalles in 1883, making it a feasible site for canneries, packers rushed to establish operations at or near indigenous fisheries. By 1900, five canneries and dozens of wheels lined the river between the Cascade Rapids and Celilo Falls.[4]

Conflict erupted immediately as the newcomers shoved aside Indian dipnetters, sometimes even dynamiting their stands to make way for wheels. Although many Native fishers would soon earn money selling salmon to the canneries, most still depended on fishing for subsistence and deeply resented the theft of their ancient fishing grounds. Before the advent of canning, some Indians had allowed local farmers to use aboriginal sites to obtain small supplies of salted salmon. These visitors only stayed a few hours, and they typically rented or borrowed nets from Native owners. The sites themselves remained in Indian hands and subject to traditional regulation. As Yakama agent James Wilbur explained in 1881,

> The Indians have always regarded these fishing stands as their own property, as much as the house or barn of any citizen; they never contemplated giving the whites the privilege of taking possession of them, but I believe when they signed the treaty supposed they were only giving the whites the privilege of taking fish at the fishery, from other stands.[5]

This culturally grounded and legally sound interpretation of the treaty phrase "in common with the citizens of the territory" held no water with white competitors, who read it to mean that they had equal standing at the tribal fisheries. They also assumed that Euro-American concepts of property ownership trumped whatever claims the Indians might have to their "usual and accustomed places." Accordingly, once individual citizens and corporations had acquired land adjoining the fisheries, they quickly moved to block tribal access to the river.

By the 1920s, confrontations between Indian fishers and white intruders had produced three federal court decisions protecting treaty fishing rights against white interference. The first case, *U.S. v. Taylor*, began when a white homesteader named Frank Taylor ran a barbed-wire fence across the main path to the Tumwater fishery near The Dalles, arguing that the barrier was necessary to stop Indians from camping and pasturing horses on his land. The Department of Justice responded with a lawsuit on behalf of the Yakama Nation, which reached the Supreme Court of Washington Territory in January 1887. While recognizing the defendant's title to the land, the Court held that "the Treaty privilege of the Indians to take fish was an easement upon it at the time the government conveyed the title and that such title did not extinguish the easement." In other words, treaty Indians had the right to cross private property when passing to and from their traditional fishing sites. Subsequent owners of the land ignored the ruling, however, forcing the federal government to bring a second lawsuit in 1897 against Audubon and Linnaeus Winans.

United States v. Winans became a milestone in the history of American Indian law and the first of nine Northwest Indian fishing rights cases to reach the U.S. Supreme Court. Hoping to overturn *Taylor*, defense attorneys Charles H. Carey and Franklin P. Mays raised several new arguments to bolster the Winans' property rights claim. First, they cited the Court's recent ruling in *Ward v. Race Horse*, which struck down Shoshone-Bannock treaty rights on the basis of the constitutional provision that new states join the Union on an equal footing with existing states. According to this line of argument, Washington's 1889 admission to statehood had abrogated treaties made during the territorial period, leaving Indians with only the common right to fish enjoyed by all citizens of the state. The defense then advanced the rather contradictory assertion that their clients' use of state-licensed fishwheels gave them a right superior to that of Native dipnetters, "since wheel fishing is one of the civilized man's methods, as legitimate as the substitution of the modern combine harvester for the ancient sickle and flail." Even when erected at traditional grounds, wheels did not deprive Indians of their common right because it supposedly applied "to no certain and defined places." In other words, the Winans' team alleged, Indians could always catch salmon somewhere else on the river.[6]

This final argument played on the notion that the fisheries had originally belonged to recognized tribes with well-defined populations and boundaries. By this logic, any member of the Yakama Nation or its fourteen constituent groups could take salmon at any usual and accustomed place within the tribes' ceded area. Fishing sites were interchangeable and open to all comers, regardless of their aboriginal ancestry and family history. In the courtroom, Native testimony exposed serious defects in this line of thinking. Take, for instance, an exchange between defense attorney Franklin Mays and Sam Tanawasha, a longtime resident of Wishram Village. When asked if he was a Yakama Indian, Tanawasha replied, "My mother is a Wisham [Wishram], I am right there at Wisham."[7] Mays then pressed him on the issue of fisheries, trying to elicit the desired response:

Q: Do you know about the fishery called Skin?

A: That is another tribe's fishing ground.

Q: Isn't there a good fishery there?

A: It is a fishing ground that belongs to another group of Indians.

Q: Couldn't you go there and fish?

A: No, I can't fish there, the Indians won't allow me, I couldn't go there.

Q: Are not the Indians that do fish there part of the Yakima Nation?

A: They used to go, some that have relatives there, go to Skin, at Wisham there is more salmon.[8]

Mays' cross-examination of other Indians produced similar results. Hoping to prove that people enrolled in the Yakama Nation could fish anywhere within their tribal territory, he instead demonstrated that indigenous conceptions of ownership still governed the fisheries almost forty years after the treaties became law.

Although Indian witnesses occasionally used the term "tribe" (or at least had their words translated that way), their testimony showed that the concept still puzzled some Native people. They understood that the Yakama treaty protected their right to fish at all usual and accustomed places. They did not assume that it dictated universal access to those sites, as Martin Speedis later explained: "The various fishing stations were the private property of individual family groups and they were handed down from generation to generation . . . it had always been that way and the Indians always recognized their own rights to family stations."[9] Residents of Wishram and their relatives fished primarily at Tumwater, whereas residents of Sk'in and their relations generally caught salmon farther upstream at Celilo Falls. White Swan, named as a plaintiff in the case, claimed fishing rights at Wishram because his wife came from that community, not because he served as head chief of the Yakama Nation. For many off-reservation Indians in particular, aboriginal attachments still mattered more than the tribal categories created by treaty. Therefore, when Mays interrogated witnesses such as Joe Kolocken about their identity, it often produced confusion and consternation on both sides:

Q: You belong to the Yakima tribe or nation of Indians?

A: Yes, I used to go there.

Q: I am asking you if you belong to the Yakima tribe or nation of Indians.

A: I don't belong, I am not a Yakima.

Q: What are you?

A: Wisham.[10]

Kolocken possessed legal rights under the Yakama treaty by virtue of his membership in the signatory and constituent Wishram "tribe," and he sometimes visited the reservation where many of his people had settled. In his view, however, traveling to that place and associating with its residents did not make him a Yakama Indian or give him the right to fish anywhere on the river. Unable to prove its claims, the defense team ultimately dismissed Indian testimony as "incompetent and inadmissible when it would tend to vary the plain stipulations of the treaty."[11]

The federal district court found for the defense, but the Supreme Court overturned that decision in 1905, setting forth two vital principles that still govern treaty interpretation. The first stated that treaties must be construed as the Indians understood them at the time and "as justice and reason demand," since the United States exerted superior power over the "unlettered" tribal representatives. The second, known as the reserved rights doctrine, held that treaties were "not a grant of rights to the Indians, but a grant of rights from them—a reservation of those not granted." Putting these principles into action, Justice Joseph McKenna declared that members of the Yakama Nation had retained their existing rights to cross the land, to fish at usual and accustomed places, and to erect temporary houses for curing their catch. Neither private property nor superior technology gave the Winans family an exclusive claim to the fishery, and they could not legally restrict the Indians in their use of it. Although Washington State might regulate tribal fishing, it too was bound to respect Indian treaties that preceded its admission to the union.[12]

Justice McKenna never explicitly addressed whether fishing rights resided in the tribe or with individuals because it did not bear directly on the issues at hand. In defining the scope of the treaties, he did recognize that they had reserved rights "to every individual Indian, as though named therein. They imposed a servitude upon every piece of land as though described therein." Throughout the opinion, however, he referred to the plaintiffs as "Yakima Indians" or "certain Indians of the Yakima Nation." Although correct in the sense intended by U.S. treaty makers, such labels flattened persistent ethnic distinctions and implied that the Wishram fishery at Tumwater belonged to all "Yakima Indians," despite substantial testimony to the contrary. This construction of the treaties, conveyed to Indians by their agents and attorneys, laid the groundwork for tribal claims to the fisheries later in the century. In the short term, most Indians still adhered to the aboriginal conception of fishing sites. Writing in 1924, Yakama superintendent Evan W. Estep professed to be "doubtful about whether any one Indian can claim the exclusive right of fishing from a particular rock or island, yet I note that numbers of them claim this right as one which descended to them from someone else." The tension between these perspectives became glaringly obvious in the conflicts to come.[13]

■ ■ ■

The *Winans* decision failed to bring lasting peace on the river. Disputes over state regulation loomed in the near future, and the ruling changed nothing on the Oregon shore, where the fraudulent Huntington Treaty still threatened Warm Springs fishing rights. Natives on that side of the river took salmon at the whim of the Seufert Brothers Company, which claimed most of the riparian property between The Dalles and Celilo Falls. By the time *Winans* went to trial, many local Indians had signed contracts to supply fish to the canneries. Seufert's sold them twine for nets, extended credit during the off-season, and allowed Indians employed by the company to take scrap lumber for fuel and scaffolding. The cannery's Chinese butchers also gave Indians discarded fish heads and tails, which they then dried and sold to visiting reservation residents.

Owner Frank Seufert even allowed Indians to camp on his land as long as they did not damage his property or interfere with the wheels. His company had a history of aggressive land acquisition, however, and many Indians already resented him for blasting traditional fishing sites near Tumwater. He antagonized them further by testifying in the Winans' defense and purchasing their land shortly before the case concluded. As his empire grew in the early twentieth century, he did not hesitate to challenge Indian fishing when it conflicted with his business interests.[14]

Seufert's principal confrontation with the treaties came in response to the activities of Sam Williams, an erstwhile company employee and the minister of the Indian Shaker Church at The Dalles. In 1907, acting on behalf of his granddaughter, Williams had filed a homestead entry for eighty acres adjoining Three Mile Rapids. Known to Native people as Waćáqs, or Lone Pine, the area had once been a traditional fishing and camping ground for villages on both sides of the river. Williams had obtained aboriginal rights to the fishery from its previous owner, Wasco Charley, but Seufert already claimed the surrounding land. By the time the General Land Office cancelled Williams's entry in 1915, he had begun operating a state-licensed fishing scow from a mooring on the contested point. Seufert tolerated his presence and even helped him secure licenses as long as he sold his catch to the company. In the summer of 1913, however, Williams switched to a buyer who offered better prices and then hired several white men to work his scow. Their vessel competed with two of Seufert's crews, which tried to stop Williams's scow from fishing that season. When his crew returned the following spring, Seufert literally took matters into his own hands by setting their boat adrift. His men repeated the offense four more times during the 1914 season, arguing that Williams had trespassed on company property. Williams sued for $2,000 in damages and requested an injunction to prevent Seufert from using the disputed river frontage. Anticipating a difficult battle, he called on the Yakama agency to help "protect my indian fishing right along river . . . I cannot fight millionaire corporation in courts without help of indian department."[15]

Throughout the ensuing trial, *United States ex. rel. Williams v. Seufert Brothers*, questions swirled around the identity of Sam Williams. Born to a Yakama father and a Cowlitz mother, he had spent part of his youth west of the Cascade Mountains. Although he had taken an allotment on the Yakama reservation in 1897, he later sold part of it and moved to an Indian homestead on the Columbia River. Consequently, his rights as a member of the Yakama Nation seemed dubious to Seufert, who exploited popular notions of "blood" and "tribe" to argue that the treaty had no bearing on the case. In an angry letter to the U.S. district attorney, he declared:

> I cannot allow Indians of the Sam Williams stripe, who really do not belong here, but belong to western Washington Agency, to come here, gather up some white trash to stand behind them, so they can ask the Government to do their lawing for them. Williams belongs to the Quinault Reservation, and they have good fishing grounds there, and he should be made to go there.[16]

Echoing this sentiment, Seufert witness Charles Switzler informed a federal attorney that Williams "hasn't any more rights on that place then [sic] I have. I told him this Sam is a different person from all the Wasco's he doesn't belong there and never was raised there. I said to the lawyer, 'even I have a little Wasco blood in me and I don't bother about any fisherys [sic].'" In fact, as a child of mixed heritage from a "pioneer" family, Switzler may have known that Williams's right to fish at Lone Pine rested on his arrangements with the late Wasco Charley and his marriage to a Wasco woman named Susie, not on any personal claim to Wasco identity. Under the government's system of tribal classification, however, Williams remained vulnerable to charges that he had no place on the Columbia River at all. Even the Justice Department harbored doubts and agreed to proceed only after the Indian Office vouched that he had been allotted as "a straight Yakima Indian."[17]

At trial, Seufert's defense team downplayed the Cowlitz identity issue and focused its attack on the rights of the Yakama Nation as a whole. Knowing that the company could not lawfully exclude treaty Indians in light of the *Winans* decision, his lawyers set out to prove that the Yakamas possessed no fishing rights south of the Columbia River. The concept of ceded areas played straight into their hands. As the treaty commissioners had rendered it on paper, Yakama territory ended at the water's northern edge. The agency superintendent, Don M. Carr, privately admitted that he understood the boundaries that way and also wondered whether the treaty applied to Indians fishing commercially with modern technology. Seufert's attorneys argued that, even if Williams was an Indian and a member of the Yakama Nation, he could not possibly have a "usual and accustomed" fishing place on the Oregon shore. Those sites belonged to the tribes of the Warm Springs reservation, which had supposedly given up their off-reservation rights in 1865. The logic was as clear and cold as the river itself. If the court accepted it, Seufert Brothers Company would become the principal owner and arbiter of Indian fishing "privileges" on the Oregon side of the Columbia.[18]

At the initial hearing on May 24, 1915, District Judge Charles E. Wolverton leaned toward the defendant's point of view. The government avowed that "the Indians upon one side went to the other side, and vice versa, and that the fishing was a right in common," but he remained skeptical. In his opinion, the Warm Springs Indians had surrendered their off-reservation rights in the Huntington Treaty, leaving "the right as claimed by the Yakimas to be established upon their own customs, and upon their own practices, in fishing upon the south side." The testimony of several non-Indian witnesses and two elderly tribal leaders failed to satisfy Wolverton. He lifted a temporary injunction against Seufert Brothers but kept the case open, giving the government a chance to produce additional evidence and initiate further proceedings. If it chose to do so, he advised, "the plaintiff should enlarge the scope of his action, and include the Yakima Indians as a tribe, or their confederated tribes, so as to secure the community right belonging to those confederated tribes, if they have one."[19]

This final word of advice reflected Wolverton's judgment that fishing rights were indeed a tribal prerogative, which Williams had forfeited by accepting U.S. citizenship. Since he was no longer a member of an Indian community, one of a tribe or band, his lawsuit could not establish any rights on behalf of the Yakama Nation. Wolverton based this opinion on the fact that Williams had received a fee patent for his allotment and had taken an Indian homestead on the public domain, which required him to swear that he had severed "tribal relations" and adopted "the habits and pursuits of civilized life." On the surface, Williams had met these stipulations. He resided off reservation, held landed property, operated a fishing scow, wore Euro-American clothing, and presided over a nominally Christian church. For making such acculturative adjustments, the government had rewarded him with citizenship. Yet there is little reason to believe that Williams had truly severed tribal relations or ceased to think of himself as an Indian. Although more "progressive" than many of his neighbors, he still spoke the Cowlitz language and lived among Indians in an off-reservation community. As a leader of the Indian Shaker Church, he ministered to Native people, healed their sick, and worked to protect their religious freedom against government persecution—all activities that entailed maintaining connections to his co-religionists on the reservations. Williams' life suggested no contradiction between "citizen" and "Indian," but the law framed them as mutually exclusive categories.[20]

The Justice Department responded to Wolverton's advice by naming the Yakama Nation as a plaintiff and broadening the pool of evidence concerning traditional fishing practices. To counter Seufert's contention that Indians from the north never fished south of the Columbia, agency superintendents recruited an army of witnesses who had seen or done that very thing.[21] Tomar Handley, a venerable Wasco resident of the Warm Springs reservation, testified to the historic mingling of diverse peoples at The Dalles:

Q. Did the Wasco Indians ever object to the Yakima Indians coming across to fish at Wah-sucks?

A. No.

Q. Well did the Yakimas ever object to the Wascos going over on their side?

A. No.

Q. Why did not one tribe, either the Yakimas or the Wascos, object to the other tribe fishing there?

A. Well, they were friendly, and they were related through marriage.[22]

By the end of the trial, fifty Indian and non-Indian witnesses had sworn that the Columbia River had never been a wall between separate and distinct tribes. "We knew no Oregon or Washington. We knew only that the shores were our fishing grounds," declared George Waters, who succeeded his brother White Swan as the head chief of the Yakama Nation. Even in 1915, said witness Doctor Shea-wa, the river remained "a table for both, both sides of the river. It laid right in between them, and they came and ate and were gone." Family relationships determined where people sat at this table, but many guests could choose from a number of different chairs.[23]

The weight of oral evidence shifted Judge Wolverton's opinion in favor of the Indians. On May 1, 1916, he ruled that Lone Pine was a traditional fishing site for the confederated tribes of the Yakama Nation and that Seufert Brothers "should be enjoined from exercising any pretended fishing right along or within this space." Citing the canons of treaty construction established in the *Winans* decision, Wolverton demolished the assumption that ceded areas limited tribal fishing grounds. "The Indian tribes did not themselves occupy definite territory with fixed and exact boundaries," he wrote, "and it is without doubt that the different tribes commingled more or less, and roamed about. . . . And so of their fishing—there was no monopoly by any one tribe of any specific and fixed territory." The ceded areas outlined in the treaties were merely a convenient device for extinguishing aboriginal title to the land. Drawn with that goal in mind, "they very naturally only followed in a general way the very general idea that the Indians had of their territorial delimitations." Native representatives agreed to these boundaries with the understanding that their people could continue to hunt, gather, and fish at their usual and accustomed places. Those rights had nothing to do with territorial boundaries, stated Wolverton, "since, to their mind, *all* such places were being reserved for their benefit anyway." The Supreme Court unanimously affirmed this opinion in 1919. Although the concept of tribal rights remained intact, the law had seemingly laid to rest the illusion of tightly bounded and mutually exclusive tribal territories.[24]

Ironically, the Columbia River Indian who had initiated the whole proceeding lost his own treaty rights as a result. Wolverton, expanding on his pronouncement at the hearing, declared that Sam Williams had become a citizen and could no longer demand government protection of his fishing rights. He had ostensibly lost his tribal status by accepting a fee patent, adopting "the habits of civilized life," and establishing his residence "separate and apart from any tribe." Thus, even as Wolverton struck down artificial geographical boundaries between tribes, he reinforced the legal barrier between Indian identity and American citizenship. Only a month later, the U.S. Supreme Court's decision in *U.S. v. Nice* removed this barrier, and in 1924 Congress conferred American citizenship on all Indians without stripping them of tribal membership. Even then, however, Seufert insisted that Williams was "not—so the court declared—an Indian." Seufert also continued to disobey the federal court order directing his company to vacate the contested river frontage, even after Judge Wolverton cited him for contempt of court in 1920. Although Williams continued to fish at Lone Pine for several years, he did so as a regular citizen under contract with Seufert Brothers Company. Clearly frustrated by the arrangement and by the decline of his Shaker congregation, he moved downstream to Hood River in the late 1920s.[25]

■ ■ ■

By the time Williams's case concluded, some Indians had already begun to act on the assumption that they could fish anywhere their tribes had recognized treaty rights. Their reasons for doing so were as varied as their origins, but the end result was generally the same: a fresh wave of trespassing disputes among Native fishers, who simultaneously confronted decreasing salmon runs and increasing harassment from state officials bent on enforcing conservation at tribal expense. In 1915, Washington State had implemented its first fisheries code, which forbade certain traditional techniques such as spearing and snaring. The following year, the state's Supreme Court ruled against two Indians convicted of fishing with illegal gear and without state licenses.[26] Meanwhile, the state fish commission began closing the Klickitat River and other tributaries to salmon fishing in order to protect spawning populations and hatchery programs supported by state license fees. Continually harassed by white sportsmen as well as game wardens, some Indian fishers quit these smaller streams and tried to subsist on spawned-out salmon carcasses from the hatcheries. Others cast their eyes upriver to the great indigenous fisheries between The Dalles and Celilo Falls, where they could more reliably find salmon and a measure of safety in numbers.[27]

A larger group of refugees came from the Umatilla and Yakima rivers, which by the 1920s had been extensively dammed to supply the irrigation demands of non-Indian farmers. Logging and ranching in the headwaters further damaged wild salmon stocks, but state authorities again blamed Indian fishers. On the Yakima River, wardens chased them away from dam spillways and fish ladders built on the very spots their ancestors had used for generations. In 1915 alone, twenty-five Indians were cited for fishing within a mile of Prosser Dam. As the arrests continued and the salmon disappeared, these people faced a stark choice: they could either stop fishing—the only way of life some had ever known—or they could find another place to do it. Over the next thirty years, hundreds of fishers from the Yakama and Umatilla reservations chose the latter option. Most gravitated to the basalt outcroppings at Celilo Falls, drawn by the festive atmosphere and the lure of ready cash during the summer and fall seasons. Cannery buyers welcomed them with open arms, but local Indians took a less charitable view.[28]

For Tommy Thompson, the headman and salmon chief at Celilo, the growing influx of outsiders created numerous headaches. During his youth in the 1870s, perhaps three to five dozen men had regularly fished the islands across from the village. By the early 1940s, there would be 200 to 300 people crowding the rocks each season. While some could claim family rights through blood or marriage, the majority possessed only the tribal right outlined in the treaties and affirmed by the courts. They could fish at traditional sites with permission or use one of five "hobo holes" on Chief Island, where Thompson allowed anyone with a net to take a turn. Rival canneries encouraged intensive commercial fishing, however, and the more aggressive newcomers simply horned in on established locations. In the worst cases, they chased away the rightful owners or erected new scaffolds that interfered with existing stands. Many visiting Indians refused to share their sites with others and ignored traditional taboos against fishing at night or after drowning deaths, which reduced escapement and risked offending the salmon people. *Núsux* is a sacred food in the Washat religion, second only to water, and practitioners believed that abusing it for the sake of profit could bring disaster upon everyone. At the very least, Thompson worried, flouting his conservation rules invited further state regulation of the fishery. Likewise, the increased traffic in illegal liquor attracted bootleggers and incurred the wrath of local law enforcement. By the fall of 1922, conditions at Celilo had deteriorated to the point that Thompson called a "general council of all Indians" to discuss what could be done to save the fishing grounds.[29]

Much of his anger focused on the large and legally assertive Yakama Nation. Emboldened by the *Seufert* decision, its members were crossing the Columbia in greater numbers each year. Thompson and other Oregon Indians tried to discourage them by resurrecting Seufert's old argument about the Yakamas' lack of fishing rights south of the river. Shortly before the 1922 council, several Yakamas complained that the Celilo chief and a Umatilla enrollee named Andrew Barnhart had tried to collect a five-dollar fee from Yakama tribal members before permitting them to fish. Two white men were also implicated in this scheme, but Yakama superintendent Don Carr singled out Barnhart, who had a reputation for bellicosity and bluster. "As a member of the Umatilla tribe," Carr scolded, "I do not understand that you have any Treaty fishing rights on the Columbia River, and certainly you do not have any under the Yakima Treaty." The reprimand made no impression. In 1925 and again in 1927, Barnhart allegedly ordered Yakamas to leave Celilo. The embarrassed Umatilla agent assured his colleague that "what [Barnhart knows] about the legal status of affairs on the Oregon side of the Columbia River would not fill a very large book." Even Thompson backed away from his erstwhile ally, informing the Umatilla agency in 1928 that Barnhart had "no authority from any Agent of the Government and none whatever from me to represent us 'Celilo Indians' in any capacity whatever." No

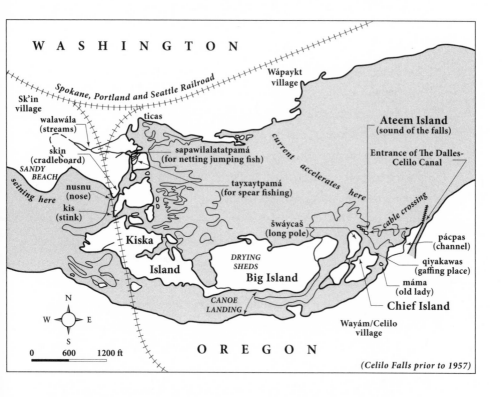

Celilo Falls. The fishing sites named by James Selam, a late elder of the John Day Indians, are only a few of the many traditional locations owned by individuals and families. Reprinted from Eugene Hunn, *Nch'i-Wána*, 1990, by permission of University of Washington Press.

reservation Indian did, in Thompson's opinion, but times were changing at Celilo.[30]

The pace of change quickened during the 1930s. After Oregon and Washington outlawed stationary fishwheels in 1926 and 1934, respectively, the Seufert Brothers Company relied more heavily on Native labor to supply fish. In 1930 Seufert's installed the first of many cableways connecting the Oregon shore to various islands in the channel. By climbing into the fish box, Indians could ride to their stands high above the roaring waters instead of braving the current in a boat. Company buyers greeted them on the return trip with the expectation that they would sell their catches to the cannery. This system opened up new locations and attracted even more fishers to Celilo. Most were local reservation residents, but non-treaty Indians from as far away as Idaho, Montana, and Alaska began appearing at Celilo Falls as well. The Great Depression also brought dozens of non-Indians seeking seasonal work. Some decided to stay for good, including hard cases such as James Marsh and Ernest and E. R. Cramer. Intent on making money, these intruders knew little and cared less about the intricate social geography of Celilo. They bullied their way into the fishery—often brazenly displacing traditional owners—and packers paid them the going rate. The resulting conflicts pitted visitors against residents, tribal rights against local prerogatives, and the practices of the modern marketplace against the customs of the aboriginal fishery.[31]

Once again, a chorus of complaints drew the Indian Office's attention to the river, stirring the usual mixture of concern and irritation. Although agency superintendents recognized the economic and cultural importance of salmon to the tribes, they soon grew tired of the endless wrangling at Celilo Falls. "At these fishing grounds there are not enough pools, rocks and rapids to go around to all the Indians who want to fish," noted the Umatilla agent in 1931. "Among themselves they regulate the time any one person may occupy a choice location and take their 'turn' at fishing. That many quarrels arise may be guessed. . . . Often the superintendent must play the part of umpire." That role required long road trips and rarely secured lasting settlements, since agents lacked the cultural knowledge and neutral status necessary to arbitrate intertribal fishing disputes. Eager to ease their burden of responsibility, the superintendents repeated their long-standing request for a permanent subagency on the Columbia River. In 1934, the year Congress passed the Indian Reorganization Act, they further suggested that "a committee of tribal representatives from Yakima, Umatilla and Warm Springs be appointed by the tribal council[s] to act on a general council at Celilo to settle local disputes." This proposal dovetailed with the federal government's recent shift toward self-determination in Indian affairs, and the tribes had to vote on it before any action could be taken. Like the tribal constitutions created under the IRA, however, the actual committee reflected American bureaucratic institutions more than it honored aboriginal practices. Consequently, it would never obtain the complete confidence and trust of many Columbia River Indians.[32]

From the outset, Chief Thompson and his allies feared that the committee would give reservation Indians the upper hand at Celilo Falls. During an August meeting to discuss the proposal, he urged the fifty or so Indians present to "work and fish in harmony with each other and to heed the traditions and customs of the fishing grounds as handed down by their ancestors." It troubled him that "Indians do not at all times govern themselves by unselfish attitudes, that oft times an Indian will claim that he has priority of rights to a desired location or eddy and will deny other Indians the opportunity to take fish." Thompson laid most of the blame at the feet of "younger Indians, mixed-bloods and visiting foreign Indians," together with the whites, but the Yakamas loomed in his mind as well. The meeting concluded with a 26 to 4 vote in favor of creating a committee to govern the Celilo fishery.[33]

Although it is not evident how or whether Thompson voted, his opposition to the plan soon became clear. In a letter to the secretary of the Interior, he protested that the Yakamas and their agent were "forcing the authority of this committee on the residents of Celilo, who do not favor the appointment of such a committee. The Celilo Indians are satisfied with the old order of things, and the rules and regulations of their Chief." The Yakamas were generally "very selfish," he further alleged, as they already had "many favorable locations at which to fish on their side of the River . . . [where] Celilo and Oregon Indians are not permitted to fish." Drawing on the River People's resentment of "rich" reservation Indians, Thompson also noted that many Yakamas and Umatillas owned allotments that furnished them sufficient income to live, whereas Celilo residents remained landless and poor. All things considered, it seemed patently unfair that they should have to submit to a committee run by such people. Thompson and Chief William Yallup tried to block further action by refusing to appoint their allotted share of committee members from Celilo and Rock Creek. By the end of the year, however, they had recognized that the proposal would go forward with or without Columbia River Indians on board. The river chiefs had no choice but to work with the Celilo Fish Committee (CFC) to uphold their traditional authority at the falls.[34]

From its inception, the CFC embodied the persistent tension between tribal management and local control. According to bylaws adopted in 1936, it had jurisdiction over fishing matters between the John Day River and Cascade Locks. The river communities below Celilo Falls did not have separate representation, however, as the committee was composed of three representatives each from the three Mid-Columbia reservations plus two from Celilo Village and one from Rock Creek. The Nez Perce tribe was also excluded due to a 1933 court ruling that claimed its treaty rights did not extend that far downriver. Together, the twelve committee members shared responsibility for five objectives: (1) advancing Indian fishing interests, (2) assisting agency superintendents with fishery administration, (3) working with state authorities to protect treaty fishing rights, (4) promoting law and order at the fisheries, and (5) prioritizing subsistence fishing ahead of commercial fishing. The committee's power to enforce specific regulations derived from the tribal councils of the three Mid-Columbia reservations, the agency superintendents, and the commissioner of Indian affairs. Significantly, the bylaws made no mention of traditional law or the salmon chief at Celilo, whose exact duties and relationship to the committee remained ambiguous. Tommy Thompson would participate actively in committee business for the next twenty years, but he never warmed to an arrangement that seemed to place the reservations and their interests ahead of his people's needs.[35]

The friction between and within its constituent groups often hindered the CFC's efforts to establish intertribal peace. Indeed, the very composition of the committee remained a source of controversy throughout its short life. At a meeting in September 1939, Umatilla delegate Andrew Barnhart charged that the Yakama tribe actually had six representatives because the acting members from Celilo and Rock Creek had enrolled on that reservation. Of the three men in question, Henry Thompson at least had good reason to laugh at the notion that enrollment determined personal loyalties. He shared his father's special antipathy toward the Yakama tribe and frequently complained of its undue influence at the falls. Meanwhile, Indians from other river communities complained that the CFC neglected their concerns because they had no seats on it. Earlier in 1939, the residents of Spearfish and Lyle, Washington, organized their own committees to handle fishing issues. Although the CFC promptly acknowledged them as intermediaries, Spearfish committeeman Otis Shilow insisted that his community should have full representation at Celilo meetings. Sally Ann Joyce, representing the Cascades people farther downstream, also wanted a delegate to look after their fisheries. When the CFC refused, Shilow called Tommy Thompson a "dictator" and said it was "unfair to have a chief who is narrow-minded and looks out for his own interests. . . . What's wrong with the Celilo Committee and its power?" Group solidarity remained elusive among Columbia River Indians, who still identified with their home villages even as they joined forces to challenge the dominance of the recognized tribes.[36]

If committee members agreed on anything, it was that whites, mixed-bloods, and non-treaty Indians had inferior rights at Celilo Falls. Clinging to their own interpretation of the "in common" language, treaty fishers maintained that they had reserved an *exclusive* right to their usual and accustomed places. Whites had to fish elsewhere. At a meeting in June 1941, Andrew Barnhart went so far as to claim that the government had added the words "in common" after the treaties were signed.[37] He also voiced widespread concerns about the presence of mixed-bloods at the fisheries, further exposing the connection between racial concepts and legal rights:

> Soon blue-eyed Indians will be fishing at Celilo altogether. It wouldn't be so bad if it were the children of these Frenchmen living on the reservation to whom allotments were given, but the white man is in question—white men who married these French women—their children are molesting us Indians.[38]

Although two committee members walked out during his remarks, perhaps showing their discomfort with such exclusionary language, the majority of those present shared his attitude toward "breeds." "I do not do any fishing myself," declared Rock Creek delegate Thomas K. Yallup, "but [I] have been here many years and have never seen mixed bloods fish here in the old days. But now that they do fish here, they should take their places [in] back of the full bloods." When federal officials explained that enrolled mixed-bloods had the same fishing rights as full-bloods, Henry Charley demanded to know who had given them such standing: "I believe they ought not to give the same privileges like the full bloods have." His logic, though legally indefensible, bore the unmistakable stamp of American racial ideology and federal identification policy. In a world defined by blood quantum, mixed-bloods seemed less Indian and therefore less entitled to a place at the fishery.[39]

Yet the racial barrier was not insurmountable. Some tribal leaders had mixed ancestry, too, and they objected to the racialized rhetoric of CFC members. As Yakama councilman Jacob Yahyowan observed in 1945, "Keeping half-breeds out means myself." Instead of attacking fellow tribal members, he urged, "We should hold our rights on [the] river and keep outside Indians from interfering [with] our rights or limit their fish." To him, blood quantum mattered less than legal affiliation with one of the treaty tribes. For others, community recognition outweighed both racial and tribal considerations. In 1941 the residents of Celilo Village adopted a non-Indian named James Dyer, who worked for the Army Corps of Engineers as the gatekeeper on the Dalles-Celilo Canal. The man they called "Jim Wildhorse" claimed no Native ancestry except "Mohawk or maybe Shawnee." Regardless, the Indian Office approved his adoption and Chief Thompson allowed him to fish "as one of the Columbia River Indian Tribe." Later, when the CFC questioned his rights at Celilo, Henry Charley emphatically stated that Dyer "was entitled to all of the privileges any other member of the band possessed." What distinguished him from other whites was not his dubious Indian heritage but rather his relationship to an indigenous community.[40]

"Outside Indians" from non-treaty tribes occupied the right side of the racial divide but the wrong side of the law. With some exceptions, they possessed neither treaty rights nor family rights at Celilo. Many were simply opportunists attracted by the commercial prospects at the fishery, and their presence irritated the CFC almost as much as the intrusion of whites. One of the committee's first resolutions in 1935 barred two Flathead Indians, P. B. Finley and George Pachite, from fishing at any usual and accustomed place. "Peanuts" Finley claimed the right to fish at Celilo because he had married a Yakama woman and bought a house for their children in the village. His kids never lived in the home, however, and he later separated from his first wife to marry a Nez Perce woman. In 1939, the CFC renewed its injunction and passed another resolution requiring every fisherman to carry an identification card certifying his enrollment in a treaty tribe. Many of the unenrolled Columbia River Indians disliked the program, however, and it soon floundered due to legal concerns and slack enforcement. That did not deter the CFC from making fresh resolutions. In 1941, the committee drafted a measure excluding fishers of less than one-half Indian blood, which Tommy Thompson amended to bar "the Idaho Indians from custom fishing rocks." When one of those Indians objected, Umatilla delegate Johnson Chapman snapped: "You heard the Chief—he don't want the Idahos to fish here." Through it all, Finley and other outsiders continued to do exactly that. Some ultimately gained acceptance, including the family of Shoshone-Bannock poet Ed Edmo, but only after they agreed to obey the CFC's rules.[41]

Finley's defiance highlighted the committee's central weaknesses: long on talk, it lacked the means to punish those who defied its resolutions. Many times, when Chief Thompson confiscated fish from offenders, they complained to the Indian Office. Tribal councils occasionally challenged committee decisions, and tribal courts lacked the jurisdiction to punish offenders. State courts, while eager to prosecute Indians who violated fish and game laws, cared little about ownership disputes unless they caused violence or property damage. That left only Congress and the federal courts to back the CFC with legal muscle. In 1939, the Indian Office finally appointed a field aide, Clarence G. Davis, to oversee the affairs of Columbia River Indians. He joined the agency superintendents in exploring the possibility of enforcing committee regulations through existing federal statutes. After a thorough investigation, the regional U.S. attorney reported that there were no current laws under which the CFC could pursue violators. Yakama superintendent M. A. Johnson saw only two alternatives, "either to secure adequate legislation through Congress to provide for the enforcement of the Fish Committee's rules and regulations . . . or frankly admit that the Fish Committee is an impotent organization without power or authority."[42]

Non-Indian intruders had already reached that conclusion. Since the early 1930s, the Indian Office had struggled without success to dislodge a number of white squatters. The Celilo Fish Committee did not frighten them, as Indian Office employee W. R. Sheldon discovered in 1938 when he investigated Indian complaints against the Cramer family. According to tribal witnesses, the Cramers had erected a cement wall behind their fishing place to prevent water from spilling over their scaffold. The barrier enabled them to reach their site earlier in the season but also diverted the current in such a way that it delayed nearby fishers for two or three weeks, a critical setback when the peak of the salmon runs lasted only a week to ten days. Furthermore, the Indians said, the Cramers had gradually expanded their operations to take over the entire rock where they fished. When Sheldon confronted them, "their attitude, especially at first, was one of bullying or bluffing the matter through." Beyond denying that the wall did any harm, they declared that the state of Oregon had given them permission to fish there and that the real trouble "was caused by various Superintendents failing to keep the Indians within the confines of the Reservations." Sheldon ended the argument with the stern warning that the Cramers would hear from the district attorney. Ten years and one lawsuit later, they were still tussling with their Native neighbors and thumbing their noses at the CFC. In the interim, several Yakama fishers vented their frustration by tossing the Cramers's scaffold into the river, only to end up in court for destruction of property.[43]

Even treaty Indians sometimes disobeyed the CFC. Many younger people ignored traditional rules, which they deemed silly superstitions; others succumbed to greed or served as the agents of meddling whites. All of these factors merged in the case of the Albert brothers, who clashed repeatedly with other fishers and the CFC from the mid-1930s to the early 1940s. In the fall of 1939, a dispute erupted over the ownership of customary fishing sites on Little Ateem Island. At the center of the controversy stood Isaac and Thomas Albert, Yakama enrollees who had started the Portland Fish Company along with several Native partners. Acting on the advice of a Seufert cannery employee, the Portland Fish Company installed cableways to Little Ateem but denied access to nonmembers and even destroyed their competitors' scaffolds. The Celilo Fish Committee revoked its earlier approval of the cables, but the Alberts defied the order and refused to attend any meetings. Bolstered by the support of Seufert's buyers, they also shrugged off a scolding letter from U.S. Attorney Carl C. Donaugh. "Under the law," he told them, "any one of the members of any one of the tribes has as much right to fish on the particular rocks that you fish on as you have. . . . I think that you should be loyal to your Yakima tribe and to the agreements that have been made on behalf of the Yakima people." In 1940, the CFC endorsed this line of reasoning by voting to give all the claimants equal privileges on Little Ateem. Threatened with exclusion if they failed to comply, the Alberts grudgingly agreed to respect the rights of others and to heed Chief Thompson's regulations—for a while.[44]

The committee's long struggle with the Alberts showcased its efforts to enforce traditional law through modern bureaucratic means. In the fall of 1939, as the brothers moved to consolidate their control of Little

Ateem, the CFC promulgated new regulations for "Tribal Fishing Sites." These locations could be privately owned, but the rules stated that all persons using them "must rotate with others who are at hand prepared to fish and who have their own equipment with which to fish." Furthermore, the CFC attempted to favor subsistence over commercial fishing by requiring everyone to yield priority to "Indians desiring to catch fish for their own food." In 1943, following another run-in between the Alberts and Ambrose Whitefoot, the committee passed a second resolution specifying certain locations as "treaty fishing places." At these select sites, all members of the confederated Umatilla, Warm Springs, and Yakama tribes had equal rights to fish on a rotating schedule. The emphasis on reciprocity and sharing reflected traditional Plateau values, but the official designation of "treaty sites" also signaled the growing acceptance of tribal sovereignty and tribal property at the fishery. Although hereditary rights remained intact, there were now places at Celilo Falls where mere membership in a recognized tribe guaranteed the right to fish.[45]

Regardless of CFC rules, many fishers continued to regard their sites as private property. They freely loaned or leased their locations to friends and relatives, and they transferred ownership through informal agreements as well as legal wills. The resulting overlay of claims frequently complicated efforts to settle disputes. For example, shortly before Jake Snidups passed away, he bequeathed his site as a gift to two young brothers from the Moses family. Their trustee, Simon George, used the site in their stead even though it technically belonged to the Yahyowan family, which had given it to Snidups under a lifetime agreement. To further complicate matters, Henry Luton and Walter Speedis asserted rights to fish the site occasionally. The delicate business of accommodating and adjudicating such tangled arrangements vexed CFC members and Indian Office agents alike. "Many places are open for everybody to fish on," reported Clarence Davis in 1941, "and it is quite confusing to me as to what the Fish Committee terms 'ownership' of the places. One time they tell me that all of them are 'tribal' places, and the next time individuals are allowed to claim ownership and management." The dual forces of colonialism and commercialism had thrown the fishery into disarray.[46]

Unable to maintain order on his own, Tommy Thompson could neither dispense with the Celilo Fish Committee nor overcome his distaste for it. On the one hand, the aging salmon chief needed it to reinforce his flagging authority and status at the falls. On the other, it partially usurped his power and yet seemed unable to rein in renegade fishers. His conflicted feelings and cantankerous character made him a gadfly to the tribal delegates. Along with William Yallup, who oversaw fishing on the Washington side of the river, Thompson tried to remain independent. The chiefs generally insisted on issuing their own statements and approving any resolutions made concerning the fisheries at Celilo and Sk'in. In 1939, for example, they authorized the Albert brothers' cableway "in our own right as Chiefs" several weeks before the CFC endorsed it. They also chastised committee members and agency officials for failing to enforce traditional regulations and control visiting Indians. "Quite a few boys from Yakima never obey tribal rule," Thompson charged during the Albert controversy. "I try to tell them and advise them in good way, but they advise me 'if you try kick me off I'll go [to] my superintendent, Mr. Johnson at Yakima and he'll tell me you can't do it.'" Yallup added, "Some people . . . they come in and say: 'I don't care about Columbia River chief, I do my way what I want.' This is not the way it used to be . . . these old people used [to] fish here without trouble." Reservation Indians had changed the rules, they insisted, and now the River People were paying the price.[47]

Although willing to share the fishery in the customary fashion, the river chiefs and their supporters still believed that local Columbia River Indians should take priority at Celilo Falls. To make that case, they appealed to a sense of difference rooted in history, culture, and place. Their ancestors had stayed on the river instead of moving to the reservations. Some had never received allotments or collected tribal benefits. They preferred to live by the "old ways," and they still depended on salmon for their subsistence as well as their limited cash income. Chief Thompson called them "home folk." Reservation residents, even those with definite rights at Celilo, were dubbed "comers."[48] They only visited the falls during the salmon runs and often ignored the traditions that governed the fishery. As Thompson told the CFC in 1940:

> I'm here as poor people [and] have no income like on Reservation—no rental—doing best I could. All that I want for is [to] support my family by fishing, and people who get Government help on Reservation come here to deprive me of my subsistence. . . . [They] have disregarded rulings here as formulated by Committee. Those so disobeying should be sent back to their Reservation.[49]

Thomas K. Yallup went a step further. At a 1944 meeting, he declared "that all River Indians had the preference on all locations and that it was only through good faith that they permitted other Indians to fish on any islands or locations." Such broad statements struck agency officials as bullying and selfish. Only the new field aide, Clarence Davis, tried to view things from the River People's perspective. "By so doing," he wrote, "you can see that they have no real animosity for Yakimas or Umatillas or Warm Springs or Idaho or California Indians—only a desire that these Indians do not entirely deprive them of their living."[50]

Their animosity seemed real enough to comers, and CFC meetings featured regular debates between defenders of individual ownership and advocates of tribal rights. In 1942, for instance, Warm Springs delegate Isaac McKinley started an argument when he proclaimed that visiting fishers should respect the salmon chief and ask his permission to use traditional locations. "You must recognize the descendants of the older people that fish here," he insisted, "and you comers should not disturb." His speech was immediately endorsed by John Whiz, a Yakama enrollee living at Celilo, but other committee members objected to McKinley's posturing. "You must stay home and work on your farm, just like I do," chided Frank Winishut, a fellow Warm Springs delegate. "I work; I never bother in fishing. . . . but I want to be fair. So let us drop all the hatred."[51] Andrew Barnhart agreed that times had changed and the old ways no longer governed the fishery:

I was appointed a fish committeeman from my Umatilla Reservation to protect my tribal rights. I can remember the old people that fished here at Celilo—Wyam Indians. But the white man has come here and ruled your location as a tribal relation . . . this Committee will not determine one individual ownership to one location. But we must rule equal right.[52]

By the 1940s, many comers had embraced the tribal framework established in the treaties, reinforced through decades of litigation, and backed by the Indian Office. For home folk and their reservation allies, however, treaty rights were merely a legal umbrella beneath which traditional rules still applied. "I recognize the treaty relations, and there is [the] Celilo chief," insisted CFC chairman Thomas K. Yallup. "He will tell you where you can fish, then you will claim ownership."[53]

Isaac McKinley's decision to side with the home folk in this dispute suggests that tribal identities remained fluid even in the 1940s. McKinley lashed out at "you comers," yet he had always lived on the Warm Springs reservation, where his parents had taken allotments after leaving Wayám. As a tribal delegate to the CFC, he nominally spoke for the interests of reservation fishers.[54] By presenting himself as one of the home folk, he rejected the government's proposition that enrollment necessarily determined personal identity and group loyalty. Columbia River Indians accepted or rejected such claims depending on the particular issues and persons involved. In 1945, when the tribes began arguing over several public domain islands near Celilo, Chief Thompson strategically aligned himself with the people of Warm Springs against the Umatillas and Yakamas. Addressing a winter meeting at Simnasho, he described the fishery as their mutual inheritance:

As long as I have lived, 80 years, I have been raised at Celilo. My people had lived there before me. . . . All of this time I did not know that Yakima and Umatilla Indians had any fishing places at Celilo. Neither did they have any drying sheds or living places there. The only people who had living places there were the Columbia River Indians, which includes the Warm Springs Indians, who were moved from the Columbia River many years ago.[55]

On other occasions, though, Thompson dismissed individual Warm Springs Indians as unwelcome comers. Three years before the speech at Simnasho, his son Henry had accused Warm Springs member Andrew David of tearing out Thompson's scaffold on Big Island and threatening to give him "a good beating up." In separate statements, Chief Thompson and Chief Yallup demanded David's return to the reservation on the grounds that he had no hereditary rights at Celilo and no regard for the rules. At the falls, insider or outsider status hinged more on personal conduct, family connection, and political interest than on the government's rigid legal categories.[56]

No one better exemplifies the contingent and contested nature of tribal identity than the enigmatic John Whiz. Though allotted and enrolled on the Yakama reservation, Whiz had lived in Celilo Village since 1911 and often represented the Columbia River Indians on the CFC. As a delegate, he joined Chief Thompson in criticizing the behavior of reservation Indians, sometimes going so far as to declare that "the Yakimas, the Umatillas, and the Warm Springs had no right to claim Celilo fishing grounds; none but the Celilo Indians themselves had such right." Even friends and allies thought he talked too much, but he made himself useful to Thompson as an interpreter and a liaison to the Oregon State legislature. During the 1940s, Whiz made numerous trips to Salem to lobby for the River People, helping to secure passage of a law to provide free hunting and fishing licenses to Columbia River Indians. These and other services earned him recognition as one of the home folk. When he overstepped his bounds and placed his own interests ahead of theirs, however, the community reminded him that his membership was conditional.[57]

Whiz soon earned a reputation on both sides of the river for self-promotion, misrepresentation, and malfeasance. To finance his frequent trips, he took up collections from the local population, sometimes in the name of the river chiefs and sometimes in his own right as "spokesman of Columbia River Indians." The money was rarely accounted for, though Whiz always avowed that he had "been working hard for my Indians [*sic*] people." The people he nominally represented also complained that he forged their names on petitions and made false statements to local newspapers. In April 1943, he went too far, reportedly insulting Tommy Thompson and the people of Celilo by saying they "live like dogs." Village residents promptly drafted their own petition to the Yakama agency enumerating Whiz's past transgressions and requesting his expulsion from the village. "We wish to remove him from here," Charley Quintocken added in separate statement, and "send him back to Yakima where he belongs." Whiz's personal stationery notwithstanding, his claim to Columbia River Indian identity had been badly tarnished. Still, he stayed at Celilo and continued to work for the river chiefs until the late 1950s. Ironically, he then moved back to the reservation and became a vocal participant in the same tribal government he had once opposed.[58]

■ ■ ■

Chiefs Thompson and Yallup probably tolerated Whiz's pretensions and periodic abuses because his skills—however tainted by greed and ego—supported their efforts to resist tribal domination. Columbia River Indians resented the assumption that the reservation governments could speak for them, and they worried that federal officials would neglect their interests.[59] Field Agent Davis recognized this defensiveness in 1939, when the Army Corps of Engineers began talks with the tribes regarding in-lieu fishing sites to replace those flooded by the recently completed Bonneville Dam:

> They feel that the residents of the River country havn't [sic] properly been represented in dealings with the War Department—that the Yakimas, the Warm Springs and the Umatillas have been allowed to send in reports to War Department as to what those people want, but that the Indians from Rock Creek, Celilo, Wishram, Spearfish, Hood River, Underwood, etc. have had no chance to voice their wishes in the matter.[60]

This attitude surfaced again during discussions about acquiring additional property around Celilo Village. In 1929, the Indian Office had purchased 7.4 acres of trust land for the use of residents and visiting fishers. Thirteen years later, when tribal delegates and agency officials visited the site to consider expansion plans, CFC member and erstwhile soda pop vendor Henry Charley alleged that they intended to allow "only certain representatives from the Agencies to speak, closing the meeting to others." Charley lived in Hood River, and his enrollment status left him open to the charge that he was in fact Yakama, as Tommy Thompson had described him the summer before. Regardless, like many who deemed themselves home folk, Charley believed that the property belonged to its permanent residents and that they should have more say in determining its future.[61]

Charley's proprietary claim revealed the extent to which Columbia River Indians had come to see themselves as distinct from the recognized tribes. In effect, the people living at Celilo regarded the trust land as their own reservation, even if the Indian Office never classified it as such. Although they hoped to expand it to relieve the cramped and unsanitary conditions in the village, they resisted doing so if that entailed surrendering control to the tribes. In the early 1940s, River Indian leaders balked at proposals to buy another 34.5 acres with tribal funds, which they assumed would give legal title to the tribes. As John Whiz protested to the CFC,

> [The land] had been set aside for the residence and use of members of the Celilo tribe of Indians and Indians from the Columbia River district . . . the visitors from the reservation had no rights on this plot of ground, and if they wanted to purchase more ground for their camps that was alright, but that Columbia River Indians were to occupy the 7.4 acres without molestation by the Reservation Indians.[62]

Whiz withdrew his objection after the chairman informed him that the tribes did not propose to exercise jurisdiction, but others were not so easily convinced. Fearing Yakama influence in particular, Chief Thompson requested a general appropriation from Congress. Chief Yallup seconded the motion, stating that "whenever general funds are used in purchasing the land, then the land shall be for the benefit of everybody." Although the CFC chose to use tribal money regardless, the chiefs continued to press for a place of their own. In 1945, Thompson even wrote to the House of Representatives asking for a separate agency at Celilo with "a competent superintendent to administer it."[63]

Columbia River Indian desires for a separate reservation were ultimately scuttled by tribal disagreements, non-Indian resistance, and shifts in federal policy. Clarence Davis, the Indian Office's field aide in The Dalles, and the agency superintendents supported the idea because it would make Celilo Village easier to administer and provide funding for much-needed services there. In 1944, the Umatilla, Warm Springs, and Yakama tribal councils began discussing the Indian Office's comprehensive plan for the "Wi-Yam Indian Reservation," but issues of jurisdiction inevitably became tangled with the question of fishing rights. The tribes spent years revising and rejecting proposals, and some Columbia River Indians continued to insist that the reservation should be theirs alone. Non-Indian opinion was also divided. Many local residents welcomed the reservation plan as an opportunity to improve a village they saw as a terrible eyesore. State authorities and white fishing interests opposed any change in legal status that would interfere with their access to and regulation of the fishery. As debate dragged into the later 1940s, the waning of the Indian New Deal heralded a national policy shift back toward assimilation and termination of the federal trust relationship with Indian tribes. Reservations were to be done away with, not created afresh. Ultimately, the newly renamed Bureau of Indian Affairs did purchase an additional 34.5 acres of land and began village renovations, but Celilo remained the shared responsibility of the existing Mid-Columbia agencies.[64]

Chief Thompson's failure to obtain a separate land base did not stop Columbia River Indians from attempting to act as an independent political body. Even though many of their people had enrolled in one of the recognized tribes, the river chiefs believed that they could handle their own affairs regardless of state and federal boundaries. In 1941, the residents of Rock Creek sent a petition to the Oregon State legislature requesting that they be notified of and allowed to testify on any bills pertaining to tribal hunting and fishing rights. Over the next several years, John Whiz and other representatives made numerous trips to lobby state and federal agen-

HOME FOLK

187

cies on behalf of the River People.[65] After one such trip in March 1945, Whiz reported that the War Department had no record of any formal tribal leaders on the Columbia River. If they wanted to deal directly with the government, he said, "they would have to establish a record in Washington, D.C., and also in the State Courts, so that such Chiefs would have a standing and be recognized by Federal and State officials."[66]

The river chiefs responded immediately with a formal assertion of independence and sovereignty. On March 20, after two days of discussing "the problem of those [I]ndians living entirely off the Reservation," William Yallup and Frank Slockish gave public statements outlining their authority as the headmen of the Rock Creek and Klickitat Indians, collectively dubbed the "Columbia River Tribe." The signed and notarized document also named their second chiefs, Gus George and Robert Quaempts, along with nine men constituting the "Council men of Columbia River Tribes." Citing their approval as proof of his mandate, Chief Yallup directly challenged the control of the recognized tribes:

> To you white people and my red people I am explaining this and asking my Government for the same power as if I live on the reservation. To be where I will be known by high Government Officials to speak for my people, and I have named my second Chief after me. I have [selected] the General Council of my Council[en], who will be known by both the State and our Government as such. ... Therefor [sic] I do not want any reservation Indians or Council Man to take up any of my Important Matters without my approval.[67]

Frank Slockish, the "Chief of Klickitat River Indians, Columbia River Tribe," followed with a speech linking his separate identity to their traditional way of life: "We are making our story of our food for our children to remember after us. And our children will carry on the way of living on this mother earth. ... I am not living like reservation Indians. I don't have any cattle or sheep or any other stock. We are all living outside of the reservation." Chief Thompson wished to make a similar statement for the Wayáms but decided to wait until he had more of his people present. Although ethnic distinctions remained important, Columbia River Indians now considered themselves a confederated tribe just like those on the reservations. By pulling together as a group, the three chiefs hoped their shadow government might break free and truly stand on its own.[68]

Their growing sense of solidarity and fear of tribal tyranny did influence an abortive effort to reorganize the Celilo Fish Committee along lines more favorable to them. In 1944, after threats of withdrawal from all sides, the committee drafted a new constitution to fix problems in the old bylaws and align them more closely with traditional practice. Unlike the original bylaws, which had not mentioned the River People specifically, the new document gave equal standing to "the Indians known as the Columbia River Indians, who have always resided on the Columbia River, and who are not enrolled at any reservation." Made at the insistence of river leaders, this concession acknowledged their distinct interests and divergent group identity. The role of salmon chief was likewise accorded official status through a provision that vested the powers of enforcement and dispute arbitration with a board of administration composed of one member from each reservation and the headman of Celilo Village, who would serve as its permanent chairman. The tribes failed to ratify the new constitution, however, because it did not address the CFC's perceived bias in favor of the Yakama Nation. Since many Columbia River Indians were enrolled in that tribe, the Umatilla and Warm Springs councils suspected the River Indians' loyalties and insisted that their delegation be composed solely of unenrolled individuals. Try as they might, the River People could not escape the orbit of the recognized tribes.[69]

By 1945, however, the unsustainable arithmetic of the fisheries had transformed their loose group affiliation into an alternative tribal identity. Continually adding people and subtracting salmon at Celilo was bound to create conflict among different user groups. Trapped within colonial categories and thrown into competition with each other, Mid-Columbia Indians divided into separate and sometimes hostile camps. Native people who had once shared the river as an extended family now sought to establish exclusive tribal claims. In doing so, they applied lessons learned through decades of litigation and exposure to federal bureaucracy. If the government treated their fishing rights as a tribal prerogative, equally available to all members, then they must follow suit or risk losing their rights. This legal reorganization of the fisheries placed Columbia River Indians in a difficult situation. Neither truly independent nor fully integrated into the recognized tribes, they struggled to defend their rights and define their place in a system that categorized them as either treaty Indians or non-treaty Indians. Accepting the former label meant acknowledging the authority of the tribal councils. Accepting the latter potentially placed their fishing rights in jeopardy. To solve this dilemma, Columbia River Indians tried to establish a tribal identity of their own.

The emergence of this identity neither severed their connections to the reservations nor precluded their membership in the recognized tribes. Since they lacked official status, Columbia River Indians had to affiliate with one of the Plateau agencies or remain as unenrolled "public domain Indians." Even if they chose not to enroll, most River People still had kinship ties to one or more of the reservations. River dwellers and reservation residents also retained a mutual commitment to the preservation of their treaty rights and their traditional fishing places. Amidst all the infighting at Celilo Falls, there were some moments of solidarity. In 1941 Native fishers showed awareness of their mutual interests as Indians and as workers by threatening a commercial boycott over low fish prices.[70] The strike quickly fizzled when some people decided to sell their catch anyway, but the following year river and reservation residents rejoiced together at the U.S. Supreme Court's favorable decision in *Tulee v. Washington*, which exempted treaty Indians from state fishing licenses.

The tribes' greatest test began in 1945, when Congress announced plans for a massive dam at the foot of Three Mile Rapids. New Deal dams at Bonneville and Grand Coulee had recently destroyed the ancient fisheries at The Cascades and Kettle Falls, displacing numerous river families and aggravating the conflict at Celilo Falls. Fearing the worst if The Dalles Dam became reality, home folk and comers alike appealed for tribal unity. "Wake up and protect the fishery at Celilo," urged Warm Springs representative Isaac McKinley at a mass meeting in April 1945. "The only way is to object to this dam. . . . We are going to [lose] it if we don't do it right. Let's get together to hold our privileges—to keep fishing in the Columbia River."[71] Chief Thompson agreed:

> Both men and women are here, and I think you all know that to-day the white man is planning to do away with the living conditions of both our men and women, and I believe we might say that if this plan of the white man is carried out we will all be made the subjects of charity. And I want you all to consider this question and the right steps to take to cooperate by joining together as a solid force. In that way something worthwhile may be accomplished.[72]

For all their differences, Mid-Columbia Indian fishers knew that they confronted a common fate if the dominant society flooded the falls. Still, the juggernaut of Euro-American progress easily smashed their unified front, and in the deluge that followed Columbia River Indians would struggle to keep their communities and their identity from being submerged.

Our people continue to refuse to leave the river and
abandon our Way of Life and our ancestors. So for the past
30 years we have had to endure dozens of attempts to
intimidate us and force us to leave, *but we remain!*

—MID-COLUMBIA RIVER COUNCIL,
STATEMENT OF UNIFICATION, 1990

7 ■ ■ ■

SUBMERGENCE AND RESURGENCE

At 10:00 a.m. on March 10, 1957, the spillway gates of The Dalles Dam
closed against the current of the Columbia River. Within minutes
the impounded waters began backing toward Celilo Falls, nine
miles upstream, where a crowd watched expectantly from the highway
and surrounding hills. Many of the Indians present refused to believe that
the dam could back up the river far enough to flood the falls. "A lot of us
weren't even worried about it," recalled Jay Minthorn, then an adolescent
boy. "'Naw, that'll never happen.' But then, sure enough, you could begin
to see the change in the water getting into the [Big Eddy] stages." Six hours
later, as a group of Indian women wailed in mourning, the last ripples of
Celilo slipped beneath the surface of its namesake reservoir. William Yallup had passed away in 1955, sparing him the sight of a slackwater pool

where the river once roared, but his friend Tommy Thompson lingered in a nursing home downstream. "There goes my life," he moaned upon hearing the dreaded news. "My people will never be the same."[1]

The dam dealt a crushing blow to the Columbia River Indians and their reservation relations. After a desperate fight to prevent its construction, they could only stare in disbelief as a man-made lake swallowed their ancestral fishing grounds in The Dalles–Celilo reach. The rising waters also flooded some of the oldest continuously inhabited settlements in North America. The ancient community of Wishram, where Lewis and Clark had stopped to trade, ceased to exist with the departure of its few remaining families. By 1957, Celilo Village had been moved three times to accommodate a railroad, a canal, and a highway; the Army Corps of Engineers moved it yet again to make way for the latest manifestation of Euro-American progress. Although a handful of families remained at the new location, sandwiched between the railroad tracks and the steep walls of the gorge, many residents drifted away and the flow of visitors dwindled. Ted Strong, whose family lost its seasonal home, remembered the uncertainty that permeated the village: "I believe that every family was faced with the same questions: Where do we go from here? Every man felt a certain loss of dignity and every woman felt a loss of family security with the disappearance of the fisheries and all of the many fish that would be yielded from these great fisheries." Unless they could afford to buy boats and gillnets, fishermen had to find employment elsewhere. Some took jobs and homes on the reservations or in neighboring towns, as others entered the federal relocation program and sampled life in the city. Those unable to adjust often fell into a cycle of drinking and despair. "I may have the wrong attitude towards life," wrote Umatilla fisherman Jack Abraham to President Dwight D. Eisenhower, "yet when your heritage has been taken away from you; and you are deprived of making a decent livelihood for your family, you wonder if life is worth it."[2]

The waters that flooded ancestral villages and lapped at the riprapped banks of the new reservoir also threatened to submerge Columbia River Indian identity. From the 1940s to the 1990s, River People faced intense pressure to abandon their off-reservation communities and assimilate into the recognized tribes, if not into the dominant society. They were simultaneously pushed from the river by the dams and pulled into the tribal orbit by a variety of incentives associated with enrollment. Financial settlements with the Corps and per capita payments from new tribal industries promised some relief from poverty, and federal and tribal attorneys offered assistance in the mounting legal battle over treaty fishing rights. As the struggle between states' rights and tribal sovereignty climaxed in the 1960s and 1970s, however, the strident activism of Columbia River Indians collided with the rising nationalism of the recognized tribes. Tribal governments, determined to exercise their sovereign powers, issued fishing regulations that threatened the traditional autonomy and spirituality of the River People. The ensuing clashes accentuated the sense of difference they had constructed between themselves and the recognized tribes. By the mid-1980s, when David Sohappy and other "renegades" went to prison for illegal fishing, the River People had revitalized their shadow government and their claim to a distinct tribal identity.

■ ■ ■

Contemporary federal and tribal officials typically regard the Columbia River Indian claim to tribal status with skepticism because most River People are now enrolled in the treaty tribes. Many had nominally accepted membership during the allotment era, but the decades following the Indian Reorganization Act of 1934 (IRA) saw a renewed campaign to bring them all into the tribal fold. It began with the bureaucratic realization that no one knew exactly how many Indians still lived in the shadowy spaces between the reservations. As the recognized tribes prepared to vote on whether to adopt new constitutions under the IRA, agency superintendents scrambled to distribute ballots to all eligible members within their respective jurisdictions. At the same time, they struggled to administer the property of public domain allottees, many of whom had since passed away without leaving legal wills to guide probate proceedings. Finding potential voters and heirs proved exceedingly difficult when agency employees had no accurate census of the off-reservation population. In 1937, the year after responsibility for The Dalles and Vancouver allotments temporarily passed to the Umatilla agency, Superintendent Omar Babcock was "still unable to state definitely how many Indians live along the Columbia River who are not enrolled anywhere else." The Yakama agency had never conducted a census either and could only provide a partial list of Dalles allottees from its files. Fortunately for Babcock, the onerous task of compiling a register of Columbia River Indians soon fell to the new field agent, Clarence Davis, who assumed his post in 1939.[3]

Although diligent and devoted to his job, Davis immediately stumbled across the numerous slippages within the Indian Office's seemingly clear system of tribal classification. Simply counting the number of Indians residing off reservation was hard enough. As visiting doctor H. U. Sanders observed of Celilo's population in 1940:

> The people are like the stars in the heavens. Now you see them; now you don't. Today there may be five hundred; tomorrow there may be only two hundred because the others have all gone to a festival or berry picking. On first thought one might think a census would be of great value, but on second thought it appears that the census would be practically useless by the time it was completed because so many of the ones enumerated would be gone, giving place to entirely new ones, who may or may not return the next year.[4]

Attempting to fix these stars in recognized tribal constellations promised to be even more frustrating. As Davis tried to corral the heavens in a tri-colored card index, he found that words such as "enrollment" and "residence" could not be easily defined in a universe where individuals continually moved and crossed paths like restless comets.

In January 1941 the new field agent confessed his confusion and asked his superior at the Yakama agency for clarification:

> The instructions say that the roll is based on enrollment and not on residence. If enrollment means enrollment on a reservation, does it follow that

no Yakima Indians, for instance, (ones enrolled at Yakima) should appear in this census I am about to take? If so, why did Mr. Babcock include, for instance, Tom Billy of the Yakima tribe, and Indian Spencer of the Warm Springs tribe? If Indians enrolled in one of the reservations, such as Abraham Showaway, for instance, is not to be included, would his wife, Minnie Wesley, who was born and raised at Tenino on the River, be included in the River census roll without mention of the name of Abraham Showaway who is or should be the head of the family? Does the caption "Residence" . . . mean that I would have to obtain the names of all Indians born on the mid-Columbia River (this area) who are now residents of a reservation, some of whom have become enrolled elsewhere such as Sampson Tulee and John Culpus, and ascertain where they now live, etc.?[5]

Superintendent M. A. Johnson did his best to answer these and other queries with bureaucratic precision. Although admitting past mistakes, such as the inclusion of Tom Billy on the Yakama roll, he assured Davis that further errors could be avoided by listing only those people not currently enrolled on any reservation. Still, Davis had questions. Did the term "reservation" embrace public domain allotments under agency jurisdiction? Should children of mixed European and Indian heritage be placed on tribal rolls if born away from the reservation? What of people from distant tribes, such as the Osage and Cherokee, who approached him "[wanting] to become identified as Indians again?" How should he identify the numerous individuals whom, it had now become apparent, were enrolled on more than one reservation under different names? The Yakama agency's palette of three colors was hardly sufficient to capture the rainbow of possibilities that arced between the reservations. By 1942, the Indian Office had abandoned the cumbersome card system altogether, though Davis doggedly persevered in creating separate census rolls for the Oregon and Washington sides of the river.[6]

The work carried Davis into communities that remained wary of outsiders as well as physically and culturally distant from centers of federal and tribal power. Columbia River Indians had always been suspicious of census takers, and some probably wondered what the busy white man would do with the information he collected. Their reticence was often compounded by cultural and linguistic differences that hindered Davis's efforts to gather the required data. Especially in the area around Rock Creek, he had to rely on interpreters to communicate with some families. Even then, many people could not provide their exact birth dates, enrollment status, or proof of legal marriage. Davis admitted early in the process: "There is about only one optimistic thing about my taking this census, I believe I know where all of the Indians in this area live when they are at home." Within a year, however, his frequent personal visits and conscientious advocacy earned the trust of many River People. They even began to seek him out, as Irene Looney George did in 1944, asking to be "taken up on some census roll." World War II had helped make them "census-conscious," Davis reported, as the U.S. military required documentary evidence to substantiate claims for allotments and "other possible emoluments of widows in case of loss of the husband while in Service." Although inclusion in a reservation census did not convey tribal benefits, which depended on membership rather than mere residence, "census consciousness" smoothed the way for the enrollment drive that followed.[7]

By the mid-1940s, several forces had converged to convince reservation leaders that they needed to clarify their tribal rolls and enrollment procedures. On the Yakama reservation, which decisively rejected the IRA, some councilmen alleged that the majority of votes in favor of the legislation had come from off-reservation members with dubious tribal connections. Suspicions regarding acculturated "half-breeds" grew as the Yakama Nation prepared to make its first per capita payment from reservation timber sales. In early 1945, anticipating an avalanche of fresh membership applications, the Yakama General Council voted to request special enrollment legislation from Congress, which enacted it the following year along with a law establishing the Indian Claims Commission (ICC). Although that tribunal took twenty-five years to fulfill its mandate, ICC proceedings raised the prospect of further per capita payments by providing a means for tribes to obtain monetary redress for lands and resources taken without just compensation. The same issues prompted action on the Warm Springs reservation, where even Tommy Thompson sought enrollment after per capita payments from timber sales began in 1943. Three years later, the Warm Springs Tribal Council established an enrollment committee to vote on applications. The constitution and bylaws of the Confederated Tribes of the Umatilla Indian Reservation (CTUIR), approved in 1949, contained a similar provision for evaluating new members. As announcements and instructions circulated in off-reservation communities, Columbia River Indians could see both tangible reasons to enroll in the recognized tribes and a clear procedure for doing so.[8]

The shift toward tribal self-determination during the Indian New Deal further underscored the importance of enrollment. As tribal governments became increasingly assertive and bureaucratic in exercising their sovereign powers, Indians learned that political rights and legal representation now hinged on tribal membership. At the February 1945 meeting of the Yakama General Council, for instance, Virgil Hunt asserted that he could vote on council matters because he had inherited property on the reservation, though he had not enrolled and did not live there. The new superintendent, L. W. Shotwell, curtly reminded him that only enrolled Yakamas could vote in general council. Resident Walter Underwood promptly affirmed this point of order with the comment that "outside persons who inherit should not vote and overrule the members of the tribe." A month later, during a joint session of the General and Tribal councils, a delegation from the river community of Lyle appeared to request tribal assistance in defending their treaty rights against continual state interference.[9] In 1944, Klickitat men had again been arrested for fishing in their namesake tributary, where the Washington State Department of Fisheries permitted only a limited sport season to conserve spawning salmon. One of the defendants, Caples Dave, complained that the U.S. Attorney had refused to represent them and "this Superintendent [Shotwell] had stated unless [there] were enrolled Indians involved in that particular case, he was in no position to extend any help to Public Domain Indians." Shotwell immediately objected to Dave's remarks, insisting he had merely noted that their case would be stronger if it involved an enrolled member. Tribal leaders had to decide whether they would spend their precious financial and legal capital on behalf of people who technically did not belong to the Yakama Nation.[10]

The ensuing discussion spoke volumes about the competing conceptions of identity that tugged at Columbia River Indians during the enrollment drive. The members of the Klickitat delegation still recognized their traditional chief, Frank Slockish, who sat on the council of the self-styled Columbia River Tribe alongside Tommy Thompson and William Yallup. Slockish's grandfather had signed the 1855 treaty that established the Yakama Nation, but much of the Slockish family had never moved to the reservation. Many other off-reservation Klickitats had yet to enroll there, and the delegates from Lyle referred to the "Klickitat Tribe" as if it was still distinct from the Yakama Nation. Eagle Seelatsee, the chairman of the fourteen-member Tribal Council, listened sympathetically before expressing his understanding of the relationship: "The Klickitat Tribe are a member of the 14 bands of Indians, known as the Yakima Nation, [and] we should protect our treaty rights." Councilman John Sockzihi added, "I consider Public Domain Indians as a member of the Yakima Nation as they are descendants of the 14 bands of Indians banded together to make [the] Yakima Nation. Therefore the council is willing to help." The Legislative Committee drafted a resolution asking the state government to set aside the recent ruling against the Lyle fishermen, as well as authorizing the use of tribal funds to defend them in future cases. Membership had its benefits, and several Klickitat delegates soon asked to have their families added to the Yakama census roll. As time would tell, however, receiving assistance from tribal governments meant accepting their authority.[11]

Tribal council minutes from this period also reveal the ambivalence with which some reservation residents viewed "Public Domain Indians." As it had during the allotment era, the issue of enrollment stirred complex and controversial questions about race and residence. Some councilmen worried that pending timber sales and tribal claims would attract a mob of "breeds" and "aliens" intent on grabbing a share of the money. Leery of outsiders who had never lived on the reservation or had moved away, all of the tribes set blood quantum requirements of one-quarter degree or higher to qualify for membership, though not without heated debate. Columbia River Indians generally cleared that bar with ease because of their familial ties to the reservations and their reputation as traditionalists, which spared them the scrutiny that more accultur- ated applicants often faced. As Yakama councilman Wilbur Meninick declared in 1945, "We should enroll the Indians from the Public Domain, and protect them from this reservation because they are full blood Indi- ans." The initial draft of the Yakima Enrollment Act required that mem- bers be born on the reservation, however, and some tribal leaders wanted to exclude people who had not taken allotments there or had sold them and left tribal lands. Such individuals were "not Yakima Indians" in the eyes of some residents because they had seemingly chosen to sever their tribal ties. River People might be unequivocally Indian, but their alle- giance to the recognized tribes remained open to question.[12]

Bonds of blood, culture, and law ultimately kept Columbia River Indi- ans in the pool of prospective tribal members. In March 1946, shortly before Congress passed it as Public Law 706, the Yakama General Coun- cil amended the enrollment bill to avoid disinheriting and disenfranchis- ing off-reservation families with demonstrable kinship connections to the confederated tribes. Anyone descended from a reservation allottee or public domain allottee and still living within the Yakama Nation's ceded area would be eligible for enrollment; those residing outside tribal terri- tory could be adopted after presenting a satisfactory family history. Con- troversy continued for years, with charges of discrimination and demands for repeal flying from various quarters, but most Columbia River Indians met the stipulations set by the Yakama Nation and the other recognized tribes. There remained some perplexing questions about their tribal affil- iations. Because residents of Celilo Village lived outside the official ceded area of the Yakama Nation, they could not enroll until the tribe further amended Public Law 706. Many applicants had mixed aboriginal heri- tage—the "blood" of many tribes in their veins—and some had received two allotments or had inherited land on multiple reservations, which potentially qualified them for membership in more than one recognized tribe. Consequently, as enrollment committees picked apart the skein of relationships that composed Native identity, unaffiliated Columbia River

Indians were asked to choose one thread over the others, to select the tribe that supposedly defined them.[13]

■ ■ ■

For all the parties concerned, enrollment questions acquired fresh urgency as the shadow of The Dalles Dam crept over the villages and fisheries between Three Mile Rapids and Celilo Falls. In 1950, despite a continual stream of Indian protest, Congress authorized the dam's construction and ordered the Army Corps of Engineers to negotiate financial settlements with the treaty tribes to mitigate the projected economic damage. Tribal leaders initially wanted none of it. As Sam Kash Kash of the CTUIR told Army Corps officials in 1952, "You can bring on your money with wagon loads, hay rack loads, you'll never satisfy my people for the loss that they are going to take in the construction of these dams."[14] The river chiefs also objected, speaking of treaty rights but staking out a position separate from the recognized tribes. "We will have nothing to depend on for our living which the reservation tribes already have," argued the Columbia River Council in one of many petitions opposing the project. "Therefor [sic] they should not be ahead to compromise for the settlement of The Dalles dam. . . . We do not want to agree for no payment in money." One by one, though, the recognized tribes began to deal with the Corps. Columbia River Indians who fished at Celilo and had not yet enrolled anywhere became coveted pawns in the compensation game, because they could increase the amount of money their chosen tribe received. The pressure to pick one or another mounted as enrollment deadlines loomed, often producing choices that seemed arbitrary and mercenary rather than genuine and heartfelt. As Willie John Culpus testified in 1950, "I am a Columbia [River] Indian. I have land in Yakima and Warm Springs. Whichever reservation comes to settlement [first], that is where I will be enrolled."[15]

His declaration reveals the continuing fluidity of Native identity even as the federal government worked to contain and regulate it like the restless current of the Columbia River. Culpus never considered himself "a true Yakima Indian" even though his parents had taken allotments on that reservation. Born on the Washington side of the river near Maryhill, he spent most of his life moving between his own home at Celilo and his wife's house at Rock Creek. In aboriginal terms, he could claim to be either Wayám or Qmitpa. The Bureau of Indian Affairs considered him a Yakama because his parents had been allotted there, though Culpus believed that he had equal rights to membership in the Warm Springs tribe. He called himself a Columbia River Indian, affirming a new identity that overlapped with persistent village affiliations and often trumped official tribal designations. Less than a year before he prepared to pick a tribe, he told the Celilo Fish Committee "with quite some force that Warm Springs and other Reservation Indians . . . should not bother the so-called Mid-Columbia Indians; that the Mid-Columbia Indians didn't go to their reservations and bother them, and why should the so-called Reservation Indians come to the Columbia." Clearly, being *in* a recognized tribe could still differ from being *of* it.[16]

Ignoring such complexities, the Army Corps of Engineers followed the lead of the courts and the BIA in treating the Celilo fishery and Indian fishing rights as tribal possessions. "Since the treaties were made with the tribes after negotiation with their chiefs and headmen," explained District Engineer Thomas H. Lipscomb in January 1954, "it is well established that the special privileges contained in the treaties are tribal privileges and any benefits under the treaties accrue to individual members only through their tribal organizations." The benefit in this case was the $23 million value the Corps attached to Celilo Falls, based on a four-year census of the fishery that weighed only its economic return and underestimated the actual tribal harvest. Having thus "determined the size of the compensation pie," in the words of historian Katrine Barber, Corps negotiators sat down with each tribe separately to determine its share. This divide-and-conquer strategy badly aggravated intertribal divisions over control of the fishery. By the early 1950s, the Celilo Fish Committee had nearly ceased to function amid persistent charges of Yakama bias.

Demands for its complete reorganization flared into bitter squabbling as each tribe jockeyed to establish its own rights to Celilo over and against the claims of others. They managed to settle the issue without going to court, which none of the tribes wanted due to the length and uncertainty of legal proceedings, but the Corps frequently exploited their disagreements to its advantage.[17]

Columbia River Indians and other unenrolled individuals got shoved to the sidelines in this bruising, four-way scrum between the recognized players. The Yakama Nation pushed hardest, arguing that it had sole rights to Celilo Falls because the Warm Springs tribes had supposedly forfeited theirs in 1865 and the fishery lay outside the official ceded area of the Umatilla confederation. Corps negotiators manipulated the smaller tribes' legal insecurities to compel settlements in 1953, whereby the Warm Springs accepted $4,451,874 and the Umatillas received $4,616,971. Yakama representatives criticized their early capitulation for undermining further opposition to the dam, but they conceded defeat a year later after securing the lion's share of $15,019,640. None of the other tribes believed the Nez Perces should receive compensation, as a 1933 federal court decision had denied their fishing rights at Celilo, but the Corps agreed to pay them $2.8 million. If distributed on a per capita basis, the dam settlements promised to yield each tribal member more than $3,000. Most of the remaining unenrolled Indians took this bait, as the Corps and the tribes expected they would, but some diehards either refused to settle or fought to secure compensation in their own right.[18]

Columbia River Indian attempts to negotiate as an independent tribe struck a series of bureaucratic and political snags rooted in their unofficial status. In early 1953, a group of approximately 327 river residents, calling themselves the Mid-Columbia River Tribe of Indians, hired the Portland law firm of Easley, Whipple & McCormick to represent them in discussions with the Army Corps of Engineers. To their dismay, the Corps would not meet with their attorneys until the BIA approved a legal contract, which it refused to do because the Mid-Columbia River Tribe lacked federal recognition. According to Director E. Morgan Pryse of the Portland Area Office, the BIA had never acknowledged any such tribe because its members were "on the whole descendants of the Indians who negotiated and executed the treaties in 1855 under which the Warm Springs, Umatilla, and Yakima Reservations were established." The fact that some 200 of the claimants were already enrolled (mostly in the Yakama Nation) further undermined their case, as the majority had a stake in the ongoing tribal negotiations. They could not be paid twice, and from the BIA's perspective their enrollment in one tribe precluded their membership in another, recognized or otherwise. Columbia River Indians were "a non-existent tribe," in Pryse's opinion, a shadow without substance that had no business darkening his door.[19]

Regardless, lead attorney Norman Easley pressed for approval of the contract and tried to vindicate his clients' claim to a distinct identity. He began with the plain, procedural argument that BIA precedent allowed claims contracts with unrecognized tribes. Furthermore, Easley contended, Columbia River Indians had a constitutional right as American citizens "to form associations of their own" apart from the tribal organizations established by treaty. "But more than that," his appeal concluded, "these Indians identify themselves as and believe themselves to be Mid-Columbia River Indians, and have so identified themselves for many years, with common interests separate and distinct from any of the three organized tribes." Although conceding that most of his clients had enrolled in one of those groups, Easley explained that "the enrollees believe themselves not properly represented by the tribal councils and legal representatives of the organized tribes." On the contrary, they distrusted reservation leaders and did "not believe that they would be fairly treated in the loss of their fishing rights if forced to seek compensation through the organized tribes." Here was a primary marker of Columbia River Indian identity, jutting from the doomed rocks of Celilo like the spars of a fishing scaffold. The chiefs and council of the Mid-Columbia River Tribe did not speak for all off-reservation Indians, but they insisted on speaking for themselves whether the BIA wished to hear it or not. Easley's firm promptly forwarded an amended contract to Washington,

DC, where the Mid-Columbia River Tribe planned to open a second front in the halls of Congress.[20]

Henry Thompson, Willie John Culpus, and John Whiz presented the case for a separate settlement at a hearing of the Senate Committee on Appropriations in May 1953. Whiz, the most fluent English speaker, read into the record a lengthy statement from their attorney reiterating their distrust of the tribal councils and their opposition to the settlements reached by the Warm Springs and Umatilla tribes. Ironically, in seeking to exclude those groups, the Mid-Columbia Indians aligned their claims with those of the Yakamas. Revising the fishery's history yet again, their statement insisted that the Yakama Nation could share in the $23 million settlement because it was composed "in part, of Indians descendant from the tribes, bands, and groups of river fishermen on the north shore of the Columbia." Nevertheless, the Mid-Columbia River Tribe sought its own monetary judgment because its members lived around Celilo and had "the most to lose as a result of the construction of the dam." Although the majority had enrolled in the Yakama Nation, they disliked the plan for per capita payments and feared discrimination at the hands of the tribal council. "The problem arises out of the inability of the engineers to look beyond the artificiality of enrollment," their statement suggested. "We perceive no practical difficulty in separating these nonreservation enrollees from the Yakima Tribe and treating them as members of the Mid-Columbia River Tribe of Indians." Easley's firm even proposed an amendment to the appropriations bill that would enable the Army Corps to negotiate with them, but Congress already had an answer for the question Henry Thompson left floating in the air: "When the dam goes in, who is going to take care of my Columbia River people?" The recognized tribes would, or they would have to fend for themselves as individuals.[21]

They could not have chosen a less opportune moment to make a bid for official recognition. After World War II, federal Indian policy again veered back toward assimilation, this time in the name of freeing Native Americans from government supervision. In 1950, under pressure from Congress to prune expenditures, the BIA closed The Dalles field office and reassigned Clarence Davis, robbing off-reservation Indians of a crucial ally. Legislative steps to terminate the federal trust relationship began in August 1953 with House Concurrent Resolution 108, authorizing individual bills to abrogate treaties and cut off services to targeted groups. Two weeks later, Congress took another swipe at tribal sovereignty through Public Law 280, which enabled states to exercise civil and criminal jurisdiction over reservations within their borders. Policymakers and bureaucrats were thus focused on "getting out of the Indian business" rather than opening new tribal franchises when Senator Wayne Morse (R-Oregon) introduced a bill providing for compensation to "those individual Indians not enrolled in any recognized tribe, but who through domicile at or in the immediate vicinity of the [Dalles Dam] reservoir and through custom and usage are found to have an equitable interest in the fishery." The measure passed in July as Public Law 153. It did not permit the Mid-Columbia River Tribe to negotiate as a group, however, and a subsequent bill to grant that authority died under suspicions of a ploy for double payment. Columbia River Indians could either go it alone against the Army Corps or throw in their lot with one of the recognized tribes.[22]

Following a spate of failed lawsuits, about forty unenrolled individuals reached settlements for roughly the same amount that tribal members had received. Some pursued this option because they could not meet tribal enrollment requirements. Others took the advice of private attorneys and tried to hold out for more money, hoping they could extract both the full value of the fishery and their personal property from the government. The Corps drove hard bargains, though, pressuring people with carrot-and-stick tactics reminiscent of the treaty talks. The agency's chief negotiator, Percy M. Othus, avoided meeting with groups and allegedly harassed vulnerable individuals. According to Irene Brunoe, a self-identified Mid-Columbia River Indian and a lifelong resident of Celilo, Othus and Warm Springs Superintendent Jasper Elliott visited her home on several occasions to demand that she "sign off [her] fishing rights for $3,750." Although she could barely read and asked to wait until her husband could be present, they alternately pressed for her signature and urged her to enroll in one of the recognized tribes. Easley's firm would lose in court, Othus assured her, and even if they won, her family "wouldn't get half as much as the lawyer would." If she would just sign, Brunoe "could have a new car, new clothes for the children and steaks every day for all the family; when I told Mr. Othus I could earn one-half of the $3,750.00 in one year on the island, he got pretty sore." Othus later denied Brunoe's account of these meetings, but stories like hers hardened the determination of some Columbia River Indians to resist any settlement.[23]

Chief Tommy Thompson, the head of the Mid-Columbia River Tribe, was among those who refused to take any money. By 1955, he had lived about a hundred years, almost as long as the treaty his uncle Stockely had signed to preserve Wayám access to Celilo Falls. Thompson resented the recognized tribes for selling out the fishery and forcing his people to move yet again. Although his second wife, Flora, later accepted Corps money to help defray the costs of his large funeral, she gleefully recalled the spirited rebuff the ailing chief gave to government officials shortly before his death in 1959:

> Different engineers came and even the judge was in this, [and] the superintendents. Last one that came [said], "I want the chief to sign this. I brought the judge along, Judge Wilson in The Dalles." Chief was lying on the bed over there. He says, "May I ask how old you are?" Colonel Parker, he says, "40 years." "Oh, you just a little boy. Now you want to buy my fishing? I'm not going to sign." . . . I was standing right there and I says, "Well, Colonel Parker, there's your answer. You're not going to get him to negotiate with you and I'm not going to persuade him either. . . . You tell your engineers, colonels never to come to interfere with him no more. That's the last big word he gave you—no, I'm not going to negotiate. So you remember that." You can pay off the reservation Indians but they were not eligible. They weren't entitled to it.[24]

The subsequent distribution of the tribal settlements on a per capita basis further angered Columbia River Indians as well as reservation fishers, since it gave equal shares to people who could not catch a salmon to save their lives. The memory still rankles with Chief Johnny Jackson, who intentionally stayed away from Celilo Falls on that fateful day so that he would not have to watch it drown. The per capita shares amounted to "just a drop in the bucket," he remarked in 1999, and thanks to tribal disbursement, "a lot of people got paid for Celilo that didn't even have a right to get anything from it."[25]

The feelings of loss and betrayal associated with the dam settlements infused a broader Columbia River Indian critique of tribal enrollment. Today, River People often insist that the federal government duped them into enrolling. As the Mid-Columbia River Council (MCRC) declared in a 1990 statement, "The Army Corps of Engineers and the Bureau of Indian Affairs worked together to trick and confuse the Indian people. The Enrollment Act was passed and the tribes on the reservations were used to try and force people off the river." Tribal leaders tend to regard such talk as conspiratorial and hypocritical, yet it fairly reflects the lingering suspicions and mixed feelings that Columbia River Indians have about tribal membership. In some cases, the allegation of deceit reflects the fact that minor children could be enrolled by legal guardians without their knowledge or consent. In others, the charge simply expresses frustration with tribal governance. Although the incentives to enroll may have been real and appealing, and the decision to do so made under duress, the long-term results have often seemed disappointing to people whose ancestors refused to be herded onto reservations "like a little pig or cattle," in the words of Ella Jim. Wilbur Slockish, Jr., the current Klickitat chief, recalled in 2000 that his grandfather stayed out of tribal politics because "they were pretty much following the government teachings that as elected officials, they had supreme authority to say what goes . . . they can do what they want regardless of your opinion." The recognized tribes seem too eager to compromise, too willing to sacrifice what little the River People have left. As Slockish quipped after a 2006 meeting between Yakama officials and the U.S. Forest Service, "Every time somebody tries to represent me, I lose something." That is why, despite his enrollment card, he insists on representing himself as a Klickitat and a Columbia River Indian.[26]

■ ■ ■

Slockish lived on his family's allotment along the Klickitat River from 1944 to 1954—the peak of the enrollment drive—and his parents experienced the loss of autonomy that followed political integration into the recognized tribes. During the first ten years of Slockish's youth, Klickitat fishers endured numerous closed seasons and state citations on the stream that provided much of their subsistence. In 1950, five years after the Lyle delegation asked the Yakama Nation for legal support, a group of local Indians led by Cecil Wesley concluded their own agreement with the Washington State Department of Fisheries. Significantly, it allowed them to fish at their traditional sites and establish their own enforcement committee. The accord folded in a matter of months, however, after Fisheries Director Alvin Anderson died in the spring of 1951. Fisherman Clefren Dave hoped that Anderson's successor would be "the same type of man to deal with, and listen to reason & agree with us Indians that lived along this river all our live[s] where our ancestor[s] were raised on Salmon and many other game & birds." But Robert Schoettler was not the same kind of man. He preferred to deal with the Yakama Tribal Council, which unanimously approved the state's fishery management program in April 1951 after finding it "in the best interests of the Tribe." The local Klickitat council proposed its own plan and challenged Yakama jurisdiction, demanding that "any negotiations for regulations should be made directly with the Klickitats and not through the Fish Committee of the Yakima Tribe." In their view, the best interests of the Yakama Nation did not necessarily coincide with the best interests of Columbia River Indians, even if their names appeared on the tribal roll.[27]

The off-reservation Klickitats grew more disenchanted as their nominal government cooperated in enforcing and expanding state oversight of their fishery. Although the local Indians wished to abide by the compact made with the late "Swede" Anderson, the Yakama council accepted increasingly restrictive agreements that cut back fishing seasons, prohibited certain gear, and curbed the sale of salmon. The tribe also stood aside while the Fisheries Department "corrected" the Klickitat River's lower falls by blasting them away—along with traditional fishing stations—to ease the migration of salmon and steelhead bound for state-run hatcheries. Klickitat leaders objected and requested meetings with Fisheries personnel, but Director Schoettler acknowledged only the Yakama Tribal Council and its fish committee. In turn, tribal officials assisted state authorities in policing the Klickitats, alternately intervening to save them from prosecution and scolding them for tarnishing tribal credibility. During the 1952 season, when six local Indians got caught dipnetting on closed days, fish committee chairman Wilson Charley urged them to consider their tribal loyalties and obligations: "You should remember that your violations are not entirely against the State of Washington but that you are acting against the Yakima Tribe. . . . We feel sure that you do not want to violate the tribal rights in any way." Arrests continued throughout the 1950s, however, earning the off-reservation Klickitats a reputation for poaching in both state and tribal offices. "They are getting out of hand," charged one Fisheries employee in 1954. "When these Klickitats go on a spree, they really get unruly," said another. In language reminiscent of the reservation period, Columbia River Indians were again being described as "renegades" unwilling to keep the agreements their appointed leaders had made.[28]

The flooding of The Dalles-Celilo reach in 1957 graphically reminded river and reservation people of their common interests, but it did not end the controversy over who owned fishing sites and controlled fishing rights. In separate negotiations, the Army Corp's Realty Division had provided minimal compensation to individuals for scaffolds, drying sheds, and other personal property destroyed or displaced by the rising waters of Lake Celilo. Among those paid were Ambrose and Minnie Whitefoot, Yakama enrollees who in 1955 received $1,050 for their shed and outhouse, but who also hoped to recoup personal damages for the loss of their fishing sites and fish-packing business. The Corps dismissed their claim and the BIA refused to intervene because of the Yakama Nation's plans to distribute the tribal settlement on a per capita basis. Like many fishing families, the Whitefoots considered this plan patently unfair, as it gave them far less than the full value of their six hereditary stations while granting equal shares to people who had lost nothing and therefore had "no compensable rights." They took their grievances to federal court in October 1957, seeking an injunction against the per capita distribution unless they received at least $70,000 for their abridged rights and $6,116 for their private property. Four years later, *Ambrose Whitefoot and Minnie Whitefoot v. United States* reached the U.S. Court of Claims, only to be dismissed on the familiar grounds that fishing sites constituted tribal property. Theirs would not be the last challenge to that assumption or to the tribal oversight that followed from it.[29]

The material and financial losses suffered by the Whitefoots signified the wider unraveling of Native economic and social networks woven during the previous century. Following the completion of The Dalles Dam and the inundation of upstream fisheries, both the salmon runs and the Indian share of the catch dropped to new lows. Most tribal families could no longer support themselves by fishing, which now required expensive investments in boats and gillnets, so many people stopped coming to the river altogether. The area's resident population also thinned and dispersed as the villages upstream from the dam lost their grip on the riverbank. Although the reservoir never fully covered the site of Spearfish (formerly Wishram), where a state park sits today, the village's fourteen families had to relocate with minimal assistance from the Corps. Under its strict criteria for residency, only eight households qualified for replacement homes, most of which were built miles downriver or up in the barren hills above the deserted village. Their owners faced uncertain futures. Old and in poor health, Willie and Annie Palmer hoped to eke out a living on the lease income they received from reservation allotments, since Willie could no longer fish. The families of George and Louis Cloud planned to move in nearby despite the lack of a reliable water supply. Community ties survived in attenuated form, but some seasonal residents retired to the reservations for good after their summer homes ceased to exist.[30]

Celilo Village escaped a similar end only because concerned citizens lobbied the government to let its residents "remain beside the bones of their ancestors." In 1955, after the Daughters of the American Revolution and other civic organizations sent petitions to Congress, the Army Corps grudgingly agreed to cover the costs of relocating families to the landward side of the state highway and the railroad tracks that bisected the community. Many residents disliked the new site, however, because it took them one step further from the river and forced them to dodge both trains and traffic to reach the water. Wasco County and BIA officials disliked the idea of reconstituting the village at all. Local administrators feared it would be an unsightly drain on county welfare rolls and difficult to provide with services. The Bureau preferred to move residents into nearby towns or distant cities, in keeping with the urban relocation program that accompanied federal termination policy. To encourage dispersal, the Celilo relocation committee offered $500 bonuses to families that moved at least ten miles away, and it prohibited unmarried couples and households with children from staying in the village. Ultimately, only five of thirty-six eligible families chose to remain there. As the rest scattered to new homes on the reservations or along the river, the community ties that affirmed Columbia River Indian identity became more strained than ever before.[31]

■ ■ ■

Some families migrated downstream to five "in-lieu" fishing sites the Army Corps had belatedly built to replace traditional locations flooded by Bonneville Dam. In 1945 the federal government had promised to purchase and improve roughly 400 acres at six locations for tribal fishing and camping; by 1960, the Corps had developed only four, amounting to less than forty acres. That year, six families moved into the drying sheds

Facing page: In-lieu Fishing Sites Present in 1970. Adapted from map of Columbia River Treaty Fishing Access Sites, U.S. Army Corps of Engineers, Portland District, no date.

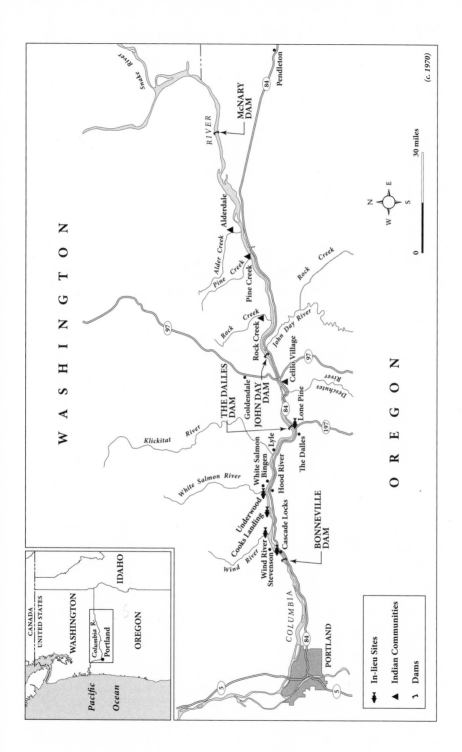

WASHINGTON

Snake River

McNARY DAM

84

Pendleton

RIVER

Alderdale

Alder Creek

Pine Creek

Pine Creek

Rock Creek

97

Rock Creek

Rock Creek

John Day River

Celilo Village

97

THE DALLES DAM

Goldendale

JOHN DAY DAM

Deschutes River

84

Lone Pine

Klickitat River

White Salmon

Bingen

Lyle

The Dalles

197

White Salmon River

Hood River

OREGON

Underwood

Cooks Landing

Cascade Locks

BONNEVILLE DAM

Wind River

Stevenson

Wind River

COLUMBIA

84

PORTLAND

5

5

N
W E
S

0   30 miles

CANADA
UNITED STATES

WASHINGTON

IDAHO

Columbia R.

Portland

OREGON

Pacific Ocean

In-lieu Sites

Indian Communities

Dams

(c. 1970)

at Lone Pine, within sight of The Dalles Dam and the weathered Indian Shaker church where Sam Williams had once preached. More than a dozen other families settled farther downstream at Underwood, Cooks (later called Cook's Landing), and Wind River. They endured awful living conditions because the sites had not been designed for year-round occupation. As fishing rights activist Randy Settler recalled of his childhood at Lone Pine, "We didn't have electricity. We did not have running water. . . . We froze in winter, roasted in summer." The Corps and the BIA refused to make improvements because they opposed the creation of permanent communities there. Johnny Jackson, whose family lived at Underwood, later explained why people refused to leave: "When they built The Dalles Dam and they finished the dam, they felt all the people would probably move away and go back to the reservation. They failed to realize that a lot of us were from that [area], we lived here, we were always here. We lived here all our lives from generation to generation. And fishing was our life, a way of fishing and taking care of the land."[32]

Their determination to keep their homes on the bank and their nets in the water turned these families into both champions and challengers of tribal treaty rights. During the early 1960s, as Indian communities across the nation fought back against termination, the long war between states and tribes over off-reservation fishing rights reached its peak in the Pacific Northwest. The American public thrilled to media reports of Indian fishers on Puget Sound protesting state regulation through "fish-ins," well-planned actions which intentionally echoed the civil rights protests then unfolding across the South. Although the issues were quite different—tribal self-determination versus black freedom from racial discrimination—the ugly state crackdowns that followed on Northwest rivers appeared to mirror the brutality of southern officials defending Jim Crow. The excesses of each helped spur federal intervention and feed the national movements for "Black Power" and "Red Power" that marked the late 1960s and early 1970s. Lost in the news coverage of these events, and in most historical accounts, was the ongoing debate among Indians regarding their treaty rights. Tribal councils, increasingly backed by the BIA and the federal courts, defended off-reservation fishing against state interference but also defined it as a tribal right subject to tribal regulation. The Mid-Columbia treaty tribes began moving to exercise that prerogative at the very same time the states tightened their grip on tribal fishing. Columbia River Indians ran afoul of both sides.[33]

The treaty battles of the postwar period unfolded along familiar lines, with individual fishers sniping at tribal authority while they engaged in a running fight with state authorities. Tribal governments, taking to heart the legal lessons of the past, sought to preempt state regulation and deflect criticism of "unrestricted" Indian fishing by demonstrating that they could control their own members. In 1962, the Yakama Tribal Council issued its first resolution setting a commercial gillnet season and requiring fishers to register their sites. Oregon and Washington immediately challenged tribal jurisdiction over off-reservation fishing, but within three years the other treaty tribes had all issued regulations more liberal than those of the states. Initially, because they lacked adequate enforcement powers, the tribal councils agreed to let state authorities arrest and prosecute Indians for fishing in violation of tribal ordinances. The states dismissed the suggestion to present trials in that way, however, and Indian fishers grew angry at the sight of council members sitting down to negotiate with state officials. During a 1963 conference on the Yakama reservation, several fishermen heralded the trouble to come with challenges hurled from the back of the room. As a state warden reported, they had "considerable to say near the end of the meeting, indicating they did not feel the tribe had any right to regulate them in their fishing outside of the Reservation and, in addition to this, did not feel either the State of Oregon or the State of Washington enforcement officers had any authority, in view of past court cases, to arrest them for fishing under the protection afforded by their treaty." There were loose cannons on the tribe's fragile ship of state.[34]

Columbia River dissidents fired their opening salvo in a series of court cases between 1963 and 1965. None of these shots even dented the legal precedent set by the *Whitefoot* decision, which judges in Wasco County and Hood River County cited to establish that fishing contrary to tribal ordinances voided an Indian's treaty rights and rendered him vulnerable to state prosecution. That did not stop one of the convicted men, Alvin Settler, from filing suit in 1965 to block the Yakama Nation from interfering with his fishing rights and confiscating his gear. The case made for some strange bedfellows. Although Settler conceded that he was a tribal member, he argued that the tribe could not regulate his off-reservation fishing. Ironically, state officials held the same view, but Settler denied state jurisdiction as well. The Yakama Nation, in turn, sought an injunction against state interference while maintaining that treaty fishing rights were subject to tribal control. The federal district court ultimately dismissed Settler's case, once again affirming the tribe's position, yet he and other fishers continued to embarrass the tribal government by racking up hundreds of citations. Robert Schoning, director of the Oregon Fish Commission, used them to attack the whole idea of tribal regulation. "If this is the Yakima tribe's concept of the way they want to cooperate with us in properly managing the Columbia River commercial fishery and the stocks involved," he grumbled in 1965, "we are not interested."[35]

Schoning had not seen anything yet. As fisheries officials on both sides of the river stepped up their efforts to break Indian resistance, the dissidents answered with more spectacular acts of defiance. Leo Alexander, a Cooks resident with a flair for the dramatic, hinted at their plans early in 1966. "I cannot at this time reveal what is taking place now amongst us," he told journalist Click Relander, "but I do know there is no turning back for the Yakima Indian fishermen and you may have a lot of Yakima Indian fishing troubles in your newspaper before the year gets old, as I think this is it and it will be to the finish." Alexander was as good as his word. In March 1966, two months after his cryptic message, some twenty-five members of the Yakama Nation petitioned the General Council to establish the Columbia River General Council Fish Commission of the Yakima Indian Nation. Alexander's name appeared on its initial slate of five members, alongside fellow fishers Clarence Tahkeal, Victor George, Lawrence Goudy, and Roger Jim. Their mandate, as expressed in a Yakama General Council executive order, was "to safeguard, protect and secure rights, privileges and benefits guaranteed to members of the Yakima Indian Nation by the treaty of June 9, 1855 for all time." The Fish Commission was likewise declared to be "perpetual" and vested with authority that superseded "any other actions taken by the Yakima Indian Agency or the Yakima Tribal Council." Dissent, it now seemed, had become outright mutiny.[36]

The dissidents' choice of language is instructive, however, for it shows the degree to which Columbia River Indians had accepted the legal ramifications of enrollment even as they challenged tribal authority. The governing council of the Mid-Columbia River Tribe had faded from view following the death of the old chiefs and the defeat of their bid for group recognition in the 1950s. The families at Cook's Landing tried to enlist the help of Chief Henry Thompson, Tommy Thompson's son and successor, but he "could not do anything about business affairs" because of poor health. His stepmother, Flora, made a few public appearances and answered questions from the press in his stead. She had no official standing, though, and the treaty papers she presented to reporters seemed to place fishing squarely under tribal control. Since the courts had repeatedly declared treaty rights to be tribal rights, only enrolled tribal members could claim protection under the treaties. Therefore, when the dissidents moved to establish the Columbia River General Council Fish Commission, they worked through the channels of their tribal government. The alternative identity Columbia River Indians had asserted so openly during the 1940s and 1950s virtually disappeared from the public record during the 1960s and 1970s, suggesting that it had been submerged along with Celilo Falls. The shadow tribe's profile shrank to the verge of disappearance as its members began to act more like a faction within the recognized tribes than like a tribe of their own.[37]

Even so, they had much in common with their "renegade" ancestors. In defying external regulation of their fishing and in the negative reactions their behavior caused, the Columbia River dissidents continued a long tradition of frustrating the powers that tried to keep them "on the reservation." Echoing the Indian agents of earlier eras, Director Schoning described the outlaw fishers as a threat to "order, system, and responsibility." If something was not done to corral them, he warned, "almost complete chaos will result." These "Rebel Indians" also spooked some white citizens with their increasingly confrontational tactics. In the spring of 1966, after a series of early morning raids by Washington Fisheries enforcement officers, the residents of Cook's Landing began guarding their nets with rifles. One local newspaper ran a photograph of a grinning Alvin Settler brandishing a chinook salmon as Leo Alexander stood watch with a loaded carbine; another paper reported that Indians had fired warning shots at state patrol boats. An angry reader clipped out both stories and sent them to Washington Fisheries Director Thor Tollefson, demanding to know how he planned to handle these actions that bordered on "armed insurrection." That fall, Tollefson also received mail from Alexander, who needled his adversary with faux condolences and a chivalrous challenge: "It is my hope the Columbia River General Council Fish Commission of the Yakima Indian Nation did not cause you, or your boys to[o] much overwork down here on the Columbia River. It is also my hope that real justice will prevail, and may the best of us win." Tweaking the noses of earnest bureaucrats remained, like fishing, an important feature of living outside the lines.[38]

Alexander's mischievous letter belied the seriousness with which he and other Columbia River Indians invested the struggle against state and tribal control. By the mid-1960s, state authorities had been arresting Indian hunters and fishers for more than half a century. They had grown tired of shouldering the burden of conservation as well as the blame for the sorry state of salmon stocks. After all, the state governments had not created the fish, and there had always been plenty to go around when only Indians caught them. "And that's why I stood up," explained Johnny Jackson:

> I didn't want to see my people going to jail, or pay[ing] for something that they didn't have to, something that we've always had here. Something that the Creator had given us, put here on this earth for us to take care of and use. . . . So when they come and ask me to stop fishing or stop hunting, that's violating my law. The Creator didn't tell me that I had to go and listen to a white man, just because he went and [made] mistakes and depleted the fish.[39]

Indians fished for a living, not for fun, yet the states regularly curtailed or closed tribal seasons while allowing white sportsmen to stay on the water. In effect, state regulations had abrogated the treaties and made it illegal to follow a way of life that still defined "being Indian" for traditionalists along the Columbia River. Breaking the law thus became a form of cultural affirmation, as anthropologist Larry Nesper has shown in his work on Indian fishing rights in the Great Lakes region. Among the Ojibways of Wisconsin, he observes, "violating" developed into a key indicator of Native identity and masculinity "because it is done to 'feed our families' and because it is against the white man's law. It is the practice of subsistence under circumstances that resemble warfare, and like warfare, it is a reproductive act." Similarly, when the Columbia River "violators" swapped stories about hiding their fish from game wardens or setting nets in prohibited locations, they were not celebrating "criminal" acts for their own sake but for the sake of their survival as River People.[40]

From the dissidents' perspective, the tribal governments failed to appreciate the stakes in this struggle "to the finish." "They didn't seem to pay any attention," complained Jackson, and when they did, it appeared their main concern was protecting their own authority. Columbia River Indians regarded tribal fishing ordinances as just another layer of restrictions, not an alternative to state law, because the states denied tribal jurisdiction and continued to arrest Indian fishers. More importantly, in their view, the bureaucrats who drafted and enforced tribal regulations had lost touch with the river, the salmon, and their culture. "Like most communities, not all people have the same religion, and this is true of the Yakima Indians. Not all Indians have the same respect for Indian culture and Indian religion," explained David Sohappy, Sr., who would soon emerge as a symbolic leader of the River People. As they saw it, fishing rights remained an individual prerogative controlled only by the rhythms of the river and the laws of the Creator. Fishing families knew better than the tribal governments how to conserve the salmon because they still lived on the river and followed the "old ways." They could be trusted to regulate themselves in accordance with traditional rules such as the prohibition against fishing on Sundays, after dark, and during funeral services. Conversely, because some tribal leaders had abandoned their traditional culture, they had no more right to control fishing than the states did. As in the past, issues of law and power became entangled with questions of racial identity and cultural authenticity.[41]

The Columbia River General Council Fish Commission represented an attempt to place fishing people in charge of fishing rights, but state and federal officials backed the Yakama Tribal Council in denying the group's legitimacy. According to tribal attorney James B. Hovis, the Yakama General Council had no executive board and therefore could not issue an executive order establishing a new tribal authority. The U.S. regional solicitor concurred, and the chairman of the General Council promptly "served notice he no longer recognized this Fish Commission." In December 1966, when the commission's members contacted the Washington State attorney general's office to solicit its opinion on the matter, Assistant Director Robert S. Robison would not even acknowledge the correspondence. "No answer. Do not wish to give this group any credence," he scribbled on the internal memo that accompanied their letter. Frustrated at every turn, the Fish Commission tried unsuccessfully to force the removal of the General Council chairman and the fourteen-member Tribal Council, alleging that they had not been properly elected in the first place. The struggle to control fishing rights had precipitated a constitutional crisis within the Yakama Nation. Once again, however, the recognized tribal authorities prevailed because powerful outsiders refused to deal with the dissidents. Columbia River Indians would have to find another way to blunt the offensive against their treaty rights and traditional way of life.[42]

The families at Cook's Landing returned to court, hoping to secure a federal decision that would at least limit the states' regulatory power. By mid-1968, the tide appeared to be turning in their favor after the U.S. Supreme Court held in *Puyallup Tribe v. Washington State Department of Game* that state regulations could not discriminate against Indians. The ruling compelled the states to open a limited commercial season for tribal fishers above Bonneville Dam, but arrests continued when they ignored the date restrictions or netted steelhead trout, which Washington had classified as a "game" fish reserved for sportsmen. Tribal leaders and river residents alike wanted a stronger statement in defense of the treaties. The Yakama Tribal Council distrusted the dissidents, however, and attorney James Hovis hesitated to support any action that might endanger tribal rights or waste tribal resources. The Interior Department's regional solicitor, George Dysart, had likewise concluded that defending individual fishers in state court constituted a legal dead end. Besides putting tribes on the defensive, that strategy placed a federal issue before state judges and limited the case to the specifics of a particular violation. Dysart sought a broad opinion that could effectively guide lower courts and bind state governments. He had begun pushing his superiors and the Justice Department to launch a federal suit when the Yakama Nation's loose cannons fired a legal broadside of their own.[43]

The case of *Sohappy v. Smith*, filed in July 1968, caught federal, state, and tribal officials by surprise. Just a month earlier, Washington Fisheries patrol officers had visited the residents of Cook's Landing to discuss the implications of the recent *Puyallup* ruling. "I talked with these people for over one and a half hours explaining the language and meaning of the decision, emphasizing the equal rights, and the fact that the river is now closed to fishing," reported Sergeant Al Dougherty. "I feel certain that the point was put across to them. . . . A feeling of friendship prevailed throughout the entire discussion. I do not feel there will be any trouble other than poaching from these people." A week later, Dougherty's partner participated in the arrest of two fishermen from Cook's, David and Richard Sohappy, for setting nets in the Bonneville pool. It seemed to be another routine violation, with the Sohappys spending several days in the Skamania County jail like dozens of Indians before them. Upon release, however, they immediately filed a federal lawsuit with twelve other Cook's residents against a slate of Oregon fish and game officials headed by Fish Commissioner McKee A. Smith. No less than Regional Solicitor Dysart, the dissident families had tired of spinning their wheels in state court. They intended to drive their treaty rights out of a rut, and the recognized tribes would be forced to come along for the ride.[44]

Although critics perceived the *Sohappy* suit as yet another sign of the renegades' recklessness, the residents of Cook's Landing had actually been planning it for months. Denied access to tribal counsel, they had talked strategy with national Indian organizations and had hired their own lawyers using money from a Ford Foundation grant. To secure additional funds and publicity, Leo Alexander incorporated Treaty Indians of the Columbia and began printing a newsletter with the masthead "Columbia River & Yakima Indian News." His appeals for sympathy and donations tapped into the growing public fascination with Native Americans, as well as the social and political ferment triggered by the Vietnam War and the Civil Rights movement. Portraying the River People as victims of "the white man's folly," Alexander strived to explain why the residents of the "Little White Salmon Indian Settlement" had taken the law into their own hands.[45] As he wrote shortly after the trial:

> Inevitably, when a combination of pressures and influences brings a status of a people and their culture into jeopardy, an explosive situation evolves. With our people and culture being subjected to repeated attacks from non-Indian fishing interests our Indian treaty fishing has reached a ruthless stage where only the hardy and determined Indian fisherman will be able to survive. Most of the Indian fishermen owe much [of] their survival to the dedicated and determined work of a few.[46]

These "dedicated and determined few" had picked their lead plaintiffs to maximize public support. Richard Sohappy, age twenty, had earned four Purple Hearts, a Bronze Star, and a Silver Star for valor in Vietnam. Home on leave to recuperate, he symbolized universal virtues of courage and sacrifice. His uncle David, with graying braids and gifted oratory, conveyed the nobility and spirituality that white liberals now associated with Indians. In time, he would become a hero to many and a martyr for the cause of Columbia River Indians.[47]

■ ■ ■

The trials and tribulations of David Sohappy provide a fitting conclusion for this history of the River People. In his life story, all the principal markers of their identity are prominently displayed: connection to the river, resistance to removal, defense of tradition and treaty rights, and estrangement from tribal government. Ironically, though, he had not grown up on the Columbia and did not trace his ancestry to one of the villages represented by the old river chiefs. A grand-nephew of Smohalla, the Wánapam prophet, Sohappy was raised on the Yakama reservation but followed the spiritual teachings and seasonal round of his ancestors. He began fishing at age five and spent much of his youth on the river at White Bluffs, where his grandparents maintained a drying shed. "That is where I learned about Indian language and religion," he later recalled. "I remember going to the longhouse from way back then, as my parents were firm believers in the Seven Drums or Washat religion. I used to attend every week. . . . We would have our ceremonies for the first food, preparing it all day Saturday for the Sunday event." Following a brief stint in the Army Air Corps, Sohappy worked various jobs and farmed his family's allotment for twenty listless years before deciding to become a full-time fisherman. In 1965, at age forty, he moved his wife, Myra, and their seven children to the in-lieu site at Cook's—just as the community landed in the crosshairs of the states' crusade against Indian fishing. His acceptance by the people there, and his identification with their cause, illustrated the continuing fluidity of Columbia River Indian identity. More than anything else, Sohappy's struggle would help to revitalize that identity after decades of quiescence.[48]

The *Sohappy* suit did not explicitly challenge tribal regulation, but the old tension between individual and tribal rights pervaded the whole proceeding. Oregon tried to have the case dismissed on the grounds that the plaintiffs lacked standing separate from the Yakama Nation in an action involving tribal rights. Meanwhile, federal and tribal attorneys debated whether to intervene in the case or bring their own suit against the state. Regional Solicitor Dysart and Sidney I. Lezak, the Justice Department's regional attorney, balked at the prospect of backing people known for resisting tribal authority. Even though the plaintiffs were all enrolled in the Yakama Nation, Lezak informed the court that they might "want relief which is greater than the Yakima Tribe and the Government itself would agree as being appropriate, considering the conservation question." Ultimately, Dysart and Lezak decided to initiate a separate suit on behalf of the four Mid-Columbia treaty tribes, allowing their attorneys to participate and circumventing the sovereign immunity provision that prevented the original plaintiffs from suing the state directly. Unlike *Sohappy v. Smith*, which named specific officials, *U.S. v. Oregon* could enjoin the entire state government. To the residents of Cook's Landing, though, it looked as if the tribes and the feds were trying to seize control of a case they had initially opposed. As Wilbur Slockish said in 2006, "They weren't interested in helping us until we started winning."[49]

U.S. District Judge Robert C. Belloni gave all of the plaintiffs some cause for celebration. In his July 1969 opinion, he merged the two cases and handed the Indians an impressive victory, ruling that the states could regulate tribal fishing only when "reasonable and necessary for conservation" and that they must guarantee the Indians a "fair and equitable share" of the salmon harvest. He held further that the tribes "must have an opportunity for meaningful participation in the rule-making process," thereby opening the door to the possibility of tribal co-management of the Columbia River runs. Judge Belloni did not explicitly address the issue of tribal regulation, however, and both the states and the *Sohappy* plaintiffs maintained their separate objections to tribal jurisdiction over off-reservation fishing. Non-Indian commercial and sport fishers chimed in as well, accusing Belloni (or "Baloney," as they preferred to call him) of extending "special rights" to the tribes. Anticipating resistance on several fronts, he kept the cases open so that the plaintiffs could "seek timely and effective judicial review." Tribal attorneys tried to assure him that the court would have no more problems on their account. The tribes had "absolute power" to cut off violators, said Warm Springs attorney Owen Panner, because without a tribal permit "they don't have any treaty rights any longer and they're not supported by the tribe." Belloni remained skeptical, though, and the *Sohappy* plaintiffs gave him good reason to be.[50]

If his decision went too far for the states, it did not go nearly far enough for the families at Cook's Landing. Still bristling over the tribes' belated intervention and the court's failure to preclude any kind of state oversight, many of them resumed fishing without regard for either state or tribal regulations. Arrests and gear confiscations resumed as well, but now the Yakama Nation's own police and courts helped enforce its ordinances. Alvin Settler returned to court in 1971, trying once more to block tribal jurisdiction, while Leo Alexander cried foul in the papers and in his newsletter. In the immediate aftermath of Belloni's ruling, the states continued to set tight seasons on the Columbia River, and the tribal proportion of the catch actually declined. Alexander took this as evidence that the states had no intention of giving Indians a fair share and that the tribes had merely succeeded in imposing more restrictions on the River People.51 Hearkening back to the debates that had riled the Celilo Fish Committee, he rejected tribal management and called for a return to traditional concepts of ownership:

> These officials are contending that Indian treaty fishing is tribal and that the Indian fisherman has no individual treaty rights to catch fish. They contend Indian fishing is communal in nature and subject to the control and regulating by the Tribal Administrative Governing Body. We now have both the State and the Yakima Tribal Council claiming they must regulate the Indian fisherman. We agree, Indian fishing was communal in nature— but by tradition it was never overall controlling.52

Their hopes rose briefly in 1974 after Judge George Boldt handed Northwest Indians another major victory in *U.S. v. Washington*, which developed from events on Puget Sound but involved the Mid-Columbia tribes as well. Building on the precedents set in the *Sohappy/Oregon* decision, Boldt ruled that a "fair and equitable share" meant 50 percent of the annual harvest and that the states could regulate Indian fishing only if all other means of conservation had been exhausted—including the restriction of non-treaty fishing "to the full extent." Boldt also affirmed the right of tribal self-regulation, however, and the subsequent failure of Settler's lawsuit effectively sealed the deal. For Indian fishers, it would be the tribes' way or no way at all.53

Still, neither the dissidents nor the states were ready to throw in the towel. During the late 1970s, as salmon runs neared the lowest levels on record, Washington's state government and congressional delegation did their best to obstruct and overturn the so-called Boldt decision. Oregon made less of a fuss but cooperated with Washington in phasing out the treaty fishing seasons above Bonneville Dam while allowing sport fishing in major tributaries. Tribal leaders objected to this clear breach of Boldt's intent, which Leo Alexander called "a backhanded way of abrogating the treaty," yet they also began developing a system of subsistence and ceremonial permits to better track the treaty harvest. It was all too much for traditional fishers like David Sohappy. "No man should be required to obtain a permit from any other man to practice his religion," he declared in 1976. "I know of no other church or religion for which to exercise it the permit of any governmental body or person or tribe is required, and I don't think it just that one be required to apply for and obtain a permit before exercising one's ceremonial fishing rites and rights." Later that year, he related the story of Ida Scowole White, an elder who collapsed and died at the Wind River in-lieu site while "bemoaning the loss of the right to fish for subsistence that has in fact existed with the closure of the Columbia River by State authorities and Tribal authorities who were not exercising the Indians' rights to fish." As Sohappy and the remaining dissidents saw it, the "old ways" that White represented would suffer the same fate if they stopped fighting for "real justice."[54]

Their continued refusal to observe closure orders outraged the states and exasperated the tribes, for whom the dissidents' defiance presented a public relations nightmare and an obstacle to productive negotiations with state officials. The governments of Oregon and Washington were in no mood to tolerate illegal Indian fishing—even as non-Indians protested the Boldt decision with their own outlaw fishery—and state enforcement officers showed their anger in a series of escalating confrontations with the people at Cook's. During one raid in 1976, David Sohappy awakened to find eighteen armed officers in flak vests, masks, and helmets searching people's homes and seizing their nets. Sohappy approached one he knew—the same officer who had arrested him in 1968—to ask what they were doing, and "he simply pointed his shot gun at me and demanded that I not come closer although he knew me to be a peace-loving person and I was unarmed with anything other than pad and a pencil." Sohappy then witnessed one of his teenage sons being tackled to the ground as he ran to warn a friend. Another officer remarked that he was "going to see that the Indian In Lieu Fishing Site at Cooks was observed 24 hours a day and that they were going to see to it that I [Sohappy] didn't get any fishing of any kind this year." Leo Alexander accused the states of embarking on "a reign of terror with the use of special tactical squads to subdue Columbia River Indian treaty fishermen." Although angered by the state's behavior, the tribal councils soon moved to disassociate their cause from the "radicals" and their headline-grabbing resistance.[55]

By 1976, tribal attorneys and officials had become fed up with the seemingly insatiable and impractical demands of the in-lieu site dissidents. Some tribal leaders actually agreed with them on certain issues, as Yakama Tribal Councilman Johnson Meninick suggested when he told Judge Belloni that indigenous customs could effectively guide tribal regulations. "I believe we've practiced lifelong [conservation]," he insisted during a hearing in May 1974. "We're born to it, we're raised with it, we die with it. Our people who were our forefathers have practiced this tradition. They know what to do, and they hand it down to us, and we're going to hand it down to the younger [generation]." The courts wanted to see effective tribal enforcement, however, and the dissidents made that difficult at best. A few weeks after vouching for the Yakama Nation's reliability, Meninick virtually disowned Alvin and Mary Settler, contending that they were not registered tribal fishers even though they were enrolled. In June 1976, the four intervening tribes further distanced themselves by moving to sever *U.S. v. Oregon* from *Sohappy v. Smith*. William C. Klein, the attorney for the original plaintiffs in *Sohappy*, opposed the motion because he suspected it would lead to the closure of their case. There were "common questions of fact and law remaining," he argued, and it would be unjust to sever given that "absent the concern of these plaintiffs pioneering in the instant case the law may not have developed and an honorable respect for their treaty rights as set forth in

227

the Court's opinion might not exist." Judge Belloni cut the cord anyway.[56]

His decision to terminate jurisdiction over *Sohappy v. Smith* reflected both his frustration with the dissidents' conduct and his conviction that they derived their individual fishing rights "from whatever rights the Yakima Nation have." In his opinion, the twelve remaining plaintiffs had adequate representation in *U.S. v. Oregon*. More importantly, he feared that they might scuttle the Columbia River Fish Management Compact that the states had signed with the treaty tribes in 1977. Clarence Tahkeal and several other *Sohappy* plaintiffs had already introduced a motion in the Yakama General Council opposing the Yakama Nation's participation in the agreement, calling it a thinly veiled capitulation to continued state regulation. "We talk about fishing," said Tahkeal during the council debate, "[but] you know we gave away our fall fishing this year all because some men put their name on a piece of paper for you." Yakama tribal chairman Watson Totus, though a strong defender of treaty rights, had committed to a compact in which the states jointly set the seasons while the tribes reserved the right to review them and seek judicial adjustments. The Yakama Tribal Council refused to back out of the compact even after Tahkeal's motion to reject it passed by a vote of 435 to 34. Still, the *Sohappy* plaintiffs had stirred up trouble again, and their separate standing in court gave them an open microphone with which to air their grievances and demand redress. The court, the states, and the tribes agreed that it was time to pull the plug.[57]

Attorney William Klein's worst fear came true in April 1978, when Judge Belloni asked all the parties concerned whether it was necessary to keep *Sohappy* open. Oregon officials proposed ending the court's jurisdiction, and Belloni accepted the motion over the plaintiffs' objections. In arguing against it, Klein made a final tilt at the windmill of tribal rights, which he said created "a situation in which the vindication of the rights of an individual Indian would depend upon the decision of his tribe to seek for him the relief to which he believes himself entitled." The *Sohappy* plaintiffs had a constitutional right to pursue action against the state independently of their tribe, he contended, and they had been forced to do so by the negligence of their federal trustees and tribal leaders. "If the

State and the Court expect to reach a negotiated settlement of the fisheries dispute which has any likelihood of surviving," Klein concluded, "they must listen to those Indians who fish as well as those Indians who 'rule.'" It was the same plea Columbia River Indians had been making for decades. Belloni had tired of hearing their complaints, though, and in June he closed the book on *Sohappy v. Smith*. David Sohappy blamed his nominal rulers on the reservation. "I wouldn't compromise with the states on a lot of issues," he later remarked, "so the intervenor tribes got tired of me and . . . [they] took over." The political subjugation of the River People appeared to be complete.[58]

■ ■ ■

Meanwhile, the process of community displacement and disruption continued with the upstream march of river development. John Day Dam, completed in 1971, eliminated the last stretch of free-flowing water between The Dalles and McNary Dam, near the town of Umatilla, Oregon. Besides inundating traditional fishing sites, the John Day pool forced the abandonment or relocation of Indian villages at Rock Creek, Pine Creek, Roosevelt, and Alderdale. Ella Jim marveled at the results in 2004: "At Rock Creek the longhouse is just sitting there. No more village. Fifty years ago I wouldn't have believed you if you told me that." Unlike the people of Celilo, the residents of these communities got little compensation for their homes and none for their fisheries. Nor did they have the opportunity to move the graves of their ancestors, which now lie beneath the waters of Lake Umatilla. By contrast, the Army Corps spent $100,000 to transplant non-Indian cemeteries at Irrigon and Boardman, Oregon, and $3 million to relocate the entire town of Arlington, Washington. New Indian communities sprang up at Georgeville and Billieville, near Goldendale, Washington, but many families moved to nearby towns or one of the reservations. By driving people away from the river, the Army Corps nearly accomplished what federal Indian policy had failed to do in the nineteenth century.[59]

As work on the John Day Dam proceeded, the Bureau of Indian Affairs initiated what Roberta Ulrich has called a "slow-motion effort" to evict the permanent residents of the five in-lieu sites along the Bonneville pool. By the late 1960s, those settlements had become cluttered with ramshackle buildings, trailers, boats, fishing nets, junked cars, and discarded equipment. They still lacked adequate services, including water and sanitation, and neither the Bureau nor the Army Corps wished to spend much money for improvements. On the contrary, both agencies wanted the year-round occupants to leave, as did some local whites, tribal officials, and visiting Indian fishers who complained of being denied access. In February 1969, as the *Sohappy* case unfolded in court, the BIA abruptly implemented new rules that required tribal identification to enter the sites, allowed the Portland Area Office to withdraw access privileges, and banned permanent structures. A few families bowed to the pressure, but most stayed and protested the rules, which the Yakama superintendent conceded "were not generally known to the people until after they became effective." Among the stalwarts were the Sohappys and the Alexanders at Cook's Landing, where around thirty people lived on a third of an acre between the river and the railroad tracks. They noted that the site had been part of an Indian village before Bonneville Dam, and they reminded the federal government that it had never fulfilled a promise to replace houses lost to the reservoir. The Little White Salmon Indian Settlement, as they preferred to call their community, was all they had left. "Let them stay," demanded Tony Hoptowit, another resident. "Just like Celilo—people lived there all their lives. They should have permanent homes."[60]

For the next twenty years, the in-lieu site controversy boiled around and through the jagged contours of the fishing rights struggle like the wild river that once tumbled over Celilo Falls. Reporting on Yakama views of the in-lieu site question in 1970, Superintendent William T. Schlick observed:

> An equitable solution of this problem is difficult at best. It is much more difficult because of the friction between a number of Yakima members involved with the in-lieu sites and the Tribal Council, basically stemming from legal battles regarding fishing rights, per capita dividends, authority of tribal police and other matters. These frictions result in the feeling that

the Superintendent is supporting a corrupt tribal government, or playing favorites with a few tribal members at the expense of the tribe, or both, depending on an individual's position in tribal politics.[61]

River residents certainly regarded the issues as one in the same, as part of a general campaign to end their way of life. During a 1972 meeting to discuss the in-lieu sites, Leo Alexander lambasted the tribes and the feds for "diverting attention from the real problems. They intend to create a climate against the Cook's people. This is an old game of outside interests, including the Bureau, to divide and conquer. Columbia River people are not against others—just trying to preserve their culture." In 1974, James Alexander, Leo's father, headed a slate of twenty-two plaintiffs in *Alexander v. Morton*, a lawsuit aimed at nullifying the BIA's regulations. Although James owned a house on the Yakama reservation and lived there part of the year, the Alexanders argued that both the 1855 treaties and the 1945 statute authorizing the sites allowed for permanent occupancy. Their attorney failed to pursue the case effectively, leading to its dismissal in 1975, but the plaintiffs and their neighbors did not budge.[62]

The final push to remove them came in the early 1980s with a federal-state crusade to suppress illegal Indian fishing and dislodge the communities that had taken root on the in-lieu sites. State officers routinely seized boats and nets—costing the Sohappys alone some $138,000 over twenty years—yet it had proven fruitless to prosecute people for illegal fishing when that carried only a misdemeanor charge in county court. The government's big break came in March 1981, when 40,000 salmon mysteriously disappeared between the fish ladders at Bonneville Dam and McNary Dam. Although biologists eventually found the missing fish in tributary streams, where they had been diverted by fluoride spills from an aluminum plant, state fisheries officials enlisted their disappearance as evidence of a massive tribal poaching ring centered on the in-lieu sites. "They labeled us as [an] Indian mafia family controlling fish prices, controlling access and all of that," remembered Wilbur Slockish, Jr. "They really tried to paint us as bad people." In April, the Washington State Department of Fisheries asked the National Marine Fisheries

Service (NMFS) to launch an undercover sting operation—soon to be dubbed "Salmonscam"—that could secure convictions under the federal Lacey Act. The state's newly elected Republican senator, Slade Gorton, had just introduced an amendment to that anti-poaching law that would make illegal fishing a felony offense. He pitched it as a way to help tribes prosecute non-Indian poachers on the reservations, but Gorton was no friend of tribal sovereignty. As the heir to a New England seafood fortune and the former attorney general of Washington State, he had nothing but contempt for treaty rights. River People would be made to suffer for the state's humiliation in the Boldt decision.[63]

Salmonscam focused all the anger and frustration that had been building within river communities since the 1940s, illustrating for them the lengths to which their enemies would go and the degree to which their own governments could not be counted on for protection. The sting operation began seven months before Congress passed the Lacey Act amendments as Public Law 97–79. Posing as fish buyers for a company called Advanced Marketing Research, two undercover NMFS agents visited the in-lieu sites to solicit sales of illegally caught salmon from the Sohappys and other residents. David and Myra were among those who suspected that their new customers were law officers—Myra even took pictures of them, as she had often done with state wardens and police—but the Sohappys sold fish anyway, including salmon that other people had asked them to sell, because they needed the money. David had no fear of going back to court; in fact, he wanted to in order to challenge the legal status quo. He soon got his wish. Early on the morning of June 17, 1982, still a full five months before President Ronald Reagan signed Public Law 97–79, two dozen NMFS agents and state officers burst into Cook's Landing and arrested the Sohappys at gunpoint. Seventy-three other members of the Yakama, Warm Springs, and Umatilla tribes were also taken into custody, nineteen of whom ultimately faced charges under the Lacey Act. Collectively, they stood accused of illegally taking and selling some 2,300 fish from the spring chinook run in a year when ocean fishers caught 129,000 fish from the same stocks. Myra Sohappy later calculated that it amounted to about two fish a month per defendant over the course of a fourteen-month investigation costing $350,000.[64]

The unspectacular nature of their crime was matched in court by the disappointing results of the government's prosecution. Myra and two other defendants were ultimately acquitted, while three others pleaded guilty to misdemeanors in state court. The remaining thirteen pleaded guilty or received felony convictions in federal trials, which the government moved to Los Angeles due to the extreme anti-Indian bias that existed in the Northwest. No one was convicted of the worst charge—conspiracy—but David Sohappy and his son each received the maximum sentence of five years for selling a combined total of 345 fish worth $10,550. Bruce Jim, whom the undercover agents had recruited as a "partner," also got five years for selling an unspecified number of fish. Of the rest, Wilbur Slockish, Jr., got three years in prison for selling sixty-three fish; Leroy Yocash got two years for seventy-eight fish; and Matthew McConville and four other Indians received one-year sentences. Most of those charged and convicted came from river communities, whose residents burned with resentment as the recognized tribes stood by, seemingly afraid to act after the federal government rebuffed their initial requests to try some of the cases in tribal court. "There's something that's gotta be done about our tribal councilmen, if they're going to send our men to prison, there is something wrong," warned Myra Sohappy during the appeals process. "They gotta right this wrong, or I'm gonna come in with a two by four."[65]

The Salmonscam convictions placed the Yakama Nation and the Confederated Tribes of Warm Springs in an awkward position. Eager to assert jurisdiction over the defendants, both tribal councils asked the federal government to transfer some of the felony cases to tribal court. They considered the offenses an internal matter because most of the fish had been caught with ceremonial permits, which the tribes issued to people who supplied salmon for Washat services and tribal feasts. Few tribal members knew of these legal maneuvers until much later, however, and the charges that the tribal courts drew up appeared to place the defendants in double jeopardy. The Warm Springs tribe dropped its case when the federal government refused to give it jurisdiction, but the

SUBMERGENCE AND RESURGENCE

Yakama Nation insisted on holding its own trial before handing over the Sohappys, Slockish, Yocash, and McConville in 1987. Outside the court building, Indian and non-Indian protesters drummed and chanted their support for the accused, whom pro bono attorney Thomas Keefe cast as defenders of traditional law. Prosecutor Jack Fiander, a tribal member, endured taunts of "pig" and "Slade Gorton" as he indicted them for violating tribal ordinances. The jury found all five men innocent, and the Yakama Tribal Council immediately requested presidential pardons, but they went to prison regardless. Further efforts to have their sentences reduced and served in Washington State failed to appease the embittered River People. Instead of standing with David Sohappy, recalled river resident Lavina Washines, the tribal government "intervened against him. That's when we lost our fishing rights."[66]

Washines and other River People also blamed Salmonscam on the Columbia River Inter-Tribal Fish Commission (CRITFC), a cooperative management organization composed of representatives from the Yakama Nation, the Confederated Tribes of the Umatilla Indian Reservation, the Confederated Tribes of Warm Springs, and the Nez Perce Tribe. Founded in 1977 to give the tribes a unified voice in resource policy, CRITFC worked with state and federal agencies in regulating the tribal harvest. Yakama fishers associated it with the reviled Columbia River Compact, and their resentment grew after CRITFC enforcement officers assisted in the search for missing Salmonscam defendants. At a Lacey Act briefing in 1986, river residents blasted the organization for failing to protect treaty rights and tradition. "Our treaty has been abrogated for quite some time," charged Cook's fisherman Lawrence Goudy, "even though the Inter-Tribal Fish Commission has maybe done some good, but have they really went behind the treaty laws and protected them[?]" Washines thought not: "This Inter-Tribal Fish Commission [that's] sitting in Portland knows more about fishing than I do. They have more authority than I as an elected official [of the General Council] to speak on behalf of my rights and it's very disturbing to me. Because they're playing with my religion." Johnny Jackson added: "People along the river suffer the most of all, through all of this and they still suffer, they will continue to suffer until this jurisdiction is straightened out. . . . If you can't represent the Indian people right, why are you there?" He had already concluded that if Columbia River Indians wanted things done right they would have to start doing things for themselves again.[67]

■ ■ ■

The last straw came when the recognized tribes supported the BIA's ongoing effort to oust Jackson and the other permanent residents of the in-lieu sites. In 1984, as Salmonscam appeals worked their way through the courts, the Portland Area Office delivered eviction notices to the families at Cascade Locks, Wind River, Cook's Landing, Underwood, and Lone Pine. The timing of the notices did not seem coincidental. "I think it's part of this entire effort," declared Sohappy's attorney, Tom Keefe, "and I think any suggestion by [Area Director Stanley] Speaks, or anyone else from the Department of the Interior that the two actions are unrelated is just a lie, and it should be treated as one." Forced to take a position on the issue, the Warm Springs and Yakama councils reluctantly backed the BIA's order. The sites belonged to the tribes as a whole, they argued, and nobody should be allowed to live there. It was one betrayal too many for people sick of sacrifice and surrender in the name of "tribal interests." As the residents dug in their heels—heels by which Myra Sohappy swore the BIA would have to drag her out—their traditional leaders broke the silence that had fallen over their council in the 1950s. At a press conference held in Celilo Village during the 1984 first-salmon feast, two Mid-Columbia chiefs vowed to fight the evictions. "They have taken everything away from us. Fishing rights, fish, the land," declared Frederick Ike, Sr., the traditional head of the Rock Creek community. "All we have left are the in-lieu sites, and we would like to hold onto them by whatever means possible." Next to him stood Howard Jim, the Wayám chief and one of the men acquitted in Salmonscam. Together, they revived and renamed the Chiefs and Council of the Columbia River Indians that had lain dormant since the death of Celilo Falls.[68]

The reawakening of Columbia River Indian political consciousness

235

had started the year before, when sympathetic members of the National Lawyers Guild helped the besieged river communities form the Columbia River Defense Project (CRDP). Its initial purpose had been to provide legal support for the Salmonscam defendants and to counteract the propaganda the government had directed at them through the press. Tapping into the national and international media attention the cases had garnered, CRDP volunteers printed pamphlets and produced films to educate the public and encourage donations. "Like it or not David Sohappy is going to become the most famous Indian in your tribal history," attorney Tom Keefe later told the Yakama General Council. "People are asking who is David Sohappy and why is he in prison?" The river chiefs also made good copy, attracting reporters and photographers with their long braids, traditional attire, and solemn invocations of the treaties and the "old ways." Working with the CRDP, Frederick Ike and Howard Jim helped turn the tide of public opinion in favor of the in-lieu site residents while also raising money for a lawsuit to stop the evictions by hosting salmon bakes and giving speeches across the Northwest. In July 1985, the Chiefs and Council of the Columbia River Indians joined the Sohappys and four other individuals in their case against the Department of the Interior. As attorney Gary Berne explained in the Council's *amicus* motion, the chiefs wished "to appear because they represent the traditional governing body of the appellants as well as other Indians who live and fish along the Columbia River."[69]

Although the BIA scoffed at their assertion of a separate tribal identity, the Columbia River Indian Council secured formal standing in the eviction case and exerted its influence in the political aftermath of Salmonscam. It also resumed its former shape when, in April 1987, Wilbur Slockish, Sr., assumed the long-vacant position of Klickitat chief. A year later, as his son and the Sohappys marked time in a federal penitentiary in Minnesota, Chief Slockish sent Georgia Goudy to represent Columbia River Indian fishers in Senate hearings on fisheries management. Appearing with other members of the "Mid-Columbia Tribe," she demanded changes in the Lacey Act and complained that her people had learned of the present proceedings only "through the grapevine."[70]

Johnny Jackson, the Klickitat sub-chief, seconded her call for direct communication between the federal government and the River People:

> I feel that I would like to ask this question: as chiefs who have always held our traditional way of life along the river, and our councils, who are not being recognized, and our chieftainship, which is not being recognized, and that Corps of Engineers and the Government claiming that they got the land, what chief ever gave that up or signed it away? I don't believe that my grandfather Slockish signed anything away, nor did Chief Tommy Thompson, nor any other chief. . . . I feel that it is time that there should be a change or changes where we should know, as individuals, that we still have a right, and that we can be recognized and known as the Indian people along the Columbia River.

After Chief Howard Jim had made a similar plea for acknowledgment, Umatilla enrollee Edith McCloud concluded her own remarks with a gesture in their direction: "I hope in the future you will listen to these gentlemen on my left here, they are the true leaders of our people—of most of our people. We try to hang on to our old ways." Significantly, the documents they submitted for the record included the statements that Frank Slockish and William Yallup had made on behalf of the "Columbia River Tribe" more than forty years earlier. The chiefs of the past and the chiefs of the present spoke with one voice, insisting that their people had a just claim to tribal status.[71]

The arguments they presented against eviction likewise referenced their distinctive history as off-reservation Indians. Attorney Jack Schwartz, representing the seven individual plaintiffs, contended that the BIA's order violated their interpretation of the treaties because the "fishing clause" had implicitly reserved the right of residence at all "usual and accustomed places" during the fishing seasons. The families at the in-lieu sites had nets in the water all the time, if one considered sturgeon and steelhead taken during the winter, so they could legally live there year-round. The residents also denied allegations that they had prevented visiting tribal fishers from using the sites, placing the blame instead on external powers that had pitted Indians against each other. As Schwartz explained, "The federal and state governments reduced the authority of the traditional river governing bodies by formalizing the elected, Bureau of Indian Affairs condoned tribal councils on the reservations. This, in turn, produced a fierce intertribal rivalry for the control of the Indian property and rights on the Columbia River." The current trouble had started not with the permanent occupants, but with the Warm Springs Tribal Council's judgment that the Yakama Nation dominated the in-lieu sites because most of the residents had enrolled in that tribe. In many ways, the controversy echoed earlier debates within the Celilo Fish Committee, and Schwartz suggested that a similar organization be created to resolve contemporary disputes over land use and fishing sites: "This could be done by the Columbia River Inter-Tribal Fish Commission . . . or by the traditional consensus process of decision-making by a council of representatives of both the on-river and reservation people and Chiefs."[72]

Attorney Gary Berne, arguing on behalf of the Chiefs and Council of the Columbia River Indians, amplified Schwartz's contention that the eviction order constituted a breach of the treaties as well an attack on their clients' traditional culture. Placing the current struggle within the context of earlier efforts to remove Columbia River Indians, Berne accused the BIA of trying to finish the bad business begun by the reservation system and the dams. The in-lieu site residents did not wish to deny anyone access to the river; they merely wished to continue their customary way of life. "The Bureau now attempts to bring these people's culture to a close by the eviction of the remaining Columbia River Indians from their dwellings and fishing sites along the River," Berne charged in the Council's *amicus* motion. If the BIA succeeded, the River People would be forced "to relinquish the last vestiges of their heritage of freedom and independence and . . . become more dependent upon the United States." They had no desire to live on the reservations, and that is why they had, "despite incredible odds and overwhelming poverty, expended considerable time, effort and resources fighting to retain their aboriginal and treaty rights to exist along the Columbia. Justice and fairness now cry out for an end to this fight; justice and fairness demand that the appellants be allowed to continue in peace the ways of their ancestors along the banks of the Columbia River." A supporting statement from David Sohappy, Jr., put the issue in even starker terms: "If I were to leave the river, I don't know what I would do, probably go crazy. . . . I am an Indian and that is the way I want to stay. A traditional Indian."[73]

The U.S. Court of Appeals for the Ninth Circuit agreed that enough was enough. After reviewing the evidence, including photographs of permanent structures that predated Bonneville Dam, a three-judge panel reversed two earlier decisions and ruled that the in-lieu site residents could stay in their homes. David Sohappy, Sr., never got to hear the good news. Although he had received parole in May 1988 after suffering a stroke, prison life had aggravated his diabetes, and he returned to Cook's Landing physically broken if spiritually unbent. Acknowledging that his health was "not so good," he nevertheless vowed in November 1990 to "keep going as long as I know I'm right. I'm right all the time. Nobody takes the time out to listen to me." Within a few months, however, his deteriorating condition forced him to leave Cook's for a nursing home in Hood River—the same place Tommy Thompson had spent his last days. Sohappy died in May 1991, just five months before the eviction case closed. At his direction, the *Oregonian* reported, "No speeches were delivered at his funeral. It followed strictly the Washat service of the Seven Drums religion founded by Sohappy's ancestor, Smohalla, the 19th-century prophet who was the leader of the Wanapum band." Many of the mourners present for his interment on the Yakama reservation blamed his death on the powerful forces that had made the last twenty years of his life a constant struggle. As one woman at the cemetery remarked bitterly, "It's like the government took a knife and turned it in his heart."[74]

■ ■ ■

The tragic ending to Sohappy's personal story should not obscure the tenacious persistence of Columbia River Indians or the dramatic resurgence of their tribal identity in the wake of Salmonscam. In early 1990, as the Sohappy family awaited word of its fate, the three traditional chiefs and their advisors formally incorporated as the Mid-Columbia River Council (MCRC). Recognizing the disparate origins and distinct interests of their scattered constituency, the council then elected a seven-member board of directors representing each of the off-reservation communities in the region. "*At this time*," the board declared, "it is not the desire of the native people of the Mid-Columbia to seek federal recognition as a distinct tribe. However, it is the will of the people that the Mid-Columbia River Council become a direct provider and broker of those services to which the native people of the Mid-Columbia are entitled by reason of their tribal membership and their status as a disadvantaged minority group." To that end, the three chiefs drafted a "Statement of Unification" outlining their people's history and calling for "our ancient rights to be recognized and respected by all." In a further challenge to the reservation governments, they insisted boldly, "We are not bound to any agreements, policies, or laws that have been passed without our participation or consent. Our people are responsible to the authority of the Mid-Columbia River Council and the sacred laws given us by the Creator." The shadow tribe had returned.[75]

CONCLUSION

Only time will tell whether the shadow tribe fades or flourishes. Today, almost two decades after its sudden resurgence, the future of Columbia River Indian identity remains uncertain. Some BIA employees believe that it has run its course and now serves merely to prop up the pretensions of a few disgruntled tribal members. Federal officials said the same thing fifty years ago, only to see the River People come roaring back in the 1980s. The revitalization of their tribal consciousness continued after David Sohappy's death, even as the Mid-Columbia River Council (MCRC) struggled to find a way around the wall that tribal enrollment had placed in its path. Shortly after issuing its provocative Statement of Unification, the MCRC hired outside consultants to write grant proposals and assist Administrative Director Ray Slockish (the brother of Wilbur, Jr.) in creating a tribal infrastructure. Slockish spearheaded a campaign to coordinate the delivery of services with the three treaty tribes whose ceded areas embrace the Mid-Columbia region. Working door-to-door in off-reservation communities, MCRC staff and board members distributed a survey to identify the most pressing needs and compile a membership roll. At that time, by the council's own estimate, it represented some 600 to 800 people scattered between the in-lieu sites on the Bonneville pool and the Umatilla reservation. More than half were enrolled in the Yakama Nation, with the remainder belonging to either the confederated Umatilla or Warm Springs tribes. Only a handful of people were still unenrolled, generally because they could not meet the criteria set by the recognized tribes. Whatever their tribal status, most survey respondents expressed a sense of being "out of sight, out of mind" for the reservations. "The three tribes use our head count to obtain federal funds," complained the MCRC, "but provide very limited services to our people."[1]

The chiefs aimed to change that. Using the survey data as a guide, Slockish and the consultants drafted a grant proposal to the Administration for Native Americans (ANA) requesting $128,770 for a pilot project. Their immediate goal was to build a cultural center in Celilo Village, a project they felt "represented the embodiment of the Council's emphasis on traditional values and customs . . . a project that would bring the people, the tribes, and the communities along the Columbia together to benefit the native peoples, and ensure the future of the place that is so important to us all." The idea had rated highly in the survey and received some conditional support from the recognized tribes. The ANA also responded favorably and awarded the grant to fund the preliminary planning. As had happened fifty years earlier, however, touchy issues of jurisdiction and recognition hindered efforts to revitalize Celilo Village. The reservation governments balked at making financial commitments to a community outside their respective service areas. Although unsure of its own authority along the river, the BIA's Portland Area Office listened sympathetically to the council's concerns, even reporting in early 1994 that its staff had "achieved the 'good will' of the River People and the avenues of communication are open." Still, when push came to shove, BIA officials concluded that "There is no relationship to MCRC—It is not a government to government issue." Columbia River Indians remained a shadow tribe, able to enter the corridors of power but only in the company of the recognized groups to which they are bound.[2]

The MCRC's failure to break through these bureaucratic barriers helped undermine the unity its members had shown since the mid-1980s. As the reservation governments and the BIA made clear to the chiefs, any governance plan for Celilo Village "must be developed within a framework of existing federal law" and "must recognize the sovereignty of the Yakama, Warm Springs and Umatilla tribes and their right to represent the Columbia River Indians, enrolled or otherwise." Frustration with the council's lack of progress aggravated personal disagreements among the chiefs and their constituents, which worsened after the founding members of the MCRC began passing away. Ultimately, the council had to return a portion of the ANA grant and shelve plans for an interpretive center, though village redevelopment went forward under the Army Corps of Engineers. Spurred by the Lewis and Clark bicentennial between 2004 and 2006, the Corps built a new longhouse and a dozen homes equipped with modern appliances and running water. Residents moved in during the summer of 2008, but the process of assigning houses left some tribal members with bruised feelings. The BIA, unable to accommodate all the requests it received, limited claims to the few verified heirs of the old homes and to people who had lived in the village since 1998. Critics deemed the policy unfair, especially to families that had been compelled to leave in 1957, but current residents defended their right to stay in the village. The chiefs began taking sides in these disputes, and their common front crumbled like the condemned buildings of the old village.[3]

Even so, the debate over housing in Celilo highlighted familiar distinctions between river and reservation people. Olsen Meanus, Jr., a lifelong village resident, echoed Tommy Thompson's view that the community belonged to those who had refused to abandon it despite the many hardships they endured:

We make up Celilo now. That's the way it is, that's the way it's got to be. There are people who are from Celilo, but they chose to go away. In my eyes, they left Celilo. . . . They got old enough, and they made a decision that the reservation was better. It might be. They've got everything they want there: jobs, houses, transportation, everything, assistance in all ways. Not like us river people, man, we rough it. We rely on that river. Whatever it provides for us—what we can make out of it, we can eat—that's what we live on.[4]

Although Johnny Jackson and Wilbur Slockish have their differences with the current village leadership, they also continue to insist that the reservation residents and tribal governments do not understand life on the river. Earlier in 2008, when the Yakama Nation shut down the spring scaffold fishery due to poor salmon runs, Jackson challenged the need for the closure and criticized its impact on fishing families. Noting that the scaffolds primarily caught steelhead for subsistence, not salmon for sale, he accused tribal leaders of taking food out of people's mouths for no good reason. "I remember when councilmen used to come around and talk to us on the river," he said. "They don't do that anymore." Jackson and the other chiefs vowed to make them listen.[5]

■ ■ ■

The Mid-Columbia River Council remains active today, though its membership has completely turned over in recent years. After Frederick Ike, Sr., passed away in 2003, the Rock Creek community named Damian Totus and Bronsco Jim to succeed him. Two years later, Olsen Meanus succeeded Howard Jim as Celilo chief, a title he now shares with Ray Colfax. Wilbur Slockish, Jr., has taken his father's position as chief of the off-reservation Klickitats, while Johnny Jackson represents the closely related Cascades people. "They elected me as secondary chief of the Klickitats," he explained of the new seat on the council, "but my Cascade people says, 'You should be our chief. We don't have a chief of the Cascade.' So I'm the chief of the Cascades." The seemingly informal nature of these arrangements leaves them open to question, and there are occasional disagreements over who is qualified to serve as chief, especially when there is no hereditary heir willing to serve. The role brings few tangible rewards, as Jackson pointed out shortly after stepping into it: "Your people come first. The welfare and the well being of your people, your children, your elders. . . . They own you, you don't own them." The chiefs help plan and preside over public events, including first-food feasts, funerals, give-aways, weddings, and other celebrations. They are also frequently called upon to settle disputes between individuals, families, and communities along the river. The formation of the MCRC simply institutionalized these traditional duties and gave political voice to people who often feel disenfranchised.[6]

The chiefs continue to speak out because the erosion of their treaty rights and traditions has not ended. At the Underwood in-lieu site, Johnny Jackson defends the tribal boat launch against non-Indian anglers and windsurfers seeking access to the river. During the 1990s, Jackson also helped lead the fight to save Lyle Point, a tribal fishing site slated for development into a premier windsurfing resort. The Yakama Nation filed and then settled a lawsuit against the proposed subdivision, but a diehard group of Columbia River Indians and non-Indian allies occupied the site until the developer backed down. Weary of compromise, Klickitat fisher-man Warren Spencer explained: "I am tired of seeing our people taking a step backwards. We don't have room to take steps backward any more. If we take another step backward, we're going to be in the water, and that'll be the end." Fellow protest leader Margaret Saluskin agreed: "If you turn your back on this river and you walk away, you turn your back on your way of life and you no longer have it, it no longer exists. So the people here by this water, they need to be here. They need to stay here. They need to survive."[7]

Besides a history of struggle, Columbia River Indians share a strong sense of community and a commitment to cultural continuity. On Sun-days and special occasions, families travel to the new longhouse at Celilo Village to attend Washat services, including a First Salmon feast held each April. The Rock Creek community has also rebuilt its longhouse just up the canyon from the original location. The new building provides a focal point for the residents of Georgeville and Billieville, as well as for members now living in the Klickitat and Yakima valleys. Another off-reservation longhouse stands near the old site of Smohalla's village, where four Wánapam households cling to a piece of land donated by the public utility district. Life is not easy in these communities, which continue to struggle with poverty, unemployment, alcohol abuse, and inadequate services. Still, many residents would never live anywhere else. "I don't have nothing against [the reservation]," said Johnny Jackson in a recent interview. "A lot of my relatives live there. I don't have nothing against it. It's just that living on land where there's no big river, I don't feel at home."[8]

The survival of Columbia River Indian identity partially depends on the continued existence of off-reservation communities. Born of resistance and resentment, its proud oppositional character owes much to a history of detachment from the centers of federal and tribal authority. Even today, though, it remains possible for individuals to live on the reservation or in the city while maintaining ties to the river and an alternative social identity. As anthropologist Morris Foster has noted in his study of the Comanches, the perpetuation of community and identity hinges on "the ability of a people to continue to associate with one another, not the preservation of a specific territory, language, or social structure through which to do so." Even for widely scattered communities, public and private gatherings provide the opportunity to renew social connections and reaffirm group membership. Columbia River Indians continue to assert their collective identity through attendance at annual first-food feasts, weekly Washat services, weddings, funerals, and other social occasions. Frederick Ike, Sr., the former leader of the Rock Creek longhouse, owned a house on the Yakama reservation and served on the tribal council until shortly before his death. He viewed Rock Creek as his true home and traveled there regularly to conduct Washat ceremonies for the community. Delsie Selam and Sara Quaempts also resided on the reservation but visited Alderdale, their birthplace, every Memorial Day to clean and decorate their families' graves. Galen Yallup, who currently lives and works on the Yakama reservation, is always asked the same question when he drives down to the Columbia: "When are you going to come home?" It is these enduring bonds and rites of renewal that enable River People to maintain group cohesion despite their geographical dispersal.[9]

From his vantage point in Toppenish, Yallup monitors tribal business and keeps the river chiefs informed about important developments. Such vigilance is necessary, they believe, if Columbia River Indians are to protect the places and resources that have sustained them for generations. As Johnny Jackson told the Senate Select Committee on Indian Affairs in 1988, "We never get to know anything that's going on because we are down on the river. We are the last ones to find out on a lot of things. There are a lot of laws being made, a lot of rules and regulations being passed, and we are the last to find out about it." Although suspicious of government in general, the chiefs must participate in political processes at the federal, state, and tribal levels. Frederick Ike worked for decades to ensure his people's access to traditional gathering sites and burial grounds located on public land. He was one of several River People elected to tribal office in recent years, yet he simultaneously represented the Rock Creek community on the Mid-Columbia River Council. Lavina Washines grew up in that community but recently occupied the chair of the Yakama Tribal Council. Johnny Jackson has never served on tribal council, but he drives up to Toppenish regularly to represent the interests of the River People. In the year 2000, having assumed the title of Cascades chief, he remained unflinching in his defense of Columbia River Indian rights: "Because we've given up enough, and if the government, if the agents, the Bureau of Indian Affairs and the tribal councils, do not want to assist and help protect those rights, then we will stand up."[10]

Although tribal recognition has become a legal impossibility for Columbia River Indians, decades of enrollment and growing participation in tribal governance have not extinguished their sense of independence. It boils to the surface whenever they perceive that some external power—federal, state, or tribal—has ignored their interests and endangered their way of life. For Jackson and the other chiefs, it is no longer a question of separate legal status, though they would accept a form of home rule for the river communities. What they really want is consideration and respect from the governments whose decisions so vitally affect life on the river. Columbia River Indians have become tribal citizens, even tribal leaders, yet they regard their own tribal councils with the same watchful eyes that other rural Westerners cast toward their state and national capitals. In spite of all they have lost, their collective identity remains afloat, anchored in the river for which they are named. "The reason why they have the [tribal] governments today, and the going governments is because a lot of the people along the Columbia River started standing up and speaking out," declared Chief Jackson in 2000. "So the [federal] government doesn't like to hear that and neither does the state governments. They talk with the tribes and say, 'Let's have a [government-to-government relationship] . . . so you can take away the right of them people to speak. You speak for them.' But that's not going to happen as long as there are people like me standing there."[11]

■ ■ ■

Whatever the future may bring for Columbia River Indians, their past holds valuable lessons about Native American history in general. In particular, their story complicates the narrative of confinement and isolation that has dominated popular understanding and representations of Indian life since the Wounded Knee Massacre of 1890. Although few scholars would deny the historical and contemporary significance of reservations, the experience of Columbia River Indians demonstrates that the removal and segregation of Native Americans remained incomplete and contested. Resistance took many forms, passive as well as active, and it did not end with the "Indian Wars" of the late nineteenth century. Wavering federal policies, weaknesses within the reservation system, and the willfulness of individual Indians prevented the solidification of racial lines. Reservation boundaries remained porous, and many Native people either refused to settle within them or never had the choice to do so. This pattern certainly holds true in the Pacific Northwest. On both sides of the Cascade Mountains and the U.S.-Canadian border, permissive treaty language and plentiful labor opportunities encouraged Indians to stay off the reservation. Moreover, in many instances the federal government's failure to authorize or ratify treaties left entire "tribes" without a land base or recognition. In southwest Washington, for example, the descendants of the Lower Chinookan people who met Lewis and Clark still wait for the U.S. government to acknowledge their continuing presence. The Columbia River Indian case, though distinctive in some ways, is representative of a much broader phenomenon in Native American history.[12]

The survival of Indian communities and identities in the absence of reservations—or in spite of them—is by no means unique to the Pacific Northwest. On the contrary, the historical record abounds with examples of Native people living in the midst of Euro-American society. In California, the flood of white settlers after 1849 overwhelmed both the Indian population and the federal government, which threw together a system of temporary reserves but left numerous treaties unratified and many Indians without refuge. Texas blocked the establishment of reservations within its borders, and Oklahoma tribes had their lands swept out from under them by allotment.[13] Alaska became a federal territory after the conclusion of formal treaty-making in 1871, so only a handful of indigenous groups there received trust land. In New England and the Mid-Atlantic region, reservations generally came as an afterthought—if at all—for the remnants of Indian groups overrun or removed in earlier periods. Scholars have also found enduring non-reservation communities in states as diverse as North and South Carolina, Michigan, and Kansas. These varied locations and situations suggest that the reservation paradigm, though useful for making historical generalizations, does not capture the complexity and diversity of modern Indian life.[14]

The same must be said of the tribal model that policymakers and historians alike have traditionally applied to the diverse inhabitants of Indian Country. Taking the terms "Indian" and "tribe" for granted, scholars have generally tried to fit indigenous peoples into the arbitrary and ahistorical categories formulated by the federal government. They have assumed, as most Americans do, that indigenous identities neatly correspond with the labels applied in treaties and bureaucratic records. The Columbia River Indians' experience shows that modern tribal identities are in fact the product of historical experiences and intercultural negotiations. Like all national identities, they are socially constructed and often hotly contested by insiders as well as outsiders.

This is not to say that Indian tribes were simply "made up" by the United States. It bears repeating here that the federal government did not give Native Americans territory, sovereignty, or identity—they already possessed all of those things. Rather, Euro-Americans took forms of social and political organization they did not fully understand and repackaged them as "tribes." Indians then had to sort out the meaning of this transformation, sparking debates that continue to this day. As historian Alexandra Harmon notes in her study of ethnic relations around Puget Sound,

> The contested or impermanent nature of some people's tribal affiliations does not mean that all tribal affiliations have been arbitrary or unimportant. It does not mean that individuals' reasons for thinking of themselves as Indians have often been spurious. Yet during decades of dialogue about where to draw lines around Indians, there have always been some people who were not sure where to stand, some who resisted pressure to stay inside official lines, and some who faced skepticism or objections when they took up a position.[15]

Columbia River Indians fall into all three categories. In the 150 years since the treaties were signed, River People have come to accept membership in the tribal nation-states that arose from those agreements. At the same time, they have maintained a certain physical and psychological distance from the reservations. Skeptical of enrollment and wary of tribal government, they have likewise faced skepticism when they asserted a separate identity. For hundreds of people today, however, being Columbia River Indian remains important to their sense of self.

Claiming this identity does not require an individual to forswear all other allegiances and associations. Although federal policy frames tribal membership as an either/or proposition, Columbia River Indians live in a more complicated world, where personal identities reflect multiple and even contradictory positions. In the context of federal-tribal relations, a question about identity could very well elicit the response, "I'm Yakama," meaning an enrolled member of the Yakama Nation. When speaking to another Indian, the same person might use an aboriginal name such as "Klickitat" or "Wayám." Columbia River Indian identity does not negate these other identities. It is not a distinct ethnicity, since reservation people share the same heritage, but rather the political expression of cultural attachments and aboriginal affiliations that remain important to River People. Their shadow tribe is no less real or meaningful to them than their recognized tribal identities, even though it lacks legal standing. Being Columbia River Indian matters because it embodies their commitment to a place and a culture they wish to preserve.

NOTES

INTRODUCTION

1   Johnny Jackson Statement, *Administrative Appeal of David Sohappy, Sr., et. al., v. Deputy Assistant Secretary—Indian Affairs (Operations)*, IBIA 85-20-A, U.S. Department of Interior—Office of Hearings and Appeals, United States District Court for the District of Oregon, Records of District Courts of the United States, Record Group 21, National Archives and Records Administration—Pacific Alaska Region (*Administrative Appeal of David Sohappy*), 222; Motion to Appear as *Amicus Curiae* and *Amicus Curiae* Brief Before the Interior Board of Indian Appeals, ibid., 132. In 1992, the Yakama Indian Nation reverted to the original spelling of its tribal name: "Yakima" is now spelled "Yakama." I have adopted this spelling to honor the tribe's decision and to distinguish the confederated tribes from the river, county, and city of the same name. Quotations and citations containing the variant spelling have not been changed.

2 Brief of Bureau of Indian Affairs, *Administrative Appeal of David Sohappy*, 74.

3 I use the terms "colonization," "colonialism," and "colonial" to describe a system of domination in which the United States appropriated Native American lands and resources, subjected Indians to policies of forced acculturation, disrupted traditional forms of social and political organization while imposing its own legal and governmental structure, and directly administered tribal affairs through a federal bureaucracy that still exists today. See, for example, Jeffrey Ostler, *The Plains Sioux and U.S. Colonialism from Lewis and Clark to Wounded Knee* (New York: Cambridge University Press, 2004).

4 Throughout the book, I use "Columbia River Indian" and "River People" interchangeably to refer to the off-reservation population concentrated along the Columbia River between the Cascade Rapids (near present-day Cascade Locks, Oregon) and Wallula Gap (near present-day Walla Walla, Washington). Although these people have sometimes called themselves "Mid-Columbia Indians," I use that term in the broader sense common among historians and anthropologists to include all aboriginal groups that historically occupied or utilized the middle stretch of the Columbia. Therefore, in this discussion, Mid-Columbia is synonymous with "southern Columbia Plateau," the southern portion of the Plateau culture area.

5 Eugene S. Hunn, "What Ever Happened to the First Peoples of the Columbia?" in *Great River of the West: Essays on the Columbia River*, ed. William L. Lang and Robert C. Carriker (Seattle: University of Washington Press, 1999), 30.

6 Patricia C. Albers, "Changing Patterns of Ethnicity in the Northeastern Plains, 1780–1870," in *History, Power, and Identity: Ethnogenesis in the Americas*, ed. Jonathan D. Hill (Iowa City: University of Iowa Press, 1996), 93–94.

7 Eugene Hunn first identified Columbia River Indians as a distinct group and briefly discussed their history in his ethnographic survey of the Mid-Columbia region, *Nch'i-Wána, "The Big River": Mid-Columbia Indians and Their Land* (Seattle: University of Washington Press, 1990), 269–74. Historian Roberta Ulrich also acknowledged the separate interests of the River People in her chronicle of the continuing struggle over in-lieu fishing sites, *Empty Nets: Indians, Dams, and the Columbia River* (Corvallis: Oregon State University Press, 1999). These accounts provide few details, however, and neither author attempts to trace the historical evolution of Columbia River Indian identity.

8 Robert H. Ruby and John A. Brown, *The Cayuse Indians: Imperial Tribesmen of Old Oregon* (Norman: University of Oklahoma Press, 1972), x. Peter

Iverson, among others, criticizes the use of Wounded Knee as a historical coda in *"We Are Still Here": American Indians in the Twentieth Century* (Wheeling, IL: Harlan Davidson, Inc., 1998), 1–4.

9   For example, in David Goldfield et. al., *The American Journey: A History of the United States* (Upper Saddle River, NJ: Prentice-Hall, Inc., 1998), Native Americans appear only four times after 1890, each occasion corresponding with a major shift in federal Indian policy; namely, the Indian New Deal of the 1930s, World War II and termination, and the "Red Power" movement of the 1970s. Brad Asher cites additional examples of the traditional textbook storyline in *Beyond the Reservation: Indians, Settlers, and the Law in Washington Territory, 1853–1889* (Norman: University of Oklahoma Press, 1999), 4. Alexandra Harmon also critiques the conventional focus on reservation confinement in *Indians in the Making: Ethnic Relations and Indian Identities around Puget Sound* (Berkeley and Los Angeles: University of California Press, 1999), 103–30.

10 Raymond D. Fogelson, "Perspectives on Native American Identity," in *Studying Native America: Problems and Prospects*, ed. Russell Thornton (Madison: University of Wisconsin Press, 1998), 40–43; Jonathan D. Hill, "Introduction: Ethnogenesis in the Americas, 1492–1992," in *History, Power, and Identity: Ethnogenesis in the Americas*, ed. Jonathan D. Hill (Iowa City: University of Iowa Press, 1996), 7–9; Edwin N. Wilmsen, "Premises of Power in Ethnic Politics," in *The Politics of Difference: Ethnic Premises in a World of Power*, ed. Edwin N. Wilmsen and Patrick McAllister (Chicago: University of Chicago Press, 1996), 2–4. On the discourse of authenticity, see Philip J. Deloria, *Indians in Unexpected Places* (Lawrence: University Press of Kansas, 2004), and Paige Raibmon, *Authentic Indians: Episodes of Encounter from the Late-Nineteenth-Century Northwest Coast* (Durham, NC: Duke University Press, 2005).

11 Among the best historical monographs on urban Indians are James B. LaGrand, *Indian Metropolis: Native Americans in Chicago, 1945–1975* (Urbana and Chicago: University of Illinois Press, 2002) and Coll Thrush, *Native Seattle: Histories from the Crossing-Over Place* (Seattle: University of Washington Press, 2007).

12 For examples of this trend among historians, see Frederick Hoxie, *Parading through History: The Making of the Crow Nation in America, 1805–1935* (New York: Cambridge University Press, 1995); John W. Heaton, *The Shoshone-Bannocks: Culture and Commerce at Fort Hall, 1870–1940* (Lawrence: University Press of Kansas, 2005); Peter Iverson, *Dinéé: A History of the Navajos* (Albuquerque: University of New Mexico Press, 2002); Paul C. Rosier, *Rebirth of the Blackfeet Nation, 1912–1954* (Lincoln: University of Nebraska Press, 2001); and Laura Woodworth-Ney, *Mapping Identity: The*

Creation of the Coeur d'Alene Indian Reservation, 1805–1902 (Boulder: University Press of Colorado, 2004).

13   Asher, *Beyond the Reservation*, 4–9; Harmon, *Indians in the Making*, 103–4.

14   Harmon, *Indians in the Making*, 247; Eugeene E. Roosens, "The Making of Natural Feelings: Problems, Concepts, and Theoretical Starting Point," in *Creating Ethnicity: The Process of Ethnogenesis, Frontiers of Anthropology*, vol. 5, ed. Eugeene E. Roosens (Newbury Park, NJ: Sage Publications, 1989), 16; Wilmsen, "Premises of Power," 4–5.

15   Morris W. Foster, *Being Comanche: A Social History of an American Indian Community* (Tucson: University of Arizona Press, 1991), 16–17; Loretta Fowler, *Shared Symbols, Contested Meanings: Gros Ventre Culture and History, 1778–1984* (Ithaca, NY: Cornell University Press, 1987), 9. For other recent studies of tribal politics and identity formation, see Thomas Biolsi, *Organizing the Lakota: The Political Economy of the New Deal on the Pine Ridge and Rosebud Reservations* (Tucson: University of Arizona Press, 1993); Melissa L. Meyer, *The White Earth Tragedy: Ethnicity and Dispossession at a Minnesota Anishinaabe Reservation, 1889–1920* (Lincoln: University of Nebraska Press, 1994); Circe Sturm, *Blood Politics: Race, Culture, and Identity in the Cherokee Nation of Oklahoma* (Berkeley: University of California Press, 2002); and Gregory E. Smoak, *Ghost Dances and Identity: Prophetic Religion and American Indian Ethnogenesis in the Nineteenth Century* (Berkeley and Los Angeles: University of California Press, 2006).

16   Wilmsen, "Premises of Power," 21. The classic studies on nationalism and ethnic identity formation are Benedict Anderson, *Imagined Communities: Reflections on the Origins and Spread of Nationalism* (New York: Verso, 1991) and Fredrik Barth, *The Social Organization of Culture Difference* (London: Allen & Unwin, 1969). For an overview of the contested history of "Americanism," see Eric Foner, *The Story of American Freedom* (New York: W.W. Norton & Company, 1998).

17   Hill, *History, Power, and Identity*, 13.

18   Harmon, *Indians in the Making*, 4–5.

1 PEOPLE OF THE RIVER

1   James P. Ronda, *Lewis and Clark among the Indians* (Lincoln: University of Nebraska Press, 1984), 217–19; Gary E. Moulton, ed., *The Journals of the Lewis & Clark Expedition*, vol. 7 (Lincoln: University of Nebraska Press, 1991), 132–39. Stick game, also known as bone or hand game, is still popular among Plateau Indians today.

2   David H. French and Katherine S. French, "Wasco, Wishram, and Cascades," in *Handbook of North American Indians*, vol. 12, ed. Deward E. Walker (Washington, DC: Smithsonian Institution, 1998), 362.

3   Robert Boyd, *People of The Dalles: The Indians of Wascopam Mission* (Lincoln: University of Nebraska Press, 1996), 4–5; Helen H. Schuster, "Yakama and Neighboring Groups," in Walker, *Handbook of North American Indians*, 327; Hunn, *Nch'i-Wána*, 216–17; Harmon, *Indians in the Making*, 8.

4   Trial Transcript, *United States of America v. Seufert Brothers Company*, vol. 2, John Wilson Special Collections, Multnomah County Library, Portland (Trial Transcript), 302; U.S. Senate, Select Committee on Indian Affairs, *Columbia River Fisheries Management: Hearing before the Select Committee on Indian Affairs*, 100th Cong., 2nd sess., 19 April 1988 (U.S. Senate, Select Committee), 45. Wanałáma is generally applied to the groups residing along the river between the former villages of Tináynu (Tenino) and Walú·la (Wallula). Wánapam is the northeast and northwest Sahaptin term, typically used to refer to the people who live on the Columbia only between Priest Rapids and the Tri-Cities area. Although the Wánapams have shared similar historical experiences and overlapping genealogies with their downstream neighbors, they remain geographically distant and politically distinct from the main body of Columbia River Indians discussed in this study. Henceforth, all indigenous words written in phonemic orthography are Columbia River Sahaptin terms adapted from Hunn, *Nch'i-Wána*, or transliterated by linguist Bruce Rigsby, University of Queensland.

5   Jarold Ramsey, ed., *Coyote Was Going There: Indian Literature of the Oregon Country* (Seattle: University of Washington Press, 1977), 43, 47.

6   Richard White, *The Organic Machine: The Remaking of the Columbia River* (New York: Hill and Wang, 1995), 18–19. See also Edward Sapir, ed., *Wishram Texts*, vol. 2 (Leyden: E. J. Brill, 1909; New York: AMS Press, Inc., 1974); Donald M. Hines, *The Forgotten Tribes: Oral Tales of the Teninos and Adjacent Mid-Columbia River Indian Nations* (Issaquah, WA: Great Eagle Publishing, Inc., 1991) and *Celilo Tales: Wasco Myths, Legends, Tales of Magic and the Marvelous* (Issaquah, WA: Great Eagle Publishing, Inc., 1996).

7   Emory and Ruth Strong, *Seeking Western Waters: The Lewis and Clark Trail from the Rockies to the Pacific* (Portland: Oregon Historical Society Press, 1995), 95–96; Hunn, *Nch'i-Wána*, 20–21; James D. Keyser, *Indian Rock Art of the Columbia Plateau* (Seattle: University of Washington Press, 1992), 23–28. For a critique of the prevailing view that Plateau culture remained relatively stable in the protohistoric period, see Sarah H. Campbell, *Post-Columbian Culture History in the Northern Columbia Plateau* (New York: Garland Publishing, 1990).

8   Eugene S. Hunn and David H. French, "Western Columbia River Sahaptins," in Walker, *Handbook of North American Indians*, 380.

9   Hunn, *Nch'i-Wána*, 119–21; Boyd, *People of The Dalles*, 63–68.

10 Angelo Anastasio, "The Southern Plateau: An Ecological Analysis of Inter-group Relations," *Northwest Anthropological Research Notes* 6, no. 2 (1972): 109–29; Slockish comment made at meeting with the U.S. Forest Service, Field Notes, Berry Field Meeting, 25 July 2006, Mt. Adams Ranger Station, Trout Lake, Washington, in author's possession (Field Notes, Berry Field Meeting); Lillian A. Ackerman, ed., *A Song to the Creator: Traditional Arts of Native American Women of the Plateau* (Norman: University of Oklahoma Press, 1996), 9–12; Hunn, *Nch'i-Wána*, 136–37.

11 Hunn and French, "Western Columbia River Sahaptins," in Walker, *Handbook of North American Indians*, 148–51; Boyd, *People of The Dalles*, 53.

12 Robert H. Ruby and John A. Brown, *Indian Slavery in the Pacific Northwest* (Spokane, WA: A. H. Clark Company, 1993), 223–27. Although most Sahaptin-speaking groups did not practice slavery on a large scale, they did hold some captives in servile positions (*ašwaníya*) and trade others to Upper Chinookan and Northwest Coast peoples. Plateau Indian slavery differed significantly from both racialized Euro-American chattel slavery and Northwest Coast varieties of "unfreedom." For information about Northwest Coast slavery, see Leland Donald, *Aboriginal Slavery on the Northwest Coast of North America* (Berkeley: University of California Press, 1997).

13 Helen Hersh Schuster, *The Yakima* (New York and Philadelphia: Chelsea House Publishers, 1990), 27; "Billingsgate" reference quoted in Boyd, *People of The Dalles*, 49.

14 Hunn, *Nch'i-Wána*, 123–27; Records of the U.S. Indian Claims Commission, Docket 47, *The Yakima Tribe of Indians v. The United States*, Transcript of Proceedings, 21 August, 1950 (New York: Clearwater Publishing Co, Inc., 1975), 100.

15 Hunn, *Nch'i-Wána*, 128–32.

16 Vivian M. Adams, "Welcome Statement," in *A Time of Gathering: Native Heritage in Washington State*, ed. Robin K. Wright (Seattle: University of Washington Press, 1991), 12; Roberta Haines, "Eastern Washington Native Peoples: A Personal Introduction," in ibid., 158–59; Boyd, *People of The Dalles*, 6.

17 Lewis and Clark quoted in Hunn, *Nch'i-Wána*, 153.

18 Perkins quoted in ibid.

19 Ibid.

20 Stephen J. Langdon, "Sustaining a Relationship: Inquiry into the Emergence of a Logic of Engagement with Salmon among the Southern Tlingits,"

in *Native Americans and the Environment: Perspectives on the Ecological Indian*, ed. Michael E. Harkin and David Rich Lewis (Lincoln: University of Nebraska Press, 2007), 238; Joseph E. Taylor III, *Making Salmon: An Environmental History of the Northwest Fisheries Crisis* (Seattle: University of Washington Press, 1999), 14.

21   Hunn and French, "Western Columbia River Sahaptins," in Walker, *Handbook of North American Indians*, 387; U.S. Senate, Select Committee on Indian Affairs, 49; Edward G. Swindell, Jr., U.S. Department of the Interior, Office of Indian Affairs, Division of Forestry and Grazing, *Report on Source, Nature, and Extent of the Fishing, Hunting, and Miscellaneous Related Rights of Certain Indian Tribes in Washington and Oregon Territory Together with Affidavits Showing the Location of a Number of Usual and Accustomed Fishing Grounds and Stations* (Los Angeles: Office of Indian Affairs, 1942), 152. On Indian conservation practices in the Northwest salmon fisheries, see Taylor, *Making Salmon*, 13–38.

22   Hunn, *Nch'i-Wána*, 59–61, 134–36; M. Dale Kinkade et al., "Languages," in Walker, *Handbook of North American Indians*, 49–72; French and French, "Wasco, Wishram, and Cascades," in ibid., 374.

23   Verne F. Ray, "Cultural Relations in the Plateau of Northwestern America," in *Publications of the Frederick Webb Hodge Anniversary Publication Fund*, vol. 3 (Los Angeles: Southwestern Museum, 1939), 9; Hunn and French, "Western Columbia River Sahaptins," in Walker, *Handbook of North American Indians*, 392; French and French, "Wasco, Wishram, and Cascades," in ibid., 374–75.

24   French and French, "Wasco, Wishram, and Cascades," in Walker, *Handbook of North American Indians*, 369–70; Hunn and French, "Western Columbia River Sahaptins," in ibid., 387; Schuster, "Yakama and Neighboring Groups," in ibid., 336; Hunn, *Nch'i-Wána*, 216–17. Bruce G. Miller and Daniel L. Boxberger refute the idea of pre-contact chiefdoms in "Creating Chiefdoms: The Puget Sound Case," *Ethnohistory* 41 (Spring 1994): 267–93.

25   Hunn, *Nch'i-Wána*, 201; Hunn and French, "Western Columbia River Sahaptins," in Walker, *Handbook of North American Indians*, 386; Swindell, *Report on Source*, 161; Boyd, *People of The Dalles*, 72–73; Harmon, *Indians in the Making*, 8.

26   Hunn, *Nch'i-Wána*, 93–94; Boyd, *People of The Dalles*, 53; Swindell, *Report on Source*, 151.

27   Hunn, *Nch'i-Wána*, 23–24.

28   Ibid., 24–25; Ruby and Brown, *Indian Slavery*, 223–27, 262–69; Robert H. Ruby and John A. Brown, *A Guide to the Indian Tribes of the Pacific Northwest* (Norman: University of Oklahoma Press, 1992), 96.

29 Hunn, *Nch'i-Wána*, 27–32; Ie-keep-swah, "Vision of Wat-til-ki," July 1918, Lucullus V. McWhorter Papers, 1918–1945, Box 43, Folder 422, Manuscripts, Archives and Special Collections, Washington State University, Pullman. Robert T. Boyd provides a detailed analysis of "virgin soil" epidemics in *The Coming of the Spirit of Pestilence: Introduced Infectious Diseases and Population Decline Among Northwest Coast Indians, 1774–1874* (Seattle: University of Washington Press, 1999).

30 Boyd, *People of The Dalles*, 38; U.S. Department of the Interior, Office of Indian Affairs, *Annual Report of the Commissioner of Indian Affairs, 1854* (Washington, DC: A.O.P. Nicholson, 1855) (ARCIA-year), 232.

31 Harmon, *Indians in the Making*, 16–17.

32 Hunn, *Nch'i-Wána*, 34–37; White, *Organic Machine*, 14. For a brief overview of the fur trade in the interior Northwest, see D. W. Meinig, *The Great Columbia Plain: A Historical Geography, 1805–1910* (Seattle: University of Washington Press, 1968). See also Theodore Stern, *Chiefs & Chief Traders: Indian Relations at Fort Nez Percés, 1818–1855* (Corvallis: Oregon State University Press, 1992).

33 Hunn, *Nch'i-Wána*, 3, 6; Theodore Stern, *Chiefs and Change in the Oregon Country: Indian Relations at Fort Nez Percés, 1818–1855*, vol. 2 (Corvallis: Oregon State University Press, 1997), xv, 7; Ronda, *Lewis and Clark among the Indians*, 171–72; White, *Organic Machine*, 13–14. On the concept of the "middle ground," see Richard White, *The Middle Ground: Indians, Empires, and Republics in the Great Lakes Region, 1650–1815* (New York: Cambridge University Press, 1991).

34 Stern, *Chiefs and Change*, xiv, 2–27.

35 Ibid., 22–27; Hunn, *Nch'i-Wána*, 216.

36 Schuster, *The Yakima*, 47–48; Stern, *Chiefs and Change*, xv; Harmon, *Indians in the Making*, 41; Hunn, *Nch'i-Wána*, 37–38. On the role of mixed bloods in the fur trade, see John C. Jackson, *Children of the Fur Trade: Forgotten Metis of the Pacific Northwest* (Missoula, MT: Mountain Press Publishing Company, 1995).

37 Hunn, *Nch'i-Wána*, 38–44. See also Christopher L. Miller, *Prophetic Worlds: Indians and Whites on the Columbia Plateau* (New Brunswick, NJ: Rutgers University Press, 1985); Boyd, *People of The Dalles*; Larry Cebula, *Plateau Indians and the Quest for Spiritual Power, 1700–1850* (Lincoln: University of Nebraska Press, 2003); Julie Roy Jeffrey, *Converting the West: A Biography of Narcissa Whitman* (Norman: University of Oklahoma Press, 1991); and John J. Killoren, *"Come, Black Robe": De Smet and the Indian Tragedy* (Norman: University of Oklahoma Press, 1994).

38 Cebula, *Plateau Indians*, 2–3, 90–127; Hunn, *Nch'i-Wána*, 40–42; Chief Joseph quoted in Alvin M. Josephy, *The Nez Perce Indians and the Open-*

ing of the Northwest (Lincoln: University of Nebraska Press, 1971), 452.

39 Stern, *Chiefs and Change*, 94–96, 107–16, 129, 247.

40 Boyd, *People of The Dalles*, 159–61; Stern, *Chiefs and Change*, 128–37.

41 Asher, *Beyond the Reservation*, 23–24; Josephy, *Nez Perce Indians*, 222–24; Stern, *Chiefs and Change*, 136–44.

2 MAKING TREATIES, MAKING TRIBES

1 Boyd, *People of The Dalles*, 329–31; copy of a letter from an Indian of the Waskopam Tribe named William Chineuch, 3 November 1853, Records of the Washington Superintendency of Indian Affairs, 1853–1874 (National Archives Microfilm Publication M5), Records of the Bureau of Indian Affairs, Record Group 75, National Archives Building, Washington, DC, Roll 608 (Records of the Washington Superintendency of Indian Affairs).

2 On the origins and evolution of the reservation policy, see Francis Paul Prucha, *The Great Father: The United States Government and the American Indians*, 2 vols. (Lincoln: University of Nebraska Press, 1986); and Robert A. Trennert, Jr., *Alternative to Extinction: Federal Indian Policy and the Beginnings of the Reservation System, 1846–51* (Philadelphia: Temple University Press, 1975). Prucha also surveys the history of treaty making in *American Indian Treaties: The History of a Political Anomaly* (Berkeley: University of California Press, 1994). On the negotiation of treaties and the creation of reservations in the Pacific Northwest, see Clifford E. Trafzer, ed., *Indians, Superintendents, and Councils: Northwestern Indian Policy, 1850–1855* (Lanham, MD and New York: University Press of America, 1986).

3 David H. French and Katherine S. French, "Wasco, Wishram, and Cascades," in Walker, *Handbook of North American Indians*, 360; Eugene S. Hunn and David H. French, "Western Columbia River Sahaptins," in ibid., 378, 392–94.

4 Robert Newell to Joel Palmer, 10 August 1849, MSS 114-2, Oregon Historical Society, Portland; Hunn, *Nch'i-Wána*, 211–14; U.S. Department of Interior, Office of Indian Affairs, ARCIA-1854, 227–28.

5 Newell to Palmer; Josephy, *Nez Perce Indians*, 278–79.

6 Isaac I. Stevens to Joel Palmer, 7 January 1854, Records of the Washington Superintendency of Indian Affairs, Roll 1; Stern, *Chiefs and Change in the Oregon Country*, 270–71. See also Kent D. Richards, *Issac I. Stevens: Young Man in a Hurry* (Provo, UT: Brigham Young University Press, 1979; repr., Pullman: Washington State University Press, 1993); Terence O'Donnell, *An Arrow in the Earth: General Joel Palmer and the Indians of Oregon* (Portland: Oregon Historical Society, 1991).

7   Isaac I. Stevens to Andrew J. Bolon, 23 March 1854, Records of the Washington Superintendency of Indian Affairs, Roll 1 [emphasis in original]; Boxberger and Miller, "Creating Chiefdoms," 273–76.

8   The Sahaptin term *Šuyápu* (white man) derived from neighboring Interior Salish languages and referred to the abundant facial hair of the newcomers. See Bruce Rigsby, "Changing Property Relations in Land and Resources in the Southern Plateau," paper presented at the Pacific Northwest Treaties in National and International Perspective Conference, Seattle, May 2005, in author's possession.

9   Schuster, *The Yakima*, 53–55; Stern, *Chiefs and Change*, 275–77; Josephy, *Nez Perce Indians*, 305–6. See Andrew J. Splawn, *Ka-mi-akin, Last Hero of the Yakimas* (Portland: Binfords and Mort for the Oregon Historical Society, 1944).

10   James Doty, *Journal of Operations of Isaac Ingalls Stevens of Washington Territory*, ed. Edward J. Kowrach (Fairfield, WA: Ye Galleon Press, 1978), 17; Stern, *Chiefs and Change*, 236–39, 282–92.

11   Treaty with the Yakima, 1855, in *Indian Affairs: Laws and Treaties*, vol. II, ed. Charles J. Kappler (Washington, DC: Government Printing Office, 1904), 698–702. As written in the treaty, the fourteen tribes and bands were the Yakama, Palouse, Pisquouse, Wenatshapam, Klikatat, Klinquit, Kow-was-say-ee, Li-ay-was, Skin-pah, Wish-ham, Shyiks, Oche-chotes, Kah-milt-pah, and Se-ap-cat.

12   Treaty with the Walla Walla, Cayuse, and Umatilla, 1855, in Kappler, *Indian Affairs*, 694–98; Treaty with the Nez Perces, 1855, in ibid., 702–6. For detailed accounts of the Walla Walla Council, see Josephy, *Nez Perce Indians*, 277–323, and Stern, *Chiefs and Change*, 293–315.

13   Treaty with the Tribes of Middle Oregon, 1855, in Kappler, *Indian Affairs*, 714–19. The treaty identified seven subdivisions within the Walla Walla (Warm Springs) and Wasco tribes: the Upper Deschutes band of Walla Wallas, the Lower Deschutes band of Walla Wallas, the Tenino band of Walla Wallas, the John Days River band of Walla Wallas, the Dalles band of Wascos, the Ki-gal-twal-la band of Wascos, and the Dog River band of Wascos.

14   Colin E. Twedell, "A Componential Analysis of the Criteria Defining an Indian 'Tribe' in Western Washington," in *Western Washington Indian Socio-Economics: Papers in Honor of Angelo Anastasio*, ed. Herbert C. Taylor, Jr., and Garland F. Grabert (Bellingham: Western Washington University, 1984), 69.

15   Harmon, *Indians in the Making*, 85. Anthropologist Russell Barsh has likewise noted the role of treaties in shaping modern Northwest tribes in "Ethnogenesis and Ethnonationalism from Competing Treaty Claims," paper

given at the Pacific Northwest Treaties in National and International Perspective Conference, Seattle, May 2005, in author's possession. See also Smoak, *Ghost Dances and Identity*, 85–112.

16   Joel Palmer to George Manypenny, 9 July 1855, Proceedings of the Wasco Council (typescript), MSS 616, Oregon Historical Society, Portland; Statement of John Skan-now-wa, 17 July 1944, Folder 155L, General Subject Correspondence, 1939–1953, Portland Area Office, Records of the Bureau of Indian Affairs, Record Group 75, National Archives and Records Administration—Pacific Alaska Region (General Subject Correspondence, 1939–1953); Virginia Bryant, "The Walla Walla Council," in Trafzer, *Indians, Superintendents, and Councils*, 77; Bruce H. Wendt, "The Dalles Treaty Council," in ibid., 87.

17   Schuster, *The Yakima*, 66; Clifford E. Trafzer and Richard D. Scheuerman, *Renegade Tribe: The Palouse Indians and the Invasion of the Inland Pacific Northwest* (Pullman: Washington State University Press, 1986), 47.

18   "Tribal Affiliations of the Yakama Signers to the Treaty of June 9, 1855 (Given by Louis Mann and other old tribesmen)," Lucullus V. McWhorter Papers; Records of the U.S. Indian Claims Commission, 81–83; Click Relander, *Strangers on the Land: A Historiette of a Longer Story of the Yakima Indian Nation's Efforts to Survive Against Great Odds* (Yakima, WA: Franklin Press, 1962), 77–79. The sixth signer, Tecolekun, cannot be positively identified, but he probably came from a river village. Testifying before the Indian Claims Commission, Jobe Charley identified Tecolekun as "Pulutkin" and placed him on the Columbia River between Rock Creek and Wallula (Records of the U.S. Indian Claims Commission, 82). Bruce Rigsby speculates that he may be Púlitqan, Owhi's son (personal communication to author, 19 April 2006).

19   Isaac I. Stevens to George W. Manypenny, 14 June 1855, Documents Relating to the Negotiation of Ratified and Unratified Treaties with Various Indian Tribes, 1801–1869 (National Archives Microfilm Publication T494), Records of the Bureau of Indian Affairs, Record Group 75, National Archives Building, Washington, DC, Roll 5.

20   Harmon, *Indians in the Making*, 85; Isaac Ingalls Stevens, *A True Copy of the Record of the Official Proceedings at the Council in the Walla Walla Valley, 1855*, ed. Darrell Scott (Fairfield, WA: Ye Galleon Press, 1985), 93.

21   Palmer to Manypenny, 9 July 1855.

22   Stevens to Bolon, 23 March 1854; Josephy, *Nez Perce Indians*, 315–20; Hunn, "What Ever Happened to the First Peoples of the Columbia?" 27; Trial Transcript, 398.

23   Rigsby, "Changing Property Relations in Land," 2–3; Stevens, *True Copy of the Record*, 82, 93; Hunn and French, "Western Columbia River

Sahaptins," in Walker, *Handbook of North American Indians*, 378; Palmer to Manypenny, 9 July 1855.

24   Stevens, *True Copy of the Record*, 80–82.

25   Clifford E. Trafzer, "Earth, Animals, and Academics: Plateau Indian Communities, Culture, and the Walla Walla Council of 1855," *American Indian Culture and Research Journal* 17, no.3 (1993): 90–92; Cebula, *Plateau Indians and the Quest for Spiritual Power*, 81–87.

26   Stevens, *True Copy of the Record*, 89; Wendt, "The Dalles Treaty Council," in Trafzer, *Indians, Superintendents, and Councils*, 92–95; Palmer to Manypenny, 9 July 1855.

27   Stevens, *True Copy of the Record*, 51–52.

28   Ibid., 52–53, 57; Palmer to Manypenny, 9 July 1855.

29   Gibbs quoted in Schuster, *The Yakima*, 55.

30   Records of the U.S. Indian Claims Commission, 102; Palmer to Manypenny, 9 July 1855.

31   Treaty with the Yakima, 1855, in Kappler, *Indian Affairs*, 699 (emphasis added).

32   Andrew H. Fisher, "'This I Know from the Old People': Yakama Indian Treaty Rights as Oral Tradition," *Montana, The Magazine of Western History* 49 (Spring 1999): 6.

33   Stevens, *True Copy of the Record*, 67; Palmer to Manypenny, 9 July 1855.

34   Fisher, "This I Know from the Old People," 9–11; Statement of John Skannowwa, 17 July 1944, General Subject Correspondence, 1939–53, 2.

35   Affidavit of Eugene S. Hunn, vol. 2, Civil 86–715, *David Sohappy, Sr., et. al. v. Donald Hodel*, United States District Court for the District of Oregon, Records of District Courts of the United States, Record Group 21, National Archives and Records Administration—Pacific Alaska Region (Civil 86–715) 7–8; Statement of John Skannowwa, 17 July 1944, General Subject Correspondence, 1939–53, 1.

36   Affidavit of Eugene S. Hunn, Civil 86–715, 4–6, 11–12. The Warm Springs treaty employs the term "suitable houses," while the other three treaties use the word "buildings," which has no equivalent in the Sahaptin language. Bruce Rigsby glosses *nišáykt* as "village, settlement" rather than "dwelling" (personal communication to author, 19 April 2006).

37   U.S. Senate, Select Committee, 148.

38   Joel Palmer to John E. Wool, 21 November 1855, Letters Received by the Office of Indian Affairs, 1824–1881, Oregon Superintendency, 1842–1880 (National Archives Microfilm Publication M234), Records of the Bureau of Indian Affairs, Record Group 75, National Archives, Washington, DC, Roll 609 (Letters Received by the Office of Indian Affairs); Schuster, *The Yakima*, 65; Trafzer, "Earth, Animals, and Academics," 95.

39   Stevens, *True Copy of the Record,* 70, 98; Schuster, *The Yakima,* 68; Stern, *Chiefs and Change,* 318–19; Joel Palmer to George Manypenny, 8 October 1853, Letters Received by the Office of Indian Affairs, Roll 11; "Indian Treaties," *(Portland) Oregonian,* 23 June 1855.

40   Schuster, *The Yakima,* 68–69; "Indian War," *(Portland) Oregonian,* 20 October 1855.

41   U.S. Department of Interior, Office of Indian Affairs, ARCIA-1855, 194; Schuster, *The Yakima,* 69–73; Richard H. Lansdale to James W. Nesmith, 20 September 1858, Records of the Washington Superintendency of Indian Affairs, Roll 17; R. R. Thompson to Joel Palmer, 28 September 1855, Letters Received by the Office of Indian Affairs, M234, Roll 608.

42   U.S. Department of Interior, Office of Indian Affairs, ARCIA-1855, 194; Stern, *Chiefs and Change,* 326; Albert H. Robie to Isaac I. Stevens, 5 September 1856, Records of the Washington Superintendency of Indian Affairs, Roll 17; Joel Palmer to George Manypenny, 25 October 1855, Letters Received by the Office of Indian Affairs, Roll 609; Annual Report of John H. Noble, 31 July 1857, ibid., Roll 610.

43   Wasco Jim, July 1918, "The Chiefs of Some of the Columbia River Tribes," Lucullus V. McWhorter Papers, Box 15, Folder 127.

44   R. R. Thompson to Joel Palmer, 31 March 1856, Letters Received by the Office of Indian Affairs, Roll 609.

45   "Clans of the Yakimas Who Were Present at the Treaty of Walla Walla, 1855, and Who Met Col. Wright in a Treaty of Peace Later in the Naches, As Given by Chief We-yallup Wa-ya-cika," Lucullus V. McWhorter Papers, Box 15, Folder 127; Nathan Olney to Joel Palmer, 30 November 1855, Letters Received by the Office of Indian Affairs, Roll 609.

46   "Indian War," *Oregonian.*

47   Relander, *Strangers on the Land,* 57; Stephen Dow Beckham, *"This Place Is Romantic and Wild": An Historical Overview of the Cascades Area, Fort Cascades, and the Cascades Townsite, Washington Territory,* Heritage Research Associates Report No. 27 (Eugene, OR: Heritage Research Associates, 1984), 56–57; Selma Neils, *The Klickitat Indians* (Portland: Binford & Mort, 1985), 90–93. On the general conduct of the Oregon Volunteers, see John C. Jackson, *A Little War of Destiny: The First Regiment of Oregon Mounted Volunteers and the Yakima Indian War of 1855–56* (Fairfield, WA: Ye Galleon Press, 1995) and William N. Bischoff, S. J., eds., *We Were Not Summer Soldiers: The Indian War Diary of Plympton J. Kelly, 1855–1856* (Tacoma: Washington State Historical Society, 1976).

48   Palmer to Manypenny, 25 October 1855, Letters Received by the Office of Indian Affairs, Roll 609; R. R. Thompson to Joel Palmer, 26 February 1856, ibid.; H. A. Porter to Don M. Carr, 21 June 1919, Wishram Tribe

Claims (1919), General Subject   Correspondence, 1908–1921, Yakima Indian Agency, Records of the Bureau of Indian Affairs, Record Group 75, National Archives and Records Administration—Pacific Alaska Region (General Subject Correspondence, 1908–1921).; Alfred Townshend to John Cain, 1 Marc h 1857, Records of the Washington Superintendency of Indian Affairs, Roll 17; R. H. Lansdale to J. W. Nesmith, 31 May 1858, ibid.

49 Isaac I. Stevens, "Notes of a Council Held with the Klickitat Indians at Vancouver, Washington Territory, October 22, 1856," typescript, Yakama Nation Archives, Toppenish, Washington; Alfred Townshend to John Cain, 1 April 1857, Records of the Washington Superintendency of Indian Affairs, Roll 17; Isaac I. Stevens to John Cain, 13 March 1857, ibid.; R. H. Lansdale to J. W. Nesmith, 23 August 1858, ibid.; R. H. Lansdale to J. W. Nesmith, 1 March 1858, ibid.

50 Harmon, *Indians in the Making*, 90; Lansdale to Nesmith, 23 August 1858, Records of the Washington Superintendency of Indian Affairs, Roll 17; R. H. Lansdale to C. H. Mott, 22 October 1858, Letters Received by the Office of Indian Affairs, Roll 611.

51 Mid-Columbia River Council, "Statement of Unification," 18 December February 1990, in Application for Federal Assistance to the Administration for Native Americans, 5 February 1993, Keith Hatch, Personal Files, Celilo Village Housing, Portland Area Office, Bureau of Indian Affairs (Hatch Files), 66–67.

52 "The Personal Narrative of Chief Spencer," Lucullus V. McWhorter Papers, Box 15, Folder 120; Mid-Columbia River Council, "Statement of Unification," Hatch Files, 67.

3 THEY MEAN TO BE INDIAN ALWAYS

1 Captain W. H. Boyle to Major A. A. Nickerson, 25 November 1878, Letters Received by the Office of Indian Affairs, Roll 628; John Smith to General Oliver O. Howard, 27 November 1878, ibid., Roll 628; U.S. Department of Interior, Office of Indian Affairs, ARCIA-1879, 134.

2 Census of Indians Refusing to Give Names or Statistics Belonging to Yakama Agency, no date (circa 1881), Yakima Indian Agency Correspondence and Records, National Archives Microfilm Publication I6, Records of the Bureau of Indian Affairs, Record Group 75, National Archives Building, Washington, DC (Yakima Indian Agency Correspondence); Clifford C. Relander Collection, Yakima Valley Regional Library, Yakima, Washington, Roll 2 (Clifford C. Relander Collection); Umatilla Indian Agency, Monthly Report for May 1878, William Cameron McKay Papers, 1824–

1893, Mss 413–1, Oregon Historical Society, Roll 2; John Smith to General Oliver O. Howard, 2 May 1879, vol. 2, July 1, 1878-Sept. 9, 1879, 229–30, Letters Sent to Commissioner of Indian Affairs, 1869–1914, Warm Springs Indian Agency, Records of the Bureau of Indian Affairs, Record Group 75, National Archives and Records Administration—Pacific Alaska Region (Letters Sent, 1869–1914).

3   U.S. Department of Interior, Office of Indian Affairs, ARCIA-1881, 174; *Report of the Commissioner of Indian Affairs for the Territories of Washington and Idaho, and the State of Oregon for the Year of 1870* (Fairfield, WA: Ye Galleon Press, 1981), 42–43.

4   U.S. Department of Interior, Office of Indian Affairs, ARCIA-1873, 317; Yakima Indian Agency Correspondence, Roll 1; William J. Pollock to Hiram Price, 19 January 1881, Records of Inspection of the Field Jurisdiction of the Office of Indian Affairs (National Archives Microfilm Publication M1070) Records of the Bureau of Indian Affairs, Record Group 75, Washington, DC, Roll 58 (Records of Inspection); Robert H. Ruby and John A. Brown, *Dreamer-Prophets of the Columbia Plateau: Smohalla and Skolaskin* (Norman: University of Oklahoma Press, 1989), 62.

5   R. H. Milroy to Hiram Price, 2 July 1884, vol. 2, Jan. 1, 1884-Jan. 8, 1885, 223–24, Press Copies of Letters Sent to Commissioner of Indian Affairs, 1882–1914, Yakima Indian Agency, Records of the Bureau of Indian Affairs, Record Group 75, National Archives and Records Administration—Pacific Alaska Region, (Press Copies of Letters Sent, 1882–1914).

6   Circular Letter to Superintendents and Agents of the Indian Department, 21 October 1873, Letters Received from the Commissioner of Indian Affairs, 1873, Yakima Indian Agency, Records of the Bureau of Indian Affairs, Record Group 75, National Archives and Records Administration—Pacific Alaska Region; John D. C. Atkins to United States Indian Agent, Warm Springs Agency, 12 March 1887, LR-CIA; Robert Newell to John D. C. Atkins, 1 May 1885, Records of Inspection, Roll 55; Pollock to Price, ibid., Roll 58.

7   U.S. Department of Interior, Office of Indian Affairs, ARCIA-1878, 122; N.A. Cornoyer to E. A. Hoyt, 29 May 1878, Letters Received by the Office of Indian Affairs, Roll 625; Captain F. K. Upham to Assistant Adjutant General J. C. Kelton, 18 March 1884, Letters Received by the Office of Adjutant General, National Archives Microfilm Publication M689, Records of the War Department, Record Group 48, National Archives Building, Washington, DC, Roll 271 (Letters Received by the Office of Adjutant General); R. H. Milroy to Hiram Price, Monthly Report, January 1885, vol. 3, Jan.1885-Dec. 1885, 31–33, Press Copies of Letters Sent, 1882–1914.

8   In 1849 the Office of Indian Affairs transferred from the Department of

War, which had administered Indian-white relations since the founding of the United States, to the newly created Department of the Interior. See Paul Prucha, *Great Father*.

9 Upham to Kelton, Letters Received by the Office of Adjutant General, Roll 271.

10 Ruby and Brown, *Dreamer-Prophets*, 90–97.

11 N. A. Cornoyer to E. A. Hoyt, 8 December 1879, Letters Received by the Office of Indian Affairs, Roll 627; U.S. Department of Interior, Office of Indian Affairs, ARCIA-1880, 145; A. B. Meacham to E. S. Parker, 25 April 1870, Letters Received by the Office of Indian Affairs, Roll 616; Ruby and Brown, *Dreamer-Prophets*, 57; Robert H. Ruby and John A. Brown, "Dreamer-Prophet Visionaries of Interior Oregon," *Oregon Humanities* (Summer 1994): 19.

12 U.S. Department of Interior, Office of Indian Affairs, ARCIA-1872, 363; Ruby and Brown, *Dreamer-Prophets*, 61–66; U.S. Census Office, *Report on Indians Taxed and Not Taxed in the United States (Except Alaska) at the Eleventh Census: 1890* (Washington, DC: Government Printing Office, 1894), S73. In 1878, for example, N. A. Cornoyer enumerated Columbia River Indians separately from the confederated Walla Walla, Cayuse, and Umatilla tribes on the reservation (U.S. Department of Interior, Office of Indian Affairs, ARCIA-1878, 122).

13 John Smith to Edward P. Smith, 24 June 1874, Letters Received by the Office of Indian Affairs, Roll 620.

14 E. S. Penham to O. A. Brown, 10 August 1878, Letters Received by the Office of Indian Affairs, Roll 622 [emphasis in original].

15 James H. Wilbur to General J. L. McKenny, 9 July 1867, Records of the Washington Superintendency of Indian Affairs, Roll 18.

16 Annual Report of James H. Wilbur, 1872, Yakima Indian Agency Correspondence and Records, Reel 1; Ruby and Brown, *Dreamer-Prophets*, 59–60. After the Modoc War, several of the Columbia River Indian scouts wanted to make a tour of eastern cities, claiming the right to go because they did not belong to any reservation and they had served in the Modoc campaign (W. B. McKay to James W. Nesmith, 18 November 1873, Letters Received by the Office of Indian Affairs, Reel 618). For a recent narrative account of the Modoc War, see Arthur Quinn, *Hell with the Fire Out: A History of the Modoc War* (Boston: Faber and Faber, 1997).

17 Deposition of W. F. Forwood and B. F. Hicks, 28 March 1883, Yakima Indian Agency Records, Cage 4375, Special Collections, Washington State University, Pullman; Stick Joe's Statement, 4 April 1883, Yakima Indian Agency Correspondence and Records, Reel 2; R. H. Milroy to Colonel C. Grover, 13 April 1883, vol. 3, June 1881–June 1885, 365–66, Press Copies of

Letters Sent, 1882–1914; Colonel C. Grover, First Endorsement, Report of investigation relative to Indian difficulties at Willows, Oregon, 16 April 1883, Letters Received by the Office of Adjutant General, Roll 271 [emphasis in original].

18 Neils, *Klickitat Indians*, 173–76; Daniel L. Boxberger, "Native American and German American Land Use Practices and Settlement in West Klickitat County," paper presented at Environmental Cultures Conference, Victoria, B.C., 27 April 1996, in author's possession; Captain J. W. MacMurray to Assistant Adjutant General J. C. Kelton, 18 August 1884, Letters Received by the Office of Adjutant General, Roll 271. See also Harmon, *Indians in the Making* and Asher, *Beyond the Reservation*.

19 Harmon, *Indians in the Making*, 62–64; Asher, *Beyond the Reservation*, 62–69. The Spino and Underwood families of the Klickitat Valley provide two examples of successful Indian-white marriage along the Columbia River. See Neils, *Klickitat Indians*, 155–58, 172–78.

20 N. A. Cornoyer to John Q. Smith, 26 March 1877, Letters Received by the Office of Indian Affairs, Reel 624; Captain J. W. MacMurray to General Nelson A. Miles, 6 July 1884, Letters Received by the Office of Adjutant General, Reel 271; Grover, First Endorsement, ibid.

21 U.S. Department of Interior, Office of Indian Affairs, ARCIA-1864, 82.

22 Penham to Brown, Letters Received by the Office of Indian Affairs, Reel 622; Horatio Gebney to John D. C. Atkins, 19 January 1885, vol. 4, Jan. 12, 1885-July 25, 1886, 27, Letters Sent, 1869–1914.

23 Ulrich, *Empty Nets*, 19; Joseph C. Dupris, Kathleen S. Hill, and William H. Rodgers, Jr., *The Si'lailo Way: Indians, Salmon and Law on the Columbia River* (Durham, NC: Carolina Academic Press, 2006), 45–49; J. W. Perit Huntington to John Smith, 22 October 1867, Letters Sent to Commissioner of Indian Affairs, 1869–1914, Warm Springs Indian Agency, Records of the Bureau of Indian Affairs, Record Group 75, National Archives and Records Administration—Pacific Alaska Region, 2; Synopsis of Report of Inspector F. C. Armstrong, 14 May 1887, Records of Inspection, Roll 55.

24 R. H. Milroy to Jason W. Hardison and Fifty Nine Others, 21 March 1883, vol. 3, June 1881–1885-June 1885, 350–51, Press Copies of Letters Sent, 1882–1914 [emphasis in original]; John Smith to General Oliver O. Howard, 27 November 1878, Letters Received by the Office of Indian Affairs, Roll 628; U.S. Department of Interior, Office of Indian Affairs, ARCIA-1883, 155.

25 R. R. Thompson to Joel Palmer, 26 February 1856, Letters Received by the Office of Indian Affairs, Roll 609; U.S. Department of Interior, Office of Indian Affairs, ARCIA-1869, 158, 161.

26 U.S. Department of Interior, Office of Indian Affairs, ARCIA-1871, 128.

27 U.S. Department of the Interior, Office of Indian Affairs, Circular No. 28,

23 December 1878, Yakima Indian Agency Records; John Smith to E. A. Hoyt, 20 January 1879, Letters Received by the Office of Indian Affairs, Roll 628. In 1880, the commissioner of Indian affairs revoked the portion of Circular Number 28 requiring Indian Office approval for off-reservation permits because it proved highly impractical and impossible to enforce.

28 A. P. Dennison to General W. P. Harney, 19 August 1859, Letters Received by the Office of Indian Affairs, Roll 611; U.S. Department of Interior, Office of Indian Affairs, ARCIA-1862, 258; ibid., ARCIA-1878, 122; Minutes of a Council Held at Umatilla Agency, 3 September 1878, for the purpose of obtaining the names of the Columbia River and Reservation Indians who joined the hostiles during the late outbreak, Letters Received by the Office of Indian Affairs, Roll 626.

29 A. J. Cain to E. R. Geary, 31 October 1859, Records of the Washington Superintendency of Indian Affairs, Roll 21; U.S. Department of Interior, Office of Indian Affairs, ARCIA-1871, 98, 118; John Smith to J. L. Smith, 9 March 1876, Letters Received by the Office of Indian Affairs, Roll 624; James B. Kennedy, "The Umatilla Indian Reservation, 1855–1975: Factors Contributing to a Diminished Land Resource Base" (Ph.D. diss., Oregon State University, 1977), 77–79, 88–90; Inspection of Yakima Agency by Inspector Ward, 23 January 1884, Records of Inspection, Roll 58. Passed on March 3, 1885, the Slater Act (23 Stat. 340) provided for the reduction and allotment of the Umatilla reservation. Although written specifically for that reservation, it strongly resembled the subsequent Dawes Act (General Allotment Act) and helped pave the way for that legislation. See Kennedy, "The Umatilla Indian Reservation," 86–90.

30 Synopsis of Report of Inspector T. D. Marcum, 26 March 1889, Records of Inspection, Roll 55.

31 Proceedings of a Council Held on the Umatilla Indian Reservation, Oregon, with the Walla Walla, Cayuse, and Umatilla Tribes of Indians, 7 August 1871–12 August 1871, Letters Received by the Office of Indian Affairs, Roll 617.

32 Kemble and Luls quoted in Ruby and Brown, *Dreamer-Prophets*, 64–65.

33 Smith to Smith, Letters Received by the Office of Indian Affairs, Roll 624. See also Frederick E. Hoxie, "From Prison to Homeland: The Cheyenne River Indian Reservation Before World War I," *South Dakota History* 10 (Winter 1979): 1–24, and Tracy Neal Leavelle, "We Will Make It Our Own Place: Agriculture and Adaptation at the Grand Ronde Reservation, 1856–1887," *American Indian Quarterly* 22 (Fall 1998): 433–56.

34 U.S. Department of Interior, Office of Indian Affairs, ARCIA-1872, 122–26; Proceedings of a Council Held on the Umatilla Indian Reservation, Letters Received by the Office of Indian Affairs, Roll 617.

35   U.S. Department of Interior, Office of Indian Affairs, ARCIA-1872, 125–26.

36   John Smith to A. B. Meacham, 18 August 1871, vol. 3, Sept. 4, 1882-Dec. 19, 1884, 277–78, Letters Sent, 1869–1914; John Smith to General Oliver O. Howard, 3 January 1879, vol. 2, July 1, 1878-Sept. 9, 1879, ibid., 1869–1914; R. H. Milroy to Hiram Price, 4 April 1883, vol. 1, Nov. 30, 1882-Jan. 13, 1884, Press Copies of Letters Sent, 1882–1914; Captain Thomas McGregor to Colonel C. Grover, 15 April 1883, Letters Received by the Office of Adjutant General, Roll 271. The other Columbia River Indian headmen present at the meeting were Waltsac, Pascappa, Stock, Callapoo, and Skamia.

37   U.S. Department of Interior, Office of Indian Affairs, ARCIA-1872, 125; Smith to Smith, Letters Received by the Office of Indian Affairs, Roll 624; Proceedings of a Council Held on the Umatilla Indian Reservation, ibid., Roll 617.

38   Smith to Smith, Letters Received by the Office of Indian Affairs, Roll 624.

39   U.S. Department of Interior, Office of Indian Affairs, ARCIA-1881, 174; Smith to Howard, 2 May 1879, vol. 2, 230, Letters Sent, 1869–1914.

40   Smith to Howard, 3 January 1879, vol. 2, July 1, 1878-Sept. 9, 1879, Letters Sent, 1869–1914,; John Smith to James Wilbur, 26 February 1879, vol. 2, July 1, 1878-Sept. 9, 1879, ibid., 1869–1914; U.S. Department of Interior, Office of Indian Affairs, ARCIA-1871, 123.

41   Smohalla quote in Lee Irwin, *Coming Down from Above: Prophecy, Resistance, and Renewal in Native American Religions* (Norman: University of Oklahoma Press, 2008), 259. For earlier interpretations of the Dreamer Religion, see Cora DuBois, "The Feather Cult of the Middle Columbia," *General Series in Anthropology* No. 7 (Menasha, WI: George Banta, 1938), and Leslie Spier, "The Prophet Dance of the Northwest and Its Derivatives: The Source of the Ghost Dance," *General Series in Anthropology* No. 1 (Menasha, WI: George Banta, 1935).

42   Clifford E. Trafzer and Margery Ann Beach, "Smohalla, the Washani, and Religion as a Factor in Northwestern Indian History," *American Indian Quarterly* 9 (Summer 1985), 309–13.

43   U.S. Department of Interior, Office of Indian Affairs, ARCIA-1872, 362; Click Relander, *Drummers and Dreamers* (Caldwell, ID: Caxton Printers, 1956), 149–61; Ruby and Brown, *Dreamer-Prophets*, 54.

44   Ruby and Brown, *Dreamer-Prophets*, 62–63; Captain Thomas McGregor to Colonel E. C. Watkins, 15 August 1878, Letters Received by the Office of Indian Affairs, Roll 626; Captain J. W. MacMurray to General Nelson A. Miles, 28 February 1885, Letters Received by the Office of Adjutant General, Reel 271.

45   N. A. Cornoyer to Edward P. Smith, 20 May 1874, Letters Received by the

Office of Indian Affairs, Reel 619; U.S. Department of Interior, Office of Indian Affairs, ARCIA-1874, 323; ibid., ARCIA-1885, 175.

46 U.S. Department of Interior, Office of Indian Affairs, ARCIA-1880, 145; William Vandever to Edward P. Smith, 20 November 1874, Records of Inspection, Roll 56; Grover, First Endorsement, Letters Received by the Office of Adjutant General, Reel 271.

47 U.S. Department of Interior, Office of Indian Affairs, ARCIA-1880, 145; R. H. Milroy to Hiram Price, 17 March 1883, vol. 1, Nov. 30, 1882-Jan. 13, 1884, 155–56, Press Copies of Letters Sent, 1882–1914; U.S. Department of Interior, Office of Indian Affairs, ARCIA-1885, 175.

48 Rusty Middleton, "View from the River," *Wana Chinook Tymoo* 1 and 2 (1993): 14.

4 PLACES OF PERSISTENCE

1 Robert H. Milroy to Hiram Price, Monthly Report, January 1885, vol. 3, Jan. 1885-Dec. 1885, Press Copies of Letters Sent to the Commissioner of Indian Affairs, 1882–1914.

2 John D. C. Atkins quote in Peter Nabokov, ed., *Native American Testimony: A Chronicle of Indian-White Relations from Prophecy to the Present, 1492–1992* (New York: Viking Penguin, 1991; reprint, New York: Penguin Books, 1992), 233; Prucha, *Great Father*, 224–28.

3 See Leonard A. Carlson, *Indians, Bureaucrats, and the Land: The Dawes Act and the Decline of Indian Farming* (Westport, CT: Greenwood Press, 1981); Janet A. McDonnell, *The Dispossession of the American Indian, 1887–1934* (Bloomington: Indiana University Press, 1991); David Rich Lewis, *Neither Wolf Nor Dog: American Indians, Environment, and Agrarian Change* (New York: Oxford University Press, 1994); Wilcomb E. Washburn, *The Assault on Indian Tribalism: The General Allotment Law (Dawes Act) of 1887* (Malabar, FL: Robert E. Krieger Publishing Company, 1986); and Meyer, *White Earth Tragedy*. For a recent reassessment of the allotment policy and Indian responses to it, see Emily Greenwald, *Reconfiguring the Reservation: The Nez Perces, Jicarilla Apaches, and the Dawes Act* (Albuquerque: University of New Mexico Press, 2002).

4 For brief discussions of off-reservation homesteads in the Northwest, see Asher, *Beyond the Reservation*; Trafzer and Scheuerman, *Renegade Tribe*; and Roberta L. Hall, *The Coquille Indians: Yesterday, Today, and Tomorrow* (Lake Oswego, OR: Smith, Smith and Smith Publishing Company, 1984).

5 Asher, *Beyond the Reservation*, 76–79; *Indian Homestead Act, Statutes at Large*, 18, sec. 15, 402 (1875).

6 "Indian Homesteads—Enabling Acts," *Oregonian* (Portland), c. 23 June 1878; Headquarters Department of the Columbia, General Order No. 7, 8 February 1878, Letters Received by the Office of Adjutant General, Roll 271.

7 General Order No. 7, Letters Received by the Office of Adjutant General; Captain J. W. MacMurray to General Nelson A. Miles, 6 July 1884, ibid.; Jade Switzler to Colonel C. Grover, 5 March 1884, ibid.; N. C. McFarland to Registers and Receivers, U.S. Land Offices, 31 May 1884, ibid.; General Nelson A. Miles to Assistant Adjutant General J. C. Kelton, 4 April 1884, ibid.

8 Captain F. K. Upham to Colonel C. Grover, 18 March 1884, Letters Received by the Office of Adjutant General; Trafzer and Scheuerman, *Renegade Tribe*, 130–32; Captain J. W. MacMurray to General Nelson A. Miles, 18 August 1884, Letters Received by the Office of Adjutant General.

9 Upham to Grover, Letters Received by the Office of Adjutant General; Cyrus Beede to Hiram Price, 28 August 1884, ibid.

10 Trafzer and Scheuerman, *Renegade Tribe*, 127–28; U.S. Department of the Interior, Office of Indian Affairs, ARCIA-1884, 173–74.

11 R. H. Milroy to Hiram Price, 8 January 1885, Yakima Indian Agency Records, Cage 4375, Manuscripts, Archives and Special Collections, Washington State University Libraries, Pullman; Circular No. 139, 2 October 1884, Yakima Indian Agency Correspondence; Clifford C. Relander Collection, Yakima Valley Regional Library, Roll 2; Trafzer and Scheuerman, *Renegade Tribe*, 131–32; Upham to Grover, Letters Received from the Office of Adjutant General; J. D. C. Atkins to Timothy A. Byrnes, Esq., 23 March 1886, Yakima Indian Agency Correspondence, Roll 2.

12 Roosevelt quoted in Prucha, *Great Father*, 227; Iverson, "We Are Still Here," 30–33. Daniel L. Boxberger and Lynn A. Robbins briefly discuss the Indian homesteads and allotments of western Klickitat County, Washington, in "An Archival and Oral History Inventory of the White Salmon and Klickitat Rivers," vol. 1, prepared for the Columbia River Gorge National Scenic Area (Bellingham, WA, 1994), 24–32. At least three hundred Mid-Columbia Indians received allotments or homesteads through the Walla Walla land office, but only a few of these fell under the jurisdiction of the Yakama, Umatilla, and Warm Springs agencies.

13 Narrative Report of the Yakima Agency, 1925, Superintendents Annual Narrative and Statistical Reports from Field Jurisdictions of the Bureau of Indian Affairs, 1907–1938, National Archives Microfilm Publication M1011, Records of the Bureau of Indian Affairs, Record Group 75, National Archives Building, Washington, DC (Superintendents Annual Narrative), Roll 171, 57. The estimate of 120 homesteads is based on a tally of the individual folders for The Dalles and Vancouver Homesteads, Allot-

ments, Records of C. G. Davis, Field Agent at The Dalles, 1939–1950, Portland Area Office, Records of the Bureau of Indian Affairs, Record Group 75, National Archives and Records Administration—Pacific Alaska Region (Allotments).

14 U.S. Department of Interior, Office of Indian Affairs, ARCIA-1890, LII-LIII; Register of Indian Allotment Applications Made at the Land Office at The Dalles, The Dalles Allottees, Allotments; Land Cards for Vancouver Allotments, ibid.; C. F. Larrabee to Jay Lynch, 11 October 1906, Letters Received from Commissioner of Indian Affairs RE: Land, Yakima Indian Agency, Records of the Bureau of Indian Affairs, Record Group 75, National Archives and Records Administration—Pacific Alaska Region; U.S. Department of the Interior, Office of Indian Affairs, *Regulations Governing Indian Allotments on the Public Domain under Section 4 of the Act of February 8, 1887 (24 Stat., 388), as Amended by the Act of February 28, 1891 (26 Stat., 794), and as Further Amended by the Act of June 25, 1910* (36 Stat., 855), Washington, DC: Government Printing Office, 1918.

15 Thomas J. Morgan to W. L. Stoble, 14 October 1889, Yakima Indian Agency Correspondence, Roll 2; Charles E. Roblin to Cato Sells, 8 May 1919, John Day—Allotments, Subject Files, 1908–25, Warm Springs Indian Agency, Records of the Bureau of Indian Affairs, Record Group 75, National Archives and Records Administration—Pacific Alaska Region (Subject Files, 1908–1925), 1–7; *Family History of George Selam and four children (Selam Family History)*, Allotment of Lands, 1906–1955, Decimal Subject Files, 1925–67, Yakima Indian Agency, Records of the Bureau of Indian Affairs, Record Group 75, National Archives and Records Administration—Pacific Alaska Region (Decimal Subject Files, 1925–1967); W. G. Flett to O. L. Babcock, ca. 1918, John Day—Allotments, Subject Files, 1908–25.

16 Roblin to Sells, 13 November 1919, The Dalles Allotments, Subject Files, 1908–25, 3–4.

17 Horace G. Wilson to Cato Sells, 1 July 1913, The Dalles—Miscellaneous, ibid.; O. F. Fithian to O. L. Babcock, 17 May 1919, John Day—Lease Inquiries, ibid.; Roblin to Sells, 13 November 1919, The Dalles Allotments, ibid., 2; W. G. Flett to O. L. Babcock, 4 March 1920, "A" Files: The Dalles, ibid.

18 Roblin to Sells, 13 November 1919, The Dalles Allotments, Subject Files, 1908–25, 6; O. L. Babcock to Cato Sells, 9 December 1918, The Dalles—Leases, Inquiries, etc., ibid.; Narrative Report of the Yakima Agency, 1917, Section VI, Superintendents Annual Narrative, Roll 171; Henry W. Thompson to Freemont W. Merewether, 13 June 1952, VA 106, General Subject Correspondence, 1939–1953; C. G. Davis to Joseph Coursey, 26 October 1940, VA 150, ibid.; Narrative Report of the Yakima Agency, 1925, Superintendents Annual Narrative, Roll 171, 58.

19   U.S. Department of Interior, Office of Indian Affairs, ARCIA-1902, 61;
       George P. Litchfield to Thomas J. Morgan, 24 September 1891, Yakima
       Indian Agency Correspondence, Roll 3. Emily Greenwald has found simi-
       lar patterns of allotment selection on the Nez Perce reservation. See Gre-
       enwald, *Reconfiguring the Reservation*, 59–89.

20   Umatilla agent to William A. Jones, 18 March 1898, vol. 2, July, 19, 1897-July
       21, 1898, Letters Sent to the Commissioner of Indian Affairs, 1880–1911,
       Umatilla Indian Agency, Records of the Bureau of Indian Affairs, Record
       Group 7, National Archives and Records Administration—Pacific Alaska
       Region (Letters Sent, 1880–1911); Lewis T. Erwin to Secretary of the Inte-
       rior, 25 October 1897, Records of Inspection, Roll 59; *Family History of
       George Selam and four children.*

21   George W. Harper to Daniel M. Browning, Letters Sent, 1880–1911, 437;
       "Chief Selatzee of the Yakimas," Lucullus V. McWhorter Papers; Sup-
       porting Affidavit of Kil-li-ish (James Takawpyicks), 29 August 1904,
       Allotment Applications and Allotment Selections, 1904-5, 1917, Umatilla
       Indian Agency, Records of the Bureau of Indian Affairs, Record Group
       75, National Archives and Records Administration—Pacific Alaska Region
       (Allotment Applications, 1904-5). Barbara Leibhardt notes the mounting
       pressure on off-reservation Indians in "Allotment Policy in an Incongru-
       ous Legal System: The Yakima Indian Nation As a Case Study, 1887–1934,"
       Agricultural History 65 (Fall 1991): 78–103.

22   D. M. Browning to Jay Lynch, 11 July 1893, Yakima Indian Agency Cor-
       respondence, Roll 3; W. A. Jones to Jay Lynch, 4 November 1897, Letters
       Received from Commissioner of Indian Affairs, Aug. 13, 1896-Nov. 30,
       1898; Leonard Underwood to Don M. Carr, 27 February 1915, Allotments—
       Public Domain, Decimal Subject Files, 1925–67; Narrative Report of the
       Warm Springs Indian Agency, 1921, Superintendents Annual Narrative,
       Roll 164; C. G. Davis to L. W. Shotwell, 31 January 1947, Heirship—no order
       determined, General Subject Correspondence, 1939–1953.

23   Leibhardt, "Allotment Policy in an Incongruous Legal System," 89–91.

24   U.S. Department of Interior, Office of Indian Affairs, ARCIA-1902, 369.

25   Claude C. Covey to Merrill E. Gates, 11 January 1906, vol. 4, Oct. 17, 1902-
       March 26, 1906, Miscellaneous Letters Sent, 1885–1914, Warm Springs
       Indian Agency, Records of the Bureau of Indian Affairs, Record Group
       75, National Archives and Records Administration—Pacific Alaska Region
       (Miscellaneous Letters Sent); Family history of Jim (Staunce) Eli and wife,
       Pop-sah-lee Eli, Allotment of Lands, Decimal Subject Files, 1925–67; Don
       M. Carr to Tommy Squimhin, 28 June 1913, Allotments—General Corre-
       spondence, 1910–1922, ibid.

26   On the creation of tribal base rolls, see Kent Carter, "Deciding Who Can

Be Cherokee: Enrollment Records of the Dawes Commission," *Chronicles of Oklahoma* 69 (1991): 174–205, and Alexandra Harmon, "Tribal Enrollment Councils: Lessons on Law and Indian Identity," *Western Historical Quarterly* 32 (Summer 2001): 175–200. On the role of allotment and blood quantum in shaping Indian identity, see Thomas Biolsi, "The Birth of the Reservation: Making the Modern Individual among the Lakota," in *American Nations: Encounters in Indian Country, 1850 to the Present*, ed. Frederick C. Hoxie, Peter C. Mancall, and James H. Merrell (New York: Routledge, 2001), 110–40, and Meyer, *White Earth Tragedy*.

27 Annual Report of Umatilla Agency, 1893, Letters Sent, 1880–1911.

28 C. F. Hawke to O. L. Babcock, 5 May 1921, Land Contracts—Double Allotments, Subject Files, 1908–25.

29 E. Morgan Pryse to Manager, Bureau of Land Management, Spokane District Land Office, 13 April 1951, VA 106, General Subject Correspondence, 1939–1953; C. G. Davis to Joseph Coursey, 26 October 1940, VA 150, ibid.; Leibhardt, "Allotment Policy in an Incongruous Legal System," 88–89.

30 Annual Narrative Report of the Yakima Indian Agency, 1912, Section VIII, Superintendents Annual Narrative, Roll 171; Harmon, "Tribal Enrollment Councils," 183–93. For examples of enrollment applications from the Umatilla agency, see Allotment Applications, 1904–5, 1917. For the Yakama reservation, see Allotments—General Correspondence, 1910–1922, Decimal Subject Files, 1925–67.

31 U.S. Department of Interior, Office of Indian Affairs, ARCIA-1893, 338.

32 L. W. Shotwell to John R. Nichols, 23 December 1949, Enrollment Legal Options, Miscellaneous Enrollment Records, Yakima Indian Agency, Records of the Bureau of Indian Affairs, Record Group 75, National Archives and Records Administration—Pacific Alaska Region (Miscellaneous Enrollment Records); Meyer, *White Earth Tragedy*, 173–75.

33 Kennedy, "Umatilla Indian Reservation," 66; William A. Jones to Charles S. McNichols, 15 October 1904, Land (General), 1879–1906, Letters Sent to Umatilla Employees, Other Government Agencies, and Private Parties, 1889–1911, Umatilla Indian Agency, Records of the Bureau of Indian Affairs, Record Group 75, National Archives and Records Administration—Pacific Alaska Region, 4.

34 Notes of a Council of the Umatilla Indians, Held in the Council-Room at the Agency, Pendleton, Oregon, December 12, 1905, Letters Sent, 1880–1911.

35 Minutes of a Council of the Indians of the Umatilla Indian Reservation, Oregon, held at the Umatilla Indian School, January 2, 1917, at which there were present 290 Indians of the full blood and mixed blood, Tribal Lands—Council Proceedings, Minutes of Tribal Councils, 1907, 1917–18, Umatilla Indian Agency, Records of the Bureau of Indian Affairs, Record

Group 75, National Archives and Records Administration—Pacific Alaska Region, 10–11 (Minutes of Tribal Councils). In March 1917, despite substantial opposition from the confederated tribes, Congress authorized the allotment of eighty acres to each unallotted Indian entitled to land on the Umatilla reservation. Over the next three years, the Indian Office allotted 61,505 of the tribes' remaining 74,000 acres (Narrative Report of the Umatilla Indian Agency, 1920, Section V, Superintendents Annual Narrative, Roll 159).

36 Harmon, "Tribal Enrollment Councils," 193.

37 Minutes of a Council of the Indians of the Umatilla Indian Reservation, Minutes of Tribal Councils, 3–4.

38 E. L. Swartzlander to Robert G. Valentine, 17 August 1909, Letters Sent, 1880–1911, vol. 1, May 3, 1909-February 19, 1910. Melinda M. Jetté analyzes the rejection of her great-grandmother's claim in "Ordinary Lives: Three Generations of a French-Indian Family in Oregon, 1827–1931 (M.A. thesis, Université Laval, 1996), 95–101.

39 Jones to McNichols, 15 October 1904, Letters Sent to Umatilla Employees, 2–3; Notes of a Council of the Umatilla Indians, December 12, 1905, Letters Sent, 1880–1911, 120.

40 Notes of a Council of the Umatilla Indians, December 12, 1905, Letters Sent, 1880–1911,121–22; ibid., December 19, 1905, 123; Kennedy, "Umatilla Indian Reservation," 65–69. The Umatilla reservation contained about 74,000 acres of tribal land in 1905. After the 1917 allotments, the confederated tribes held only 12,533 acres of low value.

41 Report of Council with Indians on Yakima Indian Reservation by Commissioners Barge and Goodwin on the 20th day of February, 1897, at Fort Simcoe, Tribal Records, 1897–1952, Yakima Indian Agency, Records of the Bureau of Indian Affairs, Record Group 75, National Archives and Records Administration—Pacific Alaska Region (Tribal Records, 1897–1952), 28–29.

42 Ibid., 28.

43 Resolution of the Wish-ham tribe, 6 January 1894, Yakima Indian Agency Correspondence; Resolution of Wisham tribe, 27 December 1915, Councils & Meetings 1913–1925, Tribal Records, 1897–1952.

44 Narrative Report of the Yakima Agency, 1915, Section VI, Superintendents Annual Narrative, Roll 171. On competition between Indian and non-Indian land users, see Barbara Leibhardt, "Law, Environment, and Social Change in the Columbia River Basin: The Yakima Indian Nation as a Case Study, 1840–1933" (Ph.D. diss., University of California at Berkeley, 1990), 383–435. Andrew H. Fisher details conflict over Native huckleberry fields in "The 1932 Handshake Agreement: Yakama Indian Treaty Rights and

Forest Service Policy in the Pacific Northwest," *Western Historical Quarterly* 28 (Summer 1997): 187–217.

45 For specific examples of trespass complaints and rent disagreements, see Folder 003, The Dalles Trespasses, Decimal Files, 1908–1952, Warm Springs Indian Agency, Records of the Bureau of Indian Affairs, Record Group 75, National Archives and Records Administration—Pacific Alaska Region (Decimal Files, 1908–1952); Allotment Case Files, ca. 1905–55, Yakima Indian Agency, Records of the Bureau of Indian Affairs, Record Group 75, National Archives and Records Administration—Pacific Alaska Region (Allotment Case Files, ca. 1905–55). Selma Neils describes clashes between farmers and root diggers in *The Klickitat Indians*, 125.

46 U.S. Department of Interior, Office of Indian Affairs, ARCIA-1886, 221.

47 A. A. Ames to Don M. Carr, 28 February 1913, Fishing Matter—Seufert vs. Olney (1912–15), General Subject Correspondence, 1908–1921, 1–2; O. L. Babcock to Cato Sells, 9 December 1918, The Dalles—Leases, Inquiries, etc., Subject Files, 1908–1925.

48 Neils, *Klickitat Indians*, 180–82; Jerry Ladiges, *Glenwood: Formerly Camas Prairie* (Glenwood, WA: privately printed, 1978), 73–75; Boxberger, "Native American and German American Land Use Practices in West Klickitat County."

49 Neils, *Klickitat Indians*, 182.

50 Evan W. Estep to J. B. Mortsolf, 19 March 1925, Correspondence, Unallotted Indians, Yakima Indian Agency, Records of the Bureau of Indian Affairs, Record Group 75, National Archives and Records Administration—Pacific Alaska Region; Melville Jacobs to Evan W. Estep, 22 March 1927, Unallotted H-M, Hunt, Joe, Allotment Case Files, ca. 1905–1955; Evan W. Estep to Melville Jacobs, 26 March 1928, Unallotted H-M, Hunt, Joe, ibid.; P. T. Lonergan to Don M. Carr, 2 February 1921, Tu-lag-us Vancouver 158 (V158), ibid.

51 O. L. Babcock to Cato Sells, 10 December 1918, "A" Files: The Dalles, Subject Files, 1908–1925; Babcock to Sells, 4 April 21, ibid.; W. A. Jones to Jay Lynch, 21 July 1899, Letters Received from the Commissioner of Indian Affairs; C. F. Larrabee, 14 April 1906, ibid.; Narrative Report of the Yakima Indian Agency, 1930, Superintendents Annual Narrative, Roll 172, 8.

52 Gilbert L. Hall to Horace G. Wilson, 17 January 1913, The Dalles-Miscellaneous, Subject Files, 1908–1925; Horace G. Wilson to Gilbert L. Hall, 20 January 1913, ibid.

53 O. L. Babcock to Cato Sells, 17 October 1918, "A" Files: The Dalles, Subject Files, 1908–1925; O. L. Babcock to Charles F. Metsker, 20 August 1936, Maps and Plats, The Dalles and Vancouver Indians 1936–1937, Decimal Subject Files, 1925–1967; Annual Narrative Report of the Umatilla Indian Agency, 1938, Superintendents Annual Narrative, Roll 160; Annual Narra-

tive Report of the Yakima Indian Agency, 1928, ibid., Roll 172, 53–54. In 1911 Yakama superintendent S. A. M. Young reported that he had *no* records for the Vancouver allotments under his jurisdiction (ibid., Section VII, Roll 171, 22–23). Three years later, his successor said the agency had "little information about Indian homesteads. In fact none at all except what is picked up through inquiry or correspondence" (Narrative Report of the Yakima Indian Agency, 1914, ibid., 31).

54 O. L. Babcock, 31 January 1921, The Dalles-Miscellaneous, Subject Files, 1908–1925; Scookum Willahee to C. F. Hauk, 4 August 1913, Berry Patches, General Subject Correspondence, 1908–1921. For specific examples of the problems associated with leasing and Individual Indian Money accounts, see Allotment Case Files, ca. 1905–55.

55 G. W. Beeks to Evan W. Estep, 20 November 1933, Che-haluck, Wanumsie, Peter, Shappalo, Willie, Vancouver 90, Allotment Case Files, ca. 1905–1955; Annual Narrative Report of the Umatilla Indian Agency, 1937, Section 1, Superintendents Annual Narrative, Roll 160; J. D. Weed to O. L. Babcock, 31 May 1922, The Dalles—Leases, Inquiries, etc., Subject Files, 1908–1925; R. A. Jackson to Evan W. Estep, 7 March 1927, Wa-ta-cinch, Vancouver 97, Allotment Case Files, ca. 1905–1955.

56 Don M. Carr to P. T. Lonergan, 15 February 1921, V158, Allotment Case Files, ca. 1905–1955; Joseph Coursey to M. A. Johnson, 22 March 1941, V.A. 150, Allotments; C. F. Hauke to Omar L. Babcock, 25 May 1922, The Dalles-Miscellaneous, Subject Files, 1908–1925; O. L. Babcock to Charles H. Burke, 30 May 1922, ibid.

57 Eugene S. Hunn, "Sk'in: The Other Side of the River," *Oregon Historical Quarterly* 108, no. 4 (Winter 2007): 618–20.

58 Willahee to Hauke, 4 August 1913; Don M. Carr to Cato Sells, 28 September 1912, Dave, Emma VHstd 3057, Allotment Case Files, ca. 1905–1955; Caples Dave to Don M. Carr, 23 October 1915, ibid.; Don M. Carr to Cato Sells, 7 September 1916, Funds for Relieving Distress Among Indians, General Subject Correspondence, 1908–1921; Tommy Thompson to Click Relander, 9 August 1954, Folder 11–10, Clifford C. Relander Collection.

59 Narrative Report of the Warm Springs Agency, 1937, Superintendents Annual Narrative, Roll 166, 4; Ed Edmo, personal communication, May 1999; Affidavit of Willie John Culpus, in Swindell, *Report on Source,* 169.

5 SPACES OF RESISTANCE

1 T. J. Smith to G. W. Rastall, 17 November 1922, The Dalles School Attendance, Subject Files, 1908–1925; John C. Veatch to O. L. Babcock, 25 Febru-

ary 1922, ibid.; O. L. Babcock to A. E. Gronewald, 27 February 1922, ibid.

2   See, for example, Robert H. Keller, Jr., *American Protestantism and United States Indian Policy, 1869–82* (Lincoln: University of Nebraska Press, 1983); Clyde A. Milner II, *With Good Intentions: Quaker Work Among the Pawnees, Otos, and Omahas in the 1870s* (Lincoln: University of Nebraska Press, 1982); and Francis Paul Prucha, *American Indian Policy in Crisis: Christian Reformers and the Indian, 1865–1900* (Norman: University of Oklahoma Press, 1976).

3   See David Wallace Adams, *Education for Extinction: American Indians and the Boarding School Experience, 1875–1928* (Lawrence: University Press of Kansas, 1995); Brenda J. Child, *Boarding School Seasons: American Indian Families, 1900–1940* (Lincoln: University of Nebraska Press, 1998); Clyde Ellis, *To Change Them Forever: Indian Education at the Rainy Mountain Boarding School, 1893–1920* (Norman: University of Oklahoma Press, 1996); K. Tsianina Lomawaima, *They Called It Prairie Light: The Story of Chilocco Indian School* (Lincoln: University of Nebraska Press, 1994); Devon A. Mihesuah, *Cultivating the Rosebuds: The Education of Women at the Cherokee Female Seminary, 1851–1909* (Urbana: University of Illinois Press, 1993); Scott Riney, *The Rapid City Indian School, 1898–1933* (Norman: University of Oklahoma Press, 1999), and Robert A. Trennert, Jr., *The Phoenix Indian School: Forced Assimilation in Arizona, 1891–1935* (Norman: University of Oklahoma Press, 1988).

4   For differing views on the issue of acculturation among off-reservation Indians, see Carlson, *Indians, Bureaucrats, and Land*, 66; Russell Lawrence Barsh, "Puget Sound Indian Demography, 1900–1920: Migration and Economic Integration," *Ethnohistory* 43 (Winter 1996): 65–97; and Hunn, *Nch'i-Wána*, 269–74.

5   For various critiques of the conventional understanding of "tradition," see Eric Hobsbawm and Terence Ranger, eds., *The Invention of Tradition* (New York: Cambridge University Press, 1992). Among the best historical studies of the concept of traditional/authentic Indians are Deloria, *Indians in Unexpected Places*, and Raibmon, *Authentic Indians*. On the shortcomings of the progressive-traditional model, see David Rich Lewis, "Reservation Leadership and the Progressive-Traditional Dichotomy: William Wash and the Northern Utes, 1865–1928," *Ethnohistory* 38 (Winter 1991): 124–42.

6   Statements of Myra Sohappy and David Sohappy, Jr., 5 April 1984, *Administrative Appeal of David Sohappy*, 223; Helen Hersh Schuster, "Yakima Indian Traditionalism: A Study in Continuity and Change" (Ph.D. diss., University of Washington, 1975), 6.

7   Prucha, *Great Father*, 218–19; Francis Paul Prucha, ed., *Americanizing the American Indians: Writings by the "Friends of the Indians"* (Cambridge,

MA: Harvard University Press, 1973), 295–305; Vine Deloria, Jr., and Clifford M. Lytle, *American Indians, American Justice* (Austin: University of Texas Press, 1983), 113–16. Frederick E. Hoxie notes the independence and initiative of Indian judges in *Parading Through History*, 308–12.

8   Schuster, "Yakima Indian Traditionalism," 6; H. G. Barnett, *Indian Shakers: A Messianic Cult of the Pacific Northwest* (Carbondale: Southern Illinois University Press, 1957), 142.

9   Ruby and Brown, *Dreamer-Prophets*, 1989, 99–102; Prucha, *Great Father*, 264–65, 275–76; Narrative Report of the Yakima Agency, 1927, Superintendents Annual Narrative, Roll 171, 17.

10   U.S. Department of the Interior, Office of Indian Affairs, ARCIA-1902, 325; Narrative Report of the Yakima Agency, 1911, Superintendents Annual Narrative, Roll 171, 3–4; ibid., 1927, Roll 171, 17–18; Don M. Carr to Commissioner of Indian Affairs, 10 August 1917, Folder 70651-17-903, Box 262, Central Classified Files, 1907–1939, Records of the Bureau of Indian Affairs, Record Group 75, National Archives Building, Washington, DC.

11   E. B. Merritt to Dick Powyowit, 14 June 1917, Ed-Law & Order, Religious Organizations, Subject Files, 1908–1925; Narrative Report of the Yakima Agency, 1927, Superintendents Annual Narrative, Roll 171, 18.

12   F. E. Perkins to the Commissioner of Indian Affairs, 25 July 1930, 072 Celebrations, Decimal Files, 1908–1952 ; C. E. Andres to F. E. Perkins, 30 July 1930, ibid., 1–5.

13   Perkins to Commissioner, 23 July 1930, Decimal Files, 1908–1952.

14   Ruby and Brown, *Dreamer-Prophets*, 97–99; Hunn, *Nch'i-Wána*, 260–61; Charles S. Heinline to Horace G. Wilson, 25 September 1915, John Day-Miscellaneous, Subject Files, 1908–1925; Narrative Report of the Yakima Agency, 1917, Superintendents Annual Narrative, Roll 171, 2. Schuster describes the modern network linking on- and off-reservation Washat longhouses in "Yakima Indian Traditionalism," 469–78.

15   Robert H. Ruby and John A. Brown, *John Slocum and the Indian Shaker Church* (Norman: University of Oklahoma Press, 1996), 1–7, 35–38; Harmon, *Indians in the Making*, 125–30.

16   Ruby and Brown, *John Slocum*, 147–149; Erna Gunther, "The Shaker Religion of the Northwest," in *Indians of the Urban Northwest*, ed. Marian W. Smith (New York: Columbia University Press, 1949), 44; Ray Harmon, "Indian Shaker Church, The Dalles," *Oregon Historical Quarterly* 72 (1971): 151–53.

17   Gunther, "Shaker Religion," 74.

18   Harmon, "Indian Shaker Church," 155.

19   *Dalles (OR) Chronicle*, 27 July 1916, 5.

20   Hunn, *Nch'i-Wána*, 237–41; David H. French and Katherine S. French, "Wasco, Wishram, and Cascades," in Walker, *Handbook of North Ameri-*

can Indians, 373; Ruby and Brown, *John Slocum,* 13; Gunther, "Shaker Religion," 42, 70–73; By-Laws of the Indian Shaker Church, 10 June 1910, Indian Shaker Church of Washington Papers, Mss 29, Washington State Historical Society, Tacoma (Indian Shaker Church), Box 6, Folder 80, 3; Harry Miller to Sargent Brown, 26 January 1920, Religious Organizations, Subject Files, 1908–1925.

21 Barnett, *Indian Shakers,* 72–73, 82–83; Narrative Report of the Yakima Agency, 1911, Superintendents Annual Narrative, Roll 171, 3; Enoch Abraham to Peter Heck, 2 May 1911, Indian Shaker Church, Box 3, Folder 46, 3.

22 Petition of Charles Pitt, O. B. Kalama, Calvin Johnson, et al., to Commissioner of Indian Affairs, 8 April 1912, Folder 33835-1912-816.2, 00-1929-810 to 39477-1933-820, Warm Springs, Central Classified Files, 1907–1939; Circular from A. M. Reynolds, "To All My Friends on the Warm Springs Reservation," 13 December 1917, Religious Organizations, Subject Files, 1908–1925; A. M. Reynolds to Commissioner of Indian Affairs, 12 February 1918, ibid.

23 E. B. Merritt to Warren McCorkle, 14 March 1920, Folder 00-1918-816, Warm Springs, Central Classified Files, 1907–1939; E. B. Merritt to A. M. Reynolds, 14 March 1918, Subject Files, 1908–1925; Miller to Brown, ibid.; Garfield Jack to Omar Babcock, 2 January 1920, ibid.; Omar Babcock to Garfield Jack, 8 January 1920, ibid.; Ruby and Brown, *John Slocum,* 167–69; George Pierre Castile, "The Indian Connection: Judge James Wickersham and the Indian Shakers," *Pacific Northwest Quarterly* 81 (October 1990): 122–29.

24 Ruby and Brown, *John Slocum,* 169–70; Minutes of the General Assembly Special Convention, 1918, John Slocum and the Indian Shaker Church Series, Box 5, Folder 260, Robert H. Ruby Papers, Ms 170, Northwest Museum of Arts & Culture, Spokane, 10–12; Harmon, "Indian Shaker Church," 157; Joe Estabrook to Peter Heck, 31 March 1932, Indian Shaker Church, Box 3, Folder 57. During the early twentieth century, the Indian Shaker Church split into Bible and non-Bible factions. For the details of this schism, see Barnett, *Indian Shakers;* Gunther, "Shaker Religion," and Ruby and Brown, *John Slocum.*

25 Clifford E. Trafzer and Margery Ann Beach, "The Waptashi Prophet and the Feather Religion: Derivative of the Washani," *American Indian Quarterly* (Summer 1985): 325–26; George W. Aguilar, Sr., *When the River Ran Wild!: Indian Traditions on the Mid-Columbia and the Warm Springs Reservation* (Portland: Oregon Historical Society Press, 2005), 152–54.

26 Hunt claimed to be the first person to witness the vision of Lishwailait, but others say that his niece, Josephine, experienced it at the funeral of Hunt's

son and that he literally took it from her hands and made it his own. See DuBois, "Feather Cult," 22.

27 Trafzer and Beach, "Waptashi Prophet," 326–29; Du Bois, "Feather Cult," 24.

28 Boxberger and Robbins, "Archival and Oral History," 31; Trafzer and Beach, "Waptashi Prophet," 329.

29 Trafzer and Beach, "Waptashi Prophet," 330; Donald M. Hines, *Magic in the Mountains: The Yakima Shaman: Power & Practice* (Issaquah, WA: Great Eagle Publishing, 1993), 231–32.

30 DuBois, "Feather Cult," 27.

31 Ibid.; Wilson Wewa, interview by Andrew H. Fisher, 26 June 2006, Warm Springs Indian Reservation, notes in author's possession.

32 DuBois, "Feather Cult," 27; O. C. Edwards to Francis E. Leupp, 27 January 1906, vol. 4, Aug. 22, 1905-Sept. 20, 1905, Letters Sent, 1880–1911, 411–12.

33 Edwards to Leupp, Letters Sent, 1880–1911.

34 O. C. Edwards to W. C. Bristol, 12 May 1906, Letters Sent to Umatilla Employees, 231–33.

35 Du Bois, "Feather Cult," 27–28.

36 Ibid., 26–27; O. L. Babcock to J. A. Speer, 12 July 1920, Religious Organizations, Subject Files, 1908–1925; Boxberger and Robbins, "Archival and Oral History," 31.

37 Hunn, *Nch'i-Wána*, 223–24; Schuster, "Yakima Indian Traditionalism," 124–25; Narrative Report of Umatilla Agency, 1911, Superintendents Annual Narrative, Roll 159, 2; E. B. Merrit to J. M. Cornielson, 16 February 1915, Records of the Bureau of Indian Affairs, Central Classified Files, 1907–1939, Series B: Indian Customs and Social Relations, Roll 22, 3.

38 U.S. Department of the Interior, Office of Indian Affairs, ARCIA-1890, 212; A. M. Reynolds to C. H. Estes, 14 December 1917, Law & Order, Marriage & Divorce, Subject Files, 1908–1925; A. M. Reynolds to E. B. Knox, 14 January 1918, ibid.; "Bigamist Gets 6 Month's Sentence," *Dalles (OR) Chronicle*, 13 February 1919, 6; Narrative Report of Warm Springs Agency, 1920, Superintendents Annual Narrative, Roll 164, 3; Narrative Report of Warm Springs Agency, 1922, ibid., 2.

39 Prucha, *Great Father*, 232–41, 280–81; Janice White Clemmer, "The Confederated Tribes of Warm Springs, Oregon: Nineteenth Century Indian Education History" (Ph.D. diss., University of Utah, 1980), 159–60.

40 Prucha, *Great Father*, 239–40; Circular No. 250, 3 April 1891, U.S. Bureau of Indian Affairs, Yakima Indian Agency Correspondence; Clifford C. Relander Collection, Roll 2; U.S. Department of the Interior, Office of Indian Affairs, ARCIA-1901, 355; J. E. Kirk to Franci E. Leupp, 16 February 1901, vol. 2, Jan. 18, 1899-May 30, 1901, Letters Sent, 1869–1914, ; O. C.

Edwards, 31 August 1906, vol. 4, Aug. 22, 1905-Sept. 20, 1905, Letters Sent, 1880–1911, , 438–39.

41   Narrative Report of the Warm Springs Agency, 1921, Superintendents Annual Narrative, Roll 164, 2–3; ibid., 1922, 5; Narrative Report of Yakima Agency, 1925, ibid., Roll 171, 29; Warm Springs Reservation School Census of Indian Children, November 1924, Ed: Schools–Census, Subject Files, 1908–1925.

42   O. L. Babcock to A. E Gronewald, 13 November 1919, The Dalles School Attendance, Subject Files, 1908–1925; Margaret Connell Szasz, *Education and the American Indian: The Road Toward Self-Determination since 1928*, 3d ed. (Albuquerque: University of New Mexico Press, 1999), 89–90; C. R. Whitlock to Clyde R. Kerr, 17 April 1931, 803—Contract & Public Schools, 1926–1941, Decimal Subject Files, 1925–1967; C. R. Whitlock to Arthur Bonney, 11 October 1934, ibid.; Evan W. Estep to Charles Rhoads, 10 January 1930, 806—Schools, 1917–1942, ibid.

43   Charles E. Frye to O. L. Babcock, 2 February 1922, The Dalles School Attendance, Subject Files, 1908–1925; Jessie L. Phipps to Victor H. Johnston, 14 September 1934, Folder 42903-36-800, Central Classified Files, 1907–1939; M. A. Johnson to C. G. Davis, 8 January 1940, 800—Education Col. River Area, Decimal Subject Files, 1925–1967; Waldo C. Zeller to Evan W. Estep, 8 December 1930, 821—Schools, 1930–1934, ibid.; Evan W. Estep to Charles Rhoads, 19 April 1930, 806—Schools, 1917–1942, ibid.

44   Robert Carlton Clark, Robert Horace Down, and George Verne Blue, *A History of Oregon* (Evanston, NY, Philadelphia, and San Francisco: Row, Peterson and Company, 1926), 17.

45   Ibid., 20, 35.

46   Chief Johnny Jackson, interview by Piper Hackett, 28 March 1999, OrHist 6208, Radical Elders Series, Oregon Historical Society, Portland (Chief Johnny Jackson), 11.

47   Bessie Quiemps to Agent of Indian Affairs, 24 April 1931, 822—Schools, 1930–1941, Decimal Subject Files, 1925–1967; Chief Johnny Jackson, 11; C. G. Davis to M. A. Johnson, 3 October 1940, 800—Education Col. River Area, Decimal Subject Files, 1925–1967.

48   Narrative Report of the Yakama Agency, 1931, Superintendents Annual Narrative, Roll 172, 23; Evan W. Estep to Charles H. Burke, 15 November 1928, 806—Schools, 1917–1942, Decimal Subject Files, 1925–1967; C. G. Davis to M. A. Johnson, 11 October 1939, 803—Contract & Public Schools, 1926–1941, ibid.; ibid., 15 April 1940; ibid., 22 August 1940.

49   Davis to Johnson, 16 October 1939, 006, Yallup, William (Chief), General Subject Correspondence, 1939–1953; Ella Jim comment in Field Notes, "Honoring the Heritage of Plateau Peoples: Past, Present, and Future"

Conference, October 2004, Pullman, Washington (in author's possession).

50   Ruth Spack, *America's Second Tongue: American Indian Education and the Ownership of English, 1860–1900* (Lincoln: University of Nebraska Press, 2002), 39–42; Ella Jim and Mavis Kindness comments made in Field Notes, "Honoring the Heritage of Plateau Peoples"; Chief Johnny Jackson 12–13; Johnny Jackson, personal communication with author, 26 July 2006. Spack points out that many Native American parents wanted their children to learn English but "*only English*—not *English only*" (41–42).

51   Walter Speedis, interview by Vivian Adams, August 1997, THPH-Elder Interviews, Yakama Reservation, transcript, The High Desert Museum, Bend, Oregon; Statement of Elsie Gibson, 10 October 1945, 803—Contract & Public Schools, 1926–1941, Decimal Subject Files, 1925–1967; Jim comment in Field Notes, "Honoring the Heritage of Plateau Peoples."

52   Davis to Johnson, 10 October 1941, 806—Schools, 1917–1942, Decimal Subject Files, 1925–1967.

53   C. G. Davis to L. W. Shotwell, 14 December 1944, General Subject Correspondence, 1939–1953; Davis to Johnson, 15 April 1940, 800—Education Col. River Area, Decimal Subject Files, 1925–1967.

54   Narrative Report of the Yakima Agency, 1917, Section VI, Superintendents Annual Narrative, Roll 171, 2.

55   Narrative Report of the Warm Springs Agency, 1921, Section IV, Superintendents Annual Narrative, Roll 164, 4; Narrative Report of the Umatilla Agency, 1914, ibid. , Roll 159, 23; Narrative Report of the Warm Springs Agency, 1932, Section IV, ibid. , Roll 165, 2. For a discussion of Native American "automobility" and representation, see Deloria, *Indians in Unexpected Places*, 136–82.

56   Narrative Report of the Yakima Agency, 1925, Superintendents Annual Narrative, Roll 171, 15; Narrative Report of the Warm Springs Agency, 1929, Section IV, ibid., Roll 160, 6; Raibmon, *Authentic Indians*, 97–99.

57   Leibhardt, "Law, Environment, and Social Change in the Columbia River Basin," 397–98; Leibhardt, "Allotment Policy in an Incongruous Legal System," 87.

58   Narrative Report of the Yakima Agency, 1929, Superintendents Annual Narrative, Roll 172, 60–61.

59   Katrine Barber, "Oregon Voices: Elsie David," 6 August 2007, *Oregon Historical Quarterly* 108, no. 4 (Winter 2007): 653.

60   Flora Thompson, interviewer unknown, no date, OHS Inv. # 9586, Oregon Historical Society, Portland (Flora Thompson), 1; Lillian A. Ackerman, *A Necessary Balance: Gender and Power among Indians of the Columbia Plateau* (Norman: University of Oklahoma Press, 2003), 150–61.

61   Statement of Elsie Gibson, 10 October 1945, 803—Contract & Public

Schools, 1926–1941, Decimal Subject Files, 1925–1967; Wilbur Slockish, Jr., interview by Michael O'Rourke, 11 February 2000, OHS Inv. #2738, Columbia River Dissenters Series, Oregon Historical Society, Portland (Wilbur Slockish interview), 1–2, 16.

62 Hunn, *Nch'i-Wána*, 131–32, 210–11; Statements of Myra Sohappy and David Sohappy, Jr., 5 April 1984, *Administrative Appeal of David Sohappy*, 223.

63 Minutes, Meeting of Celilo Fish Committee, 3 September 1941, [155], Minutes—1940, Councils—Celilo Fish Committee, General Subject Correspondence, 1939–1953; Davis to Johnson, 16 July 1941, 155-O, Councils—Celilo Fish Committee, ibid.

64 Hunn, "What Ever Happened to the First Peoples of the Columbia?" 32–33; Jim comment made in Field Notes, "Honoring the Heritage of Plateau Peoples"; U.S. Senate, Select Committee, 46.

6 HOME FOLK

1 C. G. Davis to M. A. Johnson, 16 July 1941, 155-O, Councils—Celilo Fish Committee, General Subject Correspondence, 1939–1953; Allotments.

2 Davis to Johnson, 16 July 1941, 155-O, Councils-CFC, General Subject Correspondence, 1939–1953.

3 Along with Alexandra Harmon and Russell Barsh, Susan Staiger Goodling notes the role of litigation in shaping Indian racial and tribal identities in "Place, Race, and Names: Layered Identities in *United States v. Oregon*, Confederated Tribes of the Colville Reservation, Plaintiff-Intervenor," *Law & Society Review* 28, no. 5 (1994): 1181–1230.

4 Taylor, *Making Salmon*, 62–64, 144. See also Francis Seufert, *Wheels of Fortune* (Portland: Oregon Historical Society, 1980) and Ivan J. Donaldson and Frederick K. Cramer, *Fishwheels of the Columbia* (Portland, OR: Binfords & Mort, 1971).

5 James Wilbur to Hiram Price, 21 May 1881, U.S. Bureau of Indian Affairs, Yakima Indian Agency Correspondence; Clifford C. Relander Collection, Roll 2.

6 Fay G. Cohen, *Treaties on Trial: The Continuing Controversy over Northwest Indian Fishing Rights* (Seattle: University of Washington Press, 1986), 55; United States v. Winans, 198 U.S. 317 (1905), 382.

7 Winans Testimony, 60.

8 Ibid., 64.

9 Affidavit of Martin Spedis, in Swindell, Report on Source, 175.

10 Winans Testimony, 68.

11 Ibid., 88, 18, 12–13; *U.S. v. Winans*, 382.

12 *U.S. v. Winans*, 382; Cohen, *Treaties on Trial*, 55–56.

13 *U.S. v. Winans*, 381; Evan W. Estep to Cary W. Ramsey, 15 April 1924, Fishing Matters along the Columbia River (1924), Yakima Indian Agency Correspondence, 4.

14 Winans Testimony, 203; Seufert, *Wheels of Fortune*, 45–46; F. A. Seufert to Clarence L. Reams, 15 June 1914, Box 2, Envelope 17, Seufert Brothers Company Papers, 1884–1954, MSS 1102, Oregon Historical Society, Portland (Seufert Brothers), 3; I. H. Taffe to George W. Olney, 26 July 1909, Fishing Matters along the Columbia River (1924)—Seufert v. Olney (1912–15), Yakima Indian Agency Correspondence.

15 "Indian Chief, 103, Is Erect in Court," 15 May 1915, *(Portland) Oregonian*, 12; Don M. Carr to L. A. Dorrington, 9 August 1915, Williams, Sam v. Seufert Bros. Co. (1913–18), General Subject Correspondence, 1908–1921; Seufert to Reams, 15 June 1914, Seufert Brothers, 1–2; Don M. Carr to Commissioner of Indian Affairs, 18 May 1914, Williams, Sam v. Seufert Bros. Co. (1913–18), General Subject Correspondence, 1908–1921; Dupris, Hill, and Rodgers, *Si'lailo Way*, 110–11; Sam Williams to Don M. Carr, 31 July 1913, Williams, Sam v. Seufert Bros. Co. (1913–18), General Subject Correspondence, 1908–1921.

16 Seufert to Reams, 15 June 1914, Seufert Brothers, 4.

17 Charles Switzler to F. A. Seufert, 6 April 1915, Box 2, Envelope 18, Seufert Brothers; Don M. Carr to Robert E. Rankin, 29 April 1915, Williams, Sam v. Seufert Bros. Co. (1913–18), General Subject Correspondence, 1908–1921; Dupris, Hill, and Rodgers, Si'lailo Way, 105.

18 The Trial of U.S. versus Seufert Brothers, Celilo Indian Fishermen, 1947–1951, Tribal Records, 1897–1952, 1–2; Don M. Carr to Clarence Reames, 25 May 1914, Williams, Sam v. Seufert Bros. Co. (1913–18), General Subject Correspondence, 1908–1921.

19 Opinion of Court (typescript), 24 May 1915, Trial of U.S. versus Seufert Brothers, Box 2, Envelope 19, Seufert Brothers, 1–7.

20 Ibid., 7; Dupris, Hill, and Rodgers, *Si'lailo Way*, 105; Ruby and Brown, *John Slocum and the Indian Shaker Church*, 169–70.

21 L. A. Dorrington to Gilbert L. Hall, 27 May 1915, Fishing Rights, Subject Files, 1908–1925; L. A. Dorrington to A. M. Reynolds, 15 January 1916, ibid.

22 Dorrington to Reynolds, 15 January 1916, 2.

23 "Indian Chief, 103, Is Erect in Court," 15 May 1915, *(Portland) Oregonian*, 12; Trial Transcript, *United States of America v. Seufert Brothers Company*, John Wilson Special Collections, Multnomah County Library, Portland (Trial Transcript), vol. 2, 302.

24 Trial Transcript, 583–84 [emphasis added]; *Seufert Brothers Company v. United States*, 249 U.S. 194 (1919), 198–99.

25 Transcript, 587–88; John R. Wunder, *"Retained by The People": A History of American Indians and the Bill of Rights* (New York: Oxford University Press, 1994), 49–50; Frank Seufert to Evan W. Estep, 14 August 1924, Fishing Matters along the Columbia River (1924), Yakima Indian Agency Correspondence; Don M. Carr to Commissioner of Indian Affairs, 15 May 1920, Williams, Sam v. Seufert Bros. Co. (1913–18), ibid.; Sam Williams to Evan W. Estep, 23 August 1924, ibid.

26 In both cases, *State v. Towessnute* (89 Wash. 478) and *State v. Alexis* (89 Wash. 492), the justices held that the defendant's treaty right to fish "in common" merely gave him the same privileges as non-Indian citizens. *State v. Wallahee* (143 Wash. 117) applied the same logic to Indian hunting on "open and unclaimed lands" outside reservation boundaries.

27 Don M. Carr to L. H. Darwin, 22 July 1915, Fishing Matters—State (1915–23), Yakima Indian Agency Correspondence, 1–2; L. H. Darwin to Don M. Carr, 27 July 1915, ibid.; E. B. Merritt to Don M. Carr, 27 October 1919, ibid.

28 Don M. Carr to Charles M. Buchanan, 9 June 1915, Fishing Matters, State of Washington v. H. R. Allen (1914–19), Yakima Indian Agency Correspondence, 1–3.

29 Affidavit of Tommy Thompson, in Swindell, *Report on Source*, 152; Affidavit of Isaac McKinley, ibid., 180; Aguilar, *When the River Ran Wild!*, 114, 123–26; C. W. Ramsey to Supt. Yakima Indian Reservation, 12 March 1924, Fishing Matters Along the Columbia River (1924), Yakima Indian Agency Correspondence; Evan W. Estep to Commissioner of Indian Affairs, 9 June 1924, Hunting and Fishing (1923–25), ibid.; F. E. Perkins to Commissioner of Indian Affairs, 14 October 1932, 115.1 Hunting and Fishing, Pertains to Celilo, 1932–1936, Decimal Files, 1905–1976, Umatilla Indian Agency, Records of the Bureau of Indian Affairs, Record Group 75, National Archives and Records Administration—Pacific Alaska Region (Decimal Files, 1905–1976).

30 Don M. Carr to Andrew Barnhart, 14 September 1922, Correspondence, Unallotted Indians; Evan W. Estep to O. L. Babcock, 7 May 1927, 121—Indian Troubles, Visiting Among Indians, Decimal Subject Files, 1925–1967; J. B. Mortsolf to Evan W. Estep, 13 May 1927, ibid.; Tommy Thompson to O. L. Babcock, 14 May 1928, 115.1 Hunting and Fishing, Pertains to Celilo, 1932–1936, Decimal Files, 1905–1976.

31 Seufert, *Wheels of Fortune*, 29–30, 41, 64–65; Dupris, Hill, and Rodgers, *Si'lailo Way*, 133–43; Deward E. Walker, Jr., "Productivity of Tribal Dipnet Fisheries at Celilo Falls: Analysis of the Joe Pinkham Fish Buying Records," *Northwest Anthropological Research Notes* 26, no. 2 (1992): 125; Statement of

the Yakima Indians in Support of Their Appeal to Save Their Vested Fishing Rights at Celilo Falls in the Columbia River, Box 3, Folder 18, Heister Dean Guie Papers, 1896–1978, MSS 2511, Oregon Historical Society, 1.

32 Narrative Report of the Umatilla Agency, 1931, Superintendents Annual Narrative, Roll 59, 51; ibid., 1934, 12.

33 C. R. Whitlock, F. W. Boyd, and O. L. Babcock to Commissioner of Indian Affairs, 18 August 1934, 115.1 Hunting and Fishing, Pertains to Celilo, 1932–1936, Decimal Files, 1905–1976, 1–3.

34 Tommy Thompson to Secretary of Interior, 27 August 1934, 115.1 Hunting and Fishing, Pertains to Celilo, 1932–1936, Decimal Files, 1905–1976, 1–2; C. R. Whitlock to Commissioner of Indian Affairs, 27 October 1934, ibid.; F. W. Boyd to O. L. Babcock, 15 January 1935, ibid.

35 Celilo Fish Committee By-Laws, 155-A, Councils, Celilo Fish Committee, 1939–48, Records of C. G. Davis, Field Aide at The Dalles, 1939–50, General Subject Correspondence, 1939–1953, 1–2; Dupris, Hill, and Rodgers, *Si'lailo Way*, 138–40.

36 Henry Roe Cloud to M. A. Johnson, 4 November 1939, 155-A, Celilo Fish Committee, 1939–48, Records of C. G. Davis, Field Aide at The Dalles, 1939–50, General Subject Correspondence, 1939–1953; J. W. Elliott to E. Morgan Pryse, 6 October 1949, 155-O, ibid.; Meeting of Celilo Fish Committee, 12 April 1939, Tribal Council File (1936–1939), Tribal Council Records, 1934–1951, Warm Springs Indian Agency, Records of the Bureau of Indian Affairs, Record Group 75, National Archives and Records Administration—Pacific Alaska Region (Tribal Council Records, 1934–1951), 5–6; Minutes of Meeting at Spearfish, 25 April 1939, 155, Spearfish Committee (1939–40), Records of C. G. Davis, Field Aide at The Dalles, 1939–50, General Subject Correspondence, 1939–1953.

37 Minutes of Regular Meeting of the Celilo Fish Committee, 4 June 1941, 155, Records of C. G. Davis, Field Aide at The Dalles, 1939–50, General Subject Correspondence, 1939–1953, 5.

38 Ibid., 6.

39 Ibid., 8; Allan E. Harper to M. A. Johnson, 6 October 1941, 155-I, Councils, Celilo Fish, Indian Office Letters re Resolutions, etc. (1940–46), Records of C. G. Davis, Field Aide at The Dalles, 1939–50, General Subject Correspondence, 1939–1953.

40 Minutes of Yakima Tribal Council, 27 July 1945, 064, Tribal Council Minutes, 1944–1965, Portland Area Office, Records of the Bureau of Indian Affairs, Record Group 75, National Archives and Records Administration—PacificAlaska Region (Tribal Council Minutes, 1944–1965); Minutes of Regular Meeting of the Celilo Fish Committee, 7 April 1949, Records of C. G. Davis, Field Aide at The Dalles, 1939–50, General Subject Correspon-

dence, 1939–1953, 13; Tommy Thompson to "Whom It May Concern," 31 October 1941, 155K, ibid.

41 Digest, Affairs of Indians Who Fish at Celilo and Other Points on the Columbia River, (155), Digest and By-Laws, Celilo Fish Committee, Records of C. G. Davis, Field Aide at The Dalles, 1939–50, General Subject Correspondence, 1939–1953, 30, 36–37; Minutes of Regular Meeting of the Celilo Fish Committee, 4 June 1941, ibid., 7, 14.

42 Davis to Johnson, 15 August 1941, 155-O, CFC Councils, Records of C. G. Davis, Field Aide at The Dalles, 1939–50, General Subject Correspondence, 1939–1953; M. A. Johnson to John Collier, 22 September 1939, 155-O, ibid., 2.

43 Memorandum for Mr. Babcock, 20 August 1938, 175.1, Cramer-Goudy Case 1939–48, Decimal Subject Files, 1925–1967; C. G. Davis to L. W. Shotwell, 3 May 1948, 155-Y, Celilo Fishing Commission Re—relations including fish controversies with non-Indians, private individuals, etc., Records of C. G. Davis, Field Aide at The Dalles, 1939–50, General Subject Correspondence, 1939–1953; Walker, "Productivity of Tribal Dipnet Fisheries," 125; Katrine Barber, *Death of Celilo Falls* (Seattle: University of Washington Press, 2005), 53–61.

44 Davis to Johnson, 26 October 1939, 155-O, CFC Councils, Records of C. G. Davis, Field Aide at The Dalles, 1939–50, General Subject Correspondence, 1939–1953; Minutes of Regular Meeting of the Celilo Fish Committee, 4 September 1940, ibid., 11–12; Carl C. Donaugh to Isaac Albert and the Other Members of the Fish Company, 13 September 1939, 155-E, Correspondence, Celilo Fish—Legal Matters, ibid.

45 1939 rules quoted in Dupris, Hill, and Rodgers, *Si'lailo Way*, 204; Ambrose Whitefoot to Celilo Fish Committee, 9 August 1943, 115.1, Minutes of the Celilo Fish Committee, 1942–1944, Decimal Files, 1905–1976; Celilo Fish Committee Resolution, 14 September 1943, ibid.

46 Dupris, Hill, and Rodgers, *Si'lailo Way*, 8–10, 204; C. G. Davis to Edward G. Swindell, Jr., 3 December 1941, 155-E, Councils—Celilo Fish, Legal Matters, Records of C. G. Davis, Field Aide at The Dalles, 1939–50, General Subject Correspondence, 1939–1953.

47 Davis to Shotwell, 29 July 1947, (Celilo Fish Committee, 1950), Records of C. G. Davis, Field Aide at The Dalles, 1939–50, General Subject Correspondence, 1939–1953; Agreement Between Gordon Bruce of the Portland Fish Company and Chiefs Tommy Thompson and William Yallup, 18 August 1939, 155-R, Cables operated by fish buyers at Celilo, ibid.; Minutes of Regular Meeting of the Celilo Fish Committee, 4 September 1940, ibid., 9; Statement of Willie Yallup of Rock Creek, 22 July 1939, 155-o, ibid.

48 Martha Ferguson McKeown, Report to the Special Celilo Committee Oregon Historical Society Regarding Columbia River Indians, 11 October 1956,

Celilo Falls Relocation Committee Records, MSS 2678, Oregon Historical Society (Celilo Falls Relocation Committee Records), 1.

49   Minutes of Regular Meeting of the Celilo Fish Committee, 4 September 1940, Records of C. G. Davis, Field Aide at The Dalles, 1939–50, General Subject Correspondence, 1939–1953, 10.

50   Ibid., 6 September 1944, 4; Davis to Johnson, 10 June 1939, 155-O, CFC Councils, ibid., 2.

51   Minutes of Regular Meeting of the Celilo Fish Committee, 2 September 1942, Records of C. G. Davis, Field Aide at The Dalles, 1939–50, General Subject Correspondence, 1939–1953, 4–5.

52   Ibid., 5.

53   Ibid.

54   Affidavit of Isaac McKinley, in Swindell, *Report on Source,* 177.

55   Statement of Tommy Thompson, Chief of the Celilo Indians, Celilo, Oregon, made at a general meeting of Columbia River and Warm Springs Indians, at Simnasho, Oregon, on Jan. 2, 1946, 155-L, Councils, Celilo Fish—Ownership of rocks near Celilo Falls, Records of C. G. Davis, Field Aide at The Dalles, 1939–50, General Subject Correspondence, 1939–1953.

56   Davis to Johnson, 12 May 1942, 155-O, CFC Councils, Records of C. G. Davis, Field Aide at The Dalles, 1939–50, General Subject Correspondence, 1939–1953; Statement by Henry Thompson, 12 May 1942, ibid.; Statement by Chief Willie Yallup, 12 May 1942, ibid.; Statement by Tommy Thompson, 12 May 1942, ibid.

57   Davis to Johnson, 20 April 1940, 155-J, Councils, Celilo Fish Committee, Acquisition of Land, Records of C. G. Davis, Field Aide at The Dalles, 1939–50, General Subject Correspondence, 1939–1953; S.B. 241, Chapter 409, *Oregon Laws,* 1943, 614.

58   Davis to Johnson, 20 April 1940, 155-J, Records of C. G. Davis, Field Aide at The Dalles, 1939–50, General Subject Correspondence, 1939–1953, 2; Davis to Johnson, 7 January 1941, 147, Newspaper Clippings, 1941–50, ibid., 1–2; John Whiz to Henry Charley, 6 March 1943, 006, Charley, Henry, Alice Slim Jim, ibid.; Davis to Johnson, 13 April 1943, 006, Whiz, Mary Norton, John Jr. (Billy), ibid., 1–4.

59   For a thorough discussion of the ongoing controversy over in-lieu fishing sites, see Ulrich, *Empty Nets.*

60   Davis to Johnson, 10 June 1939, 155-O, CFC Councils, Records of C. G. Davis, Field Aide at The Dalles, 1939–50, General Subject Correspondence, 1939–1953, 1.

61   Meeting of Indian representatives of the three agencies, 24 March 1942, 155-A, CFC Councils, Records of C. G. Davis, Field Aide at The Dalles, 1939–50, General Subject Correspondence, 1939–1953.

62   Minutes of Regular Meeting of the Celilo Fish Committee, 7 May 1941, Records of C. G. Davis, Field Aide at The Dalles, 1939–50, General Subject Correspondence, 1939–1953, 3.

63   Ibid., 7 May 1941, 3 September 1941; Tommy Thompson to W. J. Dunn, 5 January 1945, 155-U, What Indians Want, Records of C. G. Davis, Field Aide at The Dalles, 1939–50, General Subject Correspondence, 1939–1953; L. W. Shotwell to John Collier, 11 April 1944, 309—Islands Columbia River-Public Domain 1923–1947, Decimal Subject Files, 1925–1967.

64   Program, Wi-Yam Reservation, Oregon, Part Two—Overall Plan, 103, 10-yr. Program, Celilo, Oregon, 1944, Decimal Subject Files, 1925–1967, 1–4; L. W. Shotwell to Commissioner of Indian Affairs, 11 October 1945, 155-I, Records of C. G. Davis, Field Aide at The Dalles, 1939–50, General Subject Correspondence, 1939–1953, 1–4; ibid., 21 March 1946, 1–2; "Celilo Ready to Modernize," *(Portland) Oregon Journal*, 3 February 1940, 5; Barber, *Death of Celilo Falls*, 20–30. For an overview of termination policy, see Donald L. Fixico, *Termination and Relocation: Federal Indian Policy, 1945–1960* (Albuquerque: University of New Mexico Press, 1990).

65   Rock Creek Indians, Petition to the Honorable Members of the Oregon State Legislature, 16 January 1941, Folder 62A92, Box 8, Interim Legislature 1939–41, Oregon State Archives, Salem.

66   Davis to Shotwell, 30 March 1945, 155-O, Councils—Celilo Fish Committee, , General Subject Correspondence, 1939–1953.

67   Statements made by William Yallup, Chief of Rock Creek Indians, and Frank Slockish, Chief of the Klickitat Indians, both of which tribes are known as the Columbia River Tribe, 20 March 1945, 155-O, Councils—Celilo Fish Committee, General Subject Correspondence, 1939–1953, I-II.

68   Ibid., III; "Indians Unite Tribes," *Condon Globe-Times*, 5 March 1948, 2.

69   Affiliation of Indian Fishermen of the Columbia River, 155-A, CFC Councils, Records of C. G. Davis, Field Aide at The Dalles, 1939–50, General Subject Correspondence, 1939–1953, 1–4; Davis to Shotwell, 27 April 1944, 155-D, Councils, Celilo Fish—Marketing of Fish (1939–47), ibid., 1–2; Resolution No. 577, Warm Springs Tribal Council, 6 October 1949, 155-O, ibid.

70   "Indians Threaten Sit-Down Strike Over Fish Price," *The Dalles (OR) Chronicle*, 9 September 1941; "Indians Sell Celilo Fish," *(Portland) Oregonian*, 11 September 1941; M. A. Johnson to Kenneth R. L. Simmons, 11 September 1942, 360, Acquisition of Lands (Celilo Falls) 1937–47, Decimal Subject Files, 1925–1967. According to Superintendent Johnson, in September 1942 salmon sold for thirteen cents a pound at Astoria, Oregon, while Indians got only five cents for higher-quality fish. The previous summer, after demanding six cents a pound, most settled for only four.

71   Cohen, *Treaties on Trial*, 62–63; Minutes, Mass Meeting of Indians inter-

ested in fishing at Celilo, Ore., held April 24, 1945 at Celilo (155), Minutes—Various Meetings of Indian Fishermen, 1945–49, Records of C. G. Davis, Field Aide at The Dalles, 1939–50, General Subject Correspondence, 1939–1953, 1.

72 Minutes, Mass Meeting of Indians interested in fishing at Celilo, Ore., held April 24, 1945 at Celilo (155), Minutes—Various Meetings of Indian Fishermen, 1945–49, Records of C. G. Davis, Field Aide at The Dalles, 1939–50, General Subject Correspondence, 1939–1953, 1.

7 SUBMERGENCE AND RESURGENCE

1 Jay LaPlante, "Celilo Falls: Flooded 40 Years Ago But Not Forgotten," *Wana Chinook Tymoo* (Issue Two 1997), 10; Robert Clark, *River of the West: Stories from the Columbia* (New York: HarperCollins West, 1995), 329; Tommy Thompson quoted in Cain Allen, "'They Called It Progress': Indians, Salmon, and the Industrialization of the Columbia River" (M.A. thesis, Portland State University, 2000), 66–67.

2 Ulrich, *Empty Nets*, 90–93; Jack Abraham to the President [of the United States] and to Whom It May Concern, 15 July 1959, Folder 5-1, Clifford C. Relander Collection, 3.

3 Annual Report, Umatilla Indian Agency, 1937, Section 1, Superintendents Annual Narrative, Roll 160, 1; M. A. Johnson to O. L. Babcock, 20 March 1939, 054 Census Matters—Instruction, 1941–44, General Subject Correspondence, 1939–1953.

4 H. U. Sanders, Report on Sanitary Conditions at Celilo, Oregon, 10 October 1940, Property and Plant Management, Celilo Relocation Records, 1947–1957, Portland Area Office, Records of the Bureau of Indian Affairs, Record Group 75, National Archives and Records Administration—Pacific Alaska Region (Celilo Relocation Records), 10.

5 Davis to Johnson, 24 January 1941, Census Matters—Instruction, 1941–44, General Subject Correspondence, 1939–1953.

6 Johnson to Davis, 28 January 1941, Census Matters—Instruction, 1941–44, General Subject Correspondence, 1939–1953; Davis to Johnson, 19 February 1941, ibid.; Davis to Johnson, 28 February 1941, ibid.; C. G. Davis, Memorandum to Miss R. Bond, 26 March 1941, ibid.; Johnson to Davis, 9 April 1942, 052.9 Other Statistical Reports, Records of C. G. Davis, Field Aide at The Dalles, 1939–50, General Subject Correspondence, 1939–1953.

7 Davis to Johnson, 24 January 1941, Census Matters—Instruction, 1941–44, General Subject Correspondence, 1939–1953, 2; Report on Sanitary Conditions at Celilo, Oregon, 10 October 1940, Celilo Relocation Records,

5; Dupris, Hill, and Rodgers, *Si'lailo Way*, 147–49; Davis to Shotwell, 7 December 1944, 054 Current Census Matters, Correspondence and Instruction, 1943–48, General Subject Correspondence, 1939–1953.

8 Sharon O'Brien, *American Indian Tribal Governments* (Norman: University of Oklahoma Press, 1989), 191; Yakima General Council Meeting, 20 February 1945, 064.1, Yakima Indian Agency, Tribal Council Minutes, 1944–1965,1–2; Minutes of a Regular Tribal Council Meeting, 4 March 1946, Warm Springs Minutes, 1946–47, Tribal Council Records, 1934–1951; C. G. Davis to J. W. Elliott, 24 June 1944, Current Census Matters, Correspondence and Instruction, 1943–48; Notice to the Members of the Yakima Tribes of Indians, State of Washington, 29 July 1949, 30; Yakima Indians, Records of C. G. Davis, Field Aide at The Dalles, 1939–50, General Subject Correspondence, 1939–1953.

9 As Sharon O'Brien notes, "The Yakimas' tribal government combines a traditional structure with modern organizational practices." The fourteen-member Tribal Council, established formally in 1944, has primary responsibility for formulating policy and protecting treaty rights. The General Council is composed of all adult tribal members. During special sessions and annual meetings held in November, it discusses important policy matters and votes on resolutions intended to direct tribal policy. Although the Yakama Nation has no written constitution or bylaws specifying the separation of powers, the General Council nominally retains all governmental authority except what it has expressly delegated to the Tribal Council, including the right to annul or repeal measures passed by the Tribal Council (O'Brien, *American Indian Tribal Governments*, 189–91).

10 Yakima General Council Meeting, 6 February 1945, 064.1 Tribal Council Minutes, 1944–1965, 3–5; Yakima General Council and Tribal Council Meeting, 9 March 1945, ibid., 7.

11 Yakima General Council and Tribal Council Meeting, Tribal Council Minutes, 1944–1965, 7–9; Davis to Shotwell, 25 May 1945, 006 Dave—Sam, Annie, Harry, Lillian, General Subject Correspondence, 1939–1953.

12 Yakima General Council Meeting, 5 March 1946, 064.1, Tribal Council Minutes, 1944–1965, 5; Yakima General Council Meeting, 20 February 1945, ibid., 4; Meeting of the Fourteen Chiefs, 23 March 1944, General Council Minutes—1944, ibid., 1–5.

13 Kenneth R. L. Simmons to L. W. Shotwell, 27 August 1949, Enrollment Legal Options, Miscellaneous Enrollment Records, Yakima Indian Agency Correspondence, 1–3.

14 Conference with Umatilla Indians, 6 May 1952, Celilo Minutes 1952, Desk Files of the Realty Division, 1947–1965, Portland Area Office, Records of the Bureau of Indian Affairs, Record Group 75, National Archives and Records

Administration—Pacific Alaska Region, 5; Meeting of Wyum Indians regarding The Dalles Dam," ca. 14 April 1952, Celilo File, 1951–1952, Records of C. G. Davis, Field Aide at The Dalles, 1939–50, General Subject Correspondence, 1939–1953; Minutes of Regular Meeting of the Celilo Fish Committee, 1 June 1950, 155—Minutes of Meetings of Celilo Fish Committee, 1939–1950, ibid., 5.

15 Minutes of Yakima General Council Meeting, 20 February 1945, 064.1— General Council 1945, Tribal Council Minutes, 1944–1965, 1–6.

16 Affidavit of Willie John Culpus, in Swindell, *Report on Source*, 169; Minutes of Celilo Fish Committee Meeting, 1 September 1949, 155 Councils—Celilo Fish Committee, Records of C. G. Davis, Field Aide at The Dalles, 1939–50, General Subject Correspondence, 1939–1953, 16.

17 Colonel T. H. Lipscomb to Celilo Indians, 27 January 1954, 920 Conservation of Fish and Wildlife, Celilo Fisheries Negotiations with Unenrolled Indians, 1953–1955, Records of C. G. Davis, General Subject Correspondence, 1939–1953; Barber, *Death of Celilo Falls*, 159–61.

18 Barber, *Death of Celilo Falls*, 172; Relander, *Strangers on the Land*, 12; C. G. Davis to J. W. Elliott, 5 June 1943, 006—Thompson, Tommy, Otis and Ellen Andrews, Wilbur Kuneki, Records of C. G. Davis, Field Aide at The Dalles, 1939–50, General Subject Correspondence, 1939–1953. For a fuller discussion of the dam settlement and village relocation, see Barber, *Death of Celilo Falls*, 155–82.

19 Edward G. Swindell, for E. Morgan Pryse, to Easley, Whipple & McCormick, Attorneys at Law, 17 March 1953, Records of C. G. Davis, Field Aide at The Dalles, 1939–50, General Subject Correspondence, 1939–1953; Transcripts—Misc. Sources, Wyam Indians, Folder 60-16, Clifford C. Relander Collection, 1–3.

20 Norman L. Easley to Edward G. Swindell, 25 March 1953, 060 Tribal Relations, Celilo, 1953, Decimal Files, 1905–1976 1–2.

21 Congress, Senate, Committee on Appropriations, *Civil Functions, Department of the Army Appropriations: Hearings before the Subcommittee of the Committee on Appropriations on H.R. 5376*, 83rd Cong., 1st sess., 15–26 May 1953, 1447–52.

22 Fixico, *Termination and Relocation*, 97–99, 111–12; Barber, *Death of Celilo Falls*, 170–71; Transcripts—Misc. Sources, Clifford C. Relander Collection, 1–2; Lipscomb to Celilo Indians, 1–2, ibid.; Easley, Whipple and McCormick to Dear Friend, 16 October 1953, ibid.; File 920, Hatch, Keith, Personal Files, Celilo Village Housing, Portland Area Office, Bureau of Indian Affairs, Portland, Oregon (Hatch Files).

23 Barber, *Death of Celilo Falls*, 170–72; Dupris, Hill, and Rodgers, *Si'lailo Way*, 339–54; Affidavit of Irene Brunoe, 28 March 1954, Preliminary Correspondence, Celilo Relocation (1954–58), Celilo Relocation Records, 1940–1964.

24 Flora Thompson, 6.

25 Perry E. Skarra to Sidney A. Woodward, Sr., 11 August 1952, 921, Hunting and Fishing, Decimal Subject Files, 1925–1967, emphasis in original; Chief Johnny Jackson, 19.

26 Mid-Columbia River Council, "Statement of Unification," 18 December February 1990, in Application for Federal Assistance to the Administration for Native Americans, 5 February 1993, Hatch Files, 67; Johnny Jackson, personal communication with author, 7 May 2007; Ella Jim comment in Field Notes, "Honoring the Heritage of Plateau Peoples" Conference; Wilbur Slockish interview, 17; Slockish comment made at Field Notes, Berry Field Meeting.

27 E. M. Benn to Alvin Anderson, 12 July 1949, Folder "Yakima Indian Defiance of Yakima River closure—Klickitat River—Brown's Island, 1948–52," Box 45, Records of the Washington State Department of Fisheries, Washington State Archives, Olympia (Records of the Washington State Department of Fisheries), 1–2; Cecil Wesley and Charley Dave to Alvin Anderson, 6 June 1950, ibid.; Clefren Dave to Robert Schoettler, 12 March 1951, Folder "Yakima, Klickitat—low. Columbia Project, 1951," Box 48, Washington State Department of Fisheries, 1–3; Perry E. Skarra to Robert J. Schoettler, 12 April 1951, ibid.; Yakima Tribal Council Resolution, 11 April 1951, ibid.; Norman Riddell to Robert J. Schoettler, 11 May 1951, ibid.

28 Wilson Charley to Cecil Wesley, Roy Spino, Davis Jim, Albert Andrews, Chester Spino, James Jim, 6 May 1952, Folder "Yakima, Klickitat, 1952–53," Box 47, Washington State Department of Fisheries; Memo to M. L. Skaret, 3 May 1954, Folder "Yakima, Klickitat, 1954–56," ibid.; Frank Swick to S. P. Phillips, 4 May 1954, ibid., 2.

29 Don C. Foster to Dannie E. LeCrone, 29 October 1957, Misc. Celilo Claims (1957–58), Celilo Relocation Records; Complaint for Injunction, *Ambrose Whitefoot and Minnie Whitefoot v. Fred A. Seaton and Glen L. Emmons*, Civil No. 2658-57, ibid., 1–4; *Ambrose Whitefoot and Minnie Whitefoot v. United States*, U.S. Court of Claims, 497–57, 1961.

30 Ulrich, *Empty Nets*, 111–17; Case History of Willie and Annie Palmer, 11 February 1955, Box 1, Envelope 16, Celilo Falls Relocation Committee Records; Report on the Status of Individual Housing for Eligible Applicants under Public Law #163, 30 August 1956, Box 1, Folder 6, ibid., 2.

31 Martha Ferguson McKeown, Memo—"Regarding non-reservation Indians living in the Columbia River Gorge," ca. 1 March 1955, Preliminary Correspondence, Celilo Relocation (1954–58), Celilo Relocation Records; Barber, *Death of Celilo Falls*, 144–52; Ulrich, *Empty Nets*, 92–93.

32 Ulrich, *Empty Nets*, 36–40, 108, 112–13; Chief Johnny Jackson, 41.

33 Ulrich, *Empty Nets*, 125; Deposition of David Sohappy, 10 May 1976, vol. 3, June 17, 1974–Mar. 30, 1978, Civil 68-409, *Sohappy v. Smith*, United States

District Court for the District of Oregon, Records of District Courts of the United States, Record Group 21, National Archives and Records Administration—Pacific Alaska Region (Civil 68-409), 1. See also Cohen, *Treaties on Trial.*

34 Ulrich, *Empty Nets*, 129; Charles A. Hobbs, "Indian Hunting and Fishing Rights II," *The George Washington Law Review* 37 (July 1969): 1257; "Oregon Enlists Indian Tribes in Columbia Fish Conservation," *Oregon Journal* (Portland), 22 May 1964; George C. Starlund to George D. Dysart, 10 August 1962, Box 46, Folder "Yakima, Corr.—Attorney General on Fishing rights—Catch & Escapement, 1961-63," Washington State Department of Fisheries; R. W. Josephson to George C. Starlund, 2 August 1963, ibid., 1-2.

35 George D. Dysart to J. L. Conif, 15 April 1963, Box 9, Folder "Fishing—Columbia River, 1943-1965—Legal," Washington State Department of Fisheries; George D. Dysart to Area Director, Bureau of Indian Affairs, 21 August 1964, Box 46, Folder "Yakima, Corr.—Dept. of Interior," ibid.; Civil 65-2082, *Alvin Settler v. Yakima Tribal Council, et. al.*, United States District Court for the Eastern District of Washington Southern Division, Yakima Civil Case Files, 1938-1967, Records of District Courts of the United States, Record Group 21, National Archives and Records Administration—Pacific Alaska Region (Civil 65-2082); Robert W. Schoning to Philleo Nash, 13 May 1965, Folder 2082 (2 of 2), ibid., 1-4.

36 Leo Alexander to Click Relander, 14 January 1966, Folder 5-1, Clifford C. Relander Collection; Executive Order of the General Council of the Yakima Indian Nation, 7 March 1966, Box 46, Folder "Yakima, Corr.—Dept. of Interior/BIA Opinion on Fishing, 1966-69," Washington State Department of Fisheries, 1-2.

37 Flora Thompson, 6-7.

38 Schoning to Nash, Folder 2082 (2 of 2), Civil 65-2082, 4; Aris M. Frederick to Thor Tollefson, 27 April 1966, "Yakima Corr.—Dept. of Interior/BIA Opinion on Fishing, 1966-69," Washington State Department of Fisheries; "Fisheries Director Denies Sneak Night Attack on Gillnets of Rebel Indians," *Oregonian (Portland)*, 6 May 1966; Leo Alexander to Mr. Tollefson, 7 October 1966, "Yakima Corr.—Dept. of Interior/BIA Opinion on Fishing, 1966-69," Washington State Department of Fisheries.

39 Chief Johnny Jackson, 42.

40 Larry Nesper, *The Walleye War: The Struggle for Ojibway Spearfishing and Treaty Rights* (Lincoln: University of Nebraska Press, 2002), 55; Wilbur Slockish, personal communication with author, 28 July 2006.

41 Chief Johnny Jackson, 48; Memorandum in Opposition to Motion for Severance, 18 June 1976, Civil 68-409, 1-2.

42 Larry Coniff to Robert S. Robison, 12 December 1966, "Yakima Corr.—

Dept. of Interior/BIA Opinion on Fishing, 1966–69," Washington State Department of Fisheries; Columbia River General Council Fish Commission of the Yakima Indian Nation, 5 December 1966, Re: Yakima Indian Tribal Government & Yakima General Council Resolution T-38-56 (Umtuch), ibid., 1–2.

43   Ulrich, *Empty Nets*, 129–30; Cohen, *Treaties on Trial*, 76–77; Dysart quoted in Laura Berg, "'Let Them Do As They Have Promised': A History of *U.S. v. Oregon* and Four Tribes' Fight for Columbia River Salmon," *Hastings West-Northwest Journal of Environmental Law and Policy* 3, no. 1 (Fall 1995): 10.

44   Patrol Division, Officer's Report, 7 June 1968, Box 9, Folder "General, Fishing Sites—Columbia River, 1965–1972," Washington State Department of Fisheries; Memorandum, R. B. Gruett to Thor C. Tollefson, 14 June 1968, ibid.

45   Clark, *River of the West*, 133; "Cooks Landing," ca. 1970, in *Columbia River Indian Fishing Documents* (Vancouver, WA, 2003), ed. T. Van Arsdol, University of Washington Special Collections, 7.

46   Van Arsdol, "Cooks Landing," 8.

47   Clark, *River of the West*, 333.

48   Ulrich, *Empty Nets*, 127–28; William Dietrich, *Northwest Passage: The Great Columbia River* (New York: Simon & Schuster, 1995), 379–81; Columbia River Defense Project, *In Defense of Che Wana: Fishing Rights on the Columbia River* (Portland, OR: The Wheel Press, 1987), 7.

49   Defendants' Reply Brief in Support of Motion to Dismiss, 6 January 1969, Civil 68–409; Complaint for Declaratory Judgment and Preliminary Permanent Injunctions, 26 July 1968, *Sohappy v. Smith*, Volume 1, U.S. District Court of Oregon, Mark O. Hatfield U.S. Courthouse, Portland, 15–16; Berg, "'Let Them Do As They Have Promised,'" 11; Wilbur Slockish, personal communication with author, 28 July 2006.

50   Berg, "'Let The Do As They Have Promised,'" 12–13; Judge's Opinion, 7 July 1969, Civil No. 68–409, 23–24.

51   J. L. Coniff to Carl N. Crouse and Thor C. Tollefson, 10 May 1971, Box 46, Folder "Yakima 1970–72," Washington State Department of Fisheries; Memorandum, Yakima Tribal Law & Order Department of the Confederated Tribes and Bands of the Yakima Indian Nation, Subject: Registration—Fisherman—Sites & Nets, 1 September, 1971, ibid.; Motion for Temporary Restraining Order, 7 September 1971, Sohappy v. Smith, Volume 2 (April 14, 1970-June 17, 1974); Treaty Indians of the Columbia, Inc., "Columbia River & Yakima Indian News," Mid-December 1971, "Yakima 1970–72," Washington State Department of Fisheries, 1–2.

52   "Van Arsdol, Cooks Landing," 6.

53   Berg, "'Let Them Do As They Have Promised,.'" 13–14; *Settler v. Lameer*, 507 F.2d 231 (1974).

54   Cohen, *Treaties on Trial*, 94–106; Leo Alexander Affidavit, 26 April 1976, Civil No. 68–409; Transcript of Motion, 29 April 1974, *Sohappy v. Smith*, 42; Memorandum in Opposition to Motion for Severance, *Sohappy v. Smith*, vol. 3, 1–2; David Sohappy Affidavit, 14 May 1976, ibid.

55   David Sohappy Affidavit, 23 April 1976, *Sohappy v. Smith*, vol. 3, 1–2; Leo Alexander Affidavit, 26 April 1976, ibid., 2.

56   Civil No. 68–409, Transcript of Motion, 3 May 1974, 169; Johnson J. Meninick to Thor C. Tollefson, 14 June 1974, Box 46, Folder "Yakima 1974," Washington State Department of Fisheries; Memorandum in Opposition to Motion for Severance, *Sohappy v. Smith*, vol. 3, 1–2.

57   Excerpt from Proceedings, 4 April 1978, *Sohappy v. Smith*, vol. 4 (March 30, 1978–June 19, 1978), 2; Yakima General Council Minutes, Item 6, 29 November 1977, Carol Craig, Personal Files, Yakama Nation Fisheries Resource Management, Toppenish, Washington (Carol Craig), 89; "General Council News," *Yakama Nation Review* (Toppenish, WA), 20 December 1977, 6–7.

58   Answer to Motion for Termination of Continuing Jurisdiction and Request for Hearing, 2 May 1978, *Sohappy v. Smith*, Vol. 4; Columbia River Defense Project, *In Defense of Che Wana*, 7.

59   Ulrich, *Empty Nets*, 123–25; Ella Jim in Field Notes, "Honoring the Heritage of Plateau Peoples" conference.

60   Ulrich, *Empty Nets*, 134–39; William T. Schlick to Area Director, Portland Area Office, 11 May 1970, Exhibit 49, Affidavit of Peter A. Parnickis, Civil 86–715, *David Sohappy, Sr., et. al. v. Donald Hodel*, United States District Court for the District of Oregon, Records of District Courts of the United States, Record Group 21, National Archives and Records Administration—Pacific Alaska (Civil 86–715), 1; In-lieu Site Meeting, Stevenson, Washington, 14 April 1972, Exhibit 57, ibid., 3.

61   Schlick to Area Director, Affidavit of Peter A. Parnickis , Civil 86–715, 2.

62   In-lieu Site Meeting, ibid., 3, 11–12; *Alexander, et. al. v. Morton* (Civil No. 74–977, 1974).

63   Ulrich, *Empty Nets*, 160–62; Dietrich, *Northwest Passage*, 383–85; Clark, *River of the West*, 361–78; Columbia River Defense Project, *In Defense of Che Wana*, 21–23; Wilbur Slockish interview, 12; "Lacey Act Amendment to help Yakima Nation," 15 April 1982, *Yakima Nation Review* (Toppenish, WA),1.

64   Clark, *River of the West*, 344–53; Ulrich, *Empty Nets*, 159–63.

65   Ulrich, *Empty Nets*, 163–64; Lacey Act Workshop Minutes, 12 November 1986, Carol Craig, 63.

66   Lacey Act Workshop Minutes, Carl Craig, 8–9; Clark, *River of the West*, 367–78; Chief Johnny Jackson, 62; Lavina Washines quoted in Ulrich, *Empty Nets*, 164. The criticism directed at tribal, state, and federal officials

largely drowned out a debate among traditionalists regarding the legitimacy of Sohappy's religious defense. Some Indians took the view that the convicted fishers had brought trouble on themselves, as well as on their tribes, by selling the Creator's gifts in violation of both tribal regulations and traditional law. Ceremonial permits might be unnecessary and even objectionable, but people fishing under them were supposed to be supplying salmon for traditional feasts and ceremonies, not for the marketplace. As one longhouse member recently informed me, the dissidents "did not adhere to the tenets of the traditional values and convictions relative to the Seven Drums or Washat Religion, as claimed. I only say this because commercialism was the vacuum that brought tribal fishers to the banks of the Columbia, and it must be remembered that the true believers of our sacred religion forbids the sale of salmon in any way" (Ron Pond, personal communication with author, 30 November 2007).

67 Ted Strong, interview by Clark Hansen, 17 January 2000, OHS Inv. 2731, Columbia River Dissenters Series, Oregon Historical Society, Portland, 12–13; Lacey Act Workshop Minutes, Carol Craig, 46, 49, 79; Galen Yallup, personal communication with author, 18 July 2006.

68 Lacey Act Workshop Minutes, Carol Craig, 22; Clark, *River of the West*, 359; Ulrich, *Empty Nets*, 178–79; Daniel Spatz, "Indians Vow Opposition to Eviction Notice," *Enterprise* (White Salmon, WA), 19 April 1984, 1.

69 Columbia River Defense Project, *In Defense of Che Wana*, 1; Pat Skahan, "Yakimas Urged to Seek Lacey Act Review," *Yakima Nation Review*, 10 February 1988; Chief Johnny Jackson, 60–61; Motion to Appear as *Amicus Curiae* and *Amicus Curiae* Brief Before the Interior Board of Indian Appeals, 22 July 1985, Docket #85-20-A, U.S. Department of the Interior— Office of Hearings and Appeals, United States District Court for the District of Oregon, Records of District Courts of the United States, Record Group 21, National Archives and Records Administration—Pacific Alaska Region, 132.

70 U.S. Senate, Select Committee, 158–61.

71 Ibid., 48–51.

72 Appellant's Reply Brief, 4 November 1985, *Administrative Appeal of David Sohappy*, 34–36; Motion to Appear as *Amicus Curiae* and *Amicus Curiae* Brief Before the Interior Board of Indian Appeals, ibid., 132.

73 Motion to Appear as *Amicus Curiae* and *Amicus Curiae* Brief Before the Interior Board of Indian Appeals, Administrative Appeal of David Sohappy, 142–44, 223.

74 Clark, *River of the West*, 367; Nicholas K. Geranios, "Sohappy battles on for Indian fishing rights," 12 November 1990, *Oregonian* (Portland), A11; Jeanie Senior, "Indian leader laid to rest in tribal rite," ibid., 10 May 1991, A1.

75 Mid-Columbia River Council, Application for Federal Assistance to the

Administration for Native Americans, 5 February 1993, Hatch Files, 13, emphasis in original; Mid-Columbia River Council, "Statement of Unification," ibid., 69.

CONCLUSION

1   ANA Application, 12–15.

2   Ibid., 17–19; Charles J. Davison, United States Government Memorandum, 19 January 1994, Combined Water System for the Celilo Area, Branch of Facilities Management, Hatch Files, 1–3; Ray Slockish to Facility Management, 18 February 1994, ibid.; Keith Hatch, notes of meeting with George Gover to discuss Celilo Village and Task Force, 29 November 1994, ibid.

3   Cory Eldridge, "Enduring Village, Part 2: Intersection of Past and Future," *Dalles (OR) Chronicle*, 28 July 2008, A5.

4   Ibid.

5   Phil Ferolito, "Decision to Close Columbia Has Tribe Fishing for Answers," *Yakima (WA) Herald-Republic*, 8 June 2008.

6   Chief Johnny Jackson, 26–27.

7   Hunn, *Nch'i-Wána*, 271–73; Andrew H. Fisher, "Invasion of the Boardheads: Windsurfing and the Transformation of the Columbia Gorge," *Columbia* (Summer 2007): 27; Warren Spencer and Margaret Saluskin quoted in Peter Monahan and Danny Kepley, *The Point: Legacy of the River People* (Yakima, WA: Eastside Productions, 1996), videocassette.

8   Hunn, *Nch'i-Wána*, 27–273; Chief Johnny Jackson, 37.

9   *Being Comanche*, 20–22; Hunn, *Nch'i-Wána*, 273; Galen Yallup, personal communication with author, 18 July 2006.

10 U.S. Senate, Select Committee, 19 April 1988, 48; Chief Johnny Jackson, 28–29, 42.

11 Hunn, "What Ever Happened to the First Peoples of the Columbia?", 19; Chief Johnny Jackson, 66.

12 See Asher, *Beyond the Reservation*, and Harmon, *Indians in the Making*. See also James K. Burrows, "'A Much-Needed Class of Labour': The Economy and Income of the Southern Interior Plateau Indians, 1897–1910," *BC Studies* 71 (1986): 27–46, and Dianne Newell, *Tangled Webs of History: Indians and the Law in Canada's Pacific Coast Fisheries* (Toronto: University of Toronto Press, 1993).

13 On California, see Albert L. Hurtado, *Indian Survival on the California Frontier* (New Haven: Yale University Press, 1988), and George Harwood Phillips, *Indians and Indian Agents: The Origins of the Reservation System in California, 1849–1852* (Norman: University of Oklahoma Press, 1997). On

Texas, see Gary Clayton Anderson, *The Conquest of Texas: Ethnic Cleansing in the Promised Land, 1820–1875* (Norman: University of Oklahoma Press, 2005); Kelly F. Himmel, *The Conquest of the Karankawas and the Tonkawas, 1821–1859* (College Station: Texas A&M University Press, 1996); and F. Todd Smith, *The Caddos, the Wichitas, and the United States, 1846–1901* (College Station: Texas A&M University Press, 1999). On Indian Territory, see Jeffrey Burton, *Indian Territory and the United States, 1866–1906: Courts, Government, and the Movement for Oklahoma Statehood* (Norman: University of Oklahoma Press, 1995); and Angie Debo, *And Still the Waters Run: The Betrayal of the Five Civilized Tribes* (Princeton, NJ: Princeton University Press, 1940; repr., Norman: University of Oklahoma Press, 1984).

14   See Donald Craig Mitchell, *Sold American: The Story of Alaska Natives and Their Land, 1867–1959: The Army to Statehood* (Hanover, NH: University Press of New England, 1997). On post-colonial New England and New York, see Colin Calloway, ed., *After King Philip's War: Presence and Persistence in Indian New England* (Hanover, NH: University Press of New England, 1997); and Laurence M. Hauptman, *Conspiracy of Interests: Iroquois Dispossession and the Rise of New York State* (Syracuse, NY: Syracuse University Press, 1999). Other recent studies of Indian communities that survived without reservations include Joseph Herring, *The Enduring Indians of Kansas: A Century and a Half of Acculturation* (Lawrence: University Press of Kansas, 1990); John R. Finger, *The Eastern Band of Cherokees, 1819–1900* (Knoxville: University of Tennessee Press, 1984); James Merrell, *The Indians' New World: Catawbas and Their Neighbors from European Contact through the Era of Removal* (Chapel Hill: University of North Carolina Press, 1989); and Christopher Arris Oakley, *Keeping the Circle: American Indian Identity in Eastern North Carolina, 1885–2004* (Lincoln: University of Nebraska Press, 2007).

15   Harmon, *Indians in the Making*, 248.

BIBLIOGRAPHY

ARCHIVAL RECORDS

Administrative Appeal of David Sohappy, Sr., et. al., v. Deputy Assistant Secretary—Indian Affairs (Operations), IBIA 85-20-A, U.S. Department of Interior—Office of Hearings and Appeals, United States District Court for the District of Oregon, Records of District Courts of the United States, Record Group 21, National Archives and Records Administration—Pacific Alaska Region.

Allotment Applications and Allotment Selections, 1904–1905, 1917, Umatilla Indian Agency, Records of the Bureau of Indian Affairs, Record Group 75, National Archives and Records Administration—Pacific Alaska Region.

Allotment Case Files, ca. 1905–1955, Yakima Indian Agency, Records of the Bureau of Indian Affairs, Record Group 75, National Archives and Records Administration—Pacific Alaska Region.

Allotments, Records of C.G. Davis, Field Agent at The Dalles, 1939–1950, Portland Area Office, Records of the Bureau of Indian Affairs, Record Group 75,

National Archives and Records Administration—Pacific Alaska Region.

Carol Craig, Personal Files, Yakama Nation Fisheries Resource Management, Toppenish,Washington.

Celilo Falls Relocation Committee Records, MSS 2678, Oregon Historical Society, Portland.

Celilo Relocation Records, 1940–1964, Portland Area Office, Records of the Bureau of Indian Affairs, Record Group 75, National Archives and Records Administration—Pacific Alaska Region.

Central Classified Files, 1907–1939, Records of the Bureau of Indian Affairs, Record Group 75, National Archives Building, Washington, DC.

Civil 65-2082, *Alvin Settler v. Yakima Tribal Council, et. al.*, United States District Court for the Eastern District of Washington Southern Division, Yakima Civil Case Files, 1938–1967, Records of District Courts of the United States, Record Group 21, National Archives and Records Administration—Pacific Alaska Region.

Civil 68-409, *Sohappy v. Smith*, United States District Court for the District of Oregon, Records of District Courts of the United States, Record Group 21, National Archives and Records Administration—Pacific Alaska Region.

Civil 86-715, *David Sohappy, Sr., et. al. v. Donald Hodel*, United States District Court for the District of Oregon, Records of District Courts of the United States, Record Group 21, National Archives and Records Administration—Pacific Alaska Region.

Clifford C. Relander Collection, Yakima Valley Regional Library, Yakima, Washington.

The Dalles Allottees, Records of C. G. Davis, Field Agent at The Dalles, 1939–1950, Portland Area Office, Records of the Bureau of Indian Affairs, Record Group 75, National Archives and Records Administration—Pacific Alaska Region.

Decimal Files, 1905–1976, Umatilla Indian Agency, Records of the Bureau of Indian Affairs, Record Group 75, National Archives and Records Administration—Pacific Alaska Region.

Decimal Files, 1908–1952, Warm Springs Indian Agency, Records of the Bureau of Indian Affairs, Record Group 75, National Archives and Records Administration—Pacific Alaska Region.

Decimal Subject Files, 1925–1967, Yakima Indian Agency, Records of the Bureau of Indian Affairs, Record Group 75, National Archives and Records Administration—Pacific Alaska Region.

Desk Files of the Realty Division, 1947–1965, Portland Area Office, Records of the Bureau of Indian Affairs, Record Group 75, National Archives and Records Administration—Pacific Alaska Region.

Docket #85-20-A, U.S. Department of the Interior—Office of Hearings and

Appeals, United States District Court for the District of Oregon, Records of District Courts of the United States, Record Group 21, National Archives and Records Administration—Pacific Alaska Region.

Documents Relating to the Negotiation of Ratified and Unratified Treaties with Various Indian Tribes, 1801–1869, National Archives Microfilm Publication T494, Records of the Bureau of Indian Affairs, Record Group 75, National Archives Building, Washington, DC Roll 5.

General Subject Correspondence, 1908–1921, Yakima Indian Agency, Records of the Bureau of Indian Affairs, Record Group 75, National Archives and Records Administration—Pacific Alaska Region.

General Subject Correspondence, 1939–1953, Portland Area Office, Records of the Bureau of Indian Affairs, Record Group 75, National Archives and Records Administration—Pacific Alaska Region.

Heister Dean Guie Papers, 1896-1978, MSS 2511, Oregon Historical Society, Portland.

Indian Shaker Church of Washington Papers, Mss 29, Washington State Historical Society, Tacoma.

John Slocum and the Indian Shaker Church Series, Robert H. Ruby Papers, Ms 170, Northwest Museum of Arts & Culture, Spokane

Land Cards for Vancouver Allotments, Records of C.G. Davis, Field Agent at The Dalles, 1939–1950, Portland Area Office, Records of the Bureau of Indian Affairs, Record Group 75, National Archives and Records Administration—Pacific Alaska Region.

Letters Received by the Office of Adjutant General, National Archives Microfilm Publication M689, Records of the War Department, Record Group 48, National Archives Building, Washington, DC, Roll 271

Letters Received by the Office of Indian Affairs, 1824-1881, Oregon Superintendency, 1842-1880, National Archives Microfilm Publication M234, Records of the Bureau of Indian Affairs, Record Group 75, National Archives, Washington, DC Rolls 608–11, 617–20, 622, 624–26, 628.

Letters Received from the Commissioner of Indian Affairs, 1873, Yakima Indian Agency, Records of the Bureau of Indian Affairs, Record Group 75, National Archives and Records Administration—Pacific Alaska Region.

Letters Received from the Commissioner of Indian Affairs, July 1, 1899–August 25, 1899; February 1, 1906–April 28, 1906. Yakima Indian Agency, Records of the Bureau of Indian Affairs, Record Group 75, National Archives and Records Administration—Pacific Alaska Region.

Letters Received from Commissioner of Indian Affairs RE: Land, Yakima Indian Agency, Records of the Bureau of Indian Affairs, Record Group 75, National Archives and Records Administration—Pacific Alaska Region.

Letters Sent to Commissioner of Indian Affairs, 1869–1914, Warm Springs

Indian Agency, Records of the Bureau of Indian Affairs, Record Group 75, National Archives and Records Administration—Pacific Alaska Region.

Letters Sent to the Commissioner of Indian Affairs, 1880–1911, Umatilla Indian Agency, Records of the Bureau of Indian Affairs, Record Group 75, National Archives and Records Administration—Pacific Alaska Region.

Letters Sent to Umatilla Employees, Other Government Agencies, and Private Parties, 1889–1911, Umatilla Indian Agency, Records of the Bureau of Indian Affairs, Record Group 75, National Archives and Records Administration—Pacific Alaska Region.

Lucullus V. McWhorter Papers, 1918–1945. Manuscripts, Archives and Special Collections, Washington State University, Pullman.

Minutes of Tribal Councils, 1907, 1917–18, Umatilla Indian Agency, Records of the Bureau of Indian Affairs, Record Group 75, National Archives and Records Administration—Pacific Alaska Region.

Miscellaneous Enrollment Records, Yakima Indian Agency, Records of the Bureau of Indian Affairs, Record Group 75, National Archives and Records Administration—Pacific Alaska Region.

Miscellaneous Letters Sent, 1885–1914, Warm Springs Indian Agency, Records of the Bureau of Indian Affairs, Record Group 75, National Archives and Records Administration—Pacific Alaska Region.

Newell, Robert, to Joel Palmer, 10 August 1849. MSS 114-2, Oregon Historical Society, Portland.

Palmer, Joel, to George Manypenny, 9 July 1855. Proceedings of the Wasco Council (typescript). MSS 616, Oregon Historical Society, Portland.

Press Copies of Letters Sent to Commissioner of Indian Affairs, 1882–1914, Yakima Indian Agency, Records of the Bureau of Indian Affairs, Record Group 75, National Archives and Records Administration—Pacific Alaska Region.

Records of the Bureau of Indian Affairs, Central Classified Files, 1907-1939, Series B: Indian Customs and Social Relations, Roll 22, Record Group 75, National Archives Building, Washington, DC.

Records of Inspection of the Field Jurisdiction of the Office of Indian Affairs, National Archives Microfilm Publication M1070, Records of the Bureau of Indian Affairs, Record Group 75, National Archives Building, Washington, DC Rolls 55–56, 58–59.

Records of the Interim Legislature, 1939–41, Oregon State Archives, Salem.

Records of the Washington State Department of Fisheries, Washington State Archives, Olympia.

Records of the Washington Superintendency of Indian Affairs, 1853–1874. National Archives Microfilm Publication M5, Records of the Bureau of Indian Affairs, Record Group 75, National Archives Building, Washington, DC, Rolls 1, 17–18, 21, 608.

Seufert Brothers Company Papers, 1884-1954, MSS 1102, Oregon Historical Society, Portland.

Sohappy v. Hodel, United States District Court for the District of Oregon, Records of District Courts of the United States, Record Group 21, National Archives and Records Administration—Pacific Alaska Region.

Subject Files, 1908–1925, Warm Springs Indian Agency, Records of the Bureau of Indian Affairs, Record Group 75, National Archives and Records Administration—Pacific Alaska Region.

Superintendents Annual Narrative and Statistical Reports from Field Jurisdictions of the Bureau of Indian Affairs, 1907–1938, National Archives Microfilm Publication M1011, Records of the Bureau of Indian Affairs, Record Group 75, National Archives Building, Washington, DC. Rolls 160, 166, 171–72.

Trial Transcript, *United States of America vs. Seufert Brothers Company*, 2 vols. John Wilson Special Collections, Multnomah County Library, Portland,.

Tribal Council Minutes, 1944–1965, Portland Area Office, Records of the Bureau of Indian Affairs, Record Group 75, National Archives and Records Administration—PacificAlaska Region.

Tribal Council Records, 1934–1951, Warm Springs Indian Agency, Records of the Bureau of Indian Affairs, Record Group 75, National Archives and Records Administration—Pacific Alaska Region.

Tribal Records, 1897–1952, Yakima Indian Agency, Records of the Bureau of Indian Affairs, Record Group 75, National Archives and Records Administration—Pacific Alaska Region.

Umatilla Indian Agency, Monthly Report for May 1878, William Cameron McKay Papers, 1824-1893, MSS 413-1, Oregon Historical Society, Roll 2.

Unallotted Indians, Yakima Indian Agency, Records of the Bureau of Indian Affairs, Record Group 75, National Archives and Records Administration—Pacific Alaska Region.

Yakima Indian Agency Correspondence and Records, National Archives Microfilm Publication I6, Records of the Bureau of Indian Affairs, Record Group 75, National Archives Building, Washington, DC Rolls 1–3.

Yakima Indian Agency Records, Cage 4375, Special Collections, Washington State University, Pullman.

GOVERNMENT REPORTS AND DOCUMENTS

Doty, James. *Journal of Operations of Isaac Ingalls Stevens of Washington Territory.* Edited by Edward J. Kowrach. Fairfield, WA: Ye Galleon Press, 1978.

Hatch, Keith. Personal Files, Celilo Village Housing, Portland Area Office, Bureau of Indian Affairs, Portland, Oregon.

Indian Homestead Act, Statutes at Large, 18, sec. 15, 402 (1875).

Kappler, Charles J., ed. *Indian Affairs: Laws and Treaties,* Vol. II. Washington, DC: Government Printing Office, 1904.

Records of the U.S. Indian Claims Commission. Docket 47, *The Yakima Tribe of Indians vs. The United States.* Transcript of Proceedings, 21 August, 1950. New York: Clearwater Publishing Co, Inc., 1975.

Report of the Commissioner of Indian Affairs for the Territories of Washington and Idaho, and the State of Oregon for the Year of 1870. Fairfield, WA: Ye Galleon Press, 1981.

Settler v. Lameer, 507 F.2d 231 (1974).

Seufert Brothers Company v. United States, 249 U.S. 194 (1919).

Sohappy v. Smith, Vols. 1–4, U.S. District Court of Oregon, Mark O. Hatfield U.S. Courthouse, Portland.

Stevens, Isaac Ingalls. *A True Copy of the Record of the Official Proceedings at the Council in the Walla Walla Valley, 1855.* Edited by Darrell Scott. Fairfield, WA: Ye Galleon Press, 1985.

———. Notes of a Council Held with the Klickitat Indians at Vancouver, Washington Territory, October 22, 1856 (typescript). Yakama Nation Archives, Toppenish, Washington.

Swindell, Jr., Edward G. U.S. Department of the Interior, Office of Indian Affairs, Division of Forestry and Grazing. *Report on Source, Nature, and Extent of the Fishing, Hunting, and Miscellaneous Related Rights of Certain Indian Tribes in Washington and Oregon Territory Together with Affidavits Showing the Location of a Number of Usual and Accustomed Fishing Grounds and Stations.* Los Angeles: Office of Indian Affairs, 1942. University of Washington Library, Microfilm A-941.

United States v. Winans, 198 U.S. 317 (1905).

U.S. Census Office, *Report on Indians Taxed and Not Taxed in the United States (Except Alaska) at the Eleventh Census: 1890.* Washington, DC: Government Printing Office, 1894.

U.S. Congress, Senate, Committee on Appropriations, *Civil Functions, Department of the Army Appropriations: Hearings before the Subcommittee of the Committee on Appropriations on H.R. 5376,* 83rd Cong., 1st sess., 15–26 May 1953, 1447-52.

U.S. Department of the Interior, Office of Indian Affairs. *Annual Report of the Commissioner of Indian Affairs.* Washington, DC: A.O.P. Nicholson, 1855–1932.

U.S. Department of the Interior, Office of Indian Affairs. *Regulations Governing Indian Allotments on the Public Domain under Section 4 of the Act of February 8, 1887 (24 Stat., 388), as Amended by the Act of February 28, 1891 (26 Stat., 794), and as Further Amended by the Act of June 25, 1910 (36 Stat., 855).* Washington, DC: Government Printing Office, 1918.

U.S. Senate. Committee on Appropriations, *Civil Functions, Department of the Army Appropriations: Hearings before the Subcommittee of the Committee on Appropriations on H.R. 5376*, 83rd Cong., 1st sess., 15–26 May 1953.

U.S. Senate. Select Committee on Indian Affairs. *Columbia River Fisheries Management: Hearing before the Select Committee on Indian Affairs.* 100th Cong., 2nd sess., 19 April 1988.

NEWSPAPERS AND MAGAZINES

Condon (OR) Globe-Times, 1948.

The Dalles (OR) Chronicle, 1916, 1919, 1941, 2008.

Enterprise (White Salmon, WA), 1984.

Oregon Journal (Portland), 1964, 1966.

Oregonian (Portland), 1855, 1878, 1915, 1941, 1966, 1990, 1991.

Wana Chinook Tymoo (Columbia River Inter-Tribal Fish Commission, Portland), 1993, 1997.

Yakama Nation Review (Toppenish, WA), 1977.

Yakima (WA) Herald-Republic, 2008

ORAL HISTORIES

George Aguilar, interview by Andrew H. Fisher, 26 June 2006, Warm Springs, Oregon, notes in author's possession.

Elsie David, interview with Katrine Barber, 6 August 2007, in *Oregon Historical Quarterly* 108, no. 4 (Winter 2007): 649–54.

Field Notes, Berry Field Meeting, 25 July 2006, Mt. Adams Ranger Station, Trout Lake, Washington, in author's possession.

Field Notes, "Honoring the Heritage of Plateau Peoples: Past, Present, and Future" Conference, October 2004, Pullman, Washington, in author's possession.

Chief Johnny Jackson, interview by Piper Hackett, 28 March 1999, OrHist 6208, Radical Elders Series, Oregon Historical Society, Portland.

Wilbur Slockish, Jr., interview by Michael O'Rourke, 11 February 2000, OHS Inv. #2738, Columbia River Dissenters Series, Oregon Historical Society, Portland.

Walter Speedis, interview by Vivian Adams, August 1997, THPH-Elder Interviews, Yakama Reservation, transcript, The High Desert Museum, Bend, Oregon.

Ted Strong, interview by Clark Hansen, 17 January 2000, OHS Inv. 2731, Columbia River Dissenters Series, Oregon Historical Society, Portland.

Flora Thompson, interviewer unknown, no date, OHS Inv. # 9586, Oregon Historical Society, Portland.

Wilson Wewa, interview by Andrew H. Fisher, 26 June 2006, Warm Springs, Oregon, notes in author's possession.

BOOKS AND ARTICLES

Ackerman, Lillian A. *A Necessary Balance: Gender and Power among Indians of the Columbia Plateau*. Norman: University of Oklahoma Press, 2003.

———, ed. *A Song to the Creator: Traditional Arts of Native American Women of the Plateau*. Norman: University of Oklahoma Press, 1996.

Adams, David Wallace. *Education for Extinction: American Indians and the Boarding School Experience, 1875–1928*. Lawrence: University Press of Kansas, 1995.

Aguilar, George W., Sr. *When the River Ran Wild!: Indian Traditions on the Mid-Columbia and the Warm Springs Reservation*. Portland: Oregon Historical Society Press, 2005.

Allen, Cain. "'They Called It Progress': Indians, Salmon, and the Industrialization of the Columbia River." M.A. thesis, Portland State University, 2000.

Anastasio, Angelo. "The Southern Plateau: An Ecological Analysis of Intergroup Relations." *Northwest Anthropological Research Notes* 6, no. 2 (1972): 109–29.

Anderson, Benedict. *Imagined Communities: Reflections on the Origins and Spread of Nationalism*. New York: Verso, 1991.

Anderson, Gary Clayton. *The Conquest of Texas: Ethnic Cleansing in the Promised Land, 1820–1875*. Norman: University of Oklahoma Press, 2005.

Asher, Brad. *Beyond the Reservation: Indians, Settlers, and the Law in Washington Territory, 1853–1889*. Norman: University of Oklahoma Press, 1999.

Barber, Katrine. *Death of Celilo Falls*. Seattle: University of Washington Press, 2005.

———. "Oregon Voices: Elsie David." *Oregon Historical Quarterly* 108, no. 4 (Winter 2007): 653.

Barnett, H. G. *Indian Shakers: A Messianic Cult of the Pacific Northwest*. Carbondale: Southern Illinois University Press, 1957.

Barsh, Russell Lawrence. "Ethnogenesis and Ethnonationalism from Competing Treaty Claims." Paper presented at the Pacific Northwest Treaties in National and International Perspective Conference, Seattle, May 2005. Copy in author's possession.

———. "Puget Sound Indian Demography, 1900–1920: Migration and Economic Integration." *Ethnohistory* 43 (Winter 1996).

Barth, Fredrik. *The Social Organization of Culture Difference*. London: Allen & Unwin, 1969.

Beckham, Stephen Dow. *"This Place Is Romantic and Wild": An Historical Overview of the Cascades Area, Fort Cascades, and the Cascades Townsite, Washington Territory.* Heritage Research Associates Report No. 27. Eugene, OR: Heritage Research Associates, 1984.

Berg, Laura. "'Let Them Do As They Have Promised': A History of *U.S. v. Oregon* and Four Tribes' Fight for Columbia River Salmon." *Hastings West-Northwest Journal of Environmental Law and Policy* 3, no. 1 (Fall 1995).

Biolsi, Thomas. "The Birth of the Reservation: Making the Modern Individual among the Lakota." In Frederick C. Hoxie, Peter C. Mancall, and James H. Merrell, eds. *American Nations: Encounters in Indian Country, 1850 to the Present.* New York: Routledge, 2001), 110–40.

———. *Organizing the Lakota: The Political Economy of the New Deal on the Pine Ridge and Rosebud Reservations.* Tucson: University of Arizona Press, 1993.

Bischoff, William N., S. J., ed., *We Were Not Summer Soldiers: The Indian War Diary of Plympton J. Kelly, 1855–1856.* Tacoma: Washington State Historical Society, 1976.

Boxberger, Daniel L. "Native American and German American Land Use Practices and Settlement in West Klickitat County." Paper presented at Environmental Cultures Conference, Victoria, B.C., 27 April 1996. Copy in author's possession.

Boxberger, Daniel L., and Bruce G. Miller. "Creating Chiefdoms: The Puget Sound Case." *Ethnohistory* 41 (Spring 1994): 267–93.

Boxberger, Daniel L., and Lynn A. Robbins. "An Archival and Oral History Inventory of the White Salmon and Klickitat Rivers." Vol. 1. Prepared for the Columbia River Gorge National Scenic Area, Bellingham, WA, 1994. Copy in author's possession.

Boyd, Robert. *The Coming of the Spirit of Pestilence: Introduced Infectious Diseases and Population Decline Among Northwest Coast Indians, 1774–1874.* Seattle: University of Washington Press, 1999.

———. *People of The Dalles: The Indians of Wascopam Mission.* Lincoln: University of Nebraska Press, 1996.

Burrows, James K. "'A Much-Needed Class of Labour': The Economy and Income of the Southern Interior Plateau Indians, 1897–1910." *BC Studies* 71 (1986): 27–46.

Burton, Jeffrey. *Indian Territory and the United States, 1866–1906: Courts, Government, and the Movement for Oklahoma Statehood.* Norman: University of Oklahoma Press, 1995.

Calloway, Colin, ed. *After King Philip's War: Presence and Persistence in Indian New England.* Hanover, NH: University Press of New England, 1997.

Campbell, Sarah H. *Post-Columbian Culture History in the Northern Columbia Plateau.* New York: Garland Publishing, 1990.

Carlson, Leonard A. *Indians, Bureaucrats, and the Land: The Dawes Act and the Decline of Indian Farming.* Westport, CT: Greenwood Press, 1981.

Carter, Kent. "Deciding Who Can Be Cherokee: Enrollment Records of the Dawes Commission." *Chronicles of Oklahoma* 69 (1991): 174–205.

Castile, George Pierre. "The Indian Connection: Judge James Wickersham and the Indian Shakers." *Pacific Northwest Quarterly* 81 (October 1990): 122–29.

Cebula, Larry. *Plateau Indians and the Quest for Spiritual Power, 1700–1850.* Lincoln: University of Nebraska Press, 2003.

Child, Brenda J. *Boarding School Seasons: American Indian Families, 1900–1940.* Lincoln: University of Nebraska Press, 1998.

Clark, Robert. *River of the West: Stories from the Columbia.* New York: Harper-Collins West, 1995.

Clark, Robert Carlton, Robert Horace Down, and George Verne Blue. *A History of Oregon.* Evanston, NY, Philadelphia, and San Francisco: Row, Peterson and Company, 1926.

Clemmer, Janice White. "The Confederated Tribes of Warm Springs, Oregon: Nineteenth Century Indian Education History." Ph.D. diss., University of Utah, 1980.

Cohen, Fay G. *Treaties on Trial: The Continuing Controversy over Northwest Indian Fishing Rights.* Seattle: University of Washington Press, 1986.

Columbia River Defense Project. *In Defense of Che Wana: Fishing Rights on the Columbia River.* Portland, OR: The Wheel Press, 1987.

Debo, Angie. *And Still the Waters Run: The Betrayal of the Five Civilized Tribes.* Princeton, NJ: Princeton University Press, 1940. Reprint, Norman: University of Oklahoma Press, 1984.

Deloria, Philip J. *Indians in Unexpected Places.* Lawrence: University Press of Kansas, 2004.

Deloria, Vine, Jr., and Clifford M. Lytle. *American Indians, American Justice.* Austin: University of Texas Press, 1983.

Dietrich, William. *Northwest Passage: The Great Columbia River.* New York: Simon & Schuster, 1995.

Donald, Leland. *Aboriginal Slavery on the Northwest Coast of North America.* Berkeley: University of California Press, 1997.

Donaldson, Ivan J., and Frederick K. Cramer. *Fishwheels of the Columbia.* Portland, OR: Binfords & Mort, 1971.

DuBois, Cora. "The Feather Cult of the Middle Columbia." *General Series in Anthropology* No. 7. Menasha, WI: George Banta, 1938.

Dupris, Joseph C., Kathleen S. Hill, and William H. Rodgers, Jr. *The Si'lailo Way: Indians, Salmon and Law on the Columbia River.* Durham, NC: Carolina Academic Press, 2006.

Eickhoff, Randy Lee. *Exiled: The Tigua Indians of Ysleta del Sur.* Plano: Republic of Texas Press, 1996.

Ellis, Clyde. *To Change Them Forever: Indian Education at the Rainy Mountain Boarding School, 1893–1920.* Norman: University of Oklahoma Press, 1996.

Finger, John R. *The Eastern Band of Cherokees, 1819–1900.* Knoxville: University of Tennessee Press, 1984.

Fisher, Andrew H. "Invasion of the Boardheads: Windsurfing and the Transformation of the Columbia Gorge." *Columbia* (Summer 2007): 24–33.

———."The 1932 Handshake Agreement: Yakama Indian Treaty Rights and Forest Service Policy in the Pacific Northwest." *Western Historical Quarterly* 28 (Summer 1997): 187–217.

———. "'This I Know from the Old People': Yakama Indian Treaty Rights as Oral Tradition." *Montana, The Magazine of Western History* 49 (Spring 1999): 2–17.

Fixico, Donald L. *Termination and Relocation: Federal Indian Policy, 1945–1960.* Albuquerque: University of New Mexico Press, 1990.

Fogelson, Raymond D. "Perspectives on Native American Identity." In Russell Thornton, ed. *Studying Native America: Problems and Prospects.* Madison: University of Wisconsin Press, 1998.

Foner, Eric. *The Story of American Freedom.* New York: W. W. Norton & Company, 1998.

Foster, Morris W. *Being Comanche: A Social History of an American Indian Community.* Tucson: University of Arizona Press, 1991.

Fowler, Loretta. *Shared Symbols, Contested Meanings: Gros Ventre Culture and History, 1778–1984.* Ithaca, NY: Cornell University Press, 1987.

Goldfield, David et. al. *The American Journey: A History of the United States.* Upper Saddle River, NJ: Prentice-Hall, Inc., 1998.

Goodling, Susan Staiger. "Place, Race, and Names: Layered Identities in *United States v. Oregon*, Confederated Tribes of the Colville Reservation, Plaintiff-Intervenor." *Law & Society Review* 28, no. 5 (1994): 1181–1230.

Greenwald, Emily. *Reconfiguring the Reservation: The Nez Perces, Jicarilla Apaches, and the Dawes Act.* Albuquerque: University of New Mexico Press, 2002.

Gunther, Erna. "The Shaker Religion of the Northwest." In Marian W. Smith, ed., *Indians of the Urban Northwest.* New York: Columbia University Press, 1949.

Hall, Roberta L. *The Coquille Indians: Yesterday, Today, and Tomorrow.* Lake Oswego, OR: Smith, Smith and Smith Publishing Company, 1984.

Harkin, Michael E., and David Rich Lewis, eds. *Native Americans and the Environment: Perspectives on the Ecological Indian.* Lincoln: University of Nebraska Press, 2007.

Harmon, Alexandra. *Indians in the Making: Ethnic Relations and Indian Identities around Puget Sound.* Berkeley and Los Angeles: University of California Press, 1999.

———. "Tribal Enrollment Councils: Lessons on Law and Indian Identity." *Western Historical Quarterly* 32 (Summer 2001): 175–200.

Harmon, Ray. "Indian Shaker Church, The Dalles." *Oregon Historical Quarterly* 72 (1971).

Hauptman, Laurence M. *Conspiracy of Interests: Iroquois Dispossession and the Rise of New York State.* Syracuse, NY: Syracuse University Press, 1999.

Heaton, John W. *The Shoshone-Bannocks: Culture and Commerce at Fort Hall, 1870–1940.* Lawrence: University Press of Kansas, 2005.

Herring, Joseph. *The Enduring Indians of Kansas: A Century and a Half of Acculturation.* Lawrence: University Press of Kansas, 1990.

Hill, Jonathan D., ed. *History, Power, and Identity: Ethnogenesis in the Americas.* Iowa City: University of Iowa Press, 1996.

Himmel, Kelly F. *The Conquest of the Karankawas and the Tonkawas, 1821–1859.* College Station: Texas A&M University Press, 1996.

Hines, Donald M. *Celilo Tales: Wasco Myths, Legends, Tales of Magic and the Marvelous.* Issaquah, WA: Great Eagle Publishing, Inc., 1996.

———. *The Forgotten Tribes: Oral Tales of the Teninos and Adjacent Mid-Columbia River Indian Nations.* Issaquah, WA: Great Eagle Publishing, Inc., 1991.

———. *Magic in the Mountains: The Yakima Shaman: Power & Practice.* Issaquah, WA: Great Eagle Publishing, 1993.

Hobbs, Charles A. "Indian Hunting and Fishing Rights II." *The George Washington Law Review* 37 (July 1969).

Hobsbawm, Eric, and Terence Ranger, eds. *The Invention of Tradition.* New York: Cambridge University Press, 1992.

Hoxie, Frederick E. "From Prison to Homeland: The Cheyenne River Indian Reservation Before World War I." *South Dakota History* 10 (Winter 1979): 1-24.

———. *Parading through History: The Making of the Crow Nation in America, 1805–1935.* New York: Cambridge University Press, 1995.

Hunn, Eugene S., with James Selam and Family. *Nch'i-Wána, "The Big River": Mid-Columbia Indians and Their Land.* Seattle: University of Washington Press, 1990.

———. "Sk'in: The Other Side of the River." *Oregon Historical Quarterly* 108, no. 4 (Winter 2007): 614–23.

———. "What Ever Happened to the First Peoples of the Columbia?" In William L. Lang and Robert C. Carriker, eds. *Great River of the West: Essays on the Columbia River.* Seattle: University of Washington Press, 1999.

Hurtado, Albert L. *Indian Survival on the California Frontier.* New Haven: Yale University Press, 1988.

Irwin, Lee. *Coming Down from Above: Prophecy, Resistance, and Renewal in Native American Religions.* Norman: University of Oklahoma Press, 2008.

Iverson, Peter. *Diné: A History of the Navajos.* Albuquerque: University of New Mexico Press, 2002.

————. *"We Are Still Here": American Indians in the Twentieth Century.* Wheeling, IL: Harlan Davidson, Inc., 1998.

Jackson, John C. *Children of the Fur Trade: Forgotten Metis of the Pacific Northwest.* Missoula, MT: Mountain Press Publishing Company, 1995.

————. *A Little War of Destiny: The First Regiment of Oregon Mounted Volunteers and the Yakima Indian War of 1855–56.* Fairfield, WA: Ye Galleon Press, 1995.

Jeffrey, Julie Roy. *Converting the West: A Biography of Narcissa Whitman.* Norman: University of Oklahoma Press, 1991.

Jetté, Melinda M. "Ordinary Lives: Three Generations of a French-Indian Family in Oregon, 1827–1931." M.A. thesis, Université Laval, 1996.

Josephy, Alvin M. *The Nez Perce Indians and the Opening of the Northwest.* New Haven, CT: Yale University Press, 1965. Abridged edition, Lincoln: University of Nebraska Press, 1971.

Keller, Robert H., Jr. *American Protestantism and United States Indian Policy, 1869–82.* Lincoln: University of Nebraska Press, 1983.

Kennedy, James B. "The Umatilla Indian Reservation, 1855–1975: Factors Contributing to a Diminished Land Resource Base." Ph.D. diss., Oregon State University, 1977.

Keyser, James D. *Indian Rock Art of the Columbia Plateau.* Seattle: University of Washington Press, 1992.

Killoren, John J. *"Come, Black Robe": De Smet and the Indian Tragedy.* Norman: University of Oklahoma Press, 1994.

Ladiges, Jerry. *Glenwood: Formerly Camas Prairie.* Glenwood, WA: privately printed, 1978.

LaGrand, James B. *Indian Metropolis: Native Americans in Chicago, 1945–1975.* Urbana and Chicago: University of Illinois Press, 2002.

LaPlante, Jay. "Celilo Falls: Flooded 40 Years Ago But Not Forgotten." *Wana Chinook Tymoo* (Issue Two, 1997): 10.

Leavelle, Tracy Neal. "We Will Make It Our Own Place: Agriculture and Adaptation at the Grand Ronde Reservation, 1856–1887." *American Indian Quarterly* 22 (Fall 1998): 433-56.

Leibhardt, Barbara. "Allotment Policy in an Incongruous Legal System: The Yakima Indian Nation As a Case Study, 1887–1934." *Agricultural History* 65 (Fall 1991): 78–103.

————. "Law, Environment, and Social Change in the Columbia River Basin: The Yakima Indian Nation as a Case Study, 1840–1933." Ph.D. diss., University of California at Berkeley, 1990.

Lewis, David Rich. *Neither Wolf Nor Dog: American Indians, Environment, and Agrarian Change.* New York: Oxford University Press, 1994.

————. "Reservation Leadership and the Progressive–Traditional Dichotomy:

William Wash and the Northern Utes, 1865–1928." *Ethnohistory* 38 (Winter 1991): 124–42.

Lomawaima, K. Tsianina. *They Called It Prairie Light: The Story of Chilocco Indian School.* Lincoln: University of Nebraska Press, 1994.

McDonnell, Janet A. *The Dispossession of the American Indian, 1887–1934.* Bloomington: Indiana University Press, 1991.

Meinig, D. W. *The Great Columbia Plain: A Historical Geography, 1805–1910.* Seattle: University of Washington Press, 1968.

Merrell, James. *The Indians' New World: Catawbas and Their Neighbors from European Contact through the Era of Removal.* Chapel Hill: University of North Carolina Press, 1989.

Meyer, Melissa L. *The White Earth Tragedy: Ethnicity and Dispossession at a Minnesota Anishinaabe Reservation, 1889–1920.* Lincoln: University of Nebraska Press, 1994.

Middleton, Rusty. "View from the River." *Wana Chinook Tymoo* 1 and 2 (1993): 14.

Mihesuah, Devon A. *Cultivating the Rosebuds: The Education of Women at the Cherokee Female Seminary, 1851–1909.* Urbana: University of Illinois Press, 1993.

Miller, Bruce G., and Daniel L. Boxberger. "Creating Chiefdoms: The Puget Sound Case." *Ethnohistory* 41 (Spring 1994): 267–93.

Miller, Christopher L. *Prophetic Worlds: Indians and Whites on the Columbia Plateau.* New Brunswick, NJ: Rutgers University Press, 1985.

Milner, Clyde A., II. *With Good Intentions: Quaker Work Among the Pawnees, Otos, and Omahas in the 1870s.* Lincoln: University of Nebraska Press, 1982.

Mitchell, Donald Craig. *Sold American: The Story of Alaska Natives and Their Land, 1867–1959: The Army to Statehood.* Hanover, NH: University Press of New England, 1997.

Monahan, Peter, and Danny Kepley. *The Point: Legacy of the River People.* Eastside Productions, 1996. Videocassette.

Moulton, Gary E., ed. *The Journals of the Lewis & Clark Expedition.* Vol. 7. Lincoln: University of Nebraska Press, 1991.

Nabokov, Peter, ed. *Native American Testimony: A Chronicle of Indian-White Relations from Prophecy to the Present, 1492–1992.* New York: Viking Penguin, 1991. Reprint, New York: Penguin Books, 1992.

Neils, Selma. *The Klickitat Indians.* Portland: Binford & Mort, 1985.

Nesper, Larry. *The Walleye War: The Struggle for Ojibway Spearfishing and Treaty Rights.* Lincoln: University of Nebraska Press, 2002.

Newell, Dianne. *Tangled Webs of History: Indians and the Law in Canada's Pacific Coast Fisheries.* Toronto: University of Toronto Press, 1993.

Oakley, Christopher Arris. *Keeping the Circle: American Indian Identity in Eastern North Carolina, 1885–2004.* Lincoln: University of Nebraska Press, 2007.

O'Brien, Sharon. *American Indian Tribal Governments.* Norman: University of Oklahoma Press, 1989.

O'Donnell, Terence. *An Arrow in the Earth: General Joel Palmer and the Indians of Oregon.* Portland: Oregon Historical Society, 1991.

Ostler, Jeffrey. *The Plains Sioux and U.S. Colonialism from Lewis and Clark to Wounded Knee.* New York: Cambridge University Press, 2004.

Otis, D. S. *The Dawes Act and the Allotment of Indian Lands.* Norman: University of Oklahoma Press, 1973.

Phillips, George Harwood. *Indians and Indian Agents: The Origins of the Reservation System in California, 1849–1852.* Norman: University of Oklahoma Press, 1997.

Prucha, Francis Paul. *American Indian Policy in Crisis: Christian Reformers and the Indian, 1865–1900.* Norman: University of Oklahoma Press, 1976.

———. *American Indian Treaties: The History of a Political Anomaly.* Berkeley: University of California Press, 1994.

———. *The Great Father: The United States Government and the American Indians.* 2 vols. Lincoln: University of Nebraska Press, 1986.

———, ed. *Americanizing the American Indians: Writings by the "Friends of the Indians."* Cambridge, MA: Harvard University Press, 1973.

Quinn, Arthur. *Hell With the Fire Out: A History of the Modoc War.* Boston: Faber and Faber, 1997.

Raibmon, Paige. *Authentic Indians: Episodes of Encounter from the Late-Nineteenth-Century Northwest Coast.* Durham, NC: Duke University Press, 2005.

Ramsey, Jarold, ed. *Coyote Was Going There: Indian Literature of the Oregon Country.* Seattle: University of Washington Press, 1977.

Ray, Verne F. "Cultural Relations in the Plateau of Northwestern America." In *Publications of the Frederick Webb Hodge Anniversary Publication Fund,* vol. 3. Los Angeles: Southwestern Museum, 1939.

Relander, Click. *Drummers and Dreamers.* Caldwell, ID: Caxton Printers, 1956.

———. *Strangers on the Land: A Historiette of a Longer Story of the Yakima Indian Nation's Efforts to Survive Against Great Odds.* Yakima, WA: Franklin Press, 1962.

Richards, Kent D. *Issac I. Stevens: Young Man in a Hurry.* Provo, UT: Brigham Young University Press, 1979. Reprint, Pullman: Washington State University Press, 1993.

Rigsby, Bruce. "Changing Property Relations in Land and Resources in the Southern Plateau." Paper presented at the Pacific Northwest Treaties in National and International Perspective Conference, Seattle, May 2005. Copy in author's possession.

Riney, Scott. *The Rapid City Indian School, 1898–1933.* Norman: University of Oklahoma Press, 1999.

Ronda, James P. *Lewis and Clark among the Indians*. Lincoln: University of Nebraska Press, 1984.

Roosens, Eugeene E., ed. *Creating Ethnicity: The Process of Ethnogenesis, Frontiers of Anthropology*. Vol. 5. Newbury Park, NJ: Sage Publications, 1989.

Rosier, Paul C. *Rebirth of the Blackfeet Nation, 1912–1954*. Lincoln: University of Nebraska Press, 2001.

Ruby, Robert H., and John A. Brown. *The Cayuse Indians: Imperial Tribesmen of Old Oregon*. Norman: University of Oklahoma Press, 1972.

———. *Dreamer-Prophets of the Columbia Plateau: Smohalla and Skolaskin*. Norman: University of Oklahoma Press, 1989.

———. "Dreamer-Prophet Visionaries of Interior Oregon." *Oregon Humanities* (Summer 1994): 16–21, 52.

———. *A Guide to the Indian Tribes of the Pacific Northwest*. Norman: University of Oklahoma Press, 1992.

———. *Indian Slavery in the Pacific Northwest*. Spokane, WA: A. H. Clark Company, 1993.

———. *John Slocum and the Indian Shaker Church*. Norman: University of Oklahoma Press, 1996.

Sapir, Edward, ed. *Wishram Texts*. Vol. 2. Leyden: E. J. Brill, 1909. Reprint, New York: AMS Press, Inc., 1974.

Schuster, Helen Hersh. *The Yakima*. New York and Philadelphia: Chelsea House Publishers, 1990.

———. "Yakima Indian Traditionalism: A Study in Continuity and Change." Ph.D. diss., University of Washington, 1975.

Seufert, Francis. *Wheels of Fortune*. Portland: Oregon Historical Society, 1980.

Skahan, Pat. "Yakimas Urged to Seek Lacey Act Review." *Yakima Nation Review*, 10 February 1988.

Smith, F. Todd. *The Caddos, the Wichitas, and the United States, 1846–1901*. College Station: Texas A&M University Press, 1999.

Smoak, Gregory E. *Ghost Dances and Identity: Prophetic Religion and American Indian Ethnogenesis in the Nineteenth Century*. Berkeley and Los Angeles: University of California Press, 2006.

Spack, Ruth. *America's Second Tongue: American Indian Education and the Ownership of English, 1860–1900*. Lincoln: University of Nebraska Press, 2002.

Spier, Leslie. "The Prophet Dance of the Northwest and Its Derivatives: The Source of the Ghost Dance." *General Series in Anthropology*. No. 1. Menasha, WI: George Banta, 1935.

Splawn, Andrew J. *Ka-mi-akin, Last Hero of the Yakimas*. Portland: Binfords and Mort for the Oregon Historical Society, 1944.

Stern, Theodore. *Chiefs and Change in the Oregon Country: Indian Relations at Fort Nez Percés, 1818–1855*. Vol. 2. Corvallis: Oregon State University Press, 1997.

———. *Chiefs & Chief Traders: Indian Relations at Fort Nez Percés, 1818–1855.* Corvallis: Oregon State University Press, 1992.

Strong, Emory, and Ruth Strong. *Seeking Western Waters: The Lewis and Clark Trail from the Rockies to the Pacific.* Portland: Oregon Historical Society Press, 1995.

Sturm, Circe. *Blood Politics: Race, Culture, and Identity in the Cherokee Nation of Oklahoma.* Berkeley: University of California Press, 2002.

Szasz, Margaret Connell. *Education and the American Indian: The Road Toward Self-Determination since 1928,* 3d ed. Albuquerque: University of New Mexico Press, 1999.

Taylor, Joseph E. III. *Making Salmon: An Environmental History of the Northwest Fisheries Crisis.* Seattle: University of Washington Press, 1999.

Thrush, Coll. *Native Seattle: Histories from the Crossing-Over Place.* Seattle: University of Washington Press, 2007.

Trafzer, Clifford E., ed. "Earth, Animals, and Academics: Plateau Indian Communities, Culture, and the Walla Walla Council of 1855." *American Indian Culture and Research Journal* 17, no. 3 (1993).

———. *Indians, Superintendents, and Councils: Northwestern Indian Policy, 1850–1855.* Lanham, MD: University Press of America, 1986.

Trafzer, Clifford E., and Margery Ann Beach. "Smohalla, the Washani, and Religion as a Factor in Northwestern Indian History." *American Indian Quarterly* 9 (Summer 1985): 309–24.

———. "The Waptashi Prophet and the Feather Religion: Derivative of the Washani." *American Indian Quarterly* (Summer 1985): 325–26

Trafzer, Clifford E., and Richard D. Scheuerman. *Renegade Tribe: The Palouse Indians and the Invasion of the Inland Pacific Northwest.* Pullman: Washington State University Press, 1986.

Trennert, Robert A., Jr. *Alternative to Extinction: Federal Indian Policy and the Beginnings of the Reservation System, 1846–51.* Philadelphia: Temple University Press, 1975.

———. *The Phoenix Indian School: Forced Assimilation in Arizona, 1891–1935.* Norman: University of Oklahoma Press, 1988.

Twedell, Colin E. "A Componential Analysis of the Criteria Defining an Indian 'Tribe' in Western Washington." In Herbert C. Taylor, Jr., and Garland F. Grabert, eds., *Western Washington Indian Socio-Economics: Papers in Honor of Angelo Anastasio.* Bellingham: Western Washington University, 1984.

Ulrich, Roberta. *Empty Nets: Indians, Dams, and the Columbia River.* Corvallis: Oregon State University Press, 1999.

Van Arsdol, T., ed. *Columbia River Indian Fishing Documents.* Vancouver, WA, 2003. University of Washington Special Collections, Seattle.

Walker, Deward E., ed. *Handbook of North American Indians*. Vol. 12. Washington, DC: Smithsonian Institution, 1998.

———. "Productivity of Tribal Dipnet Fisheries at Celilo Falls: Analysis of the Joe Pinkham Fish Buying Records." *Northwest Anthropological Research Notes* 26: 2 (1992): 123-35.

Washburn, Wilcomb E. *The Assault on Indian Tribalism: The General Allotment Law (Dawes Act) of 1887*. Malabar, FL: Robert E. Krieger Publishing Company, 1986.

White, Richard. *The Middle Ground: Indians, Empires, and Republics in the Great Lakes Region, 1650–1815*. New York: Cambridge University Press, 1991.

———. *The Organic Machine: The Remaking of the Columbia River*. New York: Hill and Wang, 1995.

Wilmsen, Edwin N., and Patrick McAllister, eds. *The Politics of Difference: Ethnic Premises in a World of Power*. Chicago: University of Chicago Press, 1996.

Woodworth-Ney, Laura. *Mapping Identity: The Creation of the Coeur d'Alene Indian Reservation, 1805–1902*. Boulder: University Press of Colorado, 2004.

Wright, Robin K., ed. *A Time of Gathering: Native Heritage in Washington State*. Seattle: University of Washington Press, 1991.

Wunder, John R. *"Retained by The People": A History of American Indians and the Bill of Rights*. New York: Oxford University Press, 1994.

INDEX

Abraham, Enoch, 131
Abraham, Jack, 193
Ackerman, Lillian, 152
Adams, Mount, 20
Adams, Vivian, ix, 21
Administration for Native Americans, 242–43
Aeneas (Yakama headman), 79
agriculture: introduction of, 31; encouragement of, 49, 80; Indian labor, 110, 149–50; Indian resistance to, 82, 102, 149
Alaska, 249n14
Albert, Isaac and Thomas, 179–80, 181

alcohol: consumption, 72–73, 87, 110, 111, 124, 128, 150, 193, 246; illegal sale to Indians, 69–70, 170; religious proscriptions against, 128, 129–30, 134, 135
Alderdale (Náwawi), 44, 229
Alexander, James, 231
Alexander, Leo: and Columbia River General Council Fish Commission, 216–18; on fishing regulations, 225–26; guarding nets, 217–18; and in-lieu site eviction, 230–31; on state raids, 227; Treaty Indians of the Columbia, 222

Mid-Columbia River Council: application for federal assistance, 89, 242; current members, 244; duties, 244–45; internal tensions, 243–44; legal incorporation, 239–40; membership survey, 242; statement of unification, 13, 36, 62, 155, 192, 208, 240, 241; on Yakima War, 59–60. *See also* Columbia River Indians; Columbia River Indians, Chiefs and Council of the; Columbia Tribal Council

Middle Oregon, Treaty of: and Huntington Treaty, 73; lands ceded by, 37; reservation established by, 37, 43; signers, 45

Miles, Nelson A., 93

Miller, Harry, 130, 132

Milroy, Robert H.: and Kotiakan, 85; opposition to homesteading, 89–90, 93, 95, 118–19; and "renegades," 65, 70, 72, 74, 77, 80–81, 87, 89, 96; resignation, 67, 96; and school attendance, 66–67

Minthorn, Albert, 107

Minthorn, Jay, 192

Mission, John, 78

missionaries: agenda, 29; and Americanization policy, 121; Catholic, 30, 32, 128, 140; cultural influence, 32; Methodist, 36, 135; and Peace Policy, 83; Presbyterian, 31–32, 125, 126, 128, 131; sectarian rivalries, 32; stations established, 31–32, 36. *See also* Christianity

mixed-blood Indians: and allotment, 97, 105–8; ambiguity of identity, 31, 269n19; as cultural brokers, 260n36; fishing rights of, 173, 175–76, 177. *See also* enrollment, tribal; identity; marriage; race

Modoc War, 70

Morse, Wayne, 206

Morton, Sabina, 107

Moses, Sallie, 112

National Marine Fisheries Service, 231–32

Nesper, Larry, 219

Newell, Robert, 39

Nez Perces: aboriginal territory, 23; buffalo hunting, 27; fishing rights, 174, 203; and fur trade, 30; Nez Perce laws, 34; Nez Perce War, 93; and treaty councils, 40; treaty with, 37, 43, 45. *See also* Chief Joseph

Nez Percés, Fort, 29–30

Nixlúidix. *See* Wishram

North Carolina, 302n14

Northern Paiutes, 76, 83, 135

Northwest Coast (culture area), 25

North West Company, 29

No Shirt, 107, 108, 136

Oklahoma, 301n13

orality, 51

oral tradition, 16–17, 52

Oregon: state legislature, 184, 187; Fish Commission, 216, 221; and *Sohappy v. Smith*, 223; Territory, 34

Oregon Donation Land Act, 40

Oregon Trail, 32–33, 36, 39, 47

Oregon Volunteers, 56–57

Oregonian, The, 54, 56, 92, 239

Othus, Percy M., 206–7

Owhi (áwx̱ay), 41, 44, 46, 47, 53

Pa'kiut Village, 127

Palmer, Joel: on reaction to treaties, 53; on reserved rights, 51–52; and temporary reserves, 57; treaty nego-

Sheldon, W. R., 178–79
Shilow, Otis, 175
Shoshones, 26, 27, 33, 75–76, 79, 159, 177
Shotwell, L. W., 198
Showaway (Šáwaway, Yakama headman), 41
Simcoe, Fort: boarding school, 140; establishment of, 58; Yakama agency, 63, 68, 78, 80–81, 89, 94, 117
Simnasho, OR, 125, 126–27, 135, 183–84
Simpson, Thomas, 109–10, 130
Simtustus (Sɨmtáštaš, Tygh headman), 50
Skamania County, 221
Skamia (Sxɨmáya, Dreamer prophet), 85, 94, 271n36
Skannowa, John, 51–52
Skins (Sk'inɬáma), 40, 55
Sk'in village: connection to Wayám, 25; and Dreamer Religion, 85; fishery, 22, 160, 181; independence of, 115–16, 117; treaty signers from, 44–45; in Yakima War, 61
Skloom (Šklúum, Yakama headman), 41, 44, 53
slavery, 25, 27, 30–31, 258n12
Slockish (Šláq'iš, Klickitat headman), 44, 52–53, 237
Slockish, Frank, 116, 188, 199, 237
Slockish, Ray, 241–42
Slockish, Wilbur, Jr.: acknowledgement of, ix; and Mid-Columbia River Council, 244; and Salmonscam, 231, 233–34; on seasonal round, 18; on Sohappy v. Smith, 224; and traditionalism, 152; on tribal government, 208
Slockish, Wilbur, Sr., 236
Slocum, John (Squ-sacht-un), 128–29. See also Indian Shaker Church
smallpox, 27–28

Smith, John, 62–63, 74, 75, 86
Smith, McKee A., 221
Smohalla: creed, 82, 83–84, 239; death, 124; disciples, 84–86, 127; failure of prophecies, 123; on origins of horse, 26. See also Dreamer Religion; Washat
Snake (Indians). See Shoshones
Snake River, 40
Sockzihi, John, 199
Soctillo, Pete, 155
Sohappy, David, Jr., 122, 152, 233–34, 239
Sohappy, David, Sr.: background, 223; death, 239, 241; fishing rights activism, 194, 221–22, 226–27; and Salmonscam, 232–34; and traditionalism, 219; on tribal intervention, 229, 299n66. See also Cook's Landing: fishing rights activism; fishing; Sohappy v. Smith
Sohappy, Myra, 122, 232–33, 235
Sohappy, Richard, 221–22
Sohappy v. Smith: limited scope of, 224; plaintiffs, 222; planning for, 221–22; precedents set, 224–25; severance from U.S. v. Oregon, 227–29. See also U.S. v. Oregon
South Carolina, 302n14
sovereignty, tribal: assertion of, 214–15; basis in treaties, 59. See also fishing: tribal regulation of; treaties: reserved rights
Spalding, Henry and Eliza Hart, 31–32
Spearfish, WA. See Wishram
Speedis, Martin, 160
Speedis, Walter, 180
Spencer (Chief), 56
Spencer, Warren, 245
Splawn, Andrew, 42
steelhead trout, 20, 220, 237, 244

Wishrams, 24, 30; 40, 44, 109–10
Wolverton, Charles E., 165–68
women: as culture bearers, 152; traditional gender roles, 18–19, 151–52
World War II, 197
Wounded Knee Massacre, 248, 254n8

Yahyowan, Jacob, 176
Yakama Nation: Columbia River General Council Fish Commission, 216–17, 220; confederated tribes and bands of, viii, 262n11; Dalles Dam settlement, 203, 211; enrollment procedures, 197, 200–201; fish committee, 210; fishing regulations, 215, 244; fishing rights cases, 158–68, 198–99, 209–10, 216, 223, 227; General Council, 197, 200, 220, 228, 234, 236, 294n9; and in-lieu site eviction, 4, 235, 238; and Lyle Point, 245; per capita payments, 197; and Salmonscam, 233–34, 299n66; spelling of name, 253n1; treaty, 37, 43, 44–45, 58–59, 263n18; Tribal Council, viii, 4, 198–99, 209–10, 215, 220, 221, 228, 234, 247, 294n9
Yakama reservation: allotment, 76–77, 109–10; Indian relocation to, 58, 74; and Feather Religion, 135, 138; and Indian Shakers, 129, 130–31, 133; and Washat, 125–26

Yakamas: aboriginal territory, 23; buffalo hunting, 27; Lower confederation, 41, 44; spelling of name, 253n1; and treaty councils, 40, 44; Upper confederation, 41, 44; in Yakima War, 54–55, 58
Yakima Enrollment Act (Public Law 706), 200, 208. See also enrollment
Yakima River, 28, 169
Yakima Valley, 54, 246
Yakima War, 54–61
Yallup, Galen, ix, 246–47
Yallup, Thomas K., 176, 182, 183
Yallup, William: and Celilo Fish Committee, 174, 181; and Columbia River Tribe, 188, 199, 237; death, 192–93; and public education, 145–46, 148–49; on reservation Indians, 153, 156, 184; on reserved rights, 49, 156; on root-digging, 20; as traditional chief, 116, 185, 188. See also Celilo Fish Committee; Columbia Tribal Council
Yocash, Leroy, 233–34
Yocatowit (Klickitat headman), 57
Young Chief, 48
Young, S. A. M., 131
Yowaluch, Louis (Mud Bay Louis), 128–29. See also Indian Shaker Church

THE EMIL AND KATHLEEN SICK LECTURE-BOOK SERIES
IN WESTERN HISTORY AND BIOGRAPHY

The Great Columbia Plain: A Historical Geography, 1805–1910
    by Donald W. Meinig
Mills and Markets: A History of the Pacific Coast Lumber Industry to 1900
    by Thomas R. Cox
*Radical Heritage: Labor, Socialism, and Reform in Washington
    and British Columbia, 1885–1917* by Carlos A. Schwantes
The Battle for Butte: Mining and Politics on the Northern Frontier, 1864–1906
    by Michael P. Malone
*The Forging of a Black Community: Seattle's Central District from 1870
    through the Civil Rights Era* by Quintard Taylor
Warren G. Magnuson and the Shaping of Twentieth-Century America
    by Shelby Scates
The Atomic West, edited by Bruce Hevly and John M. Findlay
Power and Place in the North American West,
    edited by Richard White and John M. Findlay
Henry M. Jackson: A Life in Politics by Robert G. Kaufman